D1796673

Towards Supply Chain Risk Analytics

Iris Heckmann

Towards Supply Chain Risk Analytics

Fundamentals, Simulation, Optimization

Iris Heckmann
Karlsruhe, Deutschland

Von der Fakultät für Wirtschaftswissenschaften des Karlsruher Instituts für Technologie (KIT) genehmigte Dissertation.

Tag der mündlichen Prüfung: 26.10.2015
Referent: Prof. Dr. Stefan Nickel
Korreferent: Prof. Dr. Francisco Saldanha-da-Gama
Prüfer: Prof. Dr. Wolf Fichtner
Vorsitzender: Prof. Dr. Rudi Studer

ISBN 978-3-658-14869-0 ISBN 978-3-658-14870-6 (eBook)
DOI 10.1007/978-3-658-14870-6

Library of Congress Control Number: 2016945784

Springer Gabler

Printed on acid-free paper

This Springer Gabler imprint is published by Springer Nature
The registered company is Springer Fachmedien Wiesbaden GmbH

Acknowledgments

The pursuit of well-sophisticated solutions, derived from theory and made applicable in practice, led me to FZI Research Center for Information Technology. At FZI I was given the opportunity to work on improvements for logistics systems, to learn technical content, to get to know real-world problems and to experience a fruitful working environment.

During that time I worked on the topic of Supply Chain Risk which resulted in the underlying thesis. However, this work would have not been possible without the support and guidance of others, who I want to thank here.

I am indebted to Prof. Stefan Nickel for being the supervisor of this thesis and a mentor to my research work – especially for his farsighted guidance, his productive ideas, and his sincere interest in discussing (rebutting or exploring).

My thanks also go to Prof. Francisco Saldanha-da-Gama for being the co-supervisor of this work – for his calm, his profound thoughts and his ability to explain.

Thanks are due to Prof. Wolf Fichtner for being part of the examination committee and to Prof. Rudi Studer for his sincere conduct as the chairman of the examination committee.

Additionally, I thank my colleagues at the Logistics and Supply Chain Optimization Group at FZI, the Institute of Operations Research (IOR) as well as the Institute for Material Handling and Logistics (IFL) of the KIT – Karlsruhe Institute of Technology for sharing good and bad research times.

Priceless support and patient encouragement came from my family and friends. They all have never become tired to encourage me. Special thanks go to my parents, who have continuously offered me a quite and safe place for retreat.

Abstract

Unexpected deviations and disruptions, those are subsumed under the notion of supply chain risk, increasingly aggravate the planning and optimization of supply chains. Over the last decade there has been a growing interest in including risk aspects for supply chain optimization models. This development has led to the adoption of risk concepts, terminologies and methods defined and applied in a broad variety of related research fields and methodologies. However, for the purpose of supply chain risk management the suitability of risk, as it is coined in these domains, is up for discussion.

The major contribution of this thesis is given by the development of a profound conceptual basis of supply chain risk analytics and the transfer of newly defined concepts for the modeling and operationalization of supply chain risk within simulation and optimization approaches.

The first part gives an extensive analysis of fundamental concepts and approaches that surround research in the field of supply chain risk management. This includes a review of available concepts of risk in general and supply chain risk in particular. As supply chain risk is either ambiguously or incompletely defined the literature review does not only critically revise existing approaches, but also identifies essential aspects that drive the extent of supply chain risk. Part I provides adjustments of commonly used concepts and offers a new definition of supply chain risk. It is emphasized that it is the responsibility of supply chain risk analysis to evaluate the interactions of risk defining elements. Having set the foundation for future approaches the new concept of supply chain risk analytics is coined.

Using mathematically based approaches, supply chain risk analytics is tailored for the management of supply chain risk and associated sub themes. A discussion of the value of mathematically approaches in the light of risk-aware solutions and a review of existing literature within the field of operations research complete Part I.

Consistently following the discussions and conclusions provided in Part I, Part II introduces a new simulation-based procedure for identifying and assessing supply chain risks for a given supply chain, denoted by *SimSCRF*. The approach builds on existing proprietary supply chain planning engines and applies methods from design of experiments to determine weaknesses of the underlying supply chain. To align the data model for supply chain planning with the simulation-based representation of a given supply chain, an object-oriented information framework is presented. The introduction of an additional layer between planning engine and analysis algorithms offers the possibility to easily switch between different planning engines and as a result conduct risk analysis for different supply chain planning problems. An exemplary supply chain risk analysis is conducted on a real case supply chain originating from the chemical industry. The evaluation provides insights on the existence of supply chain risk and its extent as well as on potential conclusions for mitigation options.

While the solution approach of Part II is characterized by the interplay of technical entities within a consistent process flow, Part III focuses on the development of a risk-aware optimization model for supply chain network design problems. Based on contemporary research gaps identified for optimization approaches in Part I, Part III deduces a mixed-integer two-stage stochastic programming model that extends the capacitated plant location problem and additionally offers the possibility to formalize and operationalize supply chain risk. With the goal to evaluate risk-aware solutions the concept of value of risk consideration is defined. The evaluation of the developed optimization model discloses its usefulness in terms of providing risk-aware solutions and of approaching risk by stochastic programming principles.

Contents

List of Figures

List of Tables

1 Introduction

"Have Patience.
All things are difficult before they become easy."

Saadi

1.1 Motivation for Beginners

Most of us use the concept of risk frequently in daily language. *"If you decide to do this, you risk suffering negative consequences."* This sentence can be referred to a discussion with a colleague at work when talking about new business strategies, or with your partner when reflecting on financial precautions or health care, or with yourself when deliberating about whether to eat fish in a sushi restaurant. But what exactly is risk? How can we value risk? How can risk change our decisions? How can we improve our decisions through the consideration of risk? How is risk actually assessed? In terms of percentage? With the means of a linear scale form 1 to 10 or by using an ample scale from green to red? For the beginning we start with a comparison of different risk situations by using relative terms such as "lower" or "higher".

Imagine you want to assess the risk of not being able to deliver a wedding cake to an exclusive restaurant, because you were seriously injured by a car, when you cross the street without looking for approaching vehicles. We construct the circumstances that define this situation in more detail as follows: Assume the road to be a main through road of a small village in the back country. Generally, the volume of traffic is high within the week early in the morning and in the evening due to commuting, but it is only a small village such that the car frequency is moderate. Four times a year a local car racing is held in this region and the main through road of the village is part of the route. The village youngsters have just recently got their driving license and cruise through the village in the afternoons. Additionally, the village is part of a field trial, whose overall objective is to reduce CO_2-Emission. Each household is endowed with at least one electric car, which are by far more quite than diesel- or petrol-engined vehicles. So, the probability of a car arriving just in the moment you want to cross the street depends on the day of the year, the day of the week and the time of the day. The probability of being hit by an approaching car depends on your ear, your reaction, the driving skills of the driver, and the weight of the cake. If you want to cross the street on the day of the car race, the probability of being badly injured is significantly higher compared to normal weekdays.

The analysis of probability is a standard mean to assess risk, but is the risk of not delivering a wedding cake and being injured by a car higher or lower, if crossing the street is one of a series of dozen tasks that you have to pass as a participant of an extreme obstacle course? This challenging run is of course illegal, but frequently attended by extreme athletes from all over the world. Other obstacles on this run include passing a gill on a slackline and ends with a base jump from a rock. You are a person who can be described as an adrenaline junkie. Passing a road without looking for cars is nothing you would call a risk. Hence, the risk of not being able to deliver a wedding cake and additionally getting injured is lower for you than for a person that tackles tasks dutifully or a person suffering from the brittle-bone disease, who both try to avoid any danger, when passing a street.

How does the risk level change, if you are professional stunt-man just delivering a wedding cake for your friend, who is a confectioner? You are booked for years as a double for actors that have not the skills nor the ability to ride a car accident out – especially not when having a wedding cake in their hands. You have been trained for years to overcome situations in which fast approaching cars hit you. For you, crossing the through road of a backwater town while delivering a wedding cake does not pose a challenge – as long as it is not the day of the car race. So the risk of not being able to deliver and being injured is certainly lower for you than for a senior citizen. But it is higher, if you are on the run from a rabid dog. The dog is wanted for months as he has killed numerous animals in the neighborhood and already attacked other people. When you started your delivery walk at the urging of your friend and went through the fields nearby, you startled the dog under a tree while he was eating a blackbird. During your career as a stunt-man you have witnessed several stunts with mad animals. You know that a confrontation with a mad or even rabid animal can have serious consequences for your well-being, which you want to avoid. The dog is fast and if you stop or slow down before the road, he will certainly catch you. The restaurant is located on the opposite side of the road, if you run across the street (without looking), you will certainly find a shelter and be safe. Your individual objective has changed and you now want to ensure or maximize your physical inviolability, but you also try to deliver your friends cake anyway. Nevertheless, crossing the street of a small village is less dangerous than fighting with a rabid dog.

How does the risk level change, if your objective changes again? What is the risk of being injured, when you are on the way to the hospice? You had a great time as stunt-man, but those days have long since passed. The last years you fought against a serious illness and the doctors give you one or two months before your body will lose this fight. During your stay at your friends house you decided that it is time to give up. You are grateful for having such a good friend that you comply with his demand to deliver the wedding cake. When you passed the fields, you killed the rabid dog with a judo chop and are now in thoughts while approaching the road on the day of the car race. The risk of not being able to deliver the cake and

being injured or even killed by a car is – with respect to what you have to expect – considerable low.
And how does the risk of not being able to deliver a wedding cake and being injured by a car while crossing the street of a backwater town change, if all the aforementioned thoughts do not apply to your situation, because you are sitting on the veranda of your ranch house in the outback of Australia just thinking about different types of risk? As a child becoming a stunt-man has ever since been your dream, but you decided to work as research scientist at university. You wrote your PhD thesis about the concept of risk. A couple of days before submission you were sitting on some stairs at the University, felt exhausted and thought of resigning. All of a sudden a big nugget fell down on the street. You had no idea, where it came from, but you felt blessed, finished your PhD and got a great amount of money for this golden and heavy nugget. You bought this ranch house in Australia, and became a dropout before you became a beginner. Now you are sitting on a rocking chair, looking over the fields, and patting the head of your dog, who has an anti-rabies inoculation. Streets and cars are thousands of miles away. So, the risk of not being able to deliver a wedding cake and being injured by a car while crossing a street simply does not exist.

But how about the risk being not able to deliver a didgeridoo to Europe for the birthday party of your friend, because you were seriously injured by a spider sized less than four centimeters while collecting fire wood in Australia?

This constructed case demonstrates that the level of risk changes with the perspective and seemingly depends on specific circumstances that need to be known and evaluated prior to risk assessment. The consideration of risk is often treated as exaggerated, while the risk concept itself is almost always oversimplified. As incidents like the European ash cloud in 2011, Fukushima-Daiichi nuclear disaster in 2011, or the airplane crash in the French Alpes in 2015 highlight, reality is often more erratic and unimaginable than thinking up risk scenarios.

1.2 Advanced Risk

In the last decade we witnessed numerous real cases of risk – smaller and bigger ones. When these cases occurred we were stunned by their consequences or implications. Force majeur or blow of fate? How could it happen? Why were we not prepared? Why did we not evaluate the situation correctly in advance? How can we prevent or diminish such cases or their consequences?

We relate to some cases to evaluate in more detail the perspectives introduced in the previous section, which co-determine the level of risk. Certainly, probability is one major concept of risk. However, when talking about probability we immediately enter a highly discussed field. People have been arguing about the meaning of "probability" for at least 200 years. The major polarization of the notion is between the objectivist[1] and subjectivist[2] schools [171, 223, 325]. While objectivists believe that probabilities are real, subjectivists assume probabilities to reflect the degree of beliefs of rational persons. When applied in the context of risk, probability needs to be carefully defined. While the objective probability of an ash cloud forcing airplanes to stay on the ground was ever since equal to zero, there was a certain plausibility, a subjective probability, we must affirm at hindsight. Throughout this thesis we follow [146], who combines both views and defines probability as subjective in the sense that it describes a state of knowledge rather than any property of the real world; but it is objective in the sense that it is independent of the personality of the decision maker. Two rational beings faced with the same total background of knowledge must assign the same probabilities.

Consider then the risk of a deadly airplane crash. Often people start to argue that the probability of deadly accidents is extremely low

[1] Other notions related to the "objectivist's" perception of probability are "frequentist", the "aleatory" or the "physical" notion of probability.

[2] Other notions related to the "subjectivist's" perception of probability are the "Bayesian" or "evidential" notion of probability.

compared to fatal car accidents. Does that mean the risk is low, if the probability is low? When we talk about risk, there must be at least a chance that "something" happens that may result in "something" negative. The problem with the comparison between deadly car and airplane accidents is the objective of the decision maker. If he wants to travel with safe transportation means, he could decide to use that mean which is endowed with the smaller probability of deadly accidents. However, these probabilities are based on the overall amount of passengers. Naturally decision makers are not interested in the welfare of others or of the majority of people, but in their own welfare. If the decision makers have an accident with the transportation mean they are going to choose, how great is the probability of dying? Clearly, the probability of dying while having an accident is much higher, than the probability of a deadly accident. It seems to be necessary to use the right statistics, when arguing about the security and the risk of using different transportation means.
If the decision makers are the persons in charge of scrutinizing the data and calculating the probability of a deadly plane crash, they value the risk of dying in terms of absolute or relative numbers. Contrary, if the decision makers are the person in charge of the safety of thousands of airline passengers, they decide whether this probability assessment necessitates new precaution actions, i.e. the decision makers additionally value risk based on their subjective perception with respect to their responsibility. If the decision makers are private persons, like for example a parent, they value risk by reflecting the consequences for his family. Thus, compared to probability, the level of risk seems to additionally depend on the degree of the individual involvement of the decision maker.
The observation that risk is more than just one mathematical term already resulted in misleading conclusions. Right after the incidents of Fukushima the former federal secretary for the environment, nature conservation, and nuclear safety stated that security and risk are neither a mathematical nor a static concept. Instead, they are social values which can change over time [190]. Following this argumentation the risk of a nuclear meltdown has tremendously increased solely

due to the public perception. However, probability calculus indicate that a nuclear meltdown can happen every 10.000 years per reactor. With more than 400 reactors worldwide a meltdown may happen every 25 years [336]. While the Chernobyl disaster occurred on 26 April 1986, the Fukushima MCA began on 11 March 2011, roughly 25 years later. So, probability calculations seem to work. Nevertheless, more cautiousness is needed when considering risk. Although risk does not seem to depend solely on mathematical calculations, it still depends on probability.
Residual risk refers to a part of the overall risk related to a certain situation that is hardly predictable or manageable. In this sense it is often used as the scapegoat for everything the decision makers are not able to manage or do not *want* to manage. The world for example faces the risk to be hit by comets, meteorites or even asteroids. When an asteroid impact occurs there might be no necessity for risk assessment, because there is nothing left to manage. The walls of Fukushima plant were build to withstand waves of height 5.7m. It seems strange that even though mankind was able to build walls of this height in the 700th to 500th century before Christ birth that it is the fault of residual risk, when the tsunami waves hit the coast offshore the nuclear plant. This waves might have been manageable. A meteor shower can (most probably) not be managed. It seems that it is possible to be better prepared, if risk is assessed appropriately. The prophylactic mastectomy of a famous celebrity in 2013 has long been discussed quite controversial in the public. Is such a radical step exaggerated, if *only* the medical history of close relatives indicates increased cancer risk, but not the individual examination results? Is it reasonable to intervene before becoming ill? Discussion whether this was a good or a bad decision will not come to an end. What is for sure is that the risk of dying of breast cancer has not only diminished considerably, but it has also became extremely low after having had a mastectomy.
The willingness to change and learn from risky situations recedes when normality returns. Risk is more tangible, if it is not theoretically discussed, but if the decision makers are struck by its conse-

quences. Risk becomes effective, if it intervenes with the personal environment of the decision makers and results in situations they can not bear. Then he realizes that he can live with the risk to miss the bus, but not with existential threats which may strongly affect his lives. People want to avoid nuclear meltdowns that destroy the environment they live in. People want to avoid multi-million dollar losses from security funds, in which they own shares and whose developments should safeguard the financial situation of their pension. People do not want to be infected with life-threatening illnesses such as Ebola. If the only control is to live without nuclear power, without securities funds, and without traveling possibilities, then they act accordingly. However, as soon as these risks appear to be embanked and manageable, decision makers start thinking, if we only could have cheaper energy, if we could only profit from risky security funds, if we could only travel without boundaries. It seems that the longer the immediate threat has passed, the smaller is the (perceived) risk.

This discussion reveals that the level of risk is endowed with a high degree of complexity. This thesis is about risk, but it focuses on the meaning and the influence of risk as well as a *good* risk treatment within the field of supply chain management. Therein, not all, but most of the aforementioned thoughts are valid and applicable, too. The next section introduces the field of application and discloses how risk affects the management of modern supply chains.

1.3 The Real Introduction: The Name of the Game

A *supply chain* defines a network of organizations interlinked by up- and downstream connections. Each location is responsible for different processes and operations of value adding such as storing, producing, manufacturing or shipping. The goods transfered between organizations and the goods sold to the final customer can be products or services. Figure 1.1 shows a typical supply chain, its entities and flows. Therein raw materials are procured from suppliers, preliminary products are produced at distinct or among several production facilities, shipped to warehouses for storage and then forwarded to final assembly, manufacturing or production. By global and regional distribution centers or retailers the final goods are transferred to the customers. Supply chains do not only ship materials or offer services, but they are also responsible for the transfer of financial and information flows. More detailed descriptions of supply chains and their defining entities are provided by several standard works, see for example Chopra and Meindl [55], Simchi-Levi et al. [274], and Stadtler and Kilger [291].

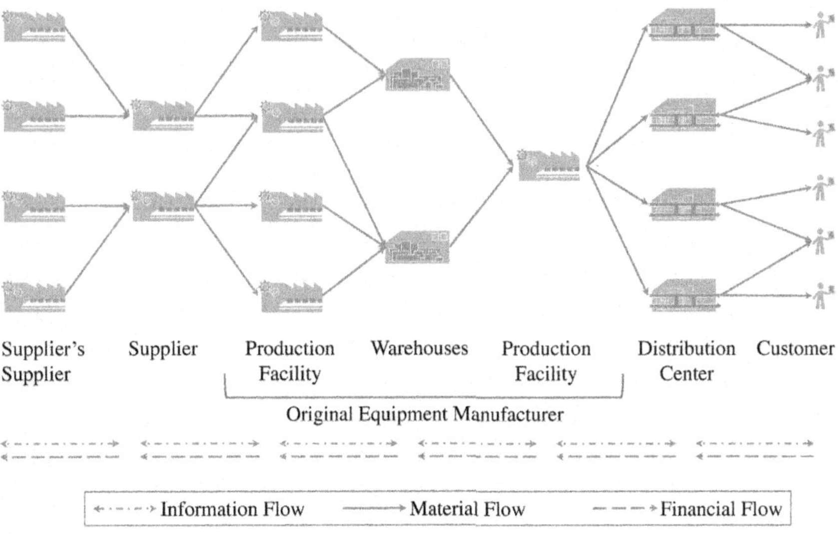

Figure 1.1: A supply chain example, see [291].

The ultimate purpose of a supply chain is to satisfy as many customer orders as possible. Decision makers need to balance the supply and the demand by efficiently allocating resources to the (expected) customer requests. Therefore, a lot of decisions have to be carried out and coordinated. These decisions comprise questions like *"Which products should be produced on which machine?"*, *"In which sequence should products be produced on a machine?"*, *"Which locations should be responsible for the production of which products?"*, *"Which transportation links and modes should be selected for shipment?"* or *"Which production facility should be opened or closed?"*. The more important a decision is, the better it has to be prepared [91]. The preparation of supply chain decisions is done by supply chain planning. In accordance with the importance and the time horizon of a decision, planning tasks are categorized upon three planning levels: long-term (strategic), mid-term (tactical), and short-term (operational) planning. Decisions of the strategic level deal with the design of a supply chain and balance different long-term effects over several years. Tactical decisions concern the assignment of regular processes, operations, and flows to available resources. They comprise the determination of approximate quantities and aggregated time frames for each resource. Decisions about daily activities are carried out on the operational level.

In order to rein the complexity of decision making on each of the aforementioned planning levels it is necessary to abstract from reality. The simplified version of reality is called a *model*. Supply chain models are descriptions of supply chain activities and desired goals. A production process, for example can be described through information about production capacity, variable production costs, or production time. Information like requested product, requested amount, and delivery date describe an activity of ordering. For planning purposes a supply chain model is created and solved by computer-based approaches.

Generally, planning can be regarded as a process of organizing, structuring, and scheduling future activities. Planning needs information about future developments to be able to consider restrictions and to achieve a favored goal. A major concern for the planning of any task or system is the treatment of information uncertainty. Usually decision makers know about the uncertain development of some distinct information. For example expectations about customer demand deviate in most cases from the initial outlook. Means for the prediction of uncertain information comprise the consideration of historic realizations or of expert knowledge. Figure 1.1 provides an aggregate snapshot of an exemplary supply chain. In reality modern supply chains can be by far more complex. Especially over the last decades supply chains evolved into internationally-acting systems and are since then caught in a crossfire of additional environmental influences. This evolution led to an increase of uncertain informations and to a broadened range of uncertainty.

In particular, incidences that lead to sudden and unexpected modifications at different locations within the supply chain attracted the attention of decision makers. Natural disasters such as earthquakes destroy production facilities or roads, and forestall the possibility to satisfy customer's needs as promised. Besides these so-called disruptions, unpredictable and slightly aggravating deviations also affect supply chain's goal achievement. Exchange rate fluctuations, variability of oil prices, or increased labor costs have the potential to reduce the profit margin and hence the competitive advantage of supply chain partners. Thus, supply chain disruptions and unknown deviations impede the availability of resources, the realization of the plan, and consequently the satisfaction of customer demand. The consideration of perils that have the potential to derogate the supply chain is carried out within the research field of *supply chain risk management*.

In order to prepare for uncertainty supply chain models need to be endowed with the information about uncertain developments. *Simulation models*, for example, re-enact decisions for supply chain processes, operations, and flows. Algorithms simulate random realizations of the uncertain information, each of which provoke different decisions. In the context of supply chain risk management simulation models provide mechanisms to understand the relationship between alternative realizations of uncertainty and their consequences on the supply chain. However, with the goal not to evaluate known solutions but to determine *risk-aware* planning solutions, *mathematical optimization models* and techniques are needed. Those approaches are often derived from the discipline of *operations research.* They determine solutions by maximizing or minimizing a mathematically formulated goal, such as cost-minimization or service-level-maximization.

Over the last years a considerable number of approaches has been published within the field of supply chain risk management. However, what is still missing is a structure that embraces these approaches or serves as a guideline for future research. The big interest for our critical review of supply chain risk [122] reveals the desire for anchors and guidance. This thesis intends to provide further steps on the research line of supply chain risk and strives for reducing the gap within the field of supply chain risk by approaching the answers to the following questions:

- *What is supply chain risk?*
- *How can simulation models support the understanding of the extent of supply chain risk?*
- *How can optimization models determine risk-aware supply chain designs?*

1.4 Outline and Course of Discussion

With the overall goal to answer the three questions posed in the previous section this thesis consists of three parts:

I Fundamentals of Supply Chain Risk,

II Simulation-based Approaches for Supply Chain Risk Identification and Assessment, and

III Optimization Approaches for Strategic Supply Chain Risk Mitigation.

Figure 1.2 highlights the structure of this thesis. The three parts are framed by an introductory discussion, Chapter 1, and a concluding debate, Chapter 13. Each part consists of one or several chapters. The methodological purpose of each chapter within the overall context of this thesis is highlighted by the legend.

The chapters of Part I review existing literature and (re-)define essential concepts. The discussion combines critical reviews of existing literature with own thoughts. The combination is intended to provide a clear structure of different topics and to deduce new definitions and conceptual approaches. Contrary, the main chapters of Part II are formed traditionally: The first two chapters provide methodological explanations and reviews, chapter three introduces the new simulation approach, which is discussed by an evaluation chapter. Additionally, two further chapters introduce accompanying research. Part III consists of one chapter, which deduces a new risk-aware stochastic optimization model for supply chain network design problems.

Chapter 2 introduces the genesis of supply chain risk. It presents trends that discover the vulnerability of modern supply chains towards uncertain deviations and classifies prominent disruptive triggers. It motivates the need for supply chain risk quantification and traces the path towards supply chain risk management. Chapter 3 provides a careful analysis of existing supply chain risk definitions and related concepts, discusses rationales of risk concepts from selected domains of application, and derives core characteristics that drive nowadays supply chain risk understanding. The chapter closes with a new definition of supply chain risk. The subsequent Chapter 4 consists of a theoretical discussion on common risk biases and main elements of supply chain risk analysis. Conceptual definitions are provided along with logistical implications. Chapter 5 coins the new concept of supply chain risk analytics. It deduces analytical insights into the capability of supply chain risk analytics to determine risk-aware supply chains. Risk measures, optimization models and

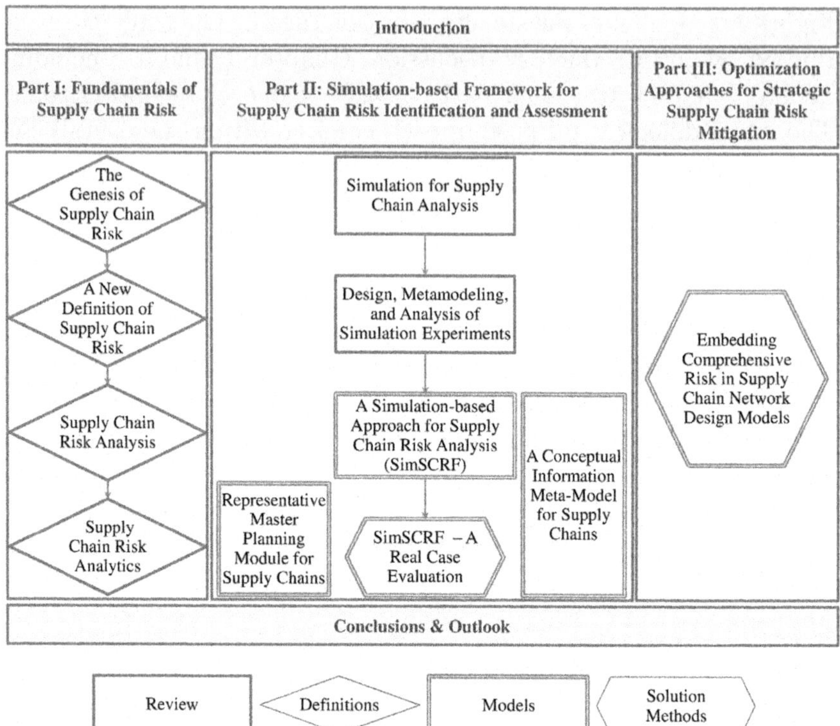

Figure 1.2: Outline

solution techniques are reviewed, which disclose relevant research gaps.

The chapters 6 and 11 present a new simulation-based framework for risk analysis. Chapter 6 introduces simulation principles especially tailored for supply chain analysis. Chapter 7 provides a basic introduction into the principles of the design of experiments used within this thesis. Consistently following the discussions and conclusions provided in Part I the Chapters 8 and 11 explain and evaluate the developed simulation-based supply chain risk analysis framework *SimSCRF*. A real case evaluation of a representative supply chain derived from chemical industry offers logistical insights and highlights the usefulness of the developed approach compared to prevailing risk approaches. Chapters 9 and 10 represent accompanying research. Chapter 9 develops a representative master planning model that replaces the (black box) proprietary planning tool within the *Sim-SCRF* approach. Chapter 10 aligns the data model for supply chain planning with the simulation-based representation of a given supply chain.

With the goal to incorporate the new supply chain risk definition not only in simulation-based, but also in optimization approaches, a risk-aware optimization model is developed during the course of Chapter 12. By extending the capacitated plant location problem a mixed-integer two-stage stochastic programming model is presented along with analytical and computational evaluations. A new concept to analyze potential risk-aware optimization solutions is defined as the value of risk consideration. The usefulness in terms of operationalization of supply chain risk and methodological appropriateness is discussed to close Part III.

In summary, the purpose of this thesis is to provide:

- fundamental knowledge about elements of supply chain risk and their dependencies by defining supply chain risk, supply chain risk analysis, and supply chain risk analytics,
- a new simulation-based procedure for supply chain risk identification and assessment by developing a framework for supply chain risk analysis and deducing managerial insights within a real case evaluation, and
- new mathematical models to determine risk-aware supply chain designs by considering supply chain risk as a holistic concept.

Part I

Supply Chain Risk Concepts – Fundamentals

2 The Genesis of Supply Chain Risk

"When anyone asks me how I can best describe my experiences in nearly 40 years at sea, I merely say, uneventful. Of course, there have been winter gales, and storms and fog and the like, but in all my experience I have never been in any accident of any sort worth speaking about. [...] I never saw a wreck and have never been wrecked, nor was I ever in any predicament that threatened to end in disaster of any sort."

Edward John Smith
Captain in command of the RMS Titanic

Supply chain officers may feel with Edward Smith. After years of un*event*ful supply chain management and after years of striving after more efficient processes, unexpected and sometimes even devastating events have derogated supply chains. A series of major disruptions like Hurricane Katrina, piracy attacks offshore Somalia, global financial crisis, flooding in Thailand, European ash-cloud, Japanese earthquake and tsunami among others have revealed a missing preparedness within today's supply and distribution networks [248]. Thus, the management of so-called supply chain risks became an issue.

This chapter briefly summarizes the genesis of supply chain risk. It starts with explaining the trends that revealed the sensitivity of modern supply chains, it revises different classes of disruptive triggers and it traces the path from the consideration of disruptions to supply chain risk management and the need for quantification.

2.1 Logistics Innovations – A Blessing and a Curse

The strategic influence of supply chain management on business performance – including not only overall logistics costs, but also customer satisfaction – is well confirmed by companies of almost all industries. Domestic firms can offer products worldwide, and hence, they compete not only with local companies on the domestic market, but also with international competitors they encounter on the world market. In order to remain competitive, while benefiting from logistics potentials, companies strive for improving and streamlining their operational processes [329, 334]. As revealed by Computer Science Corporation in 2004, companies availed themselves of the implementation of efficiency-increasing logistics innovations. While 52% of the considered companies registered an increase in their revenues, 72% stated to benefit from the new developments implemented in their supply chains. Besides the positive effects American AMR among others concluded that these new trends and strategies have a negative counterpart, which is highlighted by the increasing number of disrupted supply chains [66, 129, 149, 334, 348]. Highly efficient operations [329] expose supply chains to an environmental crossfire of different volatile influences. While disruptions do not occur everyday, supply chain strategies – also called *risk drivers* – that lead to disruptions do. When a firm takes a pure cost minimization approach in order to increase overall efficiency, it reduces excess capacity and inventory, which could make up for production losses caused by disruptions. Formerly isolated events within the supply chain can today "escalate to wide scale network disruptions" [71].

Innovation	Trend	Opportunity	Threat
Globalization	LCCS	20% to 30% lower material and labor costs	longer lead times
		supply closer to manufacturing and customer sites in emerging markets	increased risk of supply disruption and transportation capacity and performance issues
			exposure to new political, security, regulatory, tariff, and currency risk
	Outsourcing	improve operating performance and service levels	limited visibility or control of service levels or selection and performance of subtier suppliers
		lower operating costs	
Information Availability	VMI	improvespend leverage	limits ability to directly manage visibility, quality, and performance
		improve service and fill levels	
	Integrated Supply	reduce management burdens	increased reliance on single supplier for broader range of materials and services
		access "one-stop shop"	
Lean Management	JIT/JIS	reduce inventory costs	little, if any, buffer stock or time

	streamline operations	increase risk of stockouts and manufactirung disruptions due to supply or delivery glitches
Supply Base Rationalization	improve spend leverage	increased reliance on fewer or even sole-source suppliers
	reduce management burdens	links performance to financial and operational health of supplier
	improve strategic supply relationships	increased likelihood of dual- or sole-sourced suppliers relying on single sub-tier supplier

Table 2.1: Opportunities and risks of prevailing logistic best practices [see also 2, 63, 249, 329].

Popular logistics improvements, which can be derived from three main sources: globalization, lean management principles, and increased information availability, are presented in Table 2.1 [2, 63, 249, 329].

Global sourcing enables companies to follow strategies like low-cost country sourcing (LCCS), or outsourcing and off-shoring, all of which enable companies to implement cost reduction actions and to focus on their core activities. Stretched lead times, limited visibility, and difficult communications can, however, decrease flexibility and response time in case of supply chain failures. Lean management principles like Just-in-Time or Just-in-Sequence and supply base rationalization allow companies to synchronize supply with production demand more efficiently. When efficiency is the sole objective, there is very little buffer to enable recovery after a supply chain disruption has occurred. New technologies like e-business, vehicle telematics, inter-modal systems, tracking systems, and automated handling have improved information availability as well as facilitated purchasing activities for both consumers and procurement managers. However, these developments increased customer expectations. Nowadays, consumers buy more products from websites rather than visiting shops [334]. Furthermore, they want immediate gratification. Late orders caused by supply chain disruptions often result in lost customers. Additionally, information technology provides transparent and consistent support in planning, monitoring and controlling material as well as financial and information flows. As companies in the meantime rely on planning and monitoring tools, a small IT-failure could have a tremendous and immediate impact on the whole supply chain performance [249].

Logistics innovations have shifted supply and distribution processes from more or less straight chains to globally acting, complex and highly interrelated networks, most-often operating beyond consecutive company boundaries. Supply chains consequently operate in a volatile environment and are exposed to different types of potential disruptive triggers.

2.2 Supply Chain Disruptions

Disruptions like power outages, labor strikes, supplier glitches, epidemic or terrorist attacks were always considered as geographically isolated events, which executives heard about in news, but did not need to manage in their own companies nor within logistics operations. However, due to increased complexity of world-wide spread supply chains, a medical crisis in Asia became a problem for the producer of high-tech goods in the middle east. A labor strike in harbor facilities of the US affected exports coming from South Korea. The hurricane Katrina hit oil refineries in New Mexico, but oil prices increased all over the world [78]. The nature of disruption triggers varies among economic, environmental, geopolitical (as well as societal) and technological categories. Due to the ongoing change of the risk landscape all over the world, the number of triggers resulting in disruptions especially for supply networks increases and evolves constantly. Figure 2.1 presents the global risk landscape changes from 2012 to 2013 including aspects especially valid for supply chains.

According to the Supply Chain Risk Initiative of the World Economic Forum the top five external triggers among these categories in 2012 were natural disasters, extreme weather conditions, conflict and political unrest, terrorism as well as sudden demand shocks [249]. Although not yet top-ranked, IT-disruptions like IT-failure or cyber attacks can be regarded as an emerging trigger, which needs more attention. A study of the University of Minnesota concluded that 90% of companies encountering a ten day lasting IT-breakdown had to declare bankruptcy after two years at the latest. In the following paragraphs main types of disruptive triggers are further discussed. Additionally, Table 2.2 provides an overview of prominent supply chain disruptions and their impact on supply chains. For a more detailed discussion of historical disruptions and their business impacts, we refer to Punter [239].

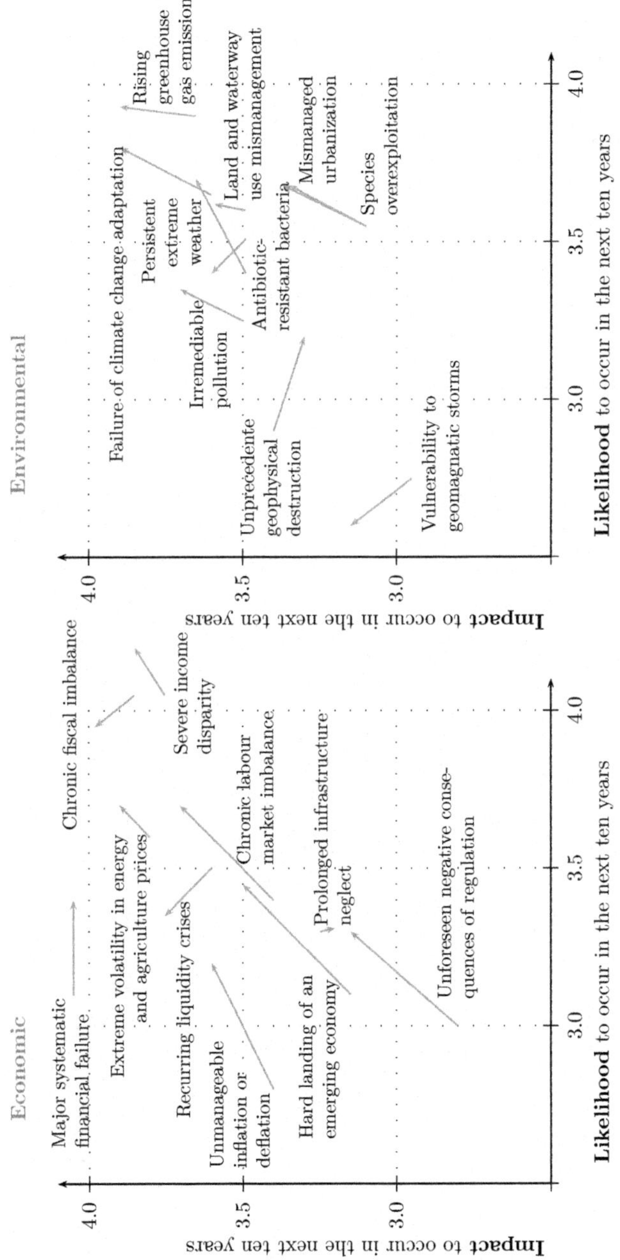

(a) Economic and Environmental

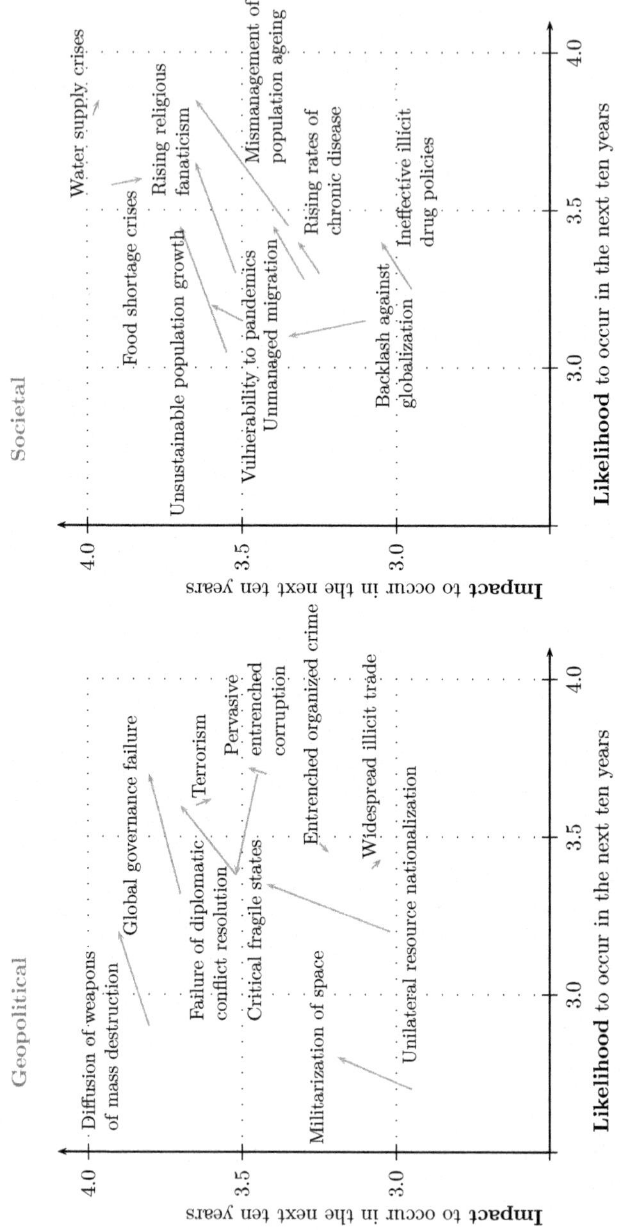

(b) Geopolitical and Societal

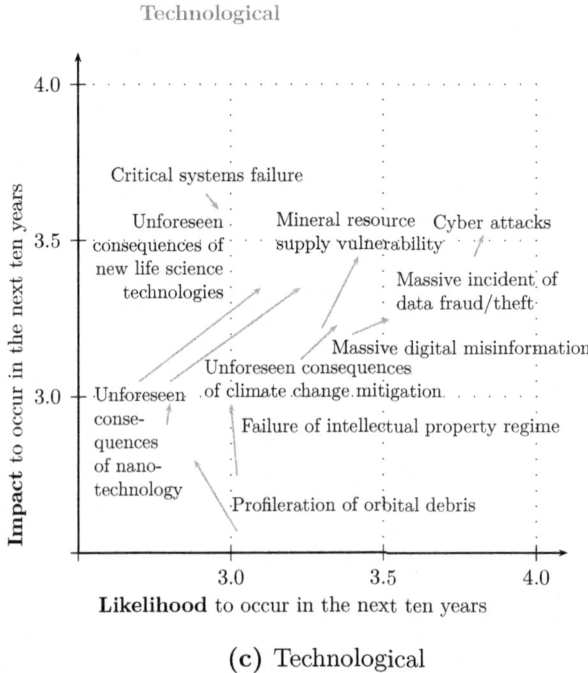

(c) Technological

Figure 2.1: Global risks landscape – movements from 2012 to 2013. Assessed on a scale between 1 and 5 [250].

Name	Incident	Description	Year
Great East Japan earthquake	seaquake and tsunami	An undersea earthquake off the Pacific coast of Tohoku occurred in March 2011. The earthquake triggered tsunami waves that reached heights of up to 40.5 meters and which flooded inland up to 10 km. Several industries such as high-tech and automotive suffered from enormous production shortages.	2011

Thailand flooding	flooding	The Thailand flooding in 2011 affected production capacity and inventory stock-out and price increase, similarly. As Thailand is the world's second major exporter of hard disk drives (HDD), an entire industrial sector was hit by the flood. According to the e-commerce tracking site Dynamite Data the price of HDD increased by 50% to 150% shortly after the flooding until 300% in the weeks afterwards.	2011
Eyjafjalla-jökull	volcanic eruption	On 14 April 2010 the eruption of the Icelandic volcano Eyjafjallajökull affected European supply chains. Due the leashed ash-cloud air travel was extensively affected by the closure of airspace over many countries. Companies such as BMW had to interrupt production in Munich, Dingolfing and Regensburg.	2010
West Coast Port Lock-out	labor strike	After weeks of negotiations between the international longshore and warehouse Union and the pacific maritime association, workers of all ports of the US West Coast went on strike for 10 days.	2002
9/11	terroristic attacks	The safety measures after the attacks of September 11 led to excessive delays in delivery within the US and abroad, and consequently to production bottlenecks at affected companies.	2001
Nokia-Philips-Ericsson	lightening bolt	A lightning bolt struck a high-voltage electricity line in New Mexico. The power fluctuation caused a fire in a Philips factory in Albuquerque. The factory produced semiconductors for mobile phones. The fire and the sprinkler destroyed around 1 million semiconductors. Nokia and Ericsson were the principle customers of Philips' semiconductors.	2000

Dell-Apple	earthquake	After an earthquake heavily affected production capacities of Taiwan's high-tech industry. Apple and Dell encountered enormous difficulties in procuring semiconductors.	1999
Toyota-Aisin	short circuit	A short circuit provoked a fire at a factory of Toyota's major p-valve supplier Aisin. P-valves are a low priced product, but essential for the production. Production was expected to halt for several weeks. Alternative valve suppliers were not immediately available and Toyota faced an increased demand, which already has led production levels reaching 115%.	1997

Table 2.2: Major disruptions from 1997 – 2011.

2.2.1 Environmental Disruptions

The recent series of natural and epidemic catastrophes affecting companies worldwide – like the Kobe earthquake in Japan in 1995, SARS in South-East Asia in 2003, the Hurricanes Katrina, Rita and Wilma in the US in 2005, the Wenchuan earthquake in China in 2008, the volcanic eruptions in Iceland 2010 and 2011, E coli outbreak in 2011 and the earthquake in Japan 2011 – are "violent reminders" [329, p. 307] that globally wide-spread supply networks are sensitive towards changes in their environment. The Chūetsu earthquake in Japan in 2004 resulted in an estimated economic loss of US$ 28 billion, 2005 Hurricanes Katrina, Rita and Wilma totaled US$ 155,3 billion, the earthquake in the Wenchuan Region in China is estimated with US$ 85 billion and the tsunami in Japan with US$ 210 billion economical loss [75].

Unfortunately, the aforementioned examples of natural and epidemic disasters are not rare events with anecdotal value. According to the International Disaster Database (EM-DAT) from the Center of Research on Epidemiology of Disasters (CRED) the long-term upward trend of frequency and economic magnitude of worldwide disasters started in 1950 and has aggravated ever since [59, 71, 75, 217, 218] see Figure 2.2. Certainly, population growth, the spread of valuable assets and improved reporting influenced this development. The exponential growth of frequency and magnitude, however, cannot be explained solely by these factors [59]. The outlook on the future of supply networks is evident: supply chains remain exposed to deviations evoked by natural and epidemic disruptions.

2.2.2 Economic Disruptions

Currency exchange rate fluctuations, commodity price volatility, global financial crises, sudden demand shocks, supplier glitches and export/import restrictions are examples of economic disruptions.

Globally-spread supply chains connect companies among diverse countries, belonging to different currency areas. Fluctuations in currency rates between procurement, production and distribution locations potentially offset margins. Competitive devaluation – sometimes referred to as *currency war* – like for example in 2010 has a great impact on supply chain profitability when procurement or distributions are concentrated overseas [248].

Additionally, cross-border movements are vulnerable to export and import restrictions or border delays evoked by customs regimes, tariff and non-tariff barriers, quota systems, security concerns and infrastructure bottlenecks [248]. According to the Supply Chain Risk Initiative of the World Economic Forum sudden new restrictions pose the main disruption trigger for cross-border material flows within supply and distributions networks [248].

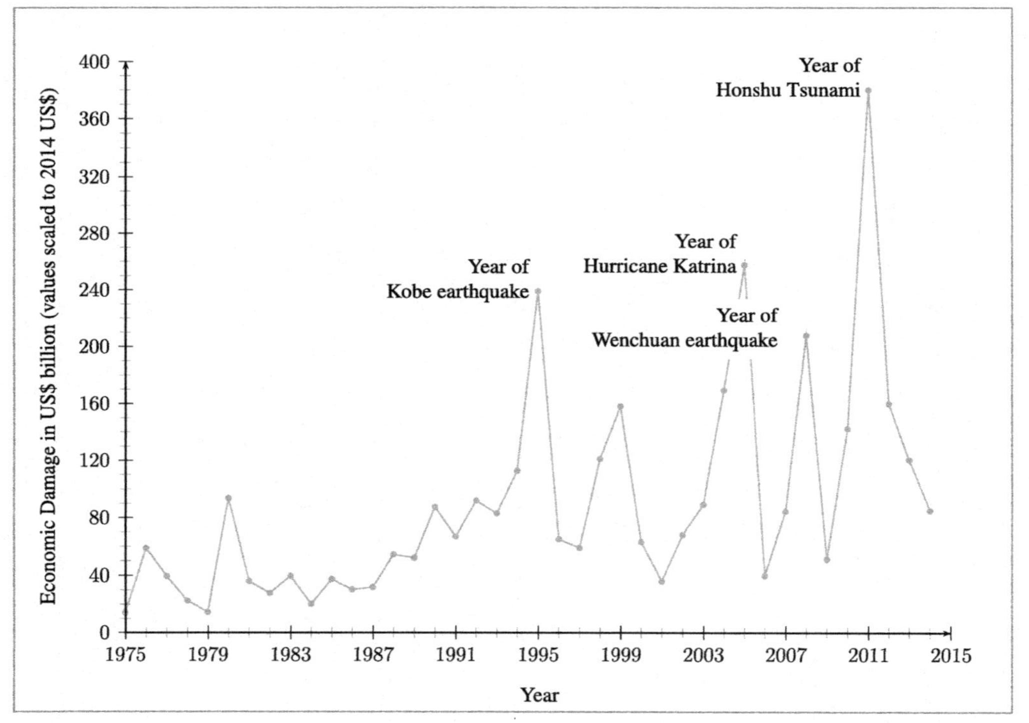

Figure 2.2: Economic damage in US$ billion caused by reported natural disaster (1975-2014) ©EM-DAT [75].

Whereas in the past fluctuations in crude oil prices and consecutively in transportation costs [276] could be solely referred to international turmoils (Gulf war I and II, OPEC embargo), today, increased investment fund activities and disruptions affecting oil production companies lead to an increase of daily crude oil price volatility. Especially the fluctuations in the years 2007 to 2009 have shown that forecasting changes and level shifts are difficult.[1] Thus crude oil prices should be assumed to remain highly volatile.

Most supply chain innovations are build on the assumption of cheap oil where lower wages embedded in a stable economy justify long transportation routes. However, at a certain point, where increased transportation costs offset benefits from outsourcing or off-shoring. Over the last decade some developing countries evolved to emerging economies, whose gross domestic product increased constantly. While the annual percentage change of real GDP growth in high-income countries declined from 4% in 2000 to 2% in 2010, it increased in developing countries from 4% in 2000 to 6% in 2010. The wage inflation of the last decade, coupled with a weaker dollar, further aggravated the cost-efficiency of sourcing from low-cost countries. According to Goel et al. a Chinese plant worker, made $1740 a year in 2003 and earned $4140 in 2008 [105]. The annual wage inflation in China has averaged 19 percent since 2003, contrary to that the US wage inflation has averaged only 3 percent [105]. Thus, besides volatile oil prices increased wages yield to offset the benefits of LCCS.

[1] In 1999, the World Bank was forecasting the nominal crude oil price to level off at US$ 18/barrel for 2005 and US$ 19/barrel for 2010. This perception reflected the one of most analysts, who assumed real prices to average between US$ 15/barrel and US$ 20/barrel in the long run [15]. When in January 15, 2002, WTI futures contract were first introduced the December 2008 futures contract opened at US$ 18.88. The average crude oil price of 2008, however, was US$ 97/barrel [15]. Although a number of regulations to financial markets are now being introduced, the effectiveness of these reforms towards excessive speculations has to be seen [110].

Economic system shifts or disruptions are difficult to predict but unfortunately remain influencing globally-spread supply chains as well.

2.2.3 Socio-Geopolitical Disruptions

Geopolitical areas – where political stability is missing, where terrorism is prevalent or where law enforcement is restricted – impose a threat to supply chain performance [248]. Socio-political turmoils, like the "Arabic Spring" for example, decreased political stability in North Africa, increased the fear of interrupted oil supply and hence raised the volatility of oil prices. Similarly, the Iraq War impaired global transport flows: Singapore Airlines – flying over the Middle East – had to choose more southerly routes, which caused a decrease of their cargo capacity for products coming from Singapore [66]. Likewise, the Ukraine conflict forced air carriers to change routes. Terrorist attacks threaten democratic societies, western citizens as well as public institutions. Additionally, companies fear attacks on production and distributions hubs. Compared to physical attacks on infrastructure, legislative responses like the safety precautions after the 9/11 attacks are considered to be more realistic. Strong restrictions at the Mexican and Canadian border and the aircraft grounding lasting several days intercepted the continuous procurement of production companies. In the fourth quarter of 2001 Ford, for example, suffered from a decline in car production of almost 13% [198]. There is no reported evidence that indicates an upcoming world-wide, perseverative, political stability. With regard to the current unrest and warlike disturbances in Iraq, Syria, Gaza, and the Ukraine one may safely assume that the uncertainty originating from the socio-geopolitical environment will (unfortunately) continue to exist – also for globally-spread supply chains.

2.2.4 Technological Disruptions

Several surveys point out that technological disruptions induced by accidental Information Technology (IT) failure, cyber attacks or corporate espionage are increasingly threatening the efficient operation of supply chains [240, 249].

Innovations like automatic identification and data acquisition, mobile devices, and cloud computing resulted in new systems such as tracking and tracing, real-time control applications, or software-as-a-service. Supply chains, therefore, evolved into interdependent systems not only with respect to material, but also information and financial flows [249]. In the meantime, cyber criminals may utilize these technologies to attack different types of flows within a supply chain. Additionally, decision and analysis tools offer planning support for production, transportation, and supply networks. EDI systems are used for the exchange of documents between suppliers and manufacturers. Both systems are indispensable in daily supply chain operations. Systematic attacks on corporate IT infrastructures may introduce computer virus or cause blackouts, and thus have tremendous effects on overall business performance. Many high-tech companies as well as legislations of large economies have already responded to the increasing potential threat imposed by cyber attacks for supply chains. The United States for example established the national cyber security division within the US Department of Homeland Security. Germany set up a national cyber response center. Both institutions are designed to create countermeasures to cyber attacks. Additionally, corporate unions such as Boeing, Cisco, IBM, Microsoft, NASA and the US Department of Defense, published a security framework for reducing the supply chain attacks and ensuring the integrity of the network [310].

Despite concerns about air traffic or rail infrastructure control or even GPS systems being hacked and manipulated too [240] – a possibility that is discussed intensively [88] – accidental IT failures might be more realistic with quite similar effects. The pursuit of developing physical secure technology should, therefore, be a major concern – especially in the light of reported traffic and logistics accidents like the mid-air collision of a passenger plane and a cargo aircraft over Überlingen in 2002, like the short circuit at British Telecom in 2004 [317], or like the collision of a carriage and a freight train in 2014 [43].

2.3 Coping with Risk

Innovations focusing on improving efficiency turned supply networks into globally operating, interrelated and complex systems, whose boundaries cross corporate entities. Formerly geographically isolated disruptions and volatilities became an issue. Both, scientific community [270, 274, 334, 349] and practitioners [129, 140] became aware of the increased number of perils that have the potential to disrupt a supply chain. The raise of decision makers' awareness, led to the application of a well-known (but not well-understood) concept: risk. The transition from disruptions to risks passed off quickly and apparently arbitrarily. Since then the management of supply chain risk is defined as one of the five fundamental challenges of supply chain management [140]. Quantitative tools are needed that support decision makers in managing those supply chain risks.

2.3.1 Enterprise Risk

Contrary to targeted holistic supply chain risk management, the treatment of perils that impede the efficient execution of atomic (logistics) sub-systems is well-established. For example, on the level of small-scale operations such as production tasks, risk is perceived as technical failures or human errors. In this context, event-related deviations from expected parameter levels are addressed by the means of scheduling systems. Scheduling tools work on an operational planning level and are executed whenever the decision maker wants to integrate new information. Managerial techniques such as Failure Mode Event Analysis (FMEA) [161, 257], Event Tree Analysis (ETA) [76] or Fault Tree Analysis (FTA) [156, 161] support decision makers in identifying potential triggering events and their related consequences. These techniques are also used for larger logistics systems crossing single locations. However, interruptions within these systems, for example in distribution networks, are quantified by frequency and estimated damage.

On an enterprise level risk management tools became necessary and were established, after major corporate and accounting scandals in the US resulted in economic crises. In the 1990, for example, companies like Enron or Tyco were struck by accounting scandals which led the US government to enact the so called Sarbanes-Oaxley Act (SOX) [242]. SOX asks for the integration of risk management in a proposed Internal Control System (ICS). The Committee of Sponsoring Organizations of the Tradeway Commission (COSO) developed an Enterprise Risk Management Integrated Framework including risk elements like event identification, risk evaluation and risk reaction. In accordance with the situation in the United States the European Union enacted several EU Directives (EU Directive 4., 7. and 8.), which hold for the implementation and control of corporate ICS [175] and led to extensions of national laws, e.g. the German Accounting Law Modernization Act (BilMoG). The compliance with these regulations impose challenges to enterprises. The occurrence of disruptive triggers is regarded as a threat that affects logistics figures which in turn influence overall corporate financial figures and need to be governed appropriately.

Today, the management of perils is even more difficult, because enterprises are parts of complex and interrelated supply chains. Disruptions occurring upstream the supply chain may affect product quality or reputation of supply chain partners downstream. Along with the growing complexity of modern supply chains, the impact of any willful action or unintended change have become hard or even impossible to predict. Figure 2.3 summarizes the aforementioned

Logistics Systems	**Characteristics**	**Risk Perception**	**Tools**
production tasks	small-scale	technical failure & human error	scheduling
distribution processes	across locations	relationship between frequency and damage	FMEA, ETA, FTA, ICS
supply chain	across companies	?	?

(a) Characteristics, risk perception, and tools of different logistics systems

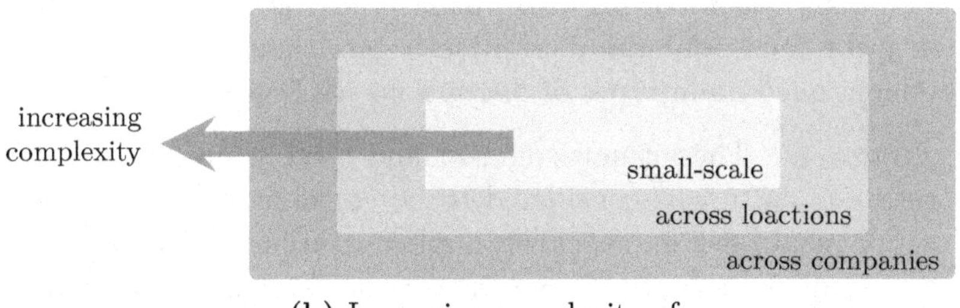

(b) Increasing complexity of logistics systems

Figure 2.3: Risk perception and complexity of different logistics systems.

thoughts and visualizes the increasing complexity of logistics system from small-scale operations over subsystems crossing single locations and business units up to the concept of a supply chain and their related perception of risk.

2.3.2 Following the footsteps of Management

Out of the literature of supply chain risk management, different streams of interest and focus developed concentrating on managing and reducing supply chain risk. Much attention has been devoted to the management of supply chain disruptions, which is referred to as *supply chain disruption risk management* [28]. Supply chain disruption management subsumes approaches that identify and assess short-term alternatives that limit the exposure to disruptive triggers and/or return supply chain execution back to a normal and/or acceptable status. The relatedness between supply chain disruption management and supply chain risk management is well elaborated by several authors [28, 66, 192, 204, 266, 282].

A generic managerial approach especially tailored for supply chain risk can be traced from diverse authors [28, 100, 109, 120, 133, 216, 334, 345, 349]. The approach is arranged as a process cycle, which encompasses the following core management steps intended to be applied for each potential disruptive trigger that evolves out of the aforementioned main types of disruption, see Figure 2.4:

- *Awareness.* The acknowledgment and establishment of a corporate risk culture is considered to be essential for the success of supply chain risk management implementations. Establishing culture implies creating risk awareness and information transparency over different business units, management levels, and supply chain partners [133, 149, 334].
- *Identification.* To install selective risk countermeasures it is indispensable to know about the threats in the environment of supply chains. Gathering and evaluating information about prospective trends or level shifts are the objectives of the identification step. Therein the supply chain, its boundaries, its processes, and its objectives are defined and described.
- *Assessment.* Then activities within the specified system are examined in order to identify potential points of weaknesses as well as threats [334]. Traditionally, the result of this step is a catalog of potential relevant threats [345]. Upon the predominant understanding of risk, identified supply chain risks are classified, assessed and ranked in accordance to their relevance. The relevance is usually quantified by the probability of a threat and its related impact.

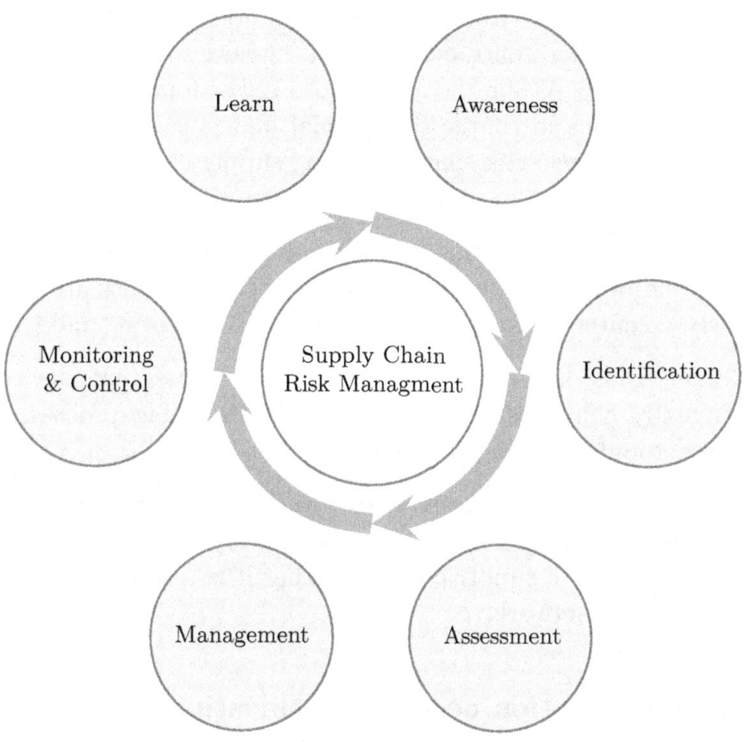

Figure 2.4: Process cycle of supply chain risk management steps based on [28, 109, 120, 133, 216, 334, 345, 349].

- *Management.* For top-prioritized supply chains efficient countermeasures need to be identified, designed and implemented. Different types of typically mentioned risk mitigation options include, but are not limited to insurance, information sharing, relationship and partnership development, design of contractual mechanisms, regular reviews and supplier audits, and pro-active assessment and planning, like flexible supply base, flexible transportation, strategic stock, or postponement [251, 307]. Ritchie and Brindley [251] as well as before Kleindorfer and Saad [168] discovered the development away from individualistic measures, such as insurance or supplier contracts, towards integrated and co-operative risk responses. While the application of the former puts external responsibilities in charge of financial and physical damages, the latter encourages risk sharing among supply chain partners.

- *Monitoring & Control.* The surveillance of relevant performance indicators, the continuous update of the relevance of identified risk, and of the developed activities for risk response are continuously executed actions and referred to as Monitoring and Control.
- *Learn.* It is emphasized by numerous authors that the course of supply chain risk management is an ongoing process, steps interact and new insights need to be considered for the execution.

Although this cycle provides a work flow of risk conduction, it lacks a quantitative treatment of risk that can be adjusted to any logistical subsystem within a supply chain, whether it is a production task or a corporate subnetwork.

2.3.3 Identification needs Quantification – Quantification needs Definition

Besides logistics operations, the performance of related business units such as finance, sales, purchasing or IT affect and depend on an effective supply chain risk management. System-inherent uncertainties that can hardly be allocated to a specific event need to be identified as well. The delimitation of different types of risks is, however, vague and hinders an efficient execution of supply chain risk management. With the intention to enhance the supply network with the capability to appropriately respond to threats, supply chain risk management has to provide reliable instruments that support the understanding and mitigation of supply chain risks. These instruments include qualitative indicators and quantitative metrics. The expertise of supply chain officers or the evaluation of real cases are valuable with regard to the understanding of risks. The need for quantitative instruments tailored for supply chains is even higher and continuously increasing, because it allows a systematic approach for risk consideration and surveillance. Consequently, the development of *risk quantification metrics* represents the most prioritized improvement need for supply chains [248]. It is due to the very nature of the term risk and the development of its understanding that results in diverse perceptions and definitions of supply chain risk and its management. As threats originate from diverse environmental categories, may affect various parts of the supply chain and have to be handled by different corporate units, this discipline attracts the attention from multiple domains and research fields. It follows that definitions of concepts related to supply chain risk depend on the methodological background and interest of research scientist as well as on cultural, industrial or geographical differences, rather than on what is actually needed or reliable.

In the following Chapter we work on the contemporary understanding of risk and re-define supply chain risk with the intention to provide the basis for what is needed most: supply chain risk quantification.

3 A New Definition of Supply Chain Risk

"We can't solve problems
by using the same kind of thinking
we used when we created them."

Albert Einstein

Each process and decision in business is prone to uncertainty. Since wrong assessments and misjudgments may lead to unforeseen developments, which may have important consequences when detected (too) late, uncertainties need to be continuously monitored and managed. Along with the increasing number of relevant uncertainties, the importance assigned to risk considerations has grown. In recent decades, we have observed this term being applied to areas such as decision theory [171, 255], finance [138, 139, 202], actuarial science [181], health care [113, 176], marketing [64, 256], management [196], emergency planning [61, 119, 131] and psychology [1, 42, 153].

Particularly in supply chain management many authors have felt the need to somehow capture risk. Due to the increasing complexity and interrelation of modern supply chains, the type and nature of uncertain developments or the impact of any action have become hard or even impossible to predict [123]. Additionally, major disruptions like Hurricane Katrina, piracy attacks offshore Somalia, global financial crisis, flooding in Thailand, European ash-cloud, Japanese earthquake and tsunami among others revealed a lack of preparedness of supply chain managers towards uncertain developments in general [248].

A close look into the use of the term risk in general and supply chain risk in particular reveals that its meaning is far from clear. The Risk Response Network of the World Economic Forum among others have just recently identified that more time and effort has to be invested not only in conceptual or methodical work but first of all in the creation of a common definition and understanding of supply chain risk [151, 249, 278, 285, 305].

The review of this chapter overcomes a gap in the literature which regards the lack of a clear definition of risk within the context of supply chain risk management. With the goal to provide a complete foundation of nowadays understanding of supply chain risk, we studied not only mathematical approaches that originate from the operations research and management science community, but also conceptual and empirical papers that provide managerial insights and risk classifications. However, the main analysis sets the focus on the mathematical body of supply chain risk literature and evaluates whether conceptual work has been transferred to mathematical approaches. Therein we reveal missing aspects of prevailing supply chain risk definitions. Since it is not possible to review all relevant literature, the analysis focuses on papers that either explicitly classify and define supply chain risk or that quantitatively model risk for supply chain design and planning problems

In this chapter we introduce and discuss the concept of supply chain risk. The remainder of this chapter is organized as follows: the next section briefly traces the development of the term risk. By doing so, it will be easier to understand the motivation for the different definitions that are presented subsequently. We focus on the use of risk in theory and practice, particularly the integration of risk management in corporate systems, and existing risk management approaches, regulations and standards. In Section 3.2 we briefly summarize main requirements for a suitable definition of supply chain risk. Section 3.3 outlines existing concepts of supply chain risk in research and practice. In Section 3.4, we derive important characteristics that drive today's understanding of risk. Presented as core concepts of risk consideration, these characteristics may also be used to define supply chain risk. Based on the main findings we provide a redefinition of supply chain risk and conclude the literature review on supply chain definitions in Section 3.5.

3.1 The Evolution of Risk

In spite (or possibly because) of its long history, the term risk is still vague and often ill-defined. Although in everyday language the term is frequently used and easily understood [213], the underlying concepts are hard to define and even harder to assess. The reason for the widespread, heterogeneous and inconsistent definitions of risk can be traced back to its evolution, the continuous change of its nature, its meaning, and its purpose of use.

The origin of the word risk cannot be clearly determined, since this term seems to have roots in different cultures. According to Adams [4] the word derives from the Arabic notion *alresk* (chance). In Chinese script, the word *crisis* consists of the signs for *risk* and *chance* [222], which implies a negative definition of risk. An etymological analysis of the European notion of risk leads to the Greek navigation term *rhizikon*, describing the need to avoid "difficulties at the sea" [279]. Understood in this sense, the best approximation of the meaning of risk would be *fear* or *adventure*. The former refers to commercial activities and implies physical and mental distress, whereas the latter means pecuniary ventures as a strategy to engross the self-worth. For a further extensive exploration of the etymological sources, evolution of meaning and role of risk in general we refer to Peter L. Bernstein's "Against the Gods" Bernstein [32]. In the

14th century, when the maritime trade between Northern Italian city states started to increase, traders adopted this perception and regarded *risk* as the danger of losing their ships. For instance a spice merchant would think of potential situations that could cause his ship to be lost: storms, piracy, mutiny of the crew, or diseases. Today, these "what-if-stories" are largely used in planning and commonly referred to as *scenarios* [54]. They reveal potential developments and their consequences [169]. However, the ultimate reason for the high risk of running a spicery business did not reside solely from external events (such as storms or piracy), but also from the fact that the merchant usually owned only one ship – a single supply channel – and all his capital had been invested in the goods transported by it. Because the consequences of losing the ship were devastating for the merchant, his business was strongly *vulnerable*. The business of a merchant who owned more ships or who additionally dealt in salt trade or had a commercial partnership – diversified business risk – was less vulnerable. Such a merchant would have less reasons to be anxious. Within this context, risk expresses the fear that economic activities lead to the loss or devaluation of an important asset or a decrease in the performance of the business. Although the supply chains have become more complex, and are caught in a crossfire of a vast amount of influences, today's supply chain managers are essentially confronted with a similar situation to the merchants in the 16th century: In order to prevent their businesses from losing value, they need to identify alternatives, before or while changes to their supply chain and its environment occur. The famous and much discussed example of supply chain risk encountered by Nokia and Ericsson reveals, how the degree of preparedness leads to different outcomes [225]. Although these organizations had to deal with the same direct consequences of an unexpected incident, Ericsson suffered deeply from a supplier shortfall possibly provoking them to leave the mobile market [225, 270, 274], while Nokia could manage to acquire backup suppliers and alternative production capacities.

While the aforementioned understanding of risk is based on the fear of losing an investment, another view focuses on the probability of events that result in loss. At the beginning of the 17th century, *risk* became prominent in mathematics, when Blaise Pascal (1623–1662) and Pierre de Fermat (1601–1665) started to measure uncertainty in gambling [96]. Their work led to the development of *Probability Theory*, which still dominates the modern concept of risk [32]. In fact, the connection between probability theory and risk has been observed since the 1950s and has been applied to many research domains. As the performance of supply chains is becoming increasingly uncertain due to unexpected changes, authors transferred this basic probability-based risk concept to supply chain risk management. The probability of flooding, earthquakes, and tsunamis in the Asian region, for example, makes supplier shortfalls more realistic and more threatening for supply chains as can be seen in a number of cases. However, less probable events like ash clouds in European air space also demand for appropriate treatment. The exclusive consideration of probabilities is not sufficient in the context of supply chain risk.

Contributions in supply chain risk management mainly discuss the identification of triggering-events and the assessment of their probabilities of occurrence – although this risk perception might be limited for supply chains. The more general concept of risk associated with the fear of losing (business) value has not evolved.

3.2 Requirements for a Definition of Supply Chain Risk

The reason for a heterogeneous and often ambiguous understanding of supply chain risk is the long history and evolution of the comprehension of risk. A standardized definition of supply chain risk would support practitioners and research scientists in developing solution approaches and methods for the management of supply chain risk.

The accuracy of risk-aware decision models depends on the possibility:

- to operationalize,
- to measure, and
- to compare supply chain risks.

The *operationalization* of supply chain risk is intended to clearly distinguish risk from other phenomena and to identify distinct types of supply chain risks. As the prevalent perception defines supply chain risk as a fuzzy concept, it is necessary with regard to the appropriateness and focus of risk-aware solutions to sharpen the understanding of supply chain risk. Closely related to the ability to operationalize supply chain risk is its *measurability*. Risk measures have a history as long as the understanding of risk. Consequently, measures differ in the concepts of describing risk they are based on. Moreover, a supply chain can be endowed or exposed to a number of risks. Similarly, different supply chains are exposed to varying extents of supply chain risks. In order to be able to differentiate between those risks a quantitative description of supply chain risk is needed.

3.3 Existing Approaches of Supply Chain Risk Definitions

Although the topic is being considered as increasingly important, there are only a few authors explicitly defining supply chain risk. Those that do, root their definition on the assumption that supply chain risk is a purely event-oriented concept. This risk perception is in accordance with the risk understanding developed over the last four centuries that strongly relates risk to the probability of occurrence of disruptive events. In the context of supply chain risk management, events are characterized by their probability of occurrence and their related consequences within the supply chain. The reasons for the occurrence of risk (i.e., the initial or so-called triggering event) is not relevant in this classification: it can be found within one firm, within its supply chain or within the supply chain environment [162]. While some authors analyze the consequences of an event for a single focal firm [329], others focus on the performance of the supply chain as a whole [162], which can be affected by the occurrence of cascading effects that propagate through the entire network.

Among the first authors to establish a supply chain risk definition were March and Shapira [196]: they define supply chain risk as the "variation in the distribution of possible supply chain outcomes, their likelihood, and their subjective values". Zsidisin [350] provides a review of literature and industrial practices derived from case studies in order to derive a definition of *supply risk*. The author proposes a definition of supply risk that relates the occurrence of an incident with the inability of the affected companies to cope with the consequences. His definition is adopted by others as well [106, 177]. Much conceptual work has been provided by Jüttner, Peck and Christopher [151]. In a common paper, the authors define supply chain risk as "the possibility and effect of mismatch between supply and demand". Likewise, Peck [231] defines supply chain risk as "anything that [disrupts or impedes] the information, material or product flows from original suppliers to the delivery of the final product to the ultimate end-user". However, most conceptual research is dedicated to the categorizations of triggering events that are often synonymously referred to as supply chain risk, which is often understood as a starting point for risk identification [170], see discussion in Section 3.4.

Figure 3.1 shows the result of the analysis of the literature with respect to the definition of supply chain risk. Articles provide (A) explicit supply chain risk definitions and define risk as a) the probability and adverse outcome, b) the supply risk by Zsidisin [350], or c) the deviation from the expected. Majority offers (B) no explicit supply chain risk definition and imply risk to be d) an event, e) a deviation from the expected/objective, f) a probability, or g) provide no further insight to the definition of risk. Note that we put the emphasis of our analysis on the evaluation of mathematical-based models, therefore, references like [151, 196, 231, 350] are missing in the Figure. Additionally, some of those papers have been selected for the analysis, although they do not directly refer to supply chain risk, but provide valuable aspects for the quantitative modeling of risk in supply chain problems. The majority of papers analyzed, however, miss to define supply chain risk, even though their emphases is put on this topic.

Taking the above references into account, we conclude that the definitions of supply chain risk are often vague, ambiguous and defy quantification. As a result, supply chain risk is still difficult to assess, monitor, control, and hardly representable in mathematical decision models.

3.4 Core Characteristics of Supply Chain Risk

So far, there is no unanimous definition of supply chain risk, but there is a vast amount of literature coming from multiple domains dealing with risk. We chose the following domains to represent the most relevant streams of the use of risk, although we acknowledge that there may be further definitions in other disciplines: finance, insurance, decision theory, utility theory, emergency management and health, safety, environmental and reliability engineering. Each of the following paragraphs outlines how risk is understood according to selected domains of application and explains the underlying rationales.

Based on this analysis we identify core characteristics that drive nowadays supply chain risk understanding: The assessment of supply chain risk is closely related to the objectives that need to be accomplished by the underlying supply chain. The degree of achievement of these objectives depends on the exposition of the underlying supply

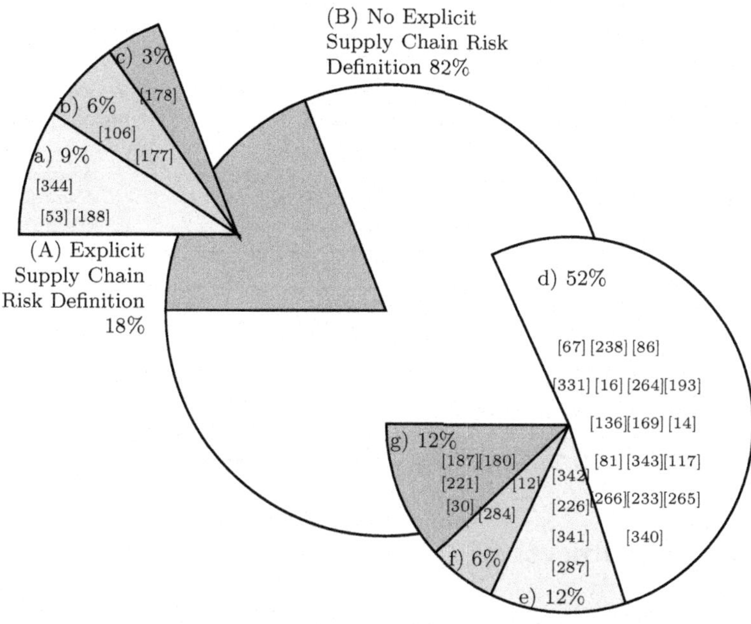

Figure 3.1: Analysis of supply chain risk definitions.

chain towards unexpected and uncertain developments. Risk exposition is further classified by potentially disrupting triggers, the ability of a supply chain to handle irritations, and time-based aspects that align the occurrence of the disruptive triggers to the current status of the supply chain. The significance of a potential non-achievement of objectives is assessed by the risk attitude of the decision maker. These characteristics are highlighted in Figure 3.2.

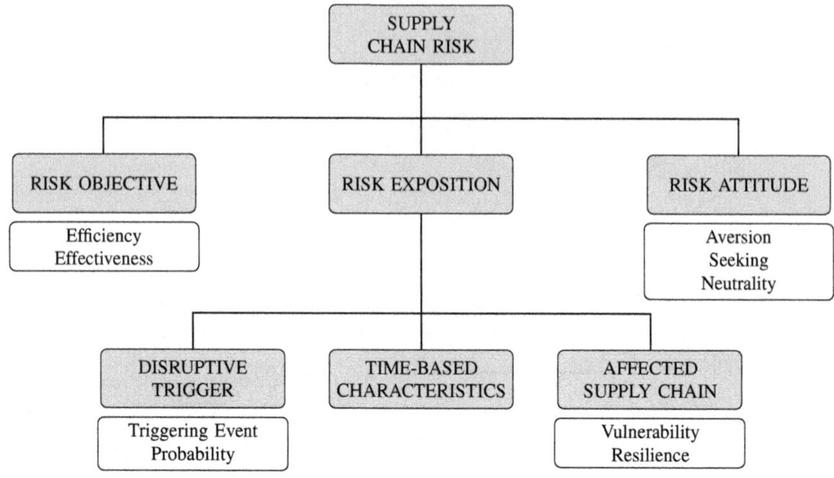

Figure 3.2: Core characteristics of supply chain risk.

3.4.1 Risk Objective

Risk considerations are very popular in financial management. The aim of this area is to efficiently plan, monitor, and control the capital resources of a company. Financial risk management then seeks to predict and to handle uncertain developments, which may lead to a degradation of company's value and forestall the achievement of corporate objectives. In finance, risk is measured as fluctuations around the expected value of financial returns. Originally, researchers considered the use of mathematical models for finding decisions which could capture this perspective of risk. In the initial models, mean-variance objective functions were considered, see for instance [68] and [197]. In finance, the understanding of risk comprises both gains and losses. Several characterizations of financial risk subsist, most of which distinguishing market, credit, currency or liquidity risk. These risks describe the potential for losses due to movements in market prices, debt payments, exchange rates, and interest in trading certain assets, respectively. Financial risk management models attempt to predict consequences of the aforementioned movements. An important indicator for market risk (the so-called systematic risk) is the volatility of an asset, usually represented by β and related to movements on the whole market. To a large extent, systematic risk is beyond the control of investors and can only be diversified by the means of derivative instruments. Modern portfolio theory, like arbitrage pricing theory, distinguish between the aforementioned systematic risk and the unsystematic risk, ϵ, which is corporate-specific. It describes the portion of the risk of an asset that is associated to negative consequences, which can be reduced or eliminated through diversification of the portfolio. In contrast to the aforementioned risks it is by far more difficult to identify, model and assess financial losses due to *operational risk*. Operational risk is defined by the Basel II Committee as "the risk of loss resulting from inadequate or failed internal processes, people and systems or from external events" [22, p.137]. In order to determine adequate capital reserves that serve as fall back positions when operations fail, organizations need to fully understand the interrelated consequences and dynamics that occur with operational risk. Operational risk reflects the complexity, uncertainty and diversity of risk sources that are valid for supply networks. It provides, therefore, a better conceptual basis for the notion of supply chain risk than financial risk as it is understood for market, credit, currency and liquidity risk.

The discussion shows that financial risk management is concerned with risk that refers to deviations of expected monetary objectives. Similarly, supply chain management has a significant influence on business goals and therefore provides competitive advantage, when designed appropriately in regards to meet business objectives [329]. However, in supply chain management goals can be achieved in two ways: efficiently or effectively [135, 210]. While effectiveness means that achieving a predefined goal can be guaranteed even if conditions are adverse, efficiency refers to minimal spending of resources to reach this goal. The primary purpose of a supply chain is to satisfy customer's demand, the availability of resources and the functionality of supply chain processes, therefore, needs to be guaranteed. The effectiveness in the context of supply chain management includes these aspects [37]. In contrast, purely efficiently designed supply chains provide the possibility of higher competitive advantages. Supply chain efficiency refers to a cost- and waste-minimal execution of supply chain activities [37]. The recent series of reported supply chain failures has shown that when efficiency is the sole objective, there is little buffer to enable continuity or recovery in the event of a disruption. It seems that the pursuit of efficiency and effectiveness are conflicting ([177]) and need to be carefully balanced.

Stock and Boyer [292] developed a consensual definition of supply chain management that incorporates the aforementioned thoughts. According to the authors, the management of supply chains seeks to plan, monitor, and control a network of interdependent organizations that facilitates different types of flows between the original producer to the final customer with the objectives to maximize profitability through efficiencies as well as to achieve customer satisfaction [292]. Consequently, a definition of supply chain risk should reflect the potential non-achievement of corporate goals due to ineffective or inefficient supply chain processes.

Meanwhile, most approaches concentrate on reducing monetary or financial consequences of uncertain and unexpected developments. Only a few authors consider effectiveness-based aspects like service level. Kull and Closs [177] for instance use discrete-event simulation with the objective of increasing customer satisfaction. Zsidisin [350] defines *supply risk* and relates the occurrence of an event to the inability of the supply chain to satisfy customer's demand. Fewer authors combine both concepts in order to truly balance supply chain efficiency with supply chain effectiveness. Peng et al. [233] develop a system dynamics model for balancing inventory level and service level. The majority of the approaches, however, focuses on a purely efficiency-based representation: when effectiveness is considered, it is measured in terms of the sighted efficiency figure (costs or profit). Figure 3.3 presents main results of this analysis with regard to the

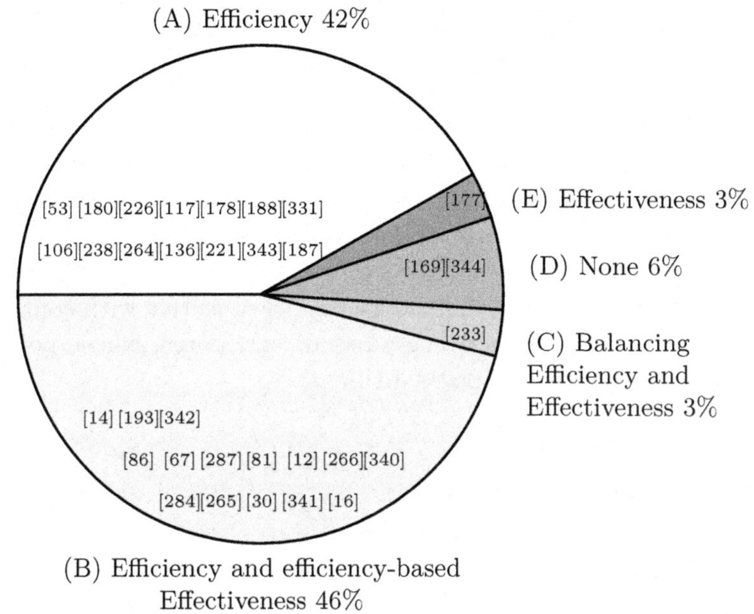

Figure 3.3: Supply chain risk objectives.

mathematical approaches considered. The predominantly objective is optimizing efficiency-based figures like costs, profit, or inventory (A). When effectiveness is considered it is transferred to efficiency-based objectives by the means of penalty or shortage cost for unmet demand (B). Efficiency and effectiveness balancing (C) as well as pure effectiveness-based approaches (E) are limited. Some work may serve for different risk-objectives (D).

Based on this discussion we define the risk objective as follows:

Definition 3.1: Risk Objective

Modern supply chains have to fulfill two types of objectives: efficiency and effectiveness. Effectiveness refers to the availability and the functionality of resources and efficiency to the profitable execution of resources. The supply chain is effective, if it is able to fulfill customer's demand. It is efficient, if it is able to provide competitive advantage. Whenever the supply chain is hindered to achieve both types of objectives, risk may arise. The risk objective is, therefore, defined as a multi-objective with conflicting (efficiency- and effectiveness-based) attributes, whose potential non-achievement imposes a threat.

3.4.2 Risk Exposition

Besides the objectives set to the supply chain, the exposition towards unexpected or uncertain developments have meaningful influence on how supply chain risk is understood. The risk exposition is specified by the occurrence of a so called-triggering event, as well as by characteristics of the underlying supply chain. While the former is further specified by the probability of occurrence and the effect within the supply chain, the latter is described by concepts like vulnerability or resilience. Additionally, time-aspects need to be considered when referring to disruptive triggers and the preparedness of the affected supply chain.

Disruptive Trigger

A disruptive trigger is further specified through the concepts of probability and event.

Probability. The central aspect of risk perception in most research areas is the availability of probability distributions. Decision theory, for instance, aims to support decision-makers in the construction or identification of an optimal or at least a satisficing decision. This is difficult in complex situations, when the assessment and evaluation of the consequence of decision is affected by different types of uncertainty [60, 93]. The effective and efficient practice of supply chain management in today's globalized world depends on the collaboration between geographically dispersed organizations [174]: (local) information must be collected, evaluated and shared across organizational boundaries [99]. Rosenhead et al. [255] were the first to classify a decision process according to the available information into three categories: certainty, risk and uncertainty. Under *certainty* all parameters are deterministic and known. The relation between information (input) and the decision (output) is unambiguous. Situations that are not certain comprehend some kind of fortuity. Reasons for the need to make decisions under these circumstances vary from lacking time and resources to collect, process and evaluate information to the inherent complexity of systems that forestalls predicting the consequences of a decision [60, 124, 184, 346]. To distinguish between these fundamentally different situations, two categories are introduced: decision making under *risk* relies on probability distributions, which govern the relation between input and output. Decision making under *uncertainty* needs to be made despite the lack of information about the likelihood of parameter changes.

Most authors adopted this categorization and refer supply chain risk to the extent of information availability about randomly changing supply chain parameters – assuming probability specifications are at hand. Yet information processing needs to respect the fact that the situation, its development and the information about both may be uncertain, fast-changing and with varying degrees of relevance and reliability. Still supply chain managers need to make decisions even when no information about the type of fortuity is available. Supply chain risk therefore addresses both decision making under risk *and* under uncertainty.

The type of fortuity used to describe the development of uncertain parameters is depicted by uncertainty models. The literature analysis follows the categorization of Owen and Daskin [227]. The authors distinguish between probabilistic approaches and scenario planning approaches. While the former explicitly consider probability distributions, the latter evaluate generated sets of possible future values, which can be weighted by discrete probability values, but do not have to [227]. Table 3.1 shows the results of this analysis.

Uncertainty model	Reference	Share
Probabilistic Approach	[16] [67] [81] [340] [344]	22%
Scenario Approach	[12] [14] [16] [30] [106] [117] [136] [178] [193] [226] [238] [265] [266] [264] [284] [287] [341] [342]	78%

Table 3.1: Uncertainty model of uncertain parameter development.

Triggering Event. The strong relation between the concepts of probability and risk is adopted by health, safety, environmental (HS&E) as well as by reliability engineering. However, a new aspect is emphasized by the implication that risk is understood as an event or a series of events. The international engineering standard ISO14971 defines and measures a risk R as the product of probability and harm of an event e: $R = P_e S_e$, where S_e and P_e refer to the severity and probability of e respectively [142]. Most of today's supply chain risk definitions start from the assumption that events are *the* decisive factor determining risk [334]. Consequently, huge efforts are invested in gathering, analyzing and assessing information to control potential triggering events that could materialize supply chain risk. To assess supply chain risk, triggering events are modeled as a function of their severity in terms of impact on the supply chain goals and their frequency of occurrence. Different terms are often used synonymously to refer to triggering events, e.g. *disturbance* [298], *disruption* [271], *disaster* [296], *hazard* or *crisis*. According to Svensson [298] a disturbance is a "random quantitative or qualitative deviation from what is normal or expected". A negative consequence of disturbance is related to "a deteriorated goal accomplishment in terms of economic costs, quantitative deviations [...] and qualitative deviations". Wagner and Bode [329] state that a disruption is characterized by its probability, severity and effects. A disruption is further described as a combination of the triggering event, which is characterized through frequency of occurrence and magnitude, and a consequential situation, which threatens the normal course of business operations. A disruption is regarded as more severe and often persist for a longer period in time than a disturbance.

Klibi and Martel [169] combine the availability of probability information and the extent of impact related to each triggering event. The authors distinguish between random, hazardous, and uncertain events. The former are described by probability distributions and occur within single periods. Hazardous events affect supply chain performance in adjacent periods. They are considered to be rare but repetitive. No probability information is available for uncertain events, however, they are considered to have enormous impact on the supply chain in adjacent periods.

Since supply chain risk is understood as a triggering event, most authors focus on categorizing supply chain risk with regards to the triggering events in order to distinguish it from other business risks [329]. This serves to better understand and manage its inherent diversity. While the majority of the approaches relate supply chain risk to the source or root causing the deviations, some authors relate risk to ultimate consequences. According to Jüttner et al. [151] and Kajüter [155] these approaches distinguish between cause- and effect-oriented definitions of supply chain risk. Major efforts in the Anglo-American supply chain risk management literature have been dedicated to cause-oriented methods. The rationale behind is that by knowing the cause, appropriate measures to reduce the likelihood of occurrence can be implemented. Additionally, the taxonomies differentiate between sources related to the supply network and to supply chain processes. Table 3.2 shows a summary of relevant supply chain risk categories and subcategories as defined in literature.

In the following the focus is set to the analysis of *risk sources.* Depending on whether the risk source lies within or beyond the supply chain boundaries, we find endogenous and exogenous origins for the supply chain risk. As a supply chain usually consists of several different interconnected companies, Götze and Mikus [109] further distinguishes endogenous risk sources as "beyond company borders" and "corporate-wide" sources. Another classification refers to the possibility of controlling the risk: Jüttner et al. [151], Waters [334], and Wagner and Bode [329] distinguish internal from external risk sources that are beyond the managers' control (e.g., policy or market risk). Christopher and Lee, Jüttner et al., and Christopher and Peck find three different types of *network related sources of supply chain risk*: lack of ownership, chaos, and inertia [57, 58, 151]. Lack of ownership refers to the increasing number of logistics partners and the resulting unclear lines of responsibilities. The increased complexity of the supply network, significant changes in the environmental conditions, and market signals drive inadequate mitigation [151], which result from over-reactions or distorted information. Among others, *process-related sources of supply chain risk* are for example referred to the Supply Chain Operations Reference (SCOR) model. Risk sources are assigned to the key processes defined within the SCOR model: plan, source, make, deliver, and return. Consequences of "SCOR-process-risks" [345] are further characterized by quality, delay, breakdown, costs etc., to facilitate analysis and communication.

Category	Subcategory	Perspective	Type of supply chain risk (characteristic of supply chain risk source)	Author
Risk sources	Network	Location	supply chain exogenous beyond company borders supply chain endogenous corporate-wide supply chain endogenous	Götze and Mikus [109]
			supply demand environmental	Jüttner [149]
			supply chain network (physical network, financial network, informational, relational, innovational network)	Cavinato [49]
		Controllability	internal	Jüttner et al. [151]
			external	Waters [334]
			internal (demand side, supply side, regulatory/legal/bureaucratic, infrastructure, catastrophic) external (regulatory/legal/bureaucratic, infrastructure, catastrophic)	Wagner and Bode [329]
			lack of ownership	Christopher and Lee [57]
			chaos	Jüttner et al. [151]
			inertia	Christopher and Peck [58]

	Assessment	quantitative qualitative	Svensson [297]
	Stakeholder	supplier-related (disruptions, delays, systems, information processing, intellectual property, procurement, receivables) internal (disruptions, delays, systems, information processing, procurement) customer-related (disruptions, delays, systems, information processing, receivables)	Chopra and Sodhi [56]
Process	SCOR levels	plan (quality, delay, breakdown, costs) source (quality, delay, breakdown, costs) make (quality, delay, breakdown, costs) deliver (quality, delay, breakdown, costs) return (quality, delay, breakdown, costs)	Ziegenbein [345]
	Controllability	environmental supply (intra-corporate) process (intra-corporate) control demand	Kersten et al. [160]
	Organizational functions	research & development supply production	Kupsch [179]

		distribution financial personal management	
	Logistical operations	order processing inventory warehouse packing transport	Götze and Mikus [109]
Target area of Risk	Location	corporate supply chain wide	Götze and Mikus [109]
	Extent of impact	operational (demand, supply and cost deviations) disruption (natural and man-mad disasters)	Tang [306]
	Controllability	known-unknown/unknown-unknown controllable/uncontrollable	Simchi-Levi [273]
	Propagation	cumulative additive singular	Kajüter [154]

Table 3.2: Supply chain risk categories.

An alternative approach categorizes supply chain risk according to the *area* that is affected by the occurrence of risk. Perspectives of this category refer to the basis of the extent, the controllability, or the network-wide location of the impact. Kajüter [154] differentiates between cumulative, additive, and singular supply chain risks. Cumulative supply chain risks intensify as they propagate along the supply chain processes. Additive supply chain risks have negative effects along the supply chain if they co-occur. Finally, singular supply chain risks are locally isolated, thus not affecting any other parts of the supply chain. Tang [306] provides a set of dimensions referring to the *extent* of impact by addressing the risk level of certain events and differentiating between operational and disruption risks. Simchi-Levi [274, 273] focuses on the role of decision-makers and provide two dimensions of analysis by distinguishing known-unknown/ unknown-unknown and controllable/uncontrollable risk. The first dimension refers to the predictability of unknown events. The latter describes the ability to manage and limit frequency and impact of risk. The unknown-unknowns are risks that can hardly be predicted. Terrorist attacks, epidemics, or geo-political instability are typical examples, but due to the climate change, also extreme weather events and related natural catastrophes will become harder to predict. The known-unknowns are risks that can be predicted from analyses of past events, for example by the means of statistical data analysis, e.g. meantime to failure, supplier lead time [273]. Controllability refers to the ability to manage and limit frequency and impact of risk. This classification is subject to individual expert assessment: the predictability and controllability of execution problems strongly depend on the nature of the business environment and the sighted level of business objectives. Moreover, the binary character makes it hard to compare the degree of control or knowledge between different events.

Based on these categorizations, Figure 3.4 shows those approaches that strongly differ between the source of uncertainty and the affected area. For instance Goh et al. [106] develop a stochastic model for a facility location and distribution planning problem under supply, demand, and exchange rate risk, where uncertainty arises from supply, demand and exchange rate, respectively. Supply chain risk is regarded as the source of uncertainty. Similarly, Mak and Shen as well as Sawik regard risk as the disruption risk, while the source of uncertainty is modeled as a distribution function of the disruption [193, 266].

Other sources of uncertainty are referred to as supply risk [67, 81, 86, 177, 178, 188, 265, 264, 344], demand risk [14, 30, 67, 106, 178, 238, 264, 284], or risk of (total) cost [14, 106, 340]. Most approaches, however, describe supply chain risk as the deviation of the affected objective, which is most often profit-, cost-, or cash-flow-oriented and therefore referred to as *monetary figure* [12, 16, 53, 117, 136, 180, 187, 221, 226, 264, 287, 341, 342, 343]. Minor work is dedicated to regard risk as customer's satisfaction [177] or supplier failures [331].

Affected Supply Chain

From emergency management another dimension of risk exposition can be identified. To prevent harm from human lives, to keep safety and to ensure sustainable growth, authorities and policy makers have sought to anticipate and prepare for the unexpected [234, 321]. Examples include emergency management plans [13] or the design of stress tests for critical infrastructures [244]. In these contexts, risk is often determined as a function of hazard, vulnerability and exposure [47, 207]. This distinction is targeted at supporting decision-makers by distinguishing the external components of risk that can hardly be influenced (such as a natural hazard) from the internal values that can be controlled or manipulated [35]. Not only does this approach regard risk as a threat deriving from triggering events, but also as a concept that depends on characteristics of the underlying organization. Only some authors have recently highlighted the correlation between magnitude of supply chain risk and the capability of resistance of the underlying system [169, 188].

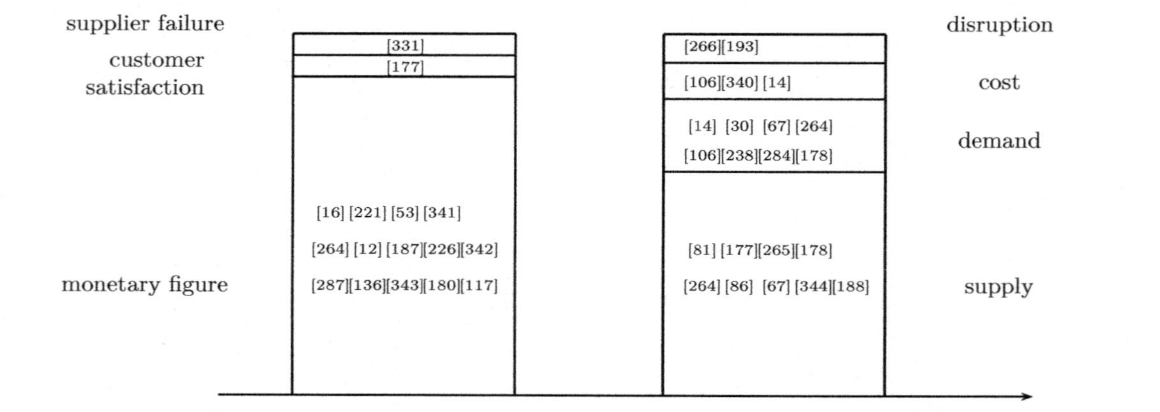

Figure 3.4: Literature analysis of supply chain risk categories: (A) Supply chain risk is classified upon the affected key performance indicator and/or (B) supply chain risk is understood as the source of uncertainty and therefore related to the uncertain parameters.

The concept used to describe the extent to which a supply chain is susceptible to a specific or unspecific risk event is called *supply chain vulnerability*. It is remarkable that prevalent definitions of both triggering event and supply chain vulnerability use concepts and computational formulae that are similar, often even identical, to supply chain risk definitions. A concept closely related to supply chain vulnerability is *supply chain resilience* describing the ability of a supply chain to overcome vulnerability. In general, vulnerability is defined as a concept that describes "the characteristics and circumstances of a community, system or asset that make it susceptible to the damaging effects of a hazard" [319]. In this sense, supply chain vulnerability can be understood as a concept that comprehends the supply chain as a system within its socio-economic environment comprising the abilities to respond to the hazard and cope with the damage that could occur. Three main perspectives of definitions describing the concept of supply chain vulnerability can be distinguished within the contemporary literature: definitions are either identical to the definition of supply chain risk, or they relate to the extent of supply chain exposure or they refer to characteristics of the underlying supply chain. Table 3.3 illustrates the prevailing perspectives on vulnerability.

The first perspective in Table 3.3 refers to the definition of supply chain risk: authors from the fields of supply chain risk management, transportation systems and network analysis understand vulnerability as a combination of the likelihood of a triggering event and its related consequence [66, 147, 271, 297, 298, 299]. Defining supply chain vulnerability as "something [that] is at risk" [231, p.132] requires an understanding of what is meant by supply chain risk. Additionally, there is no clear and unanimous distinction between the definition and understanding of supply chain vulnerability and supply chain risk.

Further work focuses on developing a conceptual and rather qualitative understanding of supply chain vulnerability by relating it for instance to *propensity*, *susceptibility* and *exposure* [19, 51, 58, 151,

Perspective	Definition of Supply Chain Vulnerability	Author
supply chain risk	Supply Chain Vulnerability = $S_e P_e$	Craighead et al. [66], Jenelius and Mattsson [147], Sheffi and Rice [271]
	"something is at risk; vulnerable: likely to be lost or damaged"	Peck [231]
	vulnerability as a construct consisting of two components, namely "disturbance" and "the negative consequence of disturbance"	Svensson [297, 298, 299]
supply chain exposure	"propensity of risk sources and risk drivers to outweigh risk mitigating strategies"	Jüttner et al. [151]
	"an exposure to serious disturbances, arising from risks within the supply-chain as well as risks external to the supply-chain"	Chapman et al. [51], Christopher and Peck [58]
	a susceptibility to incidents that can reduce availability of network resources	Berdica [31], Barnes and Oloruntoba [19]
supply chain characteristics	"is a function of certain supply chain characteristics"	Wagner and Bode [328]
	"incapacity of the supply chain to react to the disturbances at a given moment"	Barroso et al. [21]
	"characteristics and circumstances of a system [...] that make it susceptible"	United Nations Inter-Agency Secretariat of the International Strategy for Disaster Reduction (UN/ISDR) [319], Birkmann [35], Pettit et al. [235]

Table 3.3: Supply chain vulnerability definitions.

328, 330]. A first step towards a systematic understanding of supply chain vulnerability was taken by Wagner and Bode [328]. Following their argumentation certain structural supply chain characteristics can influence corporate loss given a supply chain disruption. Similarly, Barroso et al. [21] define supply chain vulnerability as the "incapacity of the supply chain to react to the disturbances at a given moment, and consequently to reach supply chain objectives".

The concept of *resilience* is applied in many different disciplines such as ecology, engineering, sociology, psychology, economics and organizational analysis. The overall understanding of resilience relates to the ability of the underlying system (material, network, individual, companies or corporate entities) to adjust or maintain essential functions under stressful and harsh conditions. In engineering resilience refers to a material's characteristic "to recover its size and shape after the deformation caused by especially compressive stress" [206]. Particularly in crisis and emergency management, resilience is often defined as the response to an actual threat, the ability to "bounce back" to the initial state [36, 61, 80, 195]. This state is considered as a point of reference, although its optimality is not guaranteed. In fact, in many situations it can be advantageous to adjust to or strive to attain a new state. In supply chain management, reasons may be that environment and operating conditions have changed in a way that turn the initial state unfavorable, or because the supply chain has learned from the disruption and adapts to the new (desired) state to improve preparedness. The first definitions of resilience referring to supply chain management were developed in 2004 at the Cranfield University [58] and in parallel studies at the MIT [271]. This work resulted in a first concise definition of supply chain resilience, which is still dominating: supply chain resilience is defined as the ability of a supply chain to return to its original or move to a new, more desirable state after being disturbed [58, 103, 231, 237]. While this understanding is uncontested in the supply chain management literature, different attitudes prevail about how supply chain resilience is related to supply chain vulnerability and to supply chain risk and how supply chain resilience can be achieved. Consequently, definitions on supply chain resilience either refer to the ability to overcome supply chain vulnerability [21, 235, 297, 298, 299] or to the ability to reduce supply chain risk [80, 150, 230]. A research analysis of current literature reveals dimensions, which are deemed to be important to increase supply chain resilience. According to Rice and Caniato the most relevant "resilience capabilities" are *flexibility* and *redundancy* [245]. Both can be further specified through flexibility-related concepts like agility [58], responsiveness [48], velocity [150], or intra-corporate concepts such as supply chain risk management culture [58], collaboration [247] and visibility [58].

Some conceptually oriented work has already described the need to combine the event-driven perception of supply chain risk with a systematic-driven view on the underlying supply chain [150, 328]. Other quantitative works pointed out the importance of combining disruptive triggers with the configuration of the supply chain [169, 177, 188, 268], but only a few applied this perception within their models, see for example [14].

Time-based Characteristics

A universal aspect of risk, which is applied in many different domains, is the consideration of time. In financial management, for example, the time horizon length has a meaningful influence on the assessment of risk and has attracted much attention [107, 326]. In emergency or disaster management early warning systems yield to increase the preparedness of a system with regard to reaction-time [241].

The literature on supply chain risk management has not yet considered in depth time-aspects, yet some authors point out their importance with respect to the modeling of supply chain risk [117, 188, 194, 270, 329]. As can be derived from the literature analysis, time-aspects are introduced for the modeling of disruptive triggers or for characterizing the affected supply chain. The magnitude of consequences, for instance, depend on the current work load of the affected supply chain (netting between demand quantity and available capacities). Considering the European ash cloud in 2010, it is quite obvious that the consequences would have been less severe if the Icelandic volcano had erupted during Christmas holidays, when many production facilities are closed anyway. The time of an impact is important in the consideration of supply chain risk [30]. Time-based characteristics that describe the ability of the affected supply chain to discover and respond to disruptive triggers are captured by Ben-Tal et al. [30] as well as Sodhi and Tang [286]. The authors distinguish between time to design a solution in response to the disruption [30], time to deploy the solution, and the time of recovery [286]. Besides characterizing the affected supply chain, time-based aspects describe properties of a disruptive trigger. For example the speed of an event captures how fast parameters change during or after the occurrence of an event [194]. The time for detection of an event formalizes the time until information about the event is available [194, 286]. The frequency captures the time between two triggering events [194]. The frequency of such events has increased considerably over the last years [59]. The duration of changes evoked by triggering events are declared as a relevant temporal aspect [270, 329, 343].

However, the classifications of time-based characteristics are of conceptual nature and have not yet been fully transfered to mathematical approaches. The description of time-based characteristics mainly relates to supply chain modifications that were evoked by triggering events, and do not relate to decisions, risk management, and required counter measures. Changes may also arise by uneventful trends or slightly varying level shifts. As the literature analysis reveals, approaches have not payed much attention to time-based characteristics of supply chain risk so far. Although mid-term problems like inventory, supply or demand planning imply the consideration of several periods, they do not employ time for capturing risk.

Definition 3.2: Risk Exposition

Risk exposition is defined as a (functional) relationship between the occurrence of a triggering event, characteristics of the underlying supply chain, and time-based characteristics. Time-based characteristics co-determine the dynamics of a trigger's effects on the supply chain status.

3.4.3 Risk Attitude

Derived from utility theory and applied in the field of financial risk management, risk is specified by the risk attitude of the decision maker. The subjective perception of the importance of risk is divided into three groups: risk-averse, risk-seeking, and risk-neutral. These attitudes drive managers' decision-making processes and lead to different solutions. Supply chain risk, as risk in general, may be regarded as a subjective concept that relies on the individual's assessment of potential outcomes, rather than an objective concepts [72]. Risk attitudes and individual or organizational preferences, therefore, have a decisive influence on the measurement of future supply chain performance and consequently co-determine supply chain decisions. While most of the approaches do not explicitly consider different risk attitudes, some authors refer to subjective perceptions of the decision maker. Liu and Nagurney [187], for instance, suggest that supply chain managers should first evaluate the risk tolerance level of the firm before making decisions that need to last for the long-run. Wakolbinger and Cruz [331] apply a weighting factor representing an adjustable risk attitude of the decision maker. Table 3.4 summarizes which of the analyzed approaches considered risk attitudes explicitly within their models.

Interestingly, risk-seeking attitudes are not considered in supply chain risk literature so far. A reason might be that supply chain risk is mainly related to negative developments of supply chain objectives.

Ref	Single risk attitude			Multiple risk attitudes
	risk-averse	risk-neutral	risk-seeking	adjustable
[14]		✓		
[16]	✓	✓		
[53]	✓			
[117]		✓		
[169]	✓	✓		
[180]	✓			
[187]	✓	✓		
[193]		✓		
[221]				✓
[226]	✓			
[266]	✓	✓		
[265]		✓		
[264]	✓	✓		
[287]	✓			
[331]				✓
[340]				✓
[342]	✓	✓		

Table 3.4: Risk attitudes considering approaches

However, to the best of our knowledge, definitions of different attitudes towards supply chain risk do not exist in the contemporary literature. As deduced in Section 3.4.1, the extent of supply chain risk strongly depends on pursued goals of the underlying supply chain. Supply chain goals are detailed by the type of objective, which can be both efficiency- or effectiveness-based, and their corresponding target-values. Based on the findings so far, we provide a definition of supply chain risk attitudes as follows.

Definition 3.3: Supply Chain Risk Attitude – Risk averse, Risk seeking, Risk neutral

The decision maker's degree of acceptance with respect to the deterioration of target-values defines his attitude towards supply chain risk. Risk-averse supply chain managers only accept a minor deterioration of target values of an efficiency- (or effectiveness-) based supply chain goal in exchange for the adherence or increase of an effectiveness- (or efficiency) based supply chain goal. Risk-seeking decision makers, however, accept higher degrees of value deterioration of a specific goal in exchange for the adherence or increase of an opposite one. Risk-neutral supply chain managers prefer neither of the two objective types.

If target values of efficient- and effective-based supply chain goals are too tight, these objectives can be mutually exclusive. For example, a targeted service level of 100% in addition with a sighted level of zero logistics cost might be impossible.

3.5 Re-defining Supply Chain Risk

An increase in observed supply chain disruptions has raised awareness towards supply chain risk management in recent years. Unfortunately, the understanding of what exactly is meant by supply chain risk, which information should be monitored, and how risk management and mitigation can be designed is heterogeneous. As risk considerations are already deeply embedded in other fields and partly applied in supply chain management, we conducted an extensive literature analysis on risk concepts in general and on conceptual as well as mathematical supply chain risk approaches in particular. Based on the literature review we identified core characteristics that are used to define, quantify and model risk. Adjusted to supply chain risk management these core characteristics can also define *supply chain risk.*

The identification and discussion of core characteristics allows for a re-definition of supply chain risk as follows:

Definition 3.4: Supply Chain Risk

Supply chain risk is the *potential loss* for a supply chain in terms of its *target values of efficiency* and *effectiveness* evoked by *uncertain* developments of supply chain *characteristics* whose changes were caused by the *occurrence* of *triggering-events.*

This re-definition allows to operationalize supply chain risk, because it is clearly distinguished from other concepts like probability or vulnerability and is additionally well-defined through major properties. We emphasize that this partition allows for a reliable risk measurement. Yet, new measures need to be developed, because existing ones can not assume this task. Due to the fact that the re-defined supply chain risk is characterized as a potential threat of a specific targeted objective, one can compare different supply chain risks. The quantification and modeling of supply chain risk, however, remain to be the real challenge in the field of supply chain risk management.

4 Supply Chain Risk Analysis – Common Flaws, Core Areas, and Main Tasks

"Mehr Licht!" – "More light!"

Johann Wolfgang von Goethe

On March 11th, 2011, a marine earthquake offshore the Japanese islands reached magnitude 9 on the Richter scale. The waves of the unleashed tsunami reached height up to 14 meter. More than 25.000 people were killed due to this natural catastrophe and its immediate consequences. Additionally, several nuclear power plants were affected by the quake and/or by the tidal wave. The emergency power generators of the Fukushima-Daiichi plant were destroyed such that they provoked the failure of the cooling system. Due to this failure a series of reactions lead to a partial core meltdown in three reactors and the escape of radioactive material to the environment.

As earthquakes and tsunamis are quite common in Japan, reactor plants have to be prepared for serious realizations of such events. The Fukushima-Daiichi plant was designed for magnitude of 8.6 on the Richter scale and tsunami waves of height 5.7 meter. Waves higher than the expected maximum of 5.7 meter have a strong potential to destroy the plant's cooling system, which is vital for nuclear safety. With the benefit of hindsight, it seems irresponsible that the plant was not designed for much higher waves. While authorities and officials declare this type of faulty preparation as a part of the unmanageable *residual risk* related to power plants [190, 336], scientists are rather questioning the usefulness of contemporary risk analysis [116]. Residual risk is often misapplied to refer not only to unmanageable developments, but additionally to those nobody is willing to manage. After such devastating events, proper emergency, safety and security plans are always discussed and put to further speculations. Compared to Japan the chance of a tsunami to occur in Germany is extremely limited. However, an advanced country like Japan was not able to properly conduct risk analysis, which could have limited the devastating incidents following the marine earthquake. This fact initiated a huge debate in Germany about natural and technical risks [85, 173]. The public dispute and perception about the dramatic events in the Fukushima nuclear power plant, prompted the German government to seal the absolute phase out of nuclear power. This event demonstrates that contemporary risk analysis is either flawed, limited or misapplied.

While the name "Fukushima" epitomizes the limitations of risk analysis in regards of public security and safety [116], events like the West coast port lockout or the European ash-cloud put the validity of contemporary supply chain risk analysis into question. The prevailing perception of risk derived from engineering assesses risk as the product of probability and impact both related to the occurrence of a disruptive event [143]. Risk analysis, thus, values expectations about future hazards. They constitute the attempt to rationalize the uncertainty of potential perils. As such, supply chain risk analysis is used as a basis for specifying mitigation options, contingency or emergency plans. Often the value of expectations provided by contemporary risk analysis is misinterpreted, because they neither predict the exact level of damage nor the precise point in time of its occurrence. The management of risks evaluated by the prevailing concept of risk analysis is therefore incomplete and non-satisfying. The benefit of contemporary risk analysis is up for debate:

- Is event-based risk analysis good enough for risk management?
- Which conclusions can be drawn from probabilistic risk analysis?
- How can risk analysis provide insights for the formulation of mathematical decision models?

In this chapter we approach the answers to the aforementioned questions with special focus on supply chains by identifying existing flaws related to the perception of risk analysis. We do not limit ourselves to the discussion of misinterpretations and missing aspects, but rather provide insights of the underlying dynamics that result in the supply chain risks. Based on the new formulated definition of supply chain risk (see Chapter 3) we present the influence of core characteristics and their interactions on the extent of supply chain risk and provide a profound and comprehensive explanation of the dynamics that should drive appropriate risk-aware solution models and methods for supply chain problems.

4.1 The Risk of Supply Chain Risk Analysis

Definitions of concepts related to supply chain risk depend on the methodological background and interest of research scientists as well as on cultural, industrial or geographical differences, as pointed out in Chapter 3. As the concept of supply chain risk is heterogeneously defined, so are derivative functions such as supply chain risk assessment, supply chain risk analysis or supply chain risk management. Often these terms are used interchangeably [216]. The Society for Risk Analysis for instance, a multidisciplinary, interdisciplinary, scholarly, international community discussing topics within the field of risk analysis, defines risk analysis as "a detailed examination including risk assessment, risk evaluation, and risk management alternatives" [283]. The International Organization for Standardization and The International Electro-technical Commission published the ISO/IEC 31010 standard on Risk Management and Risk Assessment Techniques. Therein, risk analysis is defined as a process, which supports the comprehension of risk and the determination of the level of risk [143]. Other organizations such as the European Commission (EC) or the Crisis and Risk Network (CRN), which is run by the Center for Security Studies (CSS) at ETH Zurich, similarly define risk analysis as a process encompassing three major sub-fields: risk assessment, risk management, and risk communication [121, 115].

In order to limit the confusion related to concepts and definitions we abstract commonly used steps for the analysis of supply chain risk based on the definition of managerial process steps often referred to as supply chain risk management, see Chapter 2. Correspondingly, supply chain risk analysis addresses distinct steps of the supply chain risk management cycle, see Figure 4.1.These tasks are connected to a continuously executed process.

The effective and efficient practice of this process in today's globalized world depends on the collaboration between geographically dispersed organizations [174]: (local) information must be collected, evaluated and shared across organizational boundaries [99]. Yet information processing needs to be aware of uncertainty. The status and the development of situations can be uncertain or fast-changing. The degree of relevance and reliability of information describing both status and development can be dynamic or uncertain, too.

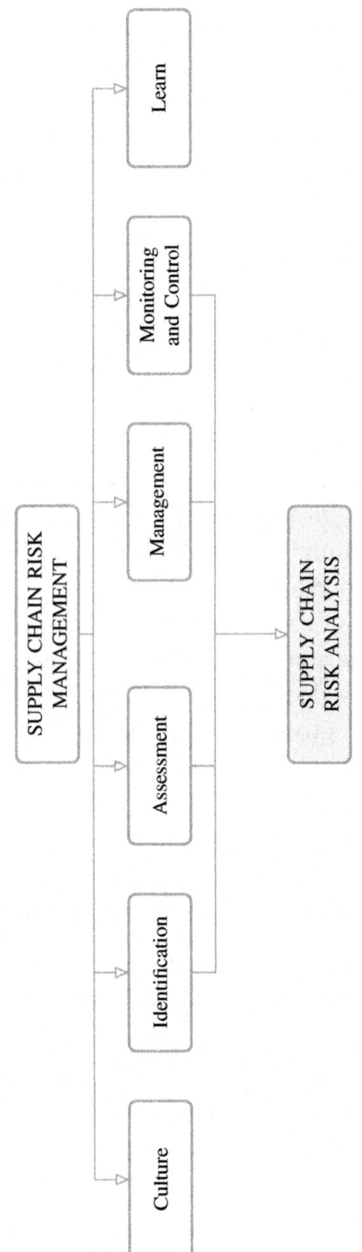

Figure 4.1: Formation of supply chain risk analysis.

These characteristics pose particular problems to supply chain managers as they make it impossible to process all available information prior to choice [199]. To deal with such situations people use heuristic forms of thinking that are relatively simple; they involve processing less of the available information and doing so in a simpler way.

These *heuristics* operate at individual and group level. For instance, individuals rely on confirmation thinking: having derived an initial interpretation of the information available, all further information searches and evaluations are biased. Falsifying information is often ignored or reinterpreted in ways that support the initial understanding. This leads to incorrect interpretations being followed with very high degrees of confidence [165]. Similarly, individuals have difficulties assessing probabilities of outcomes, so often base their judgments on subjective credibility or plausibility [152]. In other words, a plausible story is usually thought to be highly probable. There is also a range of simplifying procedures at the group level [94]. For example, groups have a strong tendency to discuss information that they hold in common without sharing information that each individual holds uniquely ('common knowledge effect') [130]. This tendency reduces the potential benefit of group decision making, which assumes that involving more individuals means that the decision is informed by more of the relevant information. Heuristics are functional, in the sense that they make complex problems tractable. However, decisions based on heuristics are prone to error and bias, which can lead to catastrophic outcomes for individuals and organizations [102].

In the following we present biases of analysis of supply chain risk which originated from heuristic thinking. We emphasize that biases of risk identification mainly arise from the definitional fiat of supply chain risk and from the simplified interpretation of probability. Biases of risk countermeasures originate from an oversimplification of risk treatment.

4.1.1 Biases of Risk Identification

The Definitional Fiat

The prevalent perception of risk, including supply chain risk, is event-related. Supply chain risk evaluation and assessment, therefore, focus on an event-by-event analysis and assume that the consequences of an initial triggering event e can be uniquely determined, see Figure 4.2 (a). The level of deterioration of relevant key performance indicators, like supplier's reliability, service-level, logistics costs, capacity utilization, production output, or inventory throughput time, are used to quantify the extent of impact on the supply chain performance, *SCP*. A single event, however, may lead to several distinct

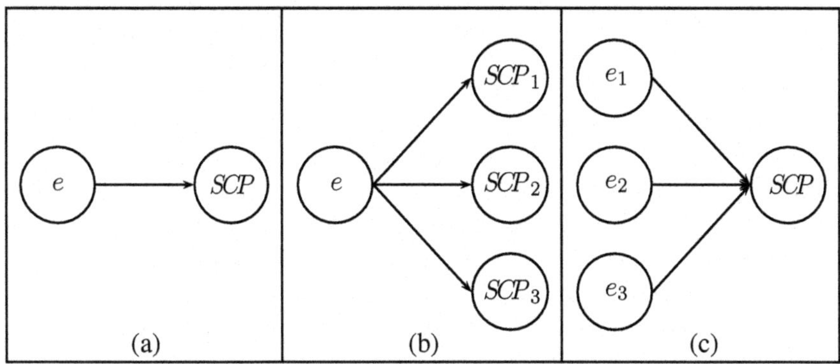

Figure 4.2: Relationship between events and their related consequences: (a) event has single outcome, (b) event has several distinct outcomes, (c) several distinct events result in the same outcome.

extents of impact on supply chain performance, see Figure 4.2 (b). An earthquake, for example, can affect production lines at core suppliers, which result in a decrease of production output at own facilities, or destroy important transportation links to customer markets, which lead to a decrease of service-level. The reverse exists too: A specific impact may be provoked by different disruptive events.

Example 4.1

The eruption of the Icelandic volcano Eyjafjallajökull led to delays of relevant production components and a halt of production [24]. In the very same year, several other, less-spectacular events occurred that had the potential to similarly affect supply chains: at the beginning of November 2010 several package bombs were detected in air cargo aircrafts; as a result cargo flights from Yemen were not allowed to enter the air space of several countries including Germany, France, the UK and the US [8, 351]. Only one month later, in December 2010, Spanish air-traffic controllers walked out on a wildcat labor strike. Spanish airspace was closed for several hours and airlines had to cancel flights [23, 25]. If the Spanish government had not authorized the military to take over flight control, the no-fly zone would have had a great impact on European supply chains.

All three examples reveal that the supply chain performance, which can be expressed by supplier's reliability, can be evoked by different triggering events. In other words, several events may result in the same single consequence for a supply chain, see Figure 4.2 (c). The reason for this ambiguity arises due to the fact that the triggering event is only the root cause of performance deterioration. In Section 4.2 we explain the dynamics that yield to negative developments after triggering events have occurred and discuss why the extent of supply chain risk depends on additional elements.

The Probability Trap

Particularly when assessing supply chain risk, probability – as measure of information uncertainty – is often inappropriately simplified or inadvertently misapplied. We denote this biased practice as *probability trap.* The following paragraphs briefly present the most important biases related to the application of the probabilistic risk definition in the context of supply chain risk management.

The explanation of the following biases highlights their similarity to existing so called *cognitive biases.* Cognitive biases describe a certain recurrent and repetitive way of heuristic thinking that results in systematic error of judgment. Based on the work of Kahneman [153] and Tversky [316] within the field of cognitive psychology, cognitive biases have been studied for years. As the definition of most cognitive biases is still controversially discussed, we limit ourselves in referring heuristic thinking within supply chain risk management to existing cognitive biases, rather than acknowledging their equality.

Ranking Bias. Global supply chains are exposed to many potential threats. It follows that the consideration and management of all risks is hardly possible. Supply chain managers, therefore, apply heuristics thinking and try to focus on managing the most important risks. To determine, what actually is most important, often the risk concept, $R = PS$, is used. The extent of a risk R is calculated by the product of probability of an event occurring, P, and the severity of its consequences, S. As the degree of uncertainty associated with a situation and its evolution may evolve over time (because new information becomes available), the probabilities associated with any risk may change, too. Often probability is considered as constant over time. Following the prevalent supply chain risk understanding that supply chain risk depends on probability, this can lead to misjudgments of risk relevance or even to its ignorance: if the probability of a highly ranked risk, R_1, decreases over time, the risk becomes less prominent and should have been rejected from the priority list. If the probability of a low-ranked risk, R_2, increases, the risk becomes more relevant and it would have been better to have considered this risk in the priority list. Instead, initial risk assessment is considered to be valid for the entire time horizon of decision level. The ranking bias resembles the *anchoring cognitive bias.* Anchoring is a cognitive bias of a decision maker that relies on the first received information (the anchor) during the decision making process. Even subsequent decisions are based on the initial information, although other (probably better) information is available. In the context of supply chain risk management anchoring, thus, originates from the need to concentrate on a subset of identified supply chain risks.

Black Swans. A decision maker underestimating the possibility and the potential consequences of a disaster might be confronted with a *Black Swan*. He assumes that a disaster that has not occurred before, will never occur in the future. If a critical situation arrives these decision makers fail to cope with the disaster. This bias arises when assessing potential triggering events. Whereas events with very low probabilities are still measurable, a phenomena exists called *Black Swans* [301]. *Black Swans* are not even represented within a distribution. Instead they are indirectly assigned a probability of zero. The reason for this is not necessarily that an event is in itself unlikely; rather its relevance is neglected either explicitly or implicitly, such as in case of emerging or unprecedented events that have not been identified yet. The *Black Swan Theory* formulated by Taleb [301] defines an event to be a *Black Swan*, when it is unexpected, has major impact and is rationalized in hindsight. The latter means that the information and data available before the event are re-interpreted in the light of the new insights. A *Black Swan*, therefore, is an event that could have been anticipated.

Example 4.2

An example is the volcanic ash cloud that affected Europe in April 2010 and is estimated to have caused losses of US$4.7 billion in global GDP [228]. Although this event has been frequently called unprecedented and unexpected [192, 253], it was neither. Volcanic activities in Iceland comparable to the 2010 eruption, occur on average every 20 to 40 years [261]. This volcanic activity only becomes a problem for air traffic in Europe when it coincides with rare north to north-westerly air movements [183]. While the ash cloud can be considered unusual, it was far from unprecedented and not unexpected: the volcano had been in eruption for four weeks before the ash cloud reached the airspace of the United Kingdom on April 15th, which was more than ample time to have put into effect contingency plans, had these existed.

In summary, *Black Swans* highlight the challenges posed by those risks for which organizations – particularly those collaborating in supply chains – and public authorities are not prepared.

Risk-elimination Bias. If, for two risks R_1 and R_2, the consequences are of equal severity ($S_1 = S_2$), the risk with higher probability is judged more important. Intuitively, however, a rare event, for which the supply chain is not prepared, is riskier than a frequent event the supply chain is already used to. Less-frequent events can have a tremendous impact on the supply chain, such that the continued non-consideration of these *unknown-unknown* events [274] can lead to the same devastating consequences as intentionally or unintentionally ignoring of risks. As risk grows with increasing impact and probability, supply chain risk management strategies aim at reducing these issues. When supply chain managers concentrate solely on the design of mitigation options for prioritized risks, they disregard the influence of those alternatives on lower-ranked risks. At best, mitigation options that reduce high-priority risks have the same impact on all other risks. In the worst case, however, mitigating one specific risk increases the impact or the probability of further risks. As these risks are usually not monitored, a change in risk relevance may go unnoticed.

Example 4.3

When, for example, the shortfall of a supplier delivering a single component is assessed to be very perilous, a prevalent mitigation strategy is to implement an alternative or backup supplier for this component [307, 303, 304]. But an additional supplier implies higher complexity and often additional costs caused by contractually specified purchase quantities or higher costs for transportation, monitoring and control. While effectiveness will improve, efficiency can aggravate.

Without a sound and careful analysis of interdependencies among *all* identified risks and identified mitigation options it is hard to assess, whether an additional supplier increases the overall resilience of the supply chain risk portfolio. Its complexity, however, has certainly increased. The risk-elimination bias has similarity with the *neglect of probability cognitive bias.* This cognitive bias relates to the tendency to completely disregard probability within the decision making process. Prioritizing the complete elimination of one risk, while a greater reduction of a group of other risks is possible, refers to the *zero-risk cognitive bias*, which could also be referred to the risk-elimination bias.

4.1.2 Biases of Risk Countermeasures

Assignment Bias

The contemporary supply chain risk analysis strictly follows the stepwise process of supply chain risk management, see Figure 2.4. Therein, each disruptive trigger is declared to be identified, assessed, and mitigated separately. Figure 4.3 highlights the allocation possibilities of identified risks– in terms of identified disruptive triggers – to available reduction strategies. Figure 4.3 (a) shows the situation where identified risks can be reduced by one or several distinct mitigation options. It might also be the case that available risk countermeasures are not appropriate for all identified risks. Only a subset of risks can be treated. This situation is depicted by Figure 4.3 (b). Figure 4.3 (c) then highlights the situation where no countermeasures are available for reducing identified risks.

Not only are disruptive triggers handled individually, but also related countermeasures. The decision maker, therefore, pre-determines which type of risk countermeasure he is willing to accept. Generally, countermeasures are categorized upon the type of supply chain process they address or upon the scope they affect. Countermeasures are not limited to supply chain processes, but can also determine engineering options for product design and production technology which in turn affect supply chain processes. Tang [305, 306, 307] gives a detailed overview of prominent quantitative approaches for mitigating the impact of supply chain risks and categorize them in accordance to supply, product, demand, and information management.

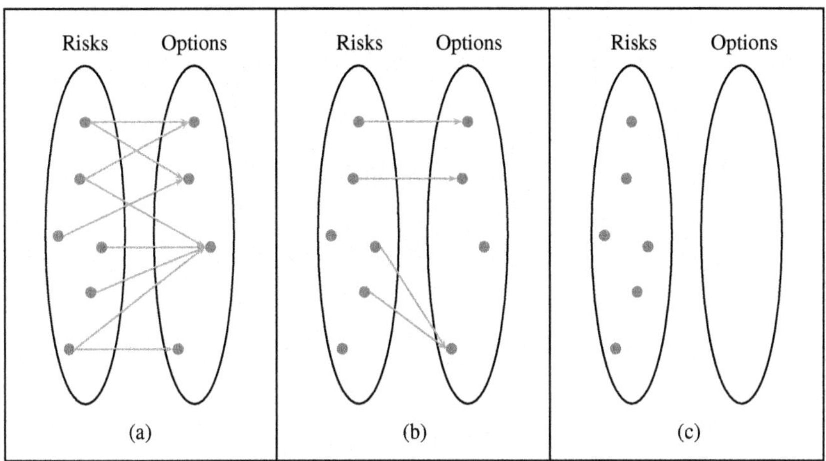

Figure 4.3: Graphical visualization of functional relation between the set of identified supply chain risks and potential mitigation options.

Figure 4.4 highlights the aforementioned risk management perspectives and related decision problems that strive for the determination of risk-aware solutions.

Table 4.1 reveals how affected companies responded to different types of disruptive triggers by applying derivatives of the aforementioned countermeasures.

Name	**Incident**	**Reaction of affected Company**	**Countermeasure**
West Coast Port Lockout	labor strike	The incident was immediately predictable. Therefore, New United Motor Manufacturing Incorporated (NUMMI) was able to increase its inventory. After inventories run empty NUMMI switched to air freight from Japan to the United States.	increased safety stock, flexible transport

9/11	terroristic attacks	Ford was not prepared with contingency plans and had to close 5 production plants. Chrysler was able to arrange direct transports from its supplier TRW in Virginia to Mexico. Continental Teves used established emergency plans with transport carriers such as Emery to compensate losses from European deliveries.	flexible transport
Nokia-Philips-Ericsson	lightening bolt	The reaction of the two main customer, Nokia and Ericsson, was very different. Nokia acted quickly and grasped the situation correctly. Due to the modular product designs of Nokia's mobile phones an alternative product specification could be created without affecting the demand of final customers. Additionally, Nokia took all available production capacities from alternative suppliers. Contrary, Ericsson could not apply postponement strategies as their product configurations did not allow alternatives and backup suppliers capacities were already blocked by Nokia.	postponement, flexible supply base
Dell-Apple	earthquake	Dell as well as Apple use a build-to-order strategy. Despite the significantly time between order and delivery date Apple was not able to isolate its customers from the consequences of the accident. Dell, however, drew the attention of customers to alternative products by advertising and strategic pricing.	postponement, flexible supply base, revenue management via dynamic pricing

Toyota-Aisin	short circuit	The close customer-supplier relationship enabled Toyota to accees the collective know-how of its suppliers, shortly implement a flexible supply base and redistribute thought lost production capacity.	flexible supply base, outsourcing

Table 4.1: Major disruptions and related countermeasures used by affected companies.

Limited Uncertainty

Uncertainty is a concept closely related to risk, see Section 3.4.2. In the context of supply chain management, uncertainty refers to the degree of not-knowing. Information about future developments within the supply chain, the occurrence of triggering-events, and the impact of any changes on supply chain performance is often limited or *uncertain*. Uncertainty can be expressed by different means, such as probability, variance, absolute or relative deviation from expected. In order to limit the size of the decision problem, decision makers limit the consideration of uncertainty to a (very) small amount of parameter types, for example customer demand or transportation lead times. The consideration of interactions between distinct uncertain and certain parameters across different parameter types is not applied. Consider the situation, where the demand of one specific type of customers is highly erratic, while the demand of another type of customers is endowed with less uncertainty. Or consider the case, where the lead times of container ships leaving the Asian region are more volatile than those of container ships leaving North America. Both cases demonstrate that approaches need to be carefully adjusted to the underlying situations. Prior to model formulation

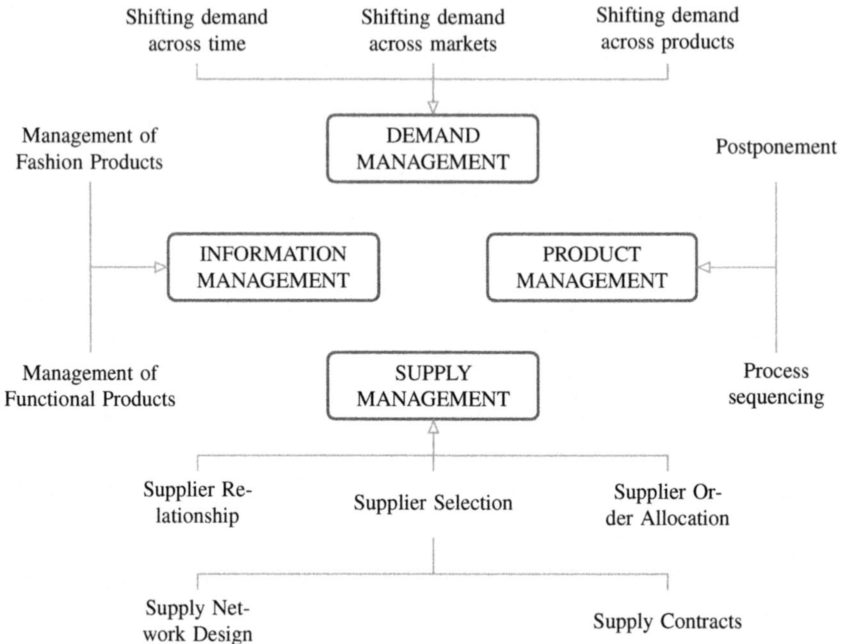

Figure 4.4: Perspectives of supply chain risk management, based on Tang [306].

it is indispensable to analyze not only which type of parameters is endowed with uncertainty, but rather which group of parameters is erratic. Similarly, the formulation of decision variables restricts the set of potential countermeasure types in advance.

Time Horizon & Planning Level

It is still an open question, for which time horizon supply chain risks should be considered and which planning level best fits for the consideration of supply chain risk. Generally, supply chain risk considerations are classified according to the decision levels: short-term, mid-term, and long-term.

Often decision makers argue that risks yielding to *huge* performance deteriorations should be handled on a strategic, *medium* risks on a tactical and *small* risks on an operational planning level. Consider the example of a Swiss chemical producer trying to limit the loss evoked by a breakdown of its production process. Typically, companies strive to limit the loss they might encounter by closing insurance contracts. However, the considered major re-insurer refused to insure the production breakdown, because the replacement time of the batch reactor was estimated to be over one year [189]. Thus, the producer had to identify another mitigation alternative in order to be prepared for disrupted production: The company established an agreement with a major competitor to share capacities in the case of production breakdown. On the contrary, the preparation on a strategic planning level for similarly *huge* risks such as the European ash cloud, might not be always sufficient. The increase of safety stock, which would have been one of the most prominent countermeasures, would yield to a constant increase of tied-up capital and consequently to an increase of overall logistic costs.

Decision models for supply chain problems consider uncertainty at distinct planning levels. Traditionally, first, strategic supply chain decisions are made. The solution of strategic decisions are used as an input for consecutive, e.g. tactical and operational, decisions, see Figure 4.5 (a). Due to the nature of most supply chain risks including the uncertainty about their future development it might be necessary to break this decision process, see Figure 4.5 (b). Most-often approaches for supply chain design are based on a problem environment where certain parameters are treated as constant over all time. Deduced supply chain structures including resource allocation are established and remain constant over years. However, product portfolio, production technology as well as international price politics change over time and other parameters such as transportation costs or supplier reliability and lead time become uncertain at once.

Disruption management is intended to overcome suddenly occurring uncertainty. It is used on the operational decision level. *Tactical*

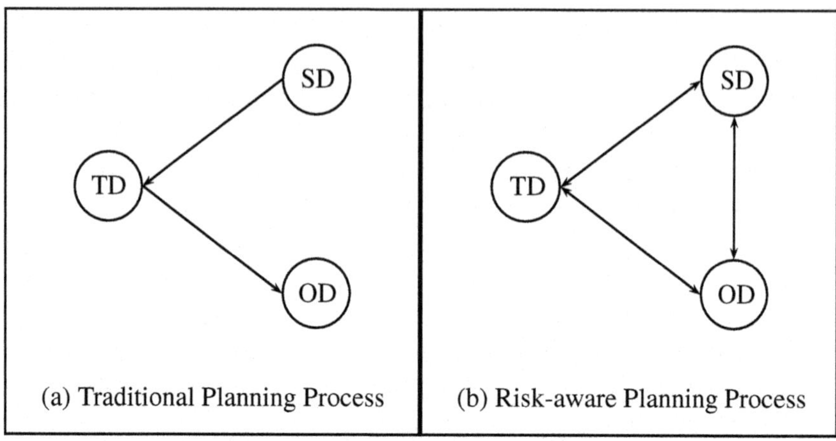

Figure 4.5: Traditional vs. risk-aware planning process (SD: Strategic Decisions, TD: Tactical Decisions, OD: Operational Decisions).

Re-planning is reasonable, if disruption management has to interfere frequently due to repeated modifications of a supply chain factor. If a periodically executed tactical re-planning is not able to reduce performance deteriorations during the execution, *Strategic Re-designs* should be carried out. If, for example, a transportation processes on a specific link is disrupted, operational disruption management could propose an alternative route or alternative means of transportation for the following transportation processes. If a delay on this transportation link needs to be managed repeatedly, it could be necessary to conduct a tactical re-planning with adjusted transportation times for this link. Earlier delivery, change of transportation means, or a modified transportation routing all reflect potential results of a re-planning step. If the tactical re-planning does not permanently reduce the performance deterioration, a strategic adjustment is recommended yielding for an increased safety stock, reallocation of resources or even closing/opening of regional distribution centers.

4.1.3 Breaking of Biases

Biases derive from heuristic forms of thinking, which aim to support the decision maker in coping with the underlying complexity.

The biases of risk identification arise due to:

- the perception of risk as a purely event-related concept,
- the perception of probability as a static rather than dynamic concept (Anchoring),
- the underestimation of event occurrence (Normalcy Bias), and due to
- the underestimation of risks with small probability of occurrence.

The biases of risk countermeasures stem from the limited consideration of complexity that:

- fades out the interaction between identified risks and appropriate countermeasures,
- bounds sources of uncertainty to distinct parameter types rather than to relevant groups of parameters,
- assigns risk to distinct planning levels.

For years it has been difficult to get access to a sufficient amount of information necessary to describe supply chain complexity and interactions. Today, due to the development of technical innovations data acquisition and preparation are more easy. What is still missing is the comprehension of the supply chain dynamics that cause the existence of supply chain risk. The missing consideration of relevant interactions forestalls the possibility to understand, model and analyze *all* potential disruptive triggers, *all* available countermeasures, and their interaction in sufficient detail. Having understood the dynamics that affect the goal attainment of underlying supply chains, formulation and solution of optimization models should resume the determination of risk-aware supply chain designs and plans.

Commonly used countermeasures such as additional suppliers, safety stock of inventory, capacity fall back positions would still be used but are determined by the mathematical model formulation, i.e. by the assignment of the degrees of freedom.

4.2 Main Elements of Supply Chain Risk Analysis

The exclusive probabilistic and event-related understanding of supply chain risk leads to an incomplete and insufficient perception and impedes the appropriate management of supply chain risks. In this section we present main elements that are needed to understand the dynamics of supply chain risk and to design appropriate risk-aware decision models.

Given the re-definition from Chapter 3 the level of supply chain risk is affected by three core characteristics: the risk objectives, the risk attitude of the decision maker, and the risk exposition of the underlying supply chain, which is further specified by disruptive triggers occurring within or exterior to the supply chain, time-based aspects having tremendous impact on the severity and characteristics of the affected supply chain. Having defined supply chain risk as a construct of interdependent elements, a profound understanding of each basic element is required as well as the analysis of their interrelations. The main tasks of supply chain risk analysis, therefore, need to be applied to these elements.

4.2.1 Analysis of Potential Triggers

Causalities

The biases discussed in Section 4.1 are based on an analysis of supply chain risk, which focuses on the simplified evaluation of the disruptive trigger and the performance deterioration. But triggering events can yield to different outcomes as well as distinct performance deteriorations may result from diverse events. This contraindication uncovers the fact that the triggering event is only the root cause of performance deterioration. A single event or a sequence of consecutive events only become a problem, when they negatively affect one or several supply chain processes and when their consequences propagate through the entire supply network. Figure 4.6 highlights this argumentation: (a) one or several events hit the supply chain and affect its functionality and/or efficiency, (b) an event triggers malfunction of a supply chain process, which propagates through the entire network

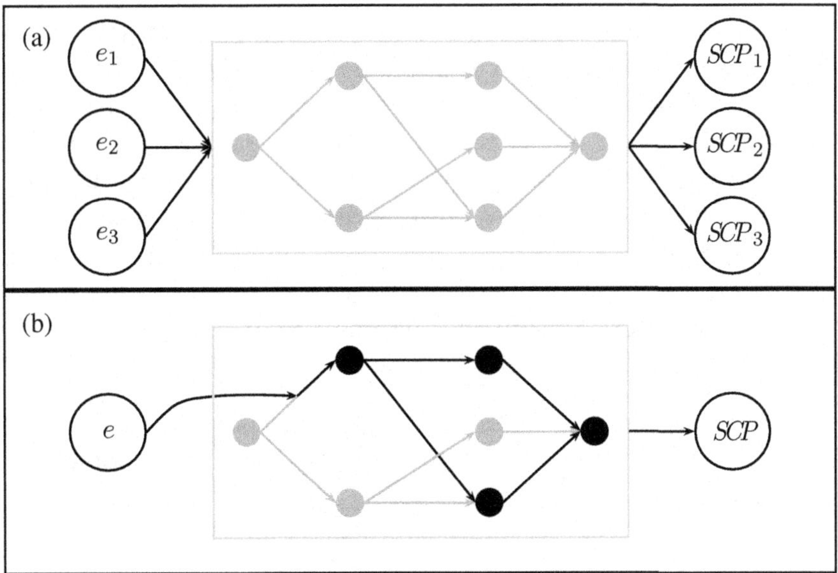

Figure 4.6: Relationship between events and their related consequences.

Definition 4.1: Supply Chain Process – SCPro

A supply chain process is defined as an individual activity involved in procuring, producing, storing, and distributing goods as well as services for the sake of goal achievement of the underlying supply chain.

Supply chain processes could be of different types of operations like transportation, production, manufacturing, storage, handling, shipment, engineering design functions, or even legal processing [132]. Once an event has occurred it is irrelevant whether it has arisen within or external to the supply chain. It is the interplay of all supply chain processes and their actual states of supply chain characteristics that defines the resilience of a supply chain towards effectiveness and efficiency. This interaction determines whether the first impact of an initial event on the supply chain provokes the inefficiency or/and ineffectiveness of consecutive processes, propagates through the entire network and finally results in a performance deterioration, see Figure 4.6 (b).

Definition 4.2: Potential Trigger – PoT

Each incident that has the potential to negatively affect the efficiency and effectiveness of a supply chain process, which may result in a performance deterioration, is defined as a potential trigger.

The eruption of the Icelandic volcano is considered to have evoked a perfect storm of consequences such as ash cloud, aircraft grounding, lead time increase, delays, halt of production and delayed customer orders. European supply chains were only hit at air transports that start or end in Europe. But for some the increase of lead time of air-shipped goods was – in this situation – large enough to result in supply chain disruptions.

We denote a potential trigger as a disruptive trigger, if its occurrence results in the deterioration of supply chain performance. Note that in Chapter 3 we introduced disruptive trigger as one element of supply chain risk. We kept its definition back to introduce it in the right context.

Definition 4.3: Disruptive Trigger – DisT
A potential trigger is defined as a disruptive trigger, if it effectively results in a deterioration of supply chain performance.

A potential trigger along with a vulnerable supply chain that is not able to handle modifications of their supply chain characteristics, both uncover the existence of one or numerous supply chain risks. However, inefficiency or ineffectiveness can be evoked by any known or unknown disruptive trigger. Instead of starting risk analyses with the identification, gathering and assessment of potential events that may serve as a disruptive trigger, we propose that it is the main task of supply chain risk analyses to evaluate the potential effect of modifications of supply chain characteristics and assess their influence on key performance indicators.

Uncertainty Profiles

The occurrence of triggering events may affect the actual status of supply chain processes and their describing characteristics. In the following we denote attributes of supply chain characteristics as *supply chain factors*. The effectiveness and efficiency of supply chain processes like transportation, production, storage, handling, or shipment are characterized by attributes like costs, capacity and time.

Definition 4.4: Supply Chain Factor – SCF

A supply chain factor is defined as the quantitative description of a specific attribute of a certain supply chain process.

Production capacity, transportation lead time, customer demand, or more detailed finished goods inventory level at an Asian distribution center are all examples of supply chain factors. In order to evaluate the potential effects of supply chain factor modifications, it is necessary to anticipate how their values may develop over time. Under the consideration of a single potential trigger the development of a supply chain factor over time can be described by temporal and quantitative aspects. In Section 3.4.2 we already introduced some of the following concepts, however, we emphasize that the elements introduced in Section 3.4.2 describe disruption profiles and present the relation between time and performance deterioration as introduced by Sheffi [270, 271] and discussed by several further authors [11, 28, 66, 192, 204, 282]. In this Section, we highlight the uncertainty development referring to the relation between time and value deviation of supply chain factors.

For the re-presentation and introduction of further concepts consider Figure 4.7. Therein, a potential deviation of a supply chain factor value from its nominal level is highlighted. This deviation may lead to specific supply chain risks, when the deviation takes positive (lead times, price) or negative values (capacity decrease). The time interval between two distinct deviations is denoted by T^a. A long time interval refers to less frequent changes of supply chain factors, while a small time interval refers to frequently occurring modifications. The duration of a value change is denoted by T^b, while this time is sub-divided by the time of major changes, T^c and a time where a deviation decays, T^d. Changes evoked by disruptive events often have a peak-moment, whose duration is described by T^e. The speed a peak is reached and left at is denoted by S^a and S^b, respectively. However,

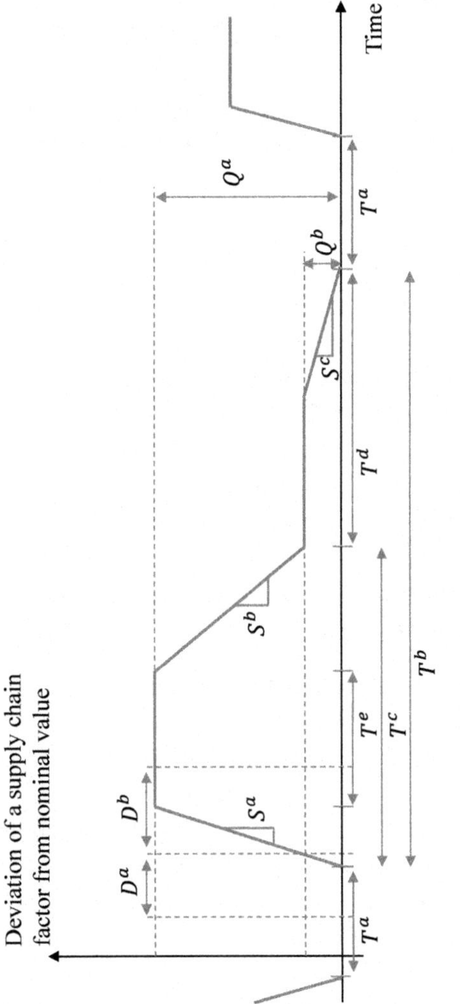

Figure 4.7: Elements of uncertainty profiles [204].

sometimes factor deviations decay in discrete steps. After a re-start of a production line, full capacity may only be reached slowly and gradually, S_c. The magnitude of deviations during its peak-moment is described by Q_a, while the magnitude during re-start or recovery is denoted by Q_b. Further, often disregarded aspects are the time of information availability or deviation detection, D_a, and the time to respond, D_b. The point in time a deviation is detected may coincide with the start of change, lie before or lie after the beginning of changing supply chain factor values.

Depending on the type of supply chain factors, uncertainty profiles look different, see Figure 4.8. They can be described by statistical moments like expected value, variance, skewness, and kurtosis. Small changes occurring frequently over time, like price or exchange rate volatilities, are exemplarily represented through the uncertainty profile (a). These often-called *operational risks* as introduced by financial risk management (see 3.4.1) relate to non-event-triggered developments that might also lead to a deterioration of supply chain performance, but also to event-based triggers like the Arabic Spring or Hurricane Katrina that affected oil production. Figure 4.9 (a) illustrates the volatility of the spot price per barrel of crude oil in terms of daily changes.

A prominent development of a tremendous deviation from nominal values is highlighted by profile (b). The uncertain development might represent a huge capacity reduction of production and transportation or an inventory stock-out. The kurtosis of this profile is high indicating a value change that occurs rarely, but is large. The profile's skewness is positive and refers to modifications that aggravate quickly but vanish slowly. Most-often major disruptive events lead to such a profile.

Example 4.4

The Thailand flooding in 2011, for example, affected production capacity and inventory stock-out and price increase, similarly. As Thailand is the world's

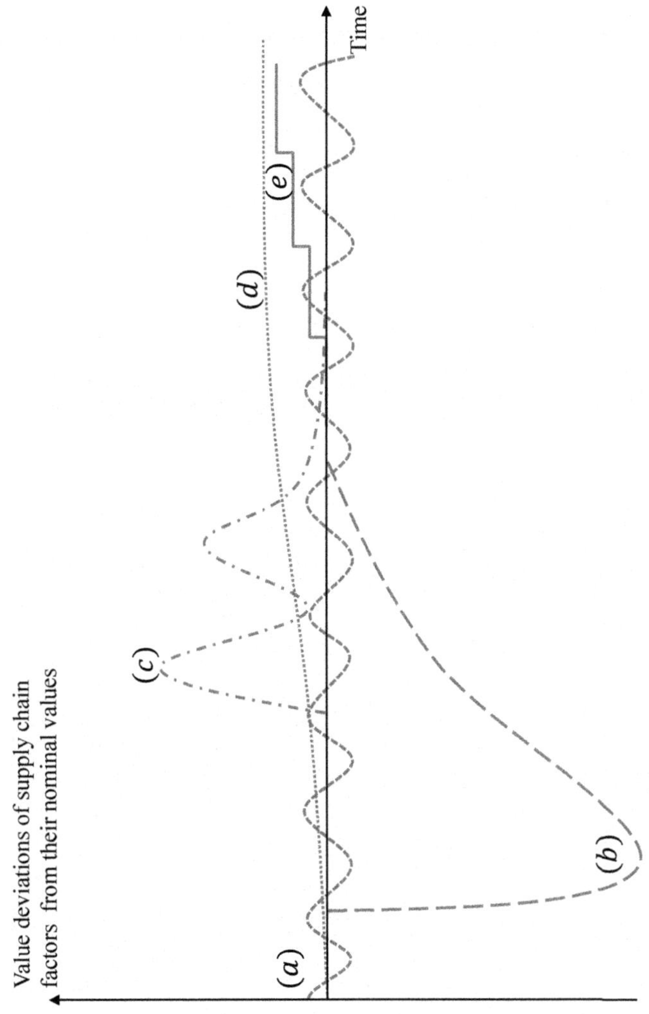

Figure 4.8: Exemplary uncertainty profiles of supply chain factor values.

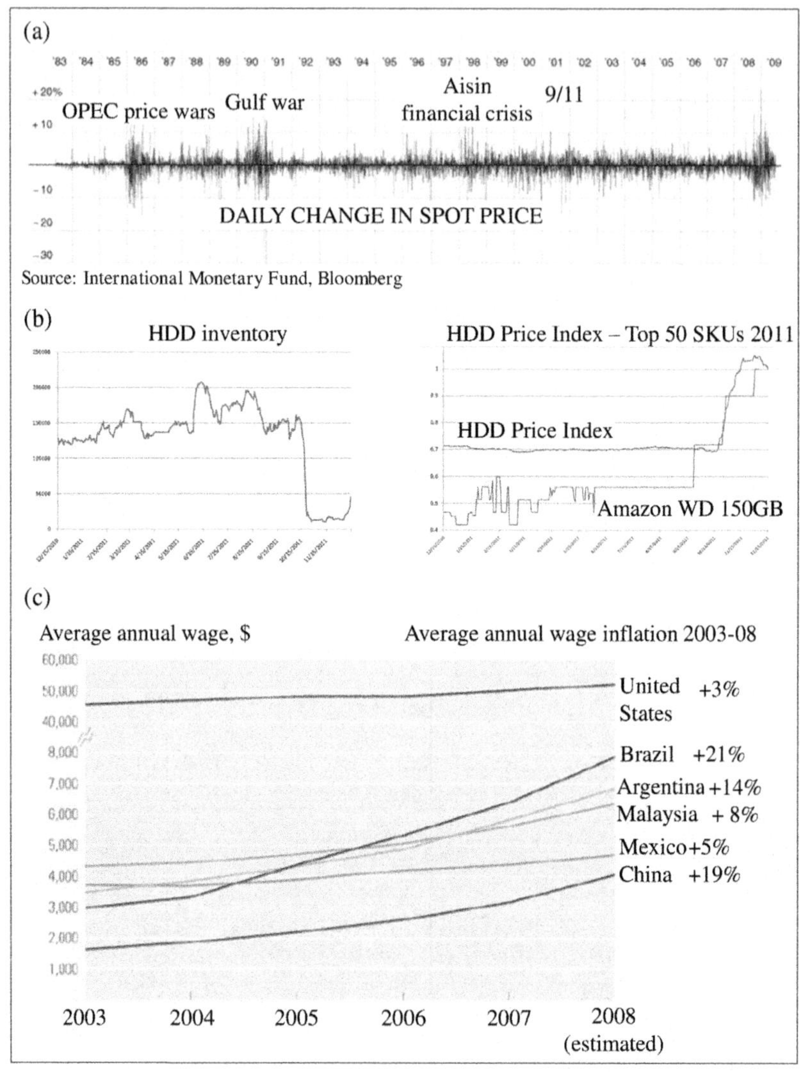

Figure 4.9: Uncertainty profiles of real-world supply chain factors: (a) daily change in spot price 1983 to 2009; Source: IMF; Bloomberg, (b) inventory level and price index of HDD; Source: Dynamite Data, and (c) average annual wage; Source: Global Insight, Economist Intelligence Unit, GIBC World Markets, McKinsey Analysis.

second major exporter of hard disk drives (HDD), an entire industrial sector was hit by the flood. According to the e-commerce tracking site Dynamite Data the price of HDD increased by 50% to 150% shortly after the flooding [203] until 300% in the weeks afterwards. The price increase originated in the sharp decline of inventory levels at both distributors and e-commerce sites. Following Dynamite Data inventory levels felt by 90% within one week.

Figure 4.9 (b) illustrates both price increase and inventory decline in the period right after the flooding. Moderate changes, (*c*), might occur less frequently than spot price modifications or more often than major deviations and have more or less severe impact on factor values of supply chains, respectively. For example, customs handling can block the export of necessary production components or can impose temporary quotes, which both result in an increased transportation time and consequently raised lead time.

Besides event-based disruptions and operational volatility, supply chain risk exists also due to changes within the supply chain or its environment that have neither the contingent nor sudden character of disruptive events. Progressing trends, (*d*), or one-directional continuous level shifts, (*e*), cannot all be allocated to specific events, but rather to creeping processes. Figure 4.9 (c) contrasts the annual wage inflation of the United States with those from countries producing high-tech goods, like Malaysia, Mexico, China, a.o..

As discussed, there might be several events having an influence on the value of the same supply chain factor. An exemplary representation of an uncertainty profile, whose development is influenced by different potential triggers, is given in Figure 4.10.

We emphasize that no matter why supply chain factors change, the supply chain constitution as well as the perception of the decision maker strongly influence the extent of supply chain risk.

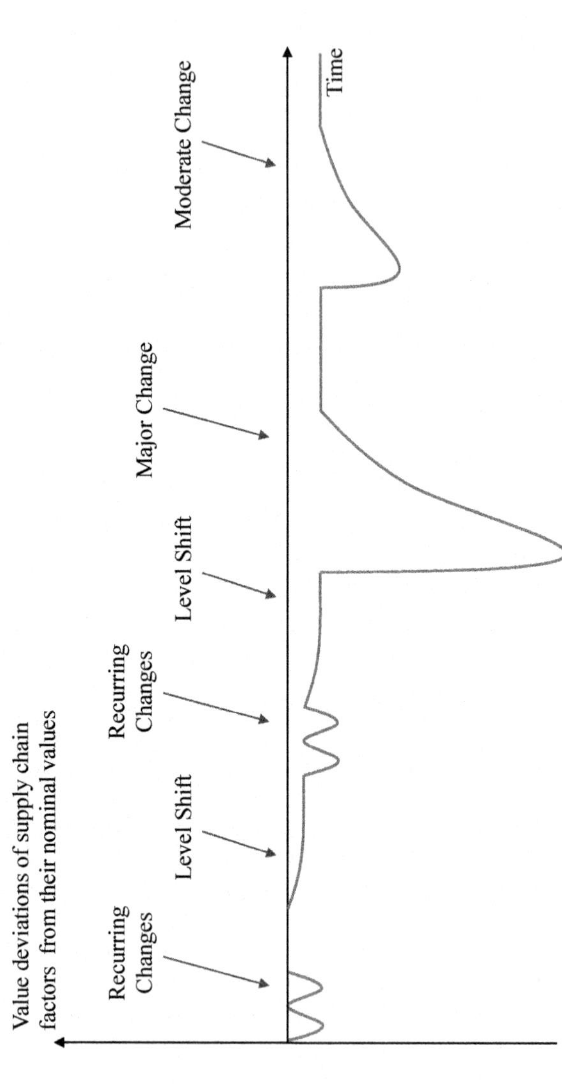

Figure 4.10: Exemplary uncertainty profiles of supply chain factor values influenced by different potential triggers.

4.2.2 Analysis of Performance Measurement

Operationalization of Efficiency and Effectiveness

We deduced that risk affected objectives can be classified into two major groups: effectiveness and efficiency, see Section 3.4.1. Effectiveness refers to the availability of resources and the functionality of supply chain processes. Effective processes are able to fulfill their functions of sourcing, producing and delivering products among others, which results in the satisfaction of customer demands on time. Whenever supply chain processes are interfered in fulfilling their functions, it could be possible that supply chain effectiveness can not be ensured. Efficiency refers to the profitable execution of supply chain processes. The efficient achievement of customer satisfaction and value creation is threatened by disruptions and failure or increasing volatility of important supply chain factors directly or indirectly related to logistics costs. In the following the focus is set to direct impacts on logistics costs. Although it may seem paradoxical, the continuous striving to be more and more efficient leads to increasing inefficiency. In the last decade supply chains were designed to be optimal with respect to their primary cost-benefit ratio. As pointed out by Simchi-Levi, the underlying rationale were "cheap oil" and "low-cost labor" [273]. Since supply chain managers based strategic decisions on the assumption of constant or slightly volatile transportation and labor costs, global sourcing and production were often among the prioritized options for supply chain design. Often offshoring or outsourcing led to reduced costs of manufacturing and inventory as well as plant rationalization, and facility consolidation offered the opportunity of realizing economies of scale [273]. These positive effects can be attained as long as the underlying assumptions are sufficiently met and prices develop as anticipated. In a world of increasing dynamics, neglecting the volatility of (oil) prices, which are today more erratic than ever before, has caused inefficiencies in the newly-formed global supply chain networks [273, 275, 276]. An alternative reason for increased logistics costs derives from the growing number of unexpected shortages and disruptions (i.e., growing uncertainty), which force the occasional reallocation of resources. Delayed inbound supply may, for instance lead to a machine disruption, which in turn delays the production, such that the company may not be able to satisfy their customers needs in time. In order to overcome this situation, a company may switch transportation mode once production is resumed; to make up for the delay, goods may be shipped by helicopter or airplane, which is much more expensive than shipment by truck or train.

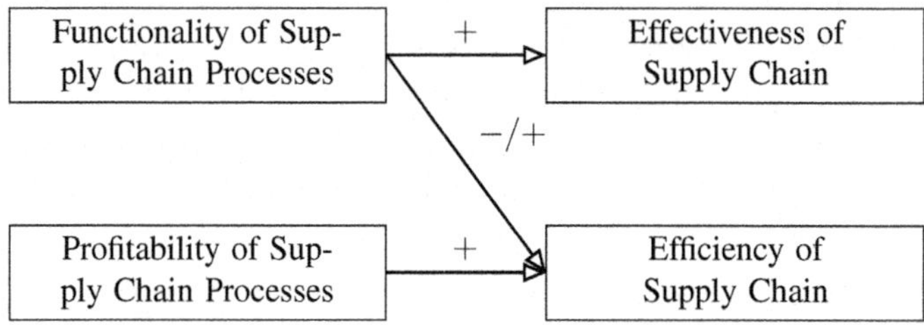

Figure 4.11: Functionality and profitability of supply chain processes affect efficiency and effectiveness.

Figure 4.11 highlights the interaction between the functionality and profitability of supply chain processes and the supply chain efficiency and effectiveness, respectively. The functionality of supply chain processes has positive as well as negative effects on supply chain efficiency. When supply chain processes are endowed with too large buffers or their functionality can only be obtained by expensive extraordinary actions, the achievement of efficiency-based objectives is threatened.

A Balanced Portfolio of Supply Chain Performance Measurement

Performance measurement provides a mean to assess supply chains with respect to improvements or to degradation of its efficiency and effectiveness. There is a vast amount of literature available that discusses both the importance of performance measurement [10, 27, 185] and the difficulty of choosing the "right" measures [70, 182]. The business performance of an organization embedded in a supply chain system depends not only on organizational efficiency, but also on the efficient and effective interplay of all supply chain entities [185]. Due to the complexity of globally operating supply chains, the variety of activities within a supply chain system as well as the subjective assessment of goal achievement of supply chain partners, the choice of supply chain performance measures is a critical task [73].

Eccles [70] among others argue that purely "accrual-based performance measures are at best obsolete – and more often harmful". Additionally, Lapide [182] states that financial accounting measures are insufficient to measure supply chain performance due to the following reasons:

- Financial measures evaluate supply chain performance in retrospect.
- Financial measures solely refer to financial goals and miss to relate to important strategic achievements like product quality and customer satisfaction.
- Financial measures prevent the assessment of operational effectiveness and efficiency.

Due to the deficiencies of traditional financial measures several measurement approaches have been developed. One of the most famous approaches in the field of performance measurement is *The Balanced Scorecard* from Richard S. Kaplan and David P. Norton [157]. The purpose of their approach is to align business activities to strategic goals by controlling non-financial and financial metrics. With respect to the measurement of supply chain performance the *Supply Chain Operations Reference (SCOR)* model has been developed by the Supply Chain Council [295]. While The Balanced Scorecard focuses on executive organizational-level measurement, the SCOR model refers to the needs of supply chain officers by comprising a set of supply chain performance measures like cycle time metrics, cost metrics, service/quality metrics, and asset metrics [182].

Performance measures should be aligned to the strategic goals of the underlying system (e.g. organization, supply chain) [157]. Supply chain strategy, however, differs among the supply chain partners and depends on a dynamic environment of competencies. Lapide [182] differentiates three stages of organizational development that determine the types of measure companies need to focus on:

- Functional Excellence
- Enterprise-Wide Integration
- Extended Enterprise Integration

A balanced portfolio of reliable supply chain performance measures is hence indispensable. The detection of poor supply chain strategies or contradicting developments *before* they become effective in poor financial results is the essence of supply chain risk analysis. Therefore, it is important to carefully select appropriate measures for supply chain performance and simultaneously exclude those that are cumbersome [182].

Performance Deterioration

Having identified which performance measures best reflect and assess supply chain strategy and related objectives of efficiency and effectiveness, it becomes necessary to determine the targeted level of these performance measures as well as the acceptable degree of level deterioration. Quite often managers know what they can bear. A service-level reduction of 2% might be acceptable, while an increase of overall logistics costs by 50% is unacceptable.

Definition 4.5: Acceptable & Critical Supply Chain Performance Deterioration – $cSCP_D$ & $aSCP_D$

A potential supply chain performance deterioration SCP_D is defined as the difference between the planned supply chain performance value SCP_P and the actual performance value SCP_A. A performance deterioration becomes critical $cSCP_D$, if it exceeds the acceptable value of performance deterioration $aSCP_D$.

The uncertainty profiles introduced in the previous section may serve as disruptive triggers and result in a deterioration of supply chain performance. Figure 4.12 (a) highlights exemplary developments of the following parameters: a factor modification over time, the planned supply chain performance, the actual supply chain performance, the resulting performance deterioration and the acceptable level of deterioration. The first minor to moderate changes can be handled by the supply chain. After the third lead time increase, however, the supply chain can not adhere to the acceptable level of performance deterioration. Based on Figure 4.9 the Figure 4.12 (b) shows the modifications of several supply chain factors over time and their implication on the degree of performance achievement. The major (capacity-) change at the beginning of the considered time horizon makes it difficult to handle moderate changes during the recovery phase.

The evaluation of the performance deterioration is a subjective concept and depends on the preferences of the decision maker [94]. The importance of a (potential) loss depends on both organizational and individual goals and constraints. Some decision makers accept only small deviations from the planned supply chain performance while others allow higher changes. In relation to a given acceptable level of supply chain performance deterioration Figure 4.13 a) presents directions towards more risk-averse and more risk-seeking levels of acceptable performance deterioration.

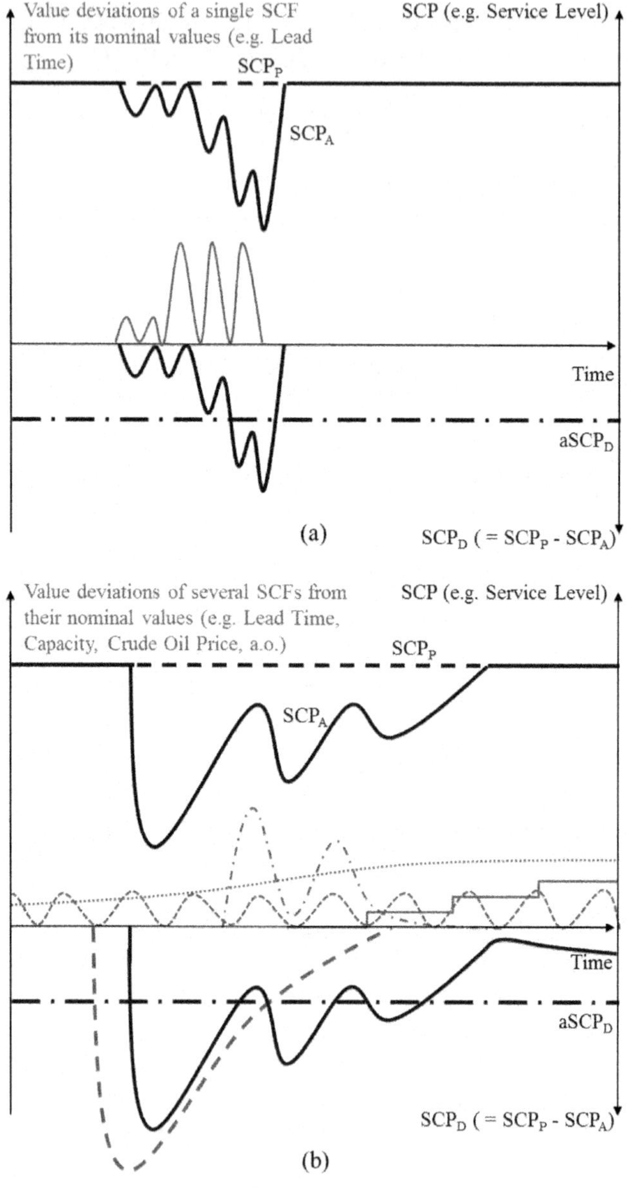

Figure 4.12: Exemplary uncertainty profiles of supply chain factor values.

As defined in Chapter 3.4.3 risk-seeking decision makers accept higher degrees of value deterioration of a specific goal in exchange for the adherence or increase of an opposite one. So, whenever a decision maker is willing to accept a higher performance deterioration, he wants something in return. To better understand the interactions behind this argument we provide the following example. Figure 4.13 b) shows the development of the performance deterioration of the service-level. At a certain point in time the service-level deterioration exceeds the acceptable level. If the acceptable level of a specific performance measure is exceeded, decision makers need to execute countermeasures that should reduce the deterioration up to an acceptable degree or should even offset the deterioration at all. However, along with the execution of recovery-enhancing countermeasures, logistics costs will rise. Figure 4.13 b) highlights the development of logistics cost that arise right after the service-level deterioration has exceeded the acceptable level. As long as the acceptable deterioration level of the performance measure *overall logistics costs* is not reached, countermeasures can be executed without impeding strategic goals of the underlying supply chain. If the performance deterioration has not yet exceeded the acceptable level of deterioration, countermeasures are not executed. In this case the decision maker prefers to maintain the level of logistics costs, even though the service-level is decreasing. It is the purpose of supply chain risk analysis to support the decision maker in evaluating how his risk attitude affects the potential non-achievement of supply chain objectives.

Note that Figure 4.13 b) presents increasing logistics costs as a consequence after a deterioration has occurred. However, increased logistics costs due to the implementation and execution of countermeasures could also arise before a deterioration occurs. In Chapter 8 we will discuss more deeply how the implementation of reactive or pro-active countermeasures affects additional expenses.

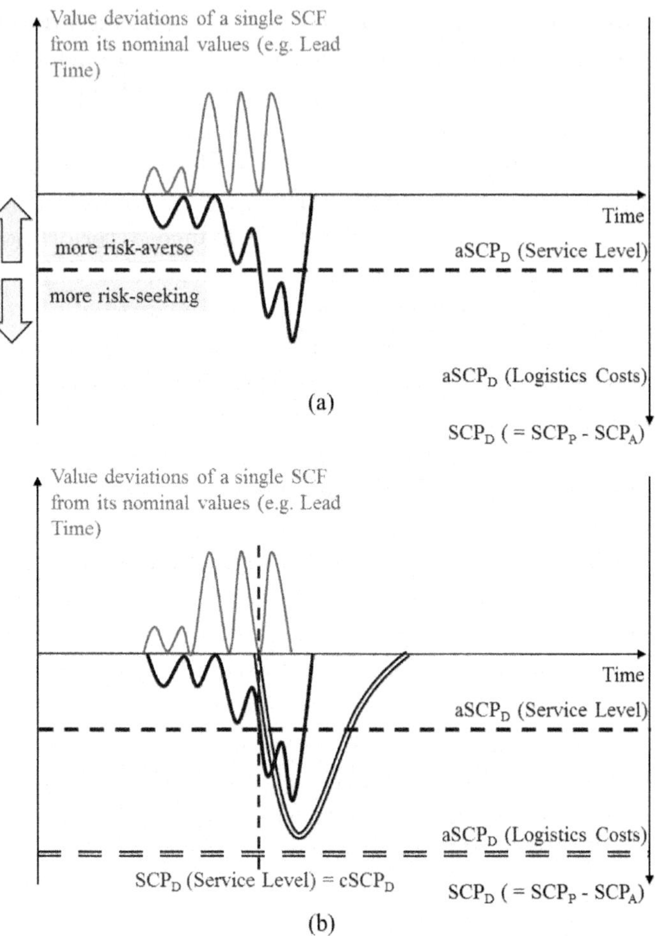

Figure 4.13: Acceptable performance deterioration levels of more risk-averse and more risk-seeking decision makers.

Risk Profiles

Modifications of supply chain factors can result in the deterioration of supply chain performance. Assuming distinct but comparable supply chains encounter the same uncertainty profile for a specific supply chain factor, their performance could evolve quite differently over time. Figure 4.14 shows how a factor change can affect the development of performance deterioration of different supply chains. The factor deviation highlighted in Figure 4.14 represents an uncertainty profile of a frequently occurring level modification, like for example small lead time fluctuations. If a supply chain ships only small amounts by the transportation link associated to the lead time fluctuations or is endowed with sufficient back-up inventory units, overall supply chain performance might not be affected. The potential loss is zero, which refers to the non-existence of supply chain risk, see Figure 4.14 (a). Other supply chains could more strongly depend on the transportation link. If a supply chain uses the transportation link rarely, for example shipments take place once in a month, the overall performance is deteriorated, but can recover, before the supply chain is hit again by a minor lead time increase. We denote this type of deterioration development as *Oscillating Supply Chain Risk*, see Figure 4.14 (b). If the transportation link is, however, used more frequently, back-up inventory units are too little or used up to early, performance deterioration builds up continuously over time. This development could take place slightly or with up and down movements. We denote this type of a risk profile as *Emerging Supply Chain Risk*, see Figure 4.14 (c). If back-up resources are too few and large amounts of goods are shipped via the affected transportation link, performance deterioration can build up quickly and severely. We denote this profile as a *Sudden Supply Chain Risk*, see Figure 4.14 (d).

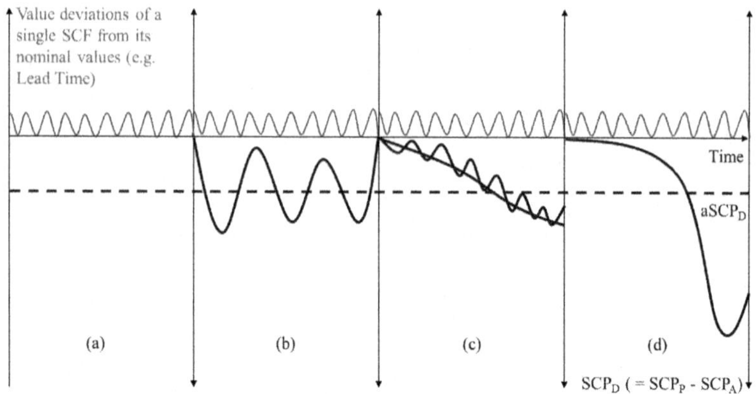

Figure 4.14: Risk profiles: (a) no supply chain risk, (b) oscillating supply chain risk, (c) (stepwise & constantly) emerging supply chain risk, and (d) sudden supply chain risk.

Definition 4.6: Oscillating, Emerging, and Sudden Supply Chain Risks

Oscillating, *emerging*, and *sudden* supply chain risks are defined as the *recurring*, *sprouting*, and *incisive* potential loss, respectively, for a supply chain in terms of its target values of efficiency and effectiveness evoked by uncertain developments of supply chain characteristics whose changes were caused by the occurrence of triggering-events.

Certainly, the magnitude of uncertain factor modifications additionally impairs the achievement of targeted supply chain objectives. An earthquake measuring 12 on the Richter scale is hardly absorbable for any competitive supply chain. Regardless of the present type of uncertainty profile it could be necessary to intervene, when the acceptable level of performance deterioration is reached and one of the presented risk profiles is realized.

Note that *Emerging Risk* is a concept used in the prevailing supply chain risk management literature. It refers to events that newly arise [61]. Typically, these risks are understood as events that have not yet been thought of or that are very uncertain, hardly understood and only vaguely defined and that thus can not be fully controlled. In consistence with the re-definition of supply chain risk, *Emerging Risk* is re-defined as stated in the Definition 4.6 and does not refer to an event.

4.2.3 Analysis of Supply Chain Constitution

The discussion so far shows that the development of factor uncertainties has an influence on the degree of performance achievement. However, it is the supply chain resilience that determines whether the targeted performance value can still be met. Supply chains are differentially endowed with the ability to absorb the consequences of potential triggers. In this section we present different elements of supply chain constitutions that favor the ability to overcome unexpected changes. Additionally, we briefly explain potential interactions and their influence on the extent of supply chain risk.

Supply Chain Structure ($\mathcal{G}(\mathcal{V}, \mathcal{E})$)

The structure of a supply chain is among the root causes of supply chain vulnerability. One particular approach to model the structure of supply chains is by means of graph theory. Here, the supply chain is modeled as a graph,$\mathcal{G}(\mathcal{V}, \mathcal{E})$, with vertices, $\mathcal{V}$, connected by edges, $\mathcal{E}$. When representing the static physical structure of the supply chain, vertices correspond to facilities like warehouses and production sites while edges correspond to transportation links. But the graph model can also represent a more abstract view of the supply chain where vertices represent markets, business units, sales channels, products or components and edges represent sales relations, distribution channels, or supply contracts. In either case, the graph models physical or conceptual elements of a supply chain and the pairwise relationships between them. By analyzing the structure of the graph model, assessments of supply chain vulnerability can be made. The theory of network metrics provides a toolbox suitable for the measurement of a graph's structural properties with respect to network size/density, network connectivity, and network complexity [66, 80]. Figure 4.15 highlights exemplary metrics with different values and corresponding degrees of supply chain resilience: The number of incoming and outgoing edges to and from a vertex is commonly regarded as an indication for the vulnerability of supply chains. The number of vertices with high importance relative to others, thus high degree of connectivity, negatively correlates with resilience. Supply chain density relates to the quantity of vertices allocated to geographical spaces. The higher the number of vertices clustered to one area, the higher supply chain density. Although small density is generally considered as more resilient than a highly dense network, this conclusion strongly depends on the type of vertices clustered to one area. Several desktop producers suffered from the Thailand flooding in 2011. Nearly all production plants of hard disk manufacturer were struck by the water. As Thailand is the world's second major exporter of hard disk drives the entire industrial sector was hit by the flood. Contrary to this situation, especially Toyota benefits from their highly dense supplier network. Short lead times and high cooperation supports the efficient and effective execution of their supply chains. Vertex connectivity together with the degree of edges refers to supply chain complexity [66]. Highly complex supply chains may be endowed with extra-capacity and buffers that compensate uncertain developments. But highly complex supply chains may also be especially prone to disruptions. This is because these metrics should be primarily used for one-product flows as in distribution or transportation networks, where the vertices and edges are of equal importance. The consideration of supply chain networks, however, involves the evaluation of different types of product flows. Highly

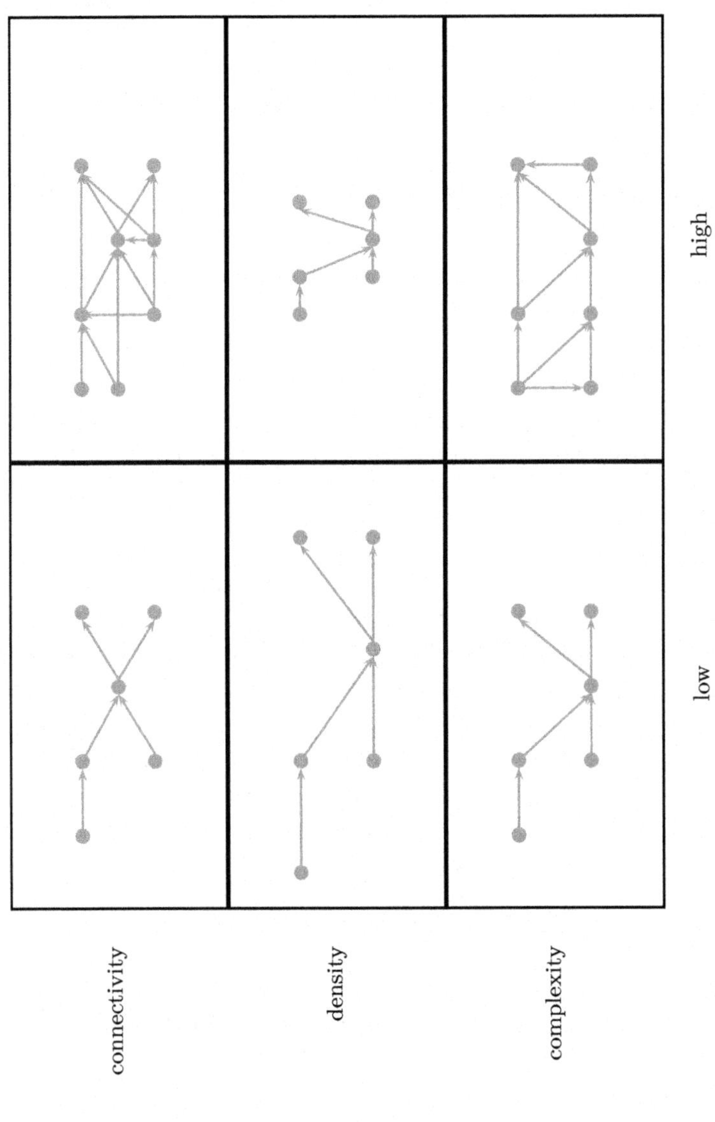

Figure 4.15: Levels of structural metrics indicating supply chain resilience: low metric value indicate less resilience [66, 80]

complex supply chains can consist of different and non-substitutable procurement channels, which have the potential to break down supply chain efficiency and effectiveness, if they are disrupted. Critical path identification is used for the identification and evaluation of vulnerable procurement channels [50, 158, 186].

Bill of Material ($\mathcal{BOM}$)

When referring to the structural characteristics of a supply network the influence of a product's bill of materials on the potential impact of an unexpected deviation is usually ignored. The number of alternative suppliers available for the procurement of one pre-product as well as the total flow of pre-products derived by the demand coefficient, related to structural characteristics such as distance, location, or alternative transportation, however, is significant for the analysis of a system's vulnerability.

Consider the following examples related to an exemplary extract of a supply chain and a bill of material, respectively, see Figure 4.16. The supply network consists of 4 nodes, namely, the original equipment manufacturer (OEM), and three suppliers (S1–S3). While the OEM produces P, each supplier is charged with the production of one or several pre-products. While the OEM, S2 and S3 produce in central Europe, S1 is located in China. In order to produce one unit of product P, the bill of materials indicates the necessity of two units of pre-product A, one unit of pre-product B and C respectively.

Example 4.5

Assume that S1 serves the OEM with product A, S2 with B, and S3 with C. System's criticality now depends on the structural allocation of the suppliers. As S1 is allocated in the Asia-Pacific region, the procurement of A is more critical than of B and C, respectively. In that case, the procurement of A is exposed to several influences that may lead to an unexpected deviation and the number of these potential influences surely exceeds the number of influences the procurement of B and C is exposed to.

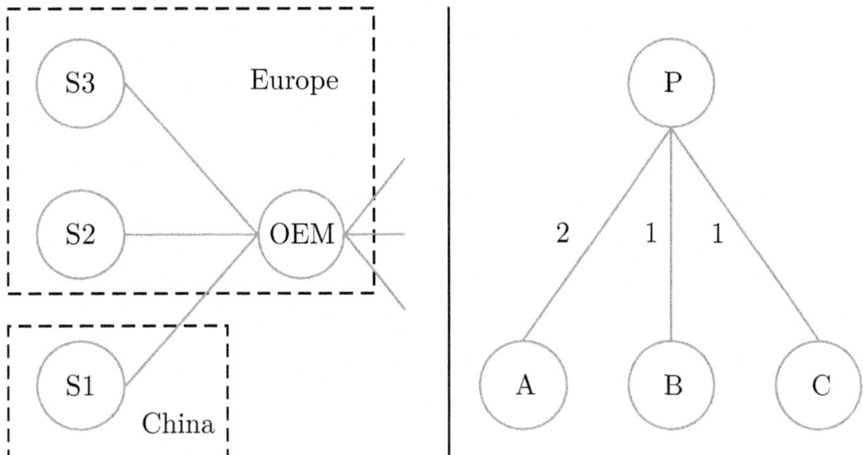

Figure 4.16: Exemplary extracts of a supply chain and a bill of material

Example 4.6

If S1 as well as S2 serves the OEM with product A and S3 provides pre-products B and C, the bill of material indicates, that the procurement of A is less critical than in example 1. If S1 fails to deliver pre-product A in time, S2 still delivers a certain amount of this pre-product. S2 may serve as a backup supplier and takes the amount of supply normally delivered by S1. Additionally, when referring the bill of material to structural characteristics, it is obvious that the OEM strongly depends on the performance of S3, because S3 now delivers 2 out of 4 parts to the OEM. System's vulnerability towards the procurement of B and C has increased.

Example 4.7

Pre-products are supplied by S1, S2 and S3 like in example 1. In the present example, however, pre-product C is defined as an optional feature of end-product P. Customers may order product P with or without this specific feature. Whether the vulnerability of the supply chain has decreased or increased compared to example 1 depends on the importance of product C. If product C is a special feature of configuration, the vulnerability has increased as the de-

mand for specific configurations is difficult to forecast and the needed amount of procurement is unknown in advance. If product C is rarely required the vulnerability has decreased

Example 4.8

Considering the production sequence assume that pre-product C is needed right at the beginning of the production process. Compared to example 1 supply chain vulnerability has increased, because, the procurement of pre-product C needs to arrive exactly on schedule. The delay of pre-products, which are manufactured later in the production process, can be less critical. However, they need to arrive before due date.

These examples highlight the influence of a product's bill of material on supply chain vulnerability, see also [300]. Minor changes of pre-product coefficients or pre-product's importance may significantly increase or decrease supply chain resilience or vulnerability, respectively.

Product Portfolio ($\mathcal{PP}$)

Analysis of supply chain resilience on the product level aims at setting the scope for the subsequent steps of the analysis process. While it may seem trivial at first sight, the basic task is to find the working definition of the term product. This definition implicitly determines the granularity of the following analysis and the amount of data needed to conduct it. For example, a product might be defined on the stock keeping unit level, the part number level or be defined as to comprise several variants, product family. The definition has important effects on the structure of the bill of materials with respect to the components and coefficients as it opens questions on the aggregation of data. For example, it is not a priori clear how material usage coefficients from several bills of materials shall be merged into a representative bill of material for the aggregated product. The aggregation of items into a product might also hide individual differences between items when analyzing developments over time, e.g. demand patterns and inventory balances.

The definition of products refers to both the demand and the supply perspective. On the demand side, finished goods and other products having primary demand, like spare parts, are aggregated into products while on the supply side, components, raw materials and auxiliary material are segmented into products as well. Pareto analysis, often referred to as 80/20 rule or ABC classification, helps to direct the analyst's attention towards those items within the product portfolio that e.g. show the highest revenue contribution or sales margin. In addition, to a certain degree uncertainty arises from the unknown behavior of demand and supply over time. An analysis of forecast errors – with respect to demand or material consumption patterns – helps to identify and cluster uncertainty related to finished goods, components, or raw materials.

After having defined the scope of product portfolio for supply chain risk analysis, the availability of assembly and manufacturing resources needs to be evaluated. Products and their pre-products compete for available production capacities distributed over the supply chain network. Thus, the extent of supply chain resilience strongly depends on the defined product portfolio.

Demand Pattern ($\mathcal{DP}$)

As introduced in Section 3.4.2, the resilience further depends on the current work load of the affected supply chain. The netting between demand quantity and available capacities within the period under consideration unveils the degree of vulnerability with respect to the functionality of the supply chain process to fulfill customer's demand. The European ash cloud in 2010 discloses the importance of the current work load. The consequences would have been less severe if the Icelandic volcano had erupted during Christmas holidays, when many production facilities are closed anyway.

Market Power ($\mathcal{MP}$)

A strong, nearly monopolistic market power of a company that offers high-end or non-substitutable products may be less affected by disruptions than companies that have to compete with numerous business rivals or than companies that offer substitutable products. When a company is the sole producer of an asset and has established and persuaded a considerable customer base, this company mainly has to deal with the immediate consequences of damaged production facilities or infrastructure, smaller margins due to price volatilities, or quality issues. Long-term and performance derogating effects of disruptions due to lost customers might be less urgent for these companies.

Similarly effects can be detected by symbiotic-like business relationships.

Example 4.9

When a fire at Aisin, a Toyota supplier of 98% of required P-valves, caused their production to stop for several days, engineers from Toyota and other suppliers achieved the implementation of alternative production lines that could compensate missing Aisin's volumes [274]. Without the large self-regula-ting cooperation among its suppliers Toyota would have suffered from shortages of several weeks.

Production Technology ($\mathcal{PT}$)

Non-substitutable products are quite often produced or manufactured by highly complex production technologies. In particular, the chemical processing industry, whose production is characterized by physically and temporally complex processes, has highly individualistic production facilities. Special chemical processors, like reactors or homogenizers, are difficult to obtain. When these components are damaged by water or fire, it often takes several months up to years to replace them [189]. Consider the example provided in Section 4.1.1 that illustrates the situation of a Swiss chemical producer having difficulties to insure a production breakdown. Such situations demand for special modeling perspectives in order to derive more resilient supply chains that overcome such disruptions.

Product Design ($\mathcal{PD}$)

One of the most famous and discussed disruptions within the field of supply chain risk analysis is the case of Nokia vs. Ericsson [274, 225, 270].

Example 4.10

After a lightning strike to a Philips factory, which manufactured semiconductors for mobile phones, the resulting fire destroyed not only production of nearly 1 million semiconductors, but also caused a contamination of the Production plant with dust and water. The reaction of the two main customers – Nokia and Ericsson – was very different. Nokia acted quickly and due to the modular product designs of its mobile phones Nokia could fall back on an alternative product specifications that did not compromise customers demand. Right after Nokia had allocated all available production capacity on the world market, Ericsson started to realize that components from Philips are not going to arrive on time. Although they reacted late, Ericsson could not fall back on similar components. In a similar way Apple encountered product issues after an earthquake had destroyed production of relevant semiconductors in 1999 (see following paragraph).

When product design allows for the implementation of alternative components and when production allows late configuration, the supply chain is more resilient [307].

Product Life Cycle ($\mathcal{PLC}$)

The product life cycle is divided into four main stages. Each stage is characterized by changes in raw material and product flow, production capacity, and network design. The cycle starts with the initial product idea, its conceptual design, development, and introduction on the market. Irrespective of the occurrence of disruptive triggers, the majority of ideas, concepts, and new products do not reach further stages. Before competitors start to replicate or further develop the new product, enterprises that have first introduced the new product have a monopolistic phase. Assuming success, sales start to grow even at other markets. This stage is characterized by high level of profit and expansion of the product, of the distributing enterprises, and of the underlying networks. The stage of maturity is reached when the product is standardized, distribution and supply channels established, and competitive pressure is high. In the last stage the product becomes obsolete and is mainly produced in low cost countries. The end of the life-cycle is reached when the product is discarded from the market.

Every stage is characterized with special challenges for the producing company. While product features, design, and promotion are essential during the first stages, overall cost efficiency as well as the establishment of supply and distribution channels become important in the latter stages in order to reach higher levels of competitiveness. A disruption has most often pure negative effects for the companies forming a supply chain. However, there are a number of documented cases that indicate that companies are particularly affected not only when a new product is in the ramp-up but also when it is in the growth stage.

Example 4.11

The "921 earthquake" occurred in Taiwan in 1999. From an industrial perspective this earthquake caused power outages, damaged infrastructure and factories and led to a production throttle of semiconductors and other PC components for two weeks [111]. Apple suffered from shortages of components that delayed production and distribution of their new products iBook (1999-2006) and Power Macintosh G4 desktop computers (1999-2004) within a period reflecting the growth stage of a product life cycle. To the fact knowing that many Apple customers want to be among the first to get an iBook, Apple permit preliminary orders. As apple was unable to change product configuration, they decided to deliver different than ordered products and received a mass of complaints [270]. A beneficiary of Apple's situation was Dell, although they suffered from shortages, too. Through dynamic pricing and promotion Dell was successful in influencing customer's product choices. For the third quarter of 1999 Dell could increase revenues by 41% [229].

A disruption of this type during the last phase of a product life cycle would result in a more rapid retirement of the product.

4.3 Tasks of Supply Chain Risk Analysis

Heuristic forms of thinking guided supply chain practitioners and scientists to oversimplifications and misinterpretations of the effects of risk. Hagman [116] concludes that the analysis of risk in general is up for debate. We emphasize that this is especially true for the analysis of supply chain risk. Due to the limits of explanatory power provided by the supply chain risk definition and the methodology deduced from this definition, numerous biases arise. The assessment of risk as a product of event-related probability and impact may lead not only to faulty identifications, but also to deficient conclusions. Statements about the future are difficult and have to be handled with care. Besides prospective developments, it is the understanding of how changes affect the supply chain, that need to be carefully evaluated. We declare the analysis of the underlying supply chain and its dynamics as the major purpose of supply chain risk analysis. In the following we summarize the main conclusions derived in this chapter:

- Instead of starting risk analysis with the identification, gathering and assessment of potential events that may serve as a disruptive trigger, we propose that it is the main task of supply chain risk analysis to evaluate the potential effect of modifications of supply chain factors and assess their influence on key performance indicators.
- Risk analysis is conducted not only on different planning levels, but also seeks for an interrelated process between all stages with the objective to identify risk-aware and efficiency-effectiveness-balanced supply chain solutions.
- The development of supply chain factors is captured by uncertainty profiles such as recurring changes, moderate changes, major changes, and level shifts.
- Effectiveness refers to the functional capability of supply chain processes which results in the satisfaction of customer demands. Efficiency refers to the profitable execution of supply chain processes. The functionality and profitability of supply chain processes operationalize both, supply chain effectiveness and efficiency.
- A balanced portfolio of reliable supply chain performance measures is indispensable for meaningful risk analysis. The detection of poor supply chain strategies or contradicting developments *before* they become effective in poor financial results is the essence of supply chain risk analysis.
- It is the purpose of supply chain risk analysis to support the decision maker in evaluating how his risk attitude affects the potential non-achievement of supply chain objectives.
- The resilience of the underlying supply chain depends on elements as different as the supply chain structure, the bills of material, the product portfolio, the demand pattern, the market power, the production technology, and the product design. The present

state of each of these elements needs to be evaluated in order to understand the underlying dynamics.

The identification and assessment of supply chain risk, therefore, should respect the influence of existing potential triggers, PoT, the prevailing portfolio of performance measures, $PPor$, and the actual constitution of the underlying supply chain, SCC, on the possible deterioration of supply chain performance. The extent of supply chain risk depends on the status of each of these elements:

$$SCR := f(PoT, PPor, SCC) \tag{4.1}$$

The status of each of these elements is described by supply chain factors that capture current element levels, i.e.
$PoT(SCF_1, SCF_2, ..., SCF_n)$, $PPor(SCF_1, SCF_2, ..., SCF_n)$, and $SCC(SCF_1, SCF_2, ..., SCF_n)$.

$$SCR := f(SCF_1, SCF_2, ..., SCF_n) \tag{4.2}$$

If these dynamics are understood, mathematical approaches can formalize these dynamics and develop appropriate model formulations. The solution of those optimization models supports decision makers in implementing reliable risk-aware supply chain designs and/or plans. Then, it is possible to overcome the biased stepwise process of assessing, identifying, and mitigating supply chain risk individually.

5 Supply Chain Risk Analytics

"The price of light is less than the cost of darkness"

Artur C. Nielsen

Over the last decades companies with the best intentions developed their supply chains into more efficient, but at the same time into more vulnerable systems, see Chapter 2. When a supply chain is faced with disruptions and its capabilities to cope with the deviations are scarce, supply chain managers may have to pay dearly [71]. Persons in charge of supply chain execution as well as risk officers have to think in terms of "not if, but when" something happens [see 78, p.26].

The newly described analysis of supply chain risk emphasizes to evaluate the effects and the interrelations of potential triggers, performance target variables, and supply chain constitution, see Chapter 4. Based on the knowledge of effects and dynamics, supply chain model formulations are needed that are able to capture supply chain risk. Although there might be approaches available that can be extracted, adapted, combined and further developed, it is an open question, whether such an effort is worth it. Rethinking supply chain strategies and restructuring globally operating networks may imply huge expenses. In order to still benefit from logistics innovations, supply chain risk has to be carefully considered when supply networks are designed and planned. Only after appropriate risk-aware solutions are implemented, a continuous monitoring of significant supply chain risk measures can assist the decision maker in identifying the point in time, where solutions have to be revised.

The remainder of this chapter is organized as follows. Based on business, supply chain, and risk analytics, the new concept of supply chain risk analytics is introduced in Section 5.1. The next section deduces first analytical insights into the capability of supply chain risk analytics to provide risk-reduced supply chain designs, plans and operations. Section 5.3 provides a short discussion on measures that are used to quantify risk in the majority of analyzed papers. Section 5.4 reviews papers classified as references of supply chain risk analytics with regard to their modeling approach and solution techniques applied. We conclude this chapter with a discussion of research gaps and development needs in Section 5.5.

5.1 Supply Chain Risk Analytics – Concept Definition

Due to the presence of risk, supply chain decision problems request solution methods that combine, adapt and further develop approaches of supply chain and risk management, respectively. We subsume mathematical methods with the objective to manage supply chain risk and emanating from both disciplines under the concept of supply chain risk analytics.

Business analytics or simply *analytics* subsume methodologies like statistics, operations research, and computer-based programming with the goal to provide a sophisticated basis for the decision-making process [79]. Analytics is classified into three major perspectives: descriptive, predictive, and prescriptive. As the nomenclature indicates descriptive analytics are used to refer to techniques that describe data: they categorize, characterize, consolidate, and classify data with the purpose to deduce useful information for the business decision ahead [79]. Predictive analytics refers to an effort invested in the analysis of historical data with the goal to detect patterns, which can be extrapolated for the future. The development of new technologies for automated data identification and acquisition (Auto-ID/RFID) and the intelligent integration of systems, assemblies, and sensors into higher-level value networks, allow to continuously process data. Predictive analytics support the evaluation and preparation of this data crowd. Having evaluated the available data base and having derived predictions for future developments, prescriptive analytics supports to determine appropriate decisions for the underlying business. The decision making process relies on different methodologies, but as the available information is often very complex, especially methods from operations research such as simulation and optimization are used. However, a KPI report may also support decision makers in determining necessary actions to take for their business. Figure 5.1 summarizes the aforementioned thoughts.

Category	**Descriptive analytics**	**Predictive analytics**	**Prescriptive analytics**
Objective	Analyzing historical data	Predicting future developments	identifying best course of actions
Techniques	regression, trend reporting, data modeling, management reports	data mining, forecasting, monte carlo simulation, pattern recognition	optimization, simulation, game theory, spreadsheet analysis
Central question	Why is this happening?	What will happen next?	What should we do next?

Table 5.1: Descriptive, predictive, and prescriptive analytics.

Analytic approaches for risk and for supply chain modeling, respectively, have been developed for years. Considering supply chain analytics, especially prescriptive analytics such as simulation techniques and mathematical optimization provide advantages for decision support. Models have been developed for facility location and network design [205], sales and operations planning [145], transportation and distribution planning [6], inventory management [272, 347], revenue management [200, 302], and production scheduling [327]. Risk analytics encompasses models for different disciplines. In finance, sophisticated mathematical models are established to assess and manage risk that exists due to fluctuations in financial markets [243]. In engineering, mathematical approaches have been developed to model the reliability of complex systems. Failure Mode and Effects Analysis (FMEA) [161, 257] originated from risk analytics in engineering as well as derivative analysis approaches like Event Tree Analysis (ETA) [76] and Fault Tree Analysis (FTA) [156, 161]. However, these approaches have been developed to address narrowly well-defined problems of specific types [243] and rely on the risk-by-risk process cycle introduced in Chapter 4.

Due to the increase of complexity and interrelatedness of supply chain networks as well as business corporations, analytics may support decision-making not only for supply chain [259, 288, 312] and risk management [243], but also for the synthesis of both: *supply chain risk analytics.*

Definition 5.1: Supply Chain Risk Analytics

Supply chain risk analytics is defined as a bundle of mathematical methods and measurement techniques tailored for determining risk-aware solutions for supply chain design, planning and execution.

The focus of this thesis is set to the analysis, conceptual design and development of new approaches tailored for supply chain risk analytics.

5.2 The Value of Supply Chain Risk Analytics

Managing supply chain risks is in itself not a process that creates value; initially it generates pure costs. It requires investing resources, time and effort into an endeavor that should enable the supply chain to avoid uncertain future losses. Highly competitive markets and pressure from shareholders require that investments made are well justified. The gathering of data, the analysis of available information, the deviation of emergency plans or the implementation of more robust supply chains need to provide benefits.

According to a study conducted by the Business Continuity Institute 85% of responding organizations had experienced at least one significant supply chain disruption in the last 12 months [44]. For example, 150 firms out of 350 had to declare bankruptcy after the bombing raid of the World Trade Center in 1993. After two years only 29% were still in business [78]. Supply chain risk management metrics that assess systemic exposure to unexpected changes are still undefined. Meanwhile, the financial impact of disruptions can be indirectly estimated. Hendricks and Singhal [125, 126, 127] determine consequences of disturbances on stock prices of affected companies. Analyses based on 827 supply chain failures and their respective consequences show that firms had to suffer a 33-40% loss in stock price compared to the benchmark within three years – as measured one year prior to the failure and two years after [126]. Accenture conducted a study for the World Economic Forum report on resilient supply chains [249]. They revealed that disruptions destroy about 7% of a company's shareholder value. Even before a disruption is announced the value started to decline. A survey conducted by FM Global Europe and the market research firm Harris Interactive among financial and risk managers at 1000 companies in North America revealed that almost three quarters of them consider hazards and supply chain disruptions as major threats to top revenues (Green, 2004).

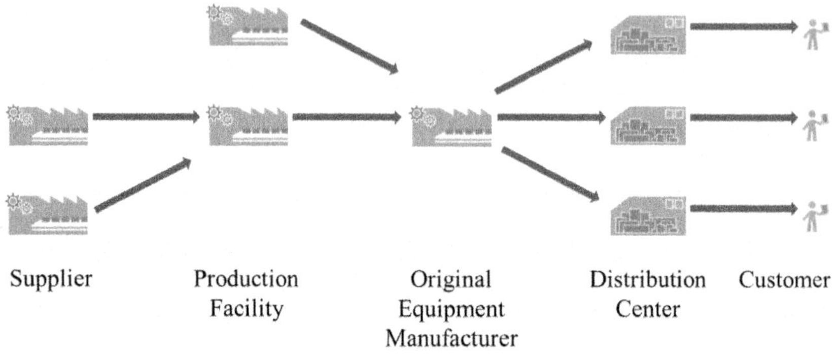

Figure 5.1: Example of a supply chain.

According to these studies there is a potential for supply chain risk analytics, if it can limit the longterm (financial) impact of supply chain disruptions. Supply chain risk analytics should endow the underlying supply network with means to reduce the influence of changing conditions, stochastic processes and shocks on supply chain performance. The value of resulting supply chain risk countermeasures can be deduced by balancing the price for the operation of mitigation alternatives and the degree of their effectiveness to reduce long-term disruption costs. In the following based on numerous classification schemes provided in the literature we evaluate the cost benefit trade-offs of different means to handle supply chain risk [77, 216, 334]. We distinguish between the option to accept, to reduce, and to spread supply chain risk.

For the sake of illustration we base our explanations on a simplified supply chain. The supply chain presented in Figure 5.1 starts at the supplier level, where their production facilities provide preproducts for a producer downstream the supply chain. A further production facility, which may act as an original equipment manufacturer, receives intermediate products. The finished good is then brought to regional distributions centers that serve customer markets.

5.2.1 Risk Acceptance

The efficient achievement of customer satisfaction and value creation is threatened by disruptions. In Chapter 2 we presented different types of disruptive triggers that might affect supply chain functionality. To evaluate the long-term consequences of a disruption, it is – in the first place – not necessary to know about its origins. The analysis has to start with the consideration of the immediate impact(s) on the supply chain. In the following we consider the situation in which a supplier is disrupted by a certain event. The immediate consequence of this trigger is delayed outbound supply. Propagating consequences might, for instance, lead to a machine disruption at the recipient's production facility, which in turn delays the production, such that the company may not be able to satisfy their customers needs in time, see Figure 5.2.

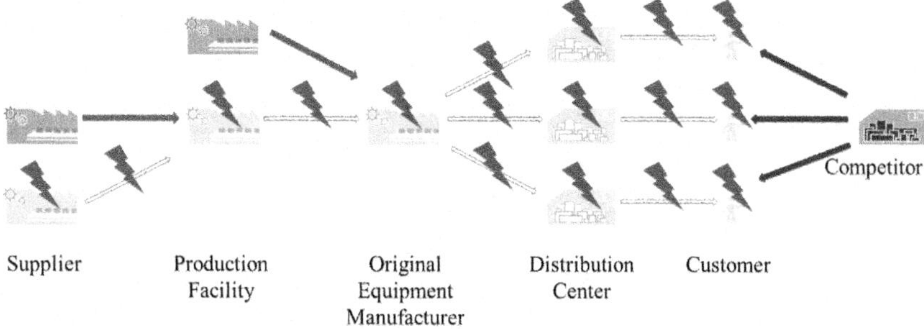

Figure 5.2: Example of a disruption propagating through the entire supply chain when risk functionalities are missing.

In order to overcome this situation, a company may switch transportation mode once production is resumed; to make up for the delay, goods may be shipped by helicopter or airplane, which is much more expensive than shipment by truck or train. Alternatively, supply chain responsibles once decided to disregard disruptions and await the end of the disruption. When supply chain operations are not endowed with risk management functionalities, disruption countermeasures are not available or the disruption is not detected, consequences can propagate through the entire network. Unsatisfied customer demand might result in lost customers, who are willing to change to other producers in the future.

The impact of disruptions in terms of performance deterioration and extra expenses is highlighted in Figure 5.3. Part a) shows the exemplary impact on supply chain performance as well as the acceptable level of performance reduction. Logistics costs, customer satisfaction, cost of working capital, or capacity utilization among others may serve as key performance indicators and depend on the business focus of the underlying supply chain partners. When supply chain risk mitigation actions are not installed the level may drop below the acceptable level. Extra expenses, Ex, that arise due to a disruption, s, that starts at $t = t_{sb}$ and ends at $t = t_{se}$, depend on direct costs that arise due to damages, $\Gamma_{s,t}$, depend on lost sales, $\Phi_{s,t}$, and depend on the loss of customer trust, $\Omega_{s,t}$, which becomes effective in the time after the disruption. Lost trust may further lead to a decline of future demand and consequently adds to lost sales. Extra expenses total to:

$$Ex := \sum_{t=t_{sb}}^{t_{se}} (\Gamma_{s,t} + \Phi_{s,t}) + \sum_{t=t_{se}}^{T} \Omega_{s,t} \tag{5.1}$$

The aforementioned example of disruption consequences is a special case of risk acceptance. More often supply chain managers accept the recurrent appearance of disruptions, but want to limit their impacts by the establishment of so-called *war-rooms*. In the case of a disruption assumed to be detected, managers come together in a room,

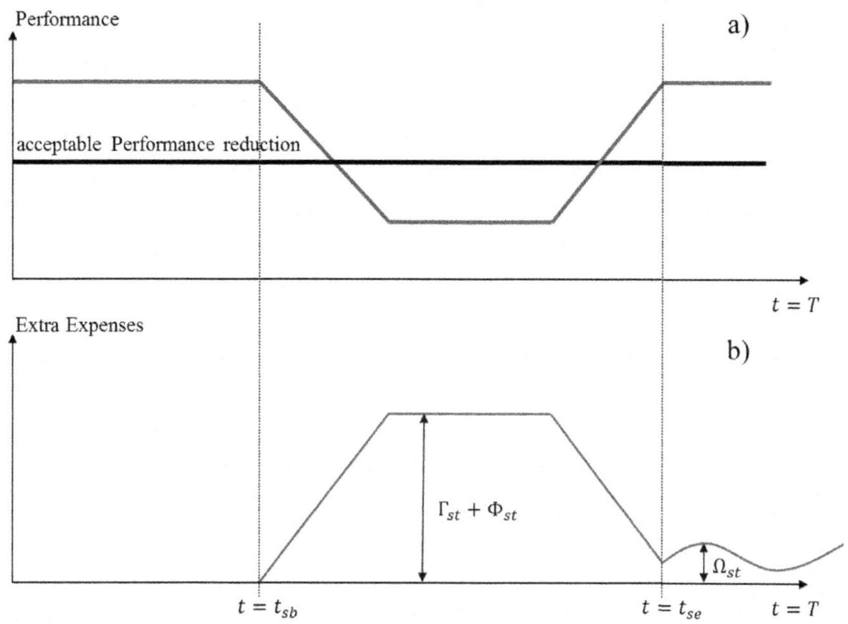

Figure 5.3: Impact of a disruption without supply chain risk management.

which provides communication tools and stock monitoring systems that support decision makers in executing supply chain risk countermeasures. These measures vary among extra tours, production synchronization with customers, purchasing capacities on the spot market and so on. The availability and efficiency of these countermeasures is often limited and costly. The costs of quickly arranged war room responses are denoted by m_{st}. However, in order to reduce time to recovery, to reestablish performance criteria, and to limit loss of customer base, supply chain partners afford countermeasures. When supply chain disruptions are detected and countermeasures are rapidly introduced the disruption profile, see Figure 5.4, and the extra expenses formula changes to:

$$Ex := \sum_{t=t_{sb}}^{t_{se}} (\Gamma_{s,t} + \Phi_{s,t} + m_{s,t}) + \sum_{t=t_{se}}^{T} \Omega_{s,t} \tag{5.2}$$

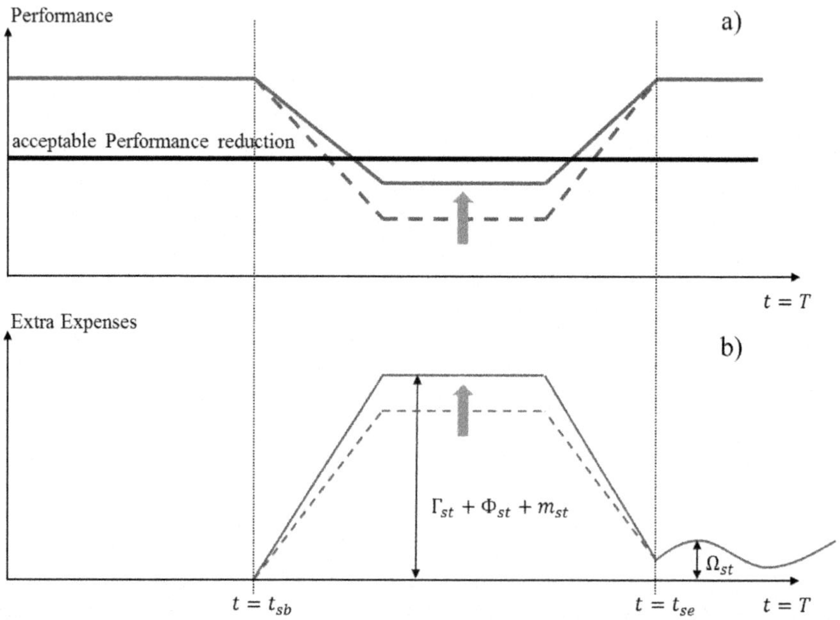

Figure 5.4: Development of performance and extra expenses in the presence of a disruption when supply chain risk management actions are not installed.

5.2.2 Risk Reduction Measures

The basis for the *implementation* of a supply chain risk system within a supply chain wide network of affiliated companies is provided by the establishment of an organizational risk culture and the integration of IT-systems that both allow for and encourage the exchange of information about financial but also physical flows. The *execution* of risk analytics encompasses the periodical identification of relevant supply chain weaknesses, the successive assessment of its resulting vulnerabilities, the implementation and update of mitigation alternatives as well as the continuous monitoring of critical processes. As the implementation and the execution are the main cost drivers, they define the price of a supply chain risk management system. Effort and costs for implementation and organizational changes cannot be neglected, however, once companies have shifted to risk-aware organizations the long-term costs of mitigation strategies define the value of supply chain risk analytics. Mitigation options differ in their ability to respond to occurring disruptions and in their costs. The latter consists of ongoing cost, c_t^r, spend for the allocation of mitigation actions as well as costs that arise when the countermeasures become effective, $m_{s,t}^r$. These costs may also be influenced by the disruption, s, itself. We distinguish between *reactive* and *pro-active* (or *absorbing*) mitigation measures. *Disruption management* and the elaboration of *business continuity plans* are reactive approaches. The development of *flexible-fall back positions* and *robust supply chain designs* demands for pro-active thinking with respect to decisions where to best place absorbing processes within the supply chain system. The notion reactiveness relates to the fact that reactive measures are executed in the presence of a disruption, while pro-active measures are executed continuously. Supply chain risk mitigation actions, r, should reduce the impact of disruptions on supply chain performance. At best they can prevent damage cost, the shortfall below acceptable levels of relevant performance metrics, which is equivalent to prevented lost sales, and similarly impede the loss of customer trust. In order to reflect the reduction of each presented cost driver we introduce the risk measures γ^r, ϕ^r, and ω^r, respectively, which may take values in the range of $[0;1]$ depending on the effectiveness of the installed supply chain risk countermeasure, r.[1]

[1] Up to this point, we kindly neglect the chance that a supply chain risk management system may also increase the aforementioned cost drivers.

Reactive Countermeasures

The objective of disruption management is to provide means to transfer the supply chain back to its original state when a disruption occurs. Business continuity plans intend to maintain supply chain functionality during a disruption. Both paradigms rely on decision support systems that appropriately allocate available resources to failed processes or to alternative processes during or right after the occurrence of a disruption. Rerouting or transferring transports to alternative transportation modes are typical examples of disruption management. Figure 5.5 presents a supply chain example endowed with transportation alternatives (modes or routes). These options are indicated by additional arrows between consecutive supply chain locations. Transportation modes are characterized by different distances, lead times and capacities for products, preproducts or intermediate products.

In case of the disruption described above preproducts still arrive late at the production facility such that production of intermediate products is delayed, see Figure 5.5. The additional transportation mode between the production facility and the OEM allows to switch transportation amounts. Anyway, some components arrive too late and production starts delayed at the OEM. As alternative transportation possibilities are available between OEM and two distributions centers an alternative transportation route may be used which results in demand fulfillment. However, there is no alternative transportation mode installed between OEM and the third distribution center, therefore goods arrive too late at customers resulting in unsatisfied demand and the possibility of lost customers.

Figure 5.6 a) illustrates the evolution of the supply chain performance, when reactive-thinking led to the implementation of disruption management or business continuity plans. When a supply chain disruption, s, occurs extra costs arise due to the execution of countermeasures, $m_{s,t}^{sr=re}$, Figure 5.6 b), and decline when performance begins to re-increase after the disruption. The allocation of reactive

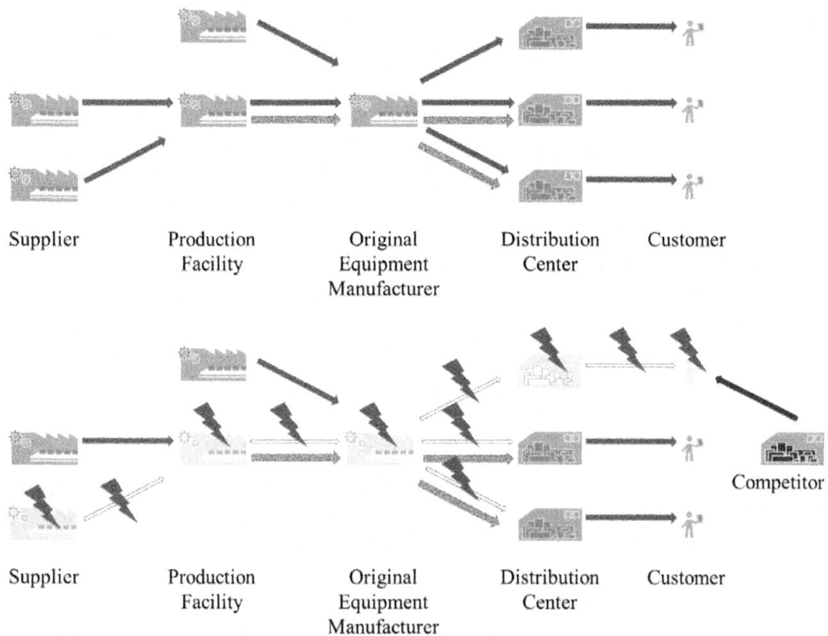

Figure 5.5: Impact of a disruption in the presence of a disruption when reactive countermeasures are installed

measures results in extra expenses for supply chain management, $c_t^{sr=re}$, which are effective during the whole planning horizon. The installation of countermeasures may also result in a decrease of costs related to damaged infrastructure $\gamma^{sr=re}$, lost sales $\phi^{sr=re}$, and loss of customer trust $\omega^{sr=re}$. Extra expenses sum up to:

$$\begin{aligned} Ex^{re} := \sum_{t=t_{sb}}^{t_{se}} \left(\gamma^{re}\Gamma_{s,t} + \phi^{re}\Phi_{s,t} + m_{s,t}^{re} \right) \\ + \sum_{t=t_{se}}^{T} \omega^{re}\Omega_{s,t} + \sum_{t}^{T} c_t^{re} \end{aligned} \tag{5.3}$$

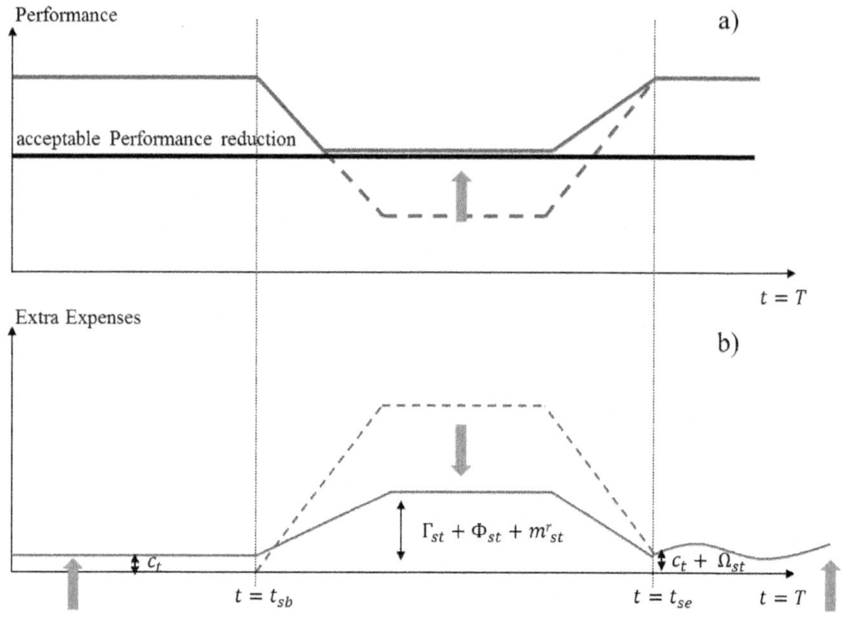

Figure 5.6: Development of performance and extra expenses in the presence of a disruption when reactive countermeasures are installed.

Pro-active Countermeasures

Often disruptions occur unexpectedly and remain temporarily undetected. Therefore, mechanisms that automatically adjust supply chain processes or compensate negative impacts are very valuable. These absorbing mitigation actions need to be implemented before disruptions occur. They require anticipatory-thinking, i.e. the ability of the decision maker to anticipate future uncertainties, to determine available mitigation actions, to analyze their potential to reduce negative impact and to assess their trade-offs. Flexible fall-back or robust positions are valuable for supply chain risk mitigation but sumptuous and need to be carefully examined. Flexible positions, such as additional suppliers or alternative production sites, provoke continuous costs, $c_t^{sr=fl}$, as well as cost that arise when the countermeasures become effective, $m_{s,t}^{sr=fl}$. Figure 5.7 presents a supply chain that is endowed with an alternative supplier.

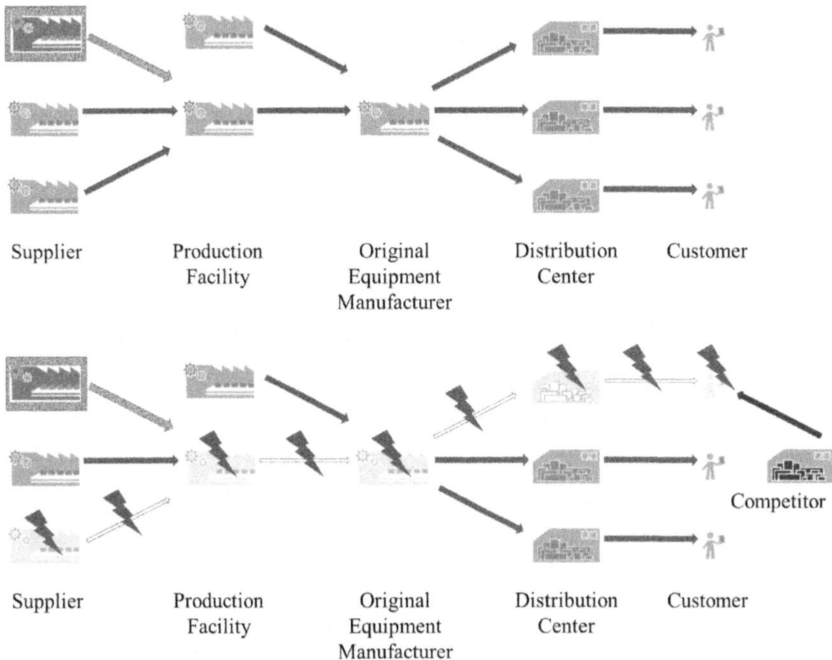

Figure 5.7: Impact of a disruption in the presence of a disruption when flexible countermeasures are installed.

When the production is impeded due to delayed components of a main supplier, supply chain sourcing may switch to the alternative supplier. Procurement may not be fully replaced, but the amount of missing parts is limited, see Figure 5.7.

$$
\begin{aligned}
Ex^{an} := \sum_{t=t_{sb}}^{t_{se}} \left(\gamma^{fl}\Gamma_{s,t} + \phi^{fl}\Phi_{s,t} + m^{fl}_{s,t}\right) \\
+ \sum_{t=t_{se}}^{T} \omega^{fl}\Omega_{s,t} + \sum_{t}^{T} c^{fl}_t
\end{aligned}
\tag{5.4}
$$

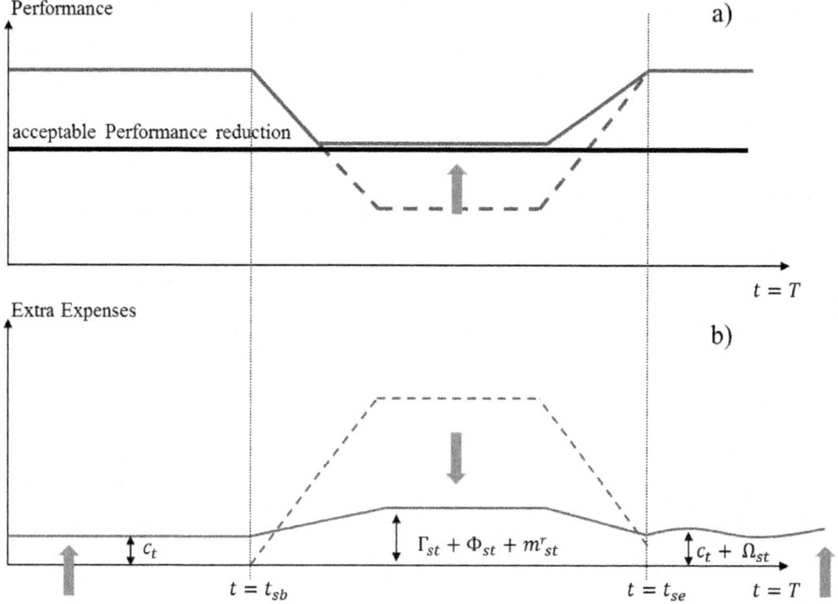

Figure 5.8: Development of performance and extra expenses in the presence of a disruption when flexible countermeasures are installed.

Robust positions include extra inventory of pre- and/or endproducts at production facilities or distribution centers, additional capacity resources for producing or manufacturing products, or time buffers before shipments to consecutive facilities, distribution centers, and customers. Figure 5.9 presents the possibility of extra inventory at the OEM.

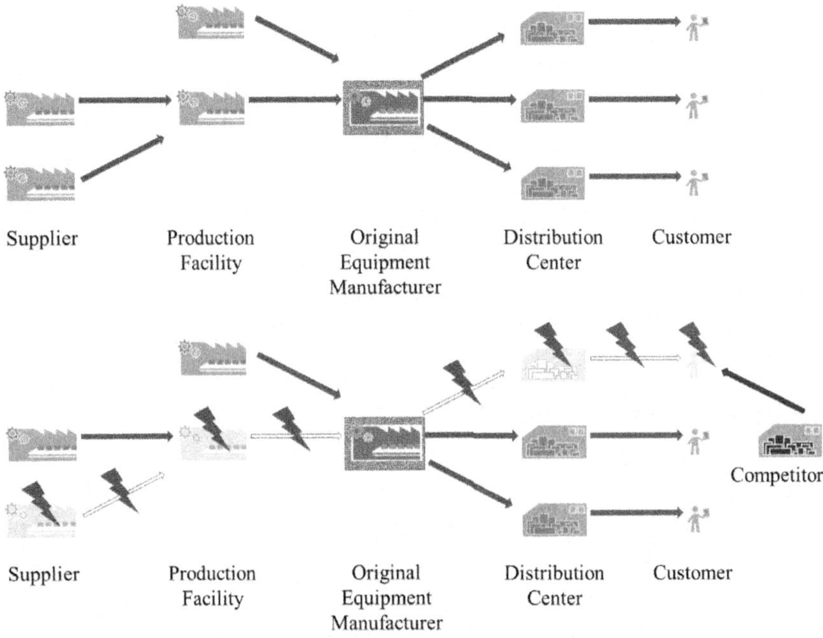

Figure 5.9: Impact of a disruption in the presence of a disruption when robust countermeasures are installed.

In case of the disruption additional inventory of components expected from the disrupted supplier can limit the production delay and consequently the dissatisfaction of customers' demand, see Figure 5.9. Robust actions are permanently installed and do not trigger costs during the disruption $c_t^{sr=ro}$.

$$Ex^{an} := \sum_{t=t_{sb}}^{t_{se}} (\gamma^{ro}\Gamma_{s,t} + \phi^{ro}\Phi_{s,t}) + \sum_{t=t_{se}}^{T} \omega^{ro}\Omega_{s,t} + \sum_{t}^{T} c_t^{ro} \tag{5.5}$$

Generally, the costs of each supply chain risk mitigation methodology must be considered for all disruption types and for several planning horizons. For the sake of simplicity we skipped the sum over all disruption, $\sum_s^S$, and multiple planning periods, $\sum_T^\Pi$.

Value of Preparedness

It is far from obvious to decide which supply chain risk mitigation strategy is the best fit for the underlying supply chain, because mitigation options are not always perfectly available or dimensioned. The flexible fall-back mitigation option discussed in the previous paragraph assumes the availability of an equally specialized additional supplier. However, sometimes specialized parts can only be produced by one company. Multiple-sourcing as an absorbing mitigation strategy is then not an option. When safety buffer is increased without a careful examination, whether it is really necessary, it might just increase logistics costs and is worthless as a mean of risk reduction. The crucial thing with supply chain risk management is to know about the risks, the vulnerabilities and the options to reduce uncertain developments. What defines good supply chain risk management is the degree of preparedness. Therefore, it is indispensable to apply analytic approaches in order to identify and assess the weaknesses of the network and the threats in its environment. This allows the determination of proper countermeasures that represent an effective portfolio, P, of mitigations actions and reduce overall extra expenses. Schmitt et al. for instance suggest to balance proactive and reactive countermeasures [267].

The risk reducing factors, γ, ϕ, and ω, therefore, highly depend on the preparedness, p, of people and systems involved.

$$
\begin{aligned}
Ex_P^{SCR} := \sum_{SCR} \sum_{t=t_{sb}}^{t_{se}} \left(\gamma(p)^{SCR} \Gamma_{s,t} + \phi(p)^{SCR} \Phi_{s,t} + m_{s,t}^{SCR} \right) \\
+ \sum_{t=t_{se}}^{T} \omega(p)^{SCR} \Omega_{s,t} + \sum_{t}^{T} c_t^{SCR}
\end{aligned}
\tag{5.6}
$$

Generally, the impact of risk mitigation strategies may have unequal effects on different supply chains. The specific situation of the supply chain under consideration, its individual uncertainties and market environments, has to be carefully analyzed before countermeasures are designed and implemented.

5.2.3 Risk Spreading Measures

Insurance

Traditionally, when thinking of limiting financial impact insurance is a prominent mean. While some companies have accepted the increased uncertainty of their supply chains as new additional costs, others rely on buying larger insurance policies [39]. The loss of customers, management time or reputation, however, can never be replaced by insurance. Since all these aspects are hard to assess, managers often fail to balance the costs and benefits of precaution measures or business contingency plans with the costs arising through insurance and uncovered losses.

Two important questions when considering insurance as a mean of supply chain risk management are: how reliable is your insurer and how good is your coverage? In terms of reliability a company needs to know whether the insurer has the financial strength to pay the loss occurred, whether it is stable enough to lean on and whether the insurer has a reputable history of payed claims [39]. Additionally, companies need to continuously monitor their coverage in accordance with the replacement value of goods and materials in order to avoid serious payments when disruptions take place. The incidents following the Great East Japan earthquake resulted in an economic loss of 210 US$ billion, but only 35 US$ billion were insured [239].

Insurance products are increasingly considered and further developed, but the market for supply chain insurance is still limited. It is assumed that difficulties in estimating the scope of potential losses and quantifying supply chain risk in general are the reasons for the limited coverages. Nevertheless, some insurers develop products that cover up to 125 US$ million of loss [7].

According to the World Economic Forum insurers reduced coverage and increased premiums due to the high costs of recent supply chain disruptions [249]. When expected losses cannot be covered through insurances, process- or purely logistic-based alternatives need to be evaluated.

There is no need to stop outsourcing to low-cost and highly-exposed countries nor to ban insurance policies as a mean of supply chain risk management [39], but as insurance can not be applied for all arising costs, it is necessary to assess and evaluate all available means of supply chain risk mitigation measures. Therefore, we regard insurance as a mean to limit some – not all – financial losses evoked by supply chain disruption. From our perspective supply chain risk management strategies could consist of a portfolio of different mitigation actions including both pure financial and additionally logistics countermeasures.

Risk Pooling

A concept initially developed to stem demand variability is risk pooling. It implies to aggregate demand over several locations and provides the possibility to offset high demand from one customer by low demand from another. Besides *demand pooling* it is possible to achieve *lead time-pooling.* Variability in lead times is offset by the aggregation of higher-than-average and below average lead times. A late shipment compensated by an early shipment. The reduction of variability allows to decrease inventory levels and increase service level.

Literature discusses different methods of risk pooling, which are either applicable for demand pooling, lead time pooling or both. Methods include, but are not limited to:

- *Inventory pooling* allows the aggregation of inventory levels, e.g. by centralization, to satisfy customer demand from centralized inventory,
- *transshipments* are transports of inventory between warehouses or retailers,
- *capacity pooling* generally refers to the association of service-, production-, and inventory-capacities over several locations,
- *order splitting* divides a single order into several partial deliveries, which allows to offset lead-time variability,
- *component commonality* suggests the manufacturing of similar rather than individualized components into their products, which allows to off-set variability of components needed for production,
- *postponement* postpones decisions for logistics, transportation, procurement, and production as long as possible.

Risk pooling is extensively considered in standard works such as [55] and [274].

5.3 Quantification Measures for Supply Chain Risk

In order to assess and compare different solutions that aim to limit the extent of risk, decision-makers need to (somehow) quantify risk. Standard deviation, mean-variance approaches, value-at-risk, conditional-value-at-risk or premiums are traditional risk measures that aim at describing the interaction of uncertainty and the extent of its related harm or benefit. Owing to the lack of quantitative measures that capture the more complex realities of supply chains, these measures – developed in finance and insurance contexts – are applied for supply chain risk, too. Starting from these concepts, supply chain risk is also measured by the likelihood and the severity of adverse effects or the extent of loss [89, 118, 213].

With respect to the aforementioned core characteristics of supply chain risk, these commonly used measures quantify the potential non-achievement of supply chain objectives while respecting given probability information. Besides the risk measures used within supply chain risk management literature we review measurement techniques from other research fields that may also serve as valuable supply chain risk measures or indicators. The transportation network literature provide so called criticality measures that focus on the assessment of the resilience of networks. Entropy-based measures additionally consider time-aspects, which is especially useful in the context of supply chain risk management.

The remainder of this section is organized as follows: In the next paragraph, several commonly used supply chain risk measures are introduced and briefly discussed. Afterwards, we review concepts from other research fields that may serve as a measure of other supply chain risk core characteristics. In the following paragraph measurement techniques from the transportation network literature are presented. The following section gives a short overview of entropy-based performance figures, before we derive general construction recommendations for supply chain risk measures.

5.3.1 Deviation Measures

Variance or *standard deviation* are widely used as a measure of supply chain risk, although several authors have been arguing that they are problematic as measures of risk in general [29, 65, 232]. Both concepts evaluate the wideness of a distribution and consider not only negative but also positive deviations from expected returns [262]. Consequently, a surplus of the expected is considered as risky as a equal-sized loss. According to Cox the most common critique in the theoretical decision analysis and financial economics literatures are the restrictions under which the mean-variance analysis is applicable [65], e.g. risk factors have normal or location-scale distributions and utility functions are quadratic, implying that less money is preferred to more, for some amounts [20, 197]. The difficulties of using probabilities in the light of growing complexity and uncertainty have already been discussed above. Deviation-based measures, like variance, standard deviation, expected or absolute values of deviation are applied by [12, 14, 16, 117, 136, 178, 193, 226, 265, 284, 331, 341, 342].

5.3.2 Downside Risk

In financial engineering and financial risk management positive and negative deviations are referred to as *upside-* and *downside-risk*, respectively. In that sense downside-risks reflects the risk associated with undesirables outcomes, i.e. losses. *Value-at-risk* (*VaR*) and *conditional-value-at-risk* (*CVaR*) are used in portfolio theory as percentile measures of downside risks. Both concepts describe different parts of a profit or loss distribution and their use is governed by the objective of the decision maker as well as by the availability and quality of distribution estimates [262]. *VaR* is defined as a threshold value associated with a specified confidence level of outcomes. Let X be a random variable most often describing a loss and $F(X) = Prob\{X \leq z\}$ the cumulative distribution function of X. The *VaR* of X with confidence level $\alpha \in [0, 1)$ is

$$VaR_\alpha(X) = \min\{z|F_X(z) \geq \alpha\}$$

By definition *VaR* is an α-percentile of X and therefore does not account for the distribution properties beyond the confidence interval. The indifference of *VaR* to extreme parts of the distribution can be both a desirable or undesirable property. When stable distribution estimates are not available *VaR* is predominantly used. However, extreme outcomes impose a particular threat and need to be explained especially if *VaR* is exceeded. $CVaR_\alpha(X)$ equals the conditional expectation of X subject to $X \geq VaR_\alpha(X)$. In other words it describes the average loss beyond the specified confidence level. Developed by Rockafellar and Uryasev [252] *CVaR* attracts much attention due to its mathematical properties that are especially suitable for optimization problems. Acerbi and Tasche [3] defined an equivalent of *CVaR* named *expected shortfall*. Sarykalin et al. [262] provide a comparative discussion of both concepts as well as suggestions of when to use which concept. For further insights we refer to their work. The application of downside risk measures within the context of supply chain problems is very common as can be deduced from the literature analysis. [188, 238, 265, 264] apply *VaR*, [238, 265, 266, 264, 287] apply *CVaR* and [53, 117, 342] use other downside risk measures.

5.3.3 Expected Values

In actuarial science risk is described by a non-negative random variable, that models a claim size caused by a policy. Actuaries develop models to quantify and price risks, i.e. they require probability distributions of the risk regarded as well as preference function to these probability distributions [181]. The price charged by the insurer for taking the risk is called a *premium*. A rule assigning a price to a risk is called a *premium calculation principle*. Goovaerts et al. [108] present various premium principles that have been proposed in insurance literature and discuss characteristics that premium principles should satisfy. In general, most premium principles transform random future loss into financial terms by applying expected values. The amount of the premium depends on the potential damage of the risk to be insured, its probability and also on the portfolio of the insurer itself. When, for example, the number of insured companies that are located within an earthquake-threatened area is higher than the number of companies in an equally threatened area, the loss for the insurer would be higher in the event of an earthquake. Relatively higher premiums for each company therefore compensate for increased expected losses [69]. Premium principles account for the portfolio of an insurer by considering a so-called additional *load*. Thus, a risk (understood as a triggering-event and its expected monetary losses) is assessed quite differently depending on the perspective of involved parties. The decision to transfer supply chain risk to an insurance has to be investigated carefully, as it does not necessarily cover the loss of the insured.

5.3.4 Probability and other measures

Other authors define approach-specific concepts like the number of hits [169] or use old-established measures like the mean-variance related to the profit [187]. Nagurney et al. [221] define risk functions for each supply chain partner that depends on the flow related to each partner and on the total flow within the network. These functions are used as an input for the model. Several authors apply probability as a measure of risk [12, 67, 81, 86, 177]. Azaron et al. [12] for instance measure the risk associated with a supply chain design problem by the probability of not meeting a certain cost level or budget. Cui et al. express supply chain risk as the probability that a certain facility serves a certain customer at a certain level [67].

Some authors do not quantify the degree of risk related to a solution, which is most-often the case, when supply chain risk is understood as the uncertainty of input parameters [30, 106, 180, 340, 343].

Figure 5.10 summarizes the analysis on risk measures applied in the literature under investigation.

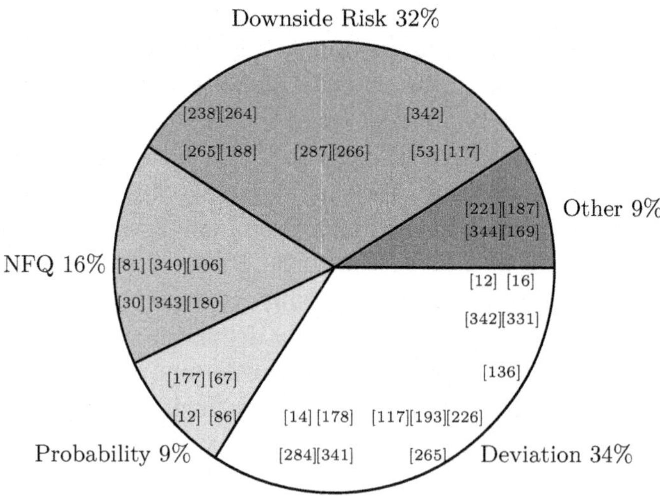

Figure 5.10: Measures applied for quantifying supply chain risk: Downside risk measures like VaR and CVaR and measures of (absolute, expected, and standard) deviation are among the most applied measures. Note that NFQ refers to "not further quantified".

5.4 Risk-aware Supply Chain Optimization

As supply chain risk management is a discipline that attracts the attention of researchers from different domains, the existing literature provides various methodological approaches. In addition, the previous discussion has shown that supply chain risk consists of several relevant aspects. There are literature reviews that analyze the existing work on some of these core characteristics: Snyder et al. [282] review papers from the operations research community that relate solely to supply chain disruption, hence that focus on *disruptive triggers*. Reviews focusing on the *affected supply chain*, discuss the design and planning of mitigation alternatives [114, 311]. Affiliated work includes topics like critical infrastructure and network reliability [219, 280].

Others classify and discuss general supply chain risk management approaches more broadly [278, 285, 305, 322] and derive managerial insights [270, 278, 306, 307]. Tang [306] classified various quantitative and qualitative approaches upon the supply chain management unit that is considered to deal with risk (supply, demand, product, or information management). Within each category the author further analyzes and differentiates available approaches upon the parameter considered as uncertain (demand, lead times, costs, yields), problem type (supply network design, supplier relationship, supplier selection process, supplier order allocation, supply contract), management strategy (postponement, process sequencing), or industry, respectively. Singhal et al. [278] provide a review that classifies literature by research approaches and key issues of supply chain risk management. They divide analytical risk modeling approaches into modeling type (mathematical, simulation, and multi-agent) and modeling settings (linear, integer, dynamic, and stochastic problem settings). According to Singhal et al. the latter refers to the nature of the study and scope/domain of the research problem.

The aforementioned surveys give a valuable overview of the supply chain risk management literature reaching across domains and methodologies. This section provides additional information and insights with the focus set to mathematical approaches that model supply chain design and planning problems and that explicitly refer to the consideration of supply chain risk. As we should be interested in how supply chain risk is defined, quantified, and modeled today, we omit the aforementioned related work. We analyze the modeling paradigms and techniques that solve the problems.

5.4.1 Modeling Approaches

In order to describe mathematical formulations for optimizing supply chain risk problems, this paragraph focuses on universal categories as well as on aspects tailored for supply chain risk considerations.

Classical categories have been proposed by Beamon [26] among others. The authors distinguishes between deterministic analytical, stochastic analytical, economic, and simulation models. Sahebi et al. just recently provided a classification based on Beamon's and Mula et. al's approaches [26, 215]. Sahebi et al.'s approach tackles relevant modeling aspects like the linearity of model formulation, dimensionality of the objective function, analytical model and purpose [260]. This classification is more suitable for the analysis of existing literature. Since the purpose of the mathematical formulation has been analyzed in Section 3.4.1, this aspect is skipped in the following presentation.

The risk statement is a further relevant aspect of description. Supply chain risk should be either minimized by the objective function, restricted by specific constraints or be balanced by its consideration in both statements. Often risk measures are introduced in the objective function and other risk related parameters are used in constraints.

linearity	linear programming non linear programming mixed integer/integer linear programming mixed integer/integer non linear programming	LP NLP MLP MNLP
objective function dimensionality	single-objective function multi-objective function	SOF MOF
risk statement placement	within objective function within constraints within constraints and objective function	OF CON OF/CON

Table 5.2: Categorization of modeling approaches.

Considering these aspects, we used the following criteria to classify the models:

- Linear programming, non-linear programming, mixed integer / integer linear programming, mixed integer / integer non-linear programming;
- Single and multi-objective functions; and
- Risk considerations within the objective function, within the constraints, or within both.

Table 5.2 summarizes the various aspects of modeling approaches that classify the reviewed papers.

Table 5.3 shows the result of this analysis. The majority of the reviewed papers applies linear programming and more precisely mixed integer programming approaches. Especially the location-allocation type of problems favors the mixed integer approach [12, 14, 67, 106, 136, 193, 238, 287]. The linear programming approaches considered tactical problems, like production, logistics or supply chain planning [30, 81, 284, 341, 342] as well as strategic decision models like supplier selection/portfolio or supply chain design problems

Ref	Linear		Nonlinear		Objective		Risk statement		
	LP	MLP	NLP	MNLP	SOF	MOF	OF	CON	OF/CON
[12]				✓		✓	✓		
[14]		✓			✓				✓
[16]				✓	✓				✓
[30]	✓				✓			✓	
[67]		✓			✓			✓	
[81]	✓				✓		✓		
[106]		✓			✓				✓
[117]		✓			✓		✓		
[136]		✓				✓	✓		
[178]		✓			✓		✓		
[193]	✓				✓				✓
[226]		✓			✓				✓
[238]		✓			✓				✓
[265]		✓			✓	✓			✓
[266]		✓			✓	✓			✓
[264]		✓			✓	✓			✓
[284]	✓				✓				✓
[287]		✓			✓				✓
[340]	✓				✓	✓			✓
[341]	✓				✓				✓
[342]	✓				✓	✓			✓
[344]	✓					✓			✓

Table 5.3: Modeling approaches of the reviewed papers.

[12, 14, 67, 106, 136, 193, 238, 264, 287, 340, 344]. Very rarely nonlinear approaches are chosen [12, 16]. Models exclusively considering multi-objective functions are of minor interest [12, 136, 344], although the need to balance different types of supply chain objectives would motivate multi-objective approaches. Therefore, the consideration of supply chain risk is stated mainly in both objective function and constraints.

Solution Technique	References	Share
General solver, exact solution	[14][16][30][117][238][265][266] [264][284][287][341]	46%
General solver, heuristic solution	[30][226][342]	13%
Specific algorithm, exact solution	[12][67][86][106][136][193]	25%
Specific algorithm, heuristic solution	[67][81][178][344]	16%

Table 5.4: Solution techniques of the reviewed papers.

5.4.2 Solution Techniques

This section follows the classification of solution methods provided by Melo et al. [205]. They defined four categories that determine different solution techniques. The first category *General solver, exact solution* refers to a problem's solution obtained by mathematical programming software. The solution is either optimal or good enough with respect to a pre-determined acceptable gap specified by the decision maker. By introducing computational time restrictions an off-the-shelf solver provides solutions of the second category, namely *heuristic solution.* Specific solution algorithms offer exact or heuristic solutions. The former are obtained by special-purpose techniques such as decomposition methods, column generation, branch-and-cut, and branch-and-bound. The latter are determined by heuristic-based approaches (Lagrangian relaxation, linear programming based heuristics and meta-heuristics) when problem sizes are huge. Table 5.4 summarizes the analysis of solution techniques.

5.5 Research Gaps

Most contemporary approaches dealing with supply chain risk concentrate on reducing monetary consequences of uncertain and unexpected developments, see Section 3.4.1. Meanwhile they predominantly evaluate the impact of changes of monetary policies (prices) or fiscal policies (taxation) with measures developed for the quantification of financial risk. However, financial risk is taken care of in financial risk management and supply chain risk management should be responsible for monetary losses within supply chain management. Additionally, we emphasize that objectives of supply chain management have different dimensions. Effectiveness-driven goals like customer satisfaction or supplier reliability ask for different measures like efficiency-based objectives.

To this date, supply chain risk management suffers from the lack of a clear and adequate quantitative measure for supply chain risk that respects the characteristics of modern supply chains. Based on the identified core characteristics defining supply chain risk that address different perspectives we suggest to quantify supply chain risk by a portfolio of different supply chain risk measures. When it is not possible to fully quantify supply chain risk through risk measures, still supply chain risk and its related core characteristics need to be represented within supply chain models. Despite the large quantity of available approaches relevant research gaps can be identified, namely:

- As nowadays supply chains need to fulfill efficiency- and effectiveness-driven objectives, approaches should account for balancing these opposite requirements.
- More advanced (context-sensitive) approaches especially with respect to the risk attitude of the decision maker and with respect to the environment of the affected supply chain are needed.
- The impact of time-aspects is evident, their integration into quantitative models, however, challenging.

Part II

Supply Chain Risk Identification and Assessment – Simulation-based Framework

6 Simulation for Supply Chain Analysis

"Do I believe, for example, that by using magic I could fly?
No. How would you get around gravity? Impossible.
Do I believe that I might be able to project my consciousness
into a very, very vivid simulation of flying?
Yeah. Yes, I've done that. Yes, that works."

Alan Moore

Supply chain management provides a means of increase the competitive position of supply chain partners by balancing conflicting business objectives of efficiency and effectiveness, see Chapter 3. However, as nowadays supply chains are surrounded by a continuously evolving environment that increases both complexity and risk exposition, the decision-making process for supply chain problems is a very challenging task. Supply chain managers have to take strategic, tactical, and operational decisions for a diversity of problems, but in such an environment it is hardly possible to completely predict all potential consequences of their decisions [191].

Decisions are made for a vast amount of supply chain parameters whose influence – especially their interacting effects – on supply chain performance change often and randomly over time. Due to the persisting complexity of supply chains that can not easily be modeled mathematical and stochastic models demand for specific solution methods tailored to the underlying problem. Restrictive assumptions facilitate the application of those solution methods, but limit a direct realization of their results. Simulation is a suitable methodology to model numerous interacting characteristics using a flexible and modular design. It allows the decision maker to create and re-create an artificial history of a real complex system [17]. Under the consideration of different constraints and objectives, simulation provides the opportunity to identify, to understand, to evaluate and to decide on different solutions [191]. Therefore, simulation is a powerful instrument for the analysis and evaluation of complex decisions as they need to be taken especially in supply chain management [191]. According to Ingalls the primary reason for using simulation is the existence of highly random supply chain parameters [141]. If demand forecasts, supplier or production reliability, distribution or procurement costs are endowed with high variance, simulation provides a realistic insight in supply chain dynamics.

The first part of this thesis pointed out that the existing literature on supply chain risk management provides insights in identifying potential triggers, but misses to rationalize underlying dynamics. In the last years the focus was primarily set to the analysis of disruptions rather on the comprehension of interactions within or in between highly complex supply chains.

In this chapter we introduce the meaning and purpose of simulation used for the analysis of typical supply chain problems. The remainder of this chapter is organized as follows: In the first section we present basic vocabulary, technical entities of simulation tools, and distinct simulation paradigms. We limit ourselves to the description of the most relevant concepts with regard to the developed simulation framework that is introduced in Chapter 8. For a closer look on simulation, we refer to Banks as well as Law et al. [17, 159]. Next, we briefly present simulation approaches for classical supply chain problems as well as solutions tailored for supply chain risk considerations.

The last part of this chapter discusses the relation of simulation and optimization.

6.1 Simulation at a Glance

Simulation is mainly used for the planning, implementation, and operation of technical systems. Simulation is especially useful, when the underlying system is assumed to be too complex to be examined by mathematical-analytical methods [323]. Such complexity arises due to time-dependent, random, and interacting effects within the system. What-if, weak-point, and sensitivity analysis are used to establish knowledge of the underlying system and to determine the degree of interaction.

The following explanations, descriptions, and definitions are mainly based on the work of Banks [17], who provides a detailed introduction to the field of discrete-event-simulation, Kleijnen [167], who gives a presentation of the design and analysis of simulation experiments and on the VDI guideline 3633 Part I and Part XII, that define important elements of the simulation technology [323, 324].

6.1.1 Basics

Based on the definitions provided by Banks [17], Kleijnen [167], and the VDI guidline 3633 Part I [323], we derive definitions of simulation and related concepts. A summary of these definitions is given in Table 6.1.

Simulation is an experimental problem solving-method, imitating the operating behavior of a technical process or system over time. The imitation implies generating artificial history of the underlying process or system and drawing conclusions [17]. Problems to be solved by simulation differ among the identification of a desirable (or even

Concept	Definition	Ref
Simulation	Simulation is an experimental problem solving-method, imitating the operating behavior of a system over time.	[17, 323]
System	A system is a set of interrelated elements separated from the environment	[62, 323]
Process	A process is the set of interacting operations in a system that process, transport, or store material, energy, or information.	[62, 323]
Model	A model is a simplified representation of the structure, function, or behavior of the underlying process or system.	[323]
Event	An event is defined as an occurrence that changes the state of a system.	[17]
System-state-variable	The system state variables are the collection of all information needed to define what ist happening within a system to a sufficient level at a given point in time.	[17]
Simulation run	Simulation is used, when the underlying system is assumed to be too complex to be examined by mathematical-analytical methods.	[323]
Simulation experiment	A simulation experiment is the targeted empirical investigation of a models behaviour by repeated simulation runs with a systematic variation of parameters or structures	[323]

Table 6.1: Simulation: terms and definitions.

optimal) solution, validation and verification, sensitivity or "what-if" analysis, and robustness, risk or uncertainty analysis of such processes or systems [166]. A simulation includes the description and the analysis of a conceptual or a real-world process or system. A *system* is defined as a set of interrelated elements separated from the environment and a *process* is a set of interacting operations in a system that process, transport, or store material, energy, or information [62]. Structure, function, or behavior of a process or system are simplified and represented by a *model*. Defining an appropriate model includes specifying its limits and boundaries. This is a challenging part of the model definition, as a model should be a simplified version of the real-world, but still complex enough to represent the dynamics or interactions within the system. The status of a model is described by *system-state-variables*. They cover all information necessary to model a system with regard to its purpose. The state of a system as well as the state of the model variables change due to the occurrence of an *event*. A *simulation experiment* investigates a model's reaction by collecting and statistically evaluating changes of state-variables over several repeated *simulation runs*. State-variables may alter within a simulation run due to the occurrence of events that are described by modified parameter values. Parametrization is a systematic variation of parameters and needs to be considered when evaluating changes of state-variables. Simulation approaches whose system-state-variables change only at discrete points of time, are called *discrete-event simulations*. Other types of simulation models are: mathematical or physical, static, dynamic, deterministic, stochastic, or continuous [18].

From the discussion so far, a generic procedure of a simulation study can be derived, see Figure 6.1.

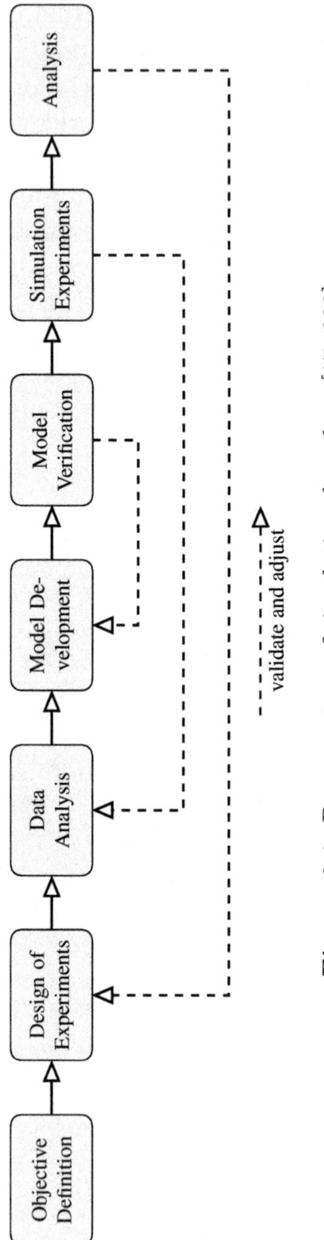

Figure 6.1: Process steps of simulation, based on [17, 323].

6.1.2 Technical entities of Simulation Tools

Available simulation software tools differ in the purpose of application and modeling philosophy, however, the VDI Guideline 3633 identifies four components that characterize the architecture of nowadays simulation software, namely: simulation kernel, data management, user interface, and interfaces to external programs philosophy [323].

The simulation kernel is responsible for the coordination and initiation of individual processes and components. Besides acting as the central control system it provides the model implementation and it executes the generation and processing of individual events.

Different types of data need to be managed within the simulation: input data is provided by the user of the model, parameter values relevant for each simulation run are referred to as experimental data, internal model data consists of absolute terms as well as variable values, and simulation result data describe the solution of the simulation run. The data management is also responsible for the assignment of different data categories to model elements and processing algorithms.

Interfaces provide access to exchange information and data. The user interface establishes a means of the user to enter input data manually or to configure data access to a data base. Interfaces to other programs are valuable for the evaluation, visualization, and further processing of simulation result data.

Figure 6.2 shows the interaction of the aforementioned core components.

Traditionally, the simulation of supply chains is realized as a whole single model executed over a single computer. This structural concept is referred to as local simulation. In order to integrate different simulation software and data sources that may exist at each supply

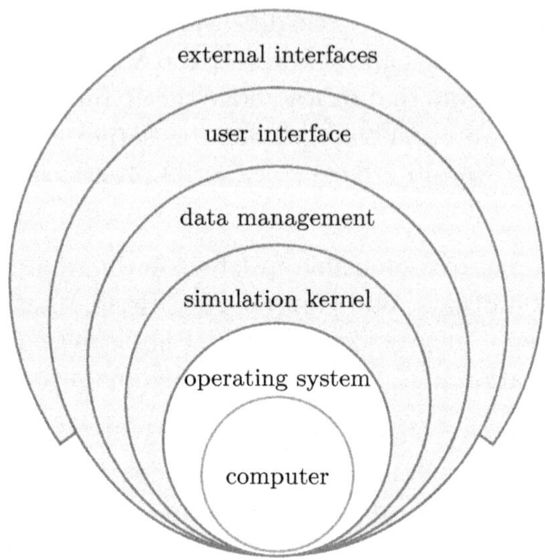

Figure 6.2: Technical components of a simulation (see [323]).

chain partner, also parallel or distributed simulation is used [98]. According to Fujimoto parallel discrete-event simulation executes simulation on multiprocessor computing platforms and distributed simulation runs on geographically distributed but connected computers [98]. Both cases imply the execution of a single main simulation model, made up by several sub-simulation models, which are executed, in a distributed manner, over multiple computing stations [309].

6.1.3 Simulation Paradigms

The main simulation paradigms of modeling complex systems are: System Dynamics (SD), Discrete Event Simulation (DES) and Agent-Based Modeling (AB). Each of these simulation approaches is based on several different assumptions. In the following paragraphs we briefly present major characteristics, assumptions and potential benefits, also summarized in Table 6.2.

System Dynamics

Primarily known under the notion "Industrial Dynamics" the paradigm was developed by engineer Jay Forrester in the 1950s. System Dynamics is defined as "the study of information-feedback characteristics of industrial activity to show how organizational structure, amplification (in policies), and time delays (in decisions and actions) interact to influence the success of the enterprise" [92]. Complex systems are modeled in terms of stocks (e.g. material, money, people), flows between stocks, and information that values the flows. The basic building block of a complex system is the "feedback loop" and the behavior of the system is described by a number of interacting feedback loops [246]. Stocks, flows, and feedback loops are visualized via causal loop diagrams. They help in analyzing the system qualitatively [28]. The mathematical formulation is based on a set of differential and algebraic equations.

Discrete Event Simulation

The name of the simulation paradigm refers to the fact that states change only at discrete points in time [18]. Between consecutive events the system does not change. The behavior of the system is analyzed by analytical or numerical methods. The former refers deductive reasoning of mathematics and the later to computational procedures. So called "runs" are generated and observations are collected to be analyzed with the goal to evaluate the system's performance [18].

System Dynamics	Discrete-Event Simulation	Agent-based Simulation
System-oriented: focus is on modeling the system observables	Process-oriented: focus is on modeling the system structure and behavior in detail	Individual-oriented: focus is on modeling the behavior of entities and interactions between them
Homogenized entities: all entities are assumed to have similar features; working with average values	Heterogeneous entities	Heterogeneous entities
No representation of micro-level entities	Micro-level entities are "passive objects" (with no intelligence or decision-making capability) that move through a system in a pre-specified process	Micro-level entities are "active objects" (agents)" that can make sense of the environment, interact with others and make autonomous decisions
"Feedback loops" are the driver of dynamic behavior	The "occurrence of events" are the driver of dynamic behavior	"Agent's decisions & interactions" are the driver of dynamic behavior
Computer formalization of underlying system is through "stock & flow"	Computer formalization of underlying system is through "event, activity, & process"	Computer formalization of underlying system is through "agents & environment"
Continuous time consideration	Discrete time consideration	Discrete time consideration
Fixed system structure	Fixed processes	system structure is not fixed

Table 6.2: Summary of major characteristics of prevailing simulation paradigms, based on [28].

Agent Based Simulation

In contrast to SD and DES agent-based simulation aims not to model and define system dynamics. Instead, individual system entities or decision makers are modeled and their interactions with each other and the environment define the global behavior [38]. While the major property of each agent is autonomy, further properties are up for debate [28]. Usually mentioned for agent-based modeling are reactivity (agents are able to react to their environment), pro-activeness (agents do not only react to changes, but also act in advance), social ability (agents communicate with each other), and adaptiveness (agents can learn and base their behavior on experience). Individual behavior or decisions are based on behavioral rules and on the current states of each agent.

6.2 Simulation of Supply Chain Problems

Simulation in the supply chain context is mainly used for the planning, the implementation, and the operation of supply chain processes [323]. Simulation, therefore, supports the analysis of various supply chain problems on different decision levels such as strategic, tactical, and operational. Especially planning problems as classified by Terzi and Cavalieri [309] for inventory, distribution and transportation, production and scheduling, demand and sales, supply chain, as well as facility location and network design are of interest. For a careful investigation of current literature with respect to classical supply chain problems and their consideration within simulation approaches we refer to Terzi and Cavalieri [309].

Behdani [28] shows that the application of simulation in its different methodological shapes is well established in literature of supply chain analysis. Over 800 papers published over 20 years have been analyzed and categorized. The amount of articles reveals the great acceptance of simulation as a mean to analyze classical supply chain problems.

Simulation is used as a methodology to deal with very complex systems that occasionally face high variance. As such, most classical simulation approaches can be suitable for the integration and consideration of uncertainty and supply chain risk, too. However, supply chain risk most often addresses additional aspects and even increases the complexity of the underlying problem. Specific approaches tailored for the analysis of supply chain risk have been developed.

For instance, Hotz [134] developed a generic architecture for simulation-based early warning systems that support operational production planning and scheduling tailored for the automotive industry. Wilson [338] applies a system dynamics approach to simulate the effects of transportation disruptions on supply chain performance. Wu and Olson [339] model a three-level supply chain and determine expected values of supply chain performance with the help of random simulated data with representative distributions. Melnyk et al. [204] design a computer-based discrete event simulation to evaluate the effects of supply chain disruptions.

6.3 Simulation and Optimization

Simulation is a method to evaluate a given solution, i.e. the assignment of values to variables, with respect to a specified objective. Simulation supports answering the question *what* the objective will look like *if* a certain solution is applied. With the goal to determine a functional relationship between input variables and the output objective many distinct runs (scenarios) need to be generated and analyzed. Simulation works efficiently when conducted as an experimental method and strongly relates to the *design of experiments*. As the simulation framework introduced in Chapter 8 works with experimental designs, Chapter 7 briefly summarizes major ideas of this research domain.

Additionally, simulation analysts often seek to identify a *good* or *desirable* solution with respect to a given objective. The purpose of simulation is then to define consecutive sets of simulation runs, while one of them may contain this solution. Approaches based on response surface approximation intended for black-box-systems support the identification of this solutions. Recently, the notion of *simulation optimization* emerged in literature referring to a process that finds the best input variable values without evaluating each assignment [97, 308]. It subsumes methodological approaches as different as response surface methodology, stochastic optimization, heuristic, and statistical methods. Although this concept seeks and theoretically is able to identify an optimal solution, because it encompasses optimization methods, we strongly emphasize that this nomenclature is misleading and therefore unfortunate. It is a simulation methodology that occasionally applies concepts of optimization and tries to determine an optimal solution for a nearly unknown system. But it is not an optimization approach in a mathematical sense that determines the best solution by the means of simulation.

In contrast to simulation, optimization is a method to determine the best solution, i.e. assignment of those values that maximize or minimize the specified objective. Sometimes it is favorable to combine both processes. For example each agent within an agent-based simulation approach can optimize their behavior with regard to his subjective goals. Or when the optimization problem is too complex, subproblems can be released from the master problem and passed to a simulation model that targets the determination of a feasible rather than an optimal solution. This process can considerably save computing time.

Today, simulation software is increasingly combined with special search processes, to guide a series of simulations to uncover optimal or near optimal scenarios [104]. While, most often simulation and optimization are used in sequence from separated software programs, the integration of both methodologies within single mathematical formalism has gained significant attention over the last decade [324].

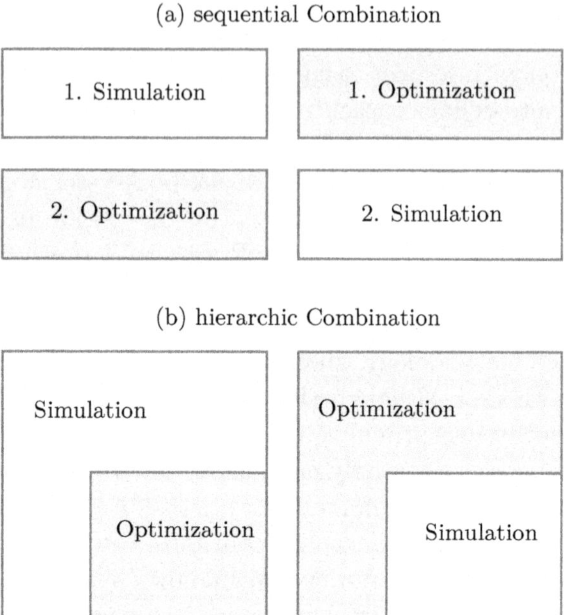

Figure 6.3: Causal and temporal classification of simulation and optimization integrating approaches (see [324]).

Especially, the aforementioned simulation paradigms have been enriched with optimization approaches.

The VDI guideline 3633 part XII provides a classification for different types of combination of simulation and optimization [324]. Accordingly, combinations can be characterized as:

- causal and temporal
- objective-oriented
- implementation determined

The former refers to the fact that single simulation- and optimization-steps should be carried out in a certain temporal order of processing, which is due to algorithm-specific requirements. A sequential combination assumes that either simulation or optimization are completed before the other can be executed. Within a hierarchical combined approach the simulation or optimization is introduced as a subclass, which can be called several times during the overall execution. Figure 6.3 gives a descriptive illustration of both alternatives.

Although an objective-oriented combination provides the possibilities to analyze distinct solutions or to find a better solution, the ultimate goal is to identify a desirable result. Therefore, all combinations fall into this category. Further classification types are determined by the degree of integration: totally separated components, coupling based on common data formats, inclusion by coordination mechanisms, or direct communication and mutual coordination of both simulation- and optimization components [324].

7 Design, Metamodeling, and Analysis of Simulation Experiments

"The experimenter, who does not know, what he is looking for, will never understand what he finds."

Claude Bernard

A simulation-based approach does not solve the underlying model by the means of mathematical calculus [167], but rather by varying different values for the input parameters of the model and analyzing the resulting outputs. Due to the complexity of supply chain systems, a simulation model needs to be endowed with an appropriate experiment setup for the efficient identification and assessment of the dynamics we want to find.

The *design of experiments* is a branch of statistics applied within agriculture, engineering and psychology for decades. Comprehensive introductions to the topic are provided by Montgomery [211] and Ghosh and Rao [101]. Traditionally, experiments were conducted in real and non-simulated setups. These experiments are called *physical experiments.* Physical experiments are exposed to a number of uncontrollable influences from the environment, which always lead to random errors. Identical settings of an experiment, thus, might

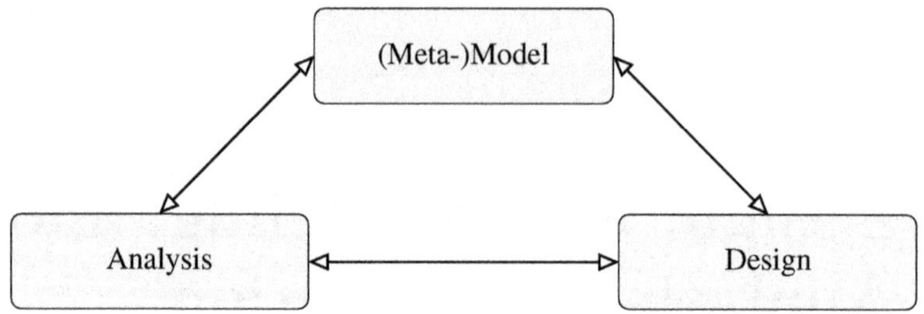

Figure 7.1: Main elements of an experimental setup.

provide different results. For the purpose of both a dependable result generation and interpretation appropriate statistical methods are needed.

The foundation of the design of experiments is the statistical model. Fang et al. [83] define a good design as one which is optimal with respect to the statistical model under consideration. For physical experiments there exist many statistical models. The *fractional factorial design* – based on an ANOVA model – and the *optimum design* – based on a regression model – are the most widely used statistical models in practice [83]. Main effects, interactions, regression coefficients, and variance of random error are considered parameters in these models. Good designs, such as orthogonal arrays, may provide unbiased estimators of the parameters with smaller or even the smallest variance-covariance matrix under certain conditions [83]. Conducting an experiment, therefore, consists of the interplay between the underlying statistical model (the so called meta-model), the design, and the analysis, see Figure 7.1.

Owing to increased computing power *computer experiments* or *computer- based simulations* become popular [83]. The statistical model of a computer-based experiment is deterministic. In contrast to physical experiments that consider only a small set of factors (ten is a maximum [167]) combined with a small number of values (five values per factor seems the limit [167]), in computer-based simulation these assumptions do not hold. Indeed, computer experiments are developed for a large amount of factors each of which has many different values [167]. The management and analysis of simulation concerned with supply chains is especially complicated: In each time period each process, each capacity resource and each order for a specific product determine a supply chain factor. Supply chains, therefore, consist of hundreds or even thousands of supply chain factors. The number of supply chain factors may decrease according to the level of detail related to the performance indicator chosen as objective. Generally, the higher the granularity specified for supply chain describing factors (production capacity at each facility is more granular then overall production capacity in a specific region) the larger the number of factors to be varied for simulation.

It is hardly possible to provide a complete overview of all approaches related to the design and analysis of computer-based simulation. Additionally it is not the purpose of this thesis to develop new or more advanced algorithms for the design and analysis of supply chain experiments. We rather transfer some of the existing approaches to the field of risk-aware supply chain analysis with the goal to support the assessment of supply chain dynamics. Therefore, we limit ourselves in presenting those approaches that are valuable for the understanding of the developed simulation model.

The remainder of this chapter is organized as follows: Section 7.1 provides further insights in different types of meta-models. Section 7.2 introduces different layouts of classical factorial designs and their purpose. Section 7.3 summarizes different modes of analysis. Next, we provide an illustrative example combining the afore explained steps for conducting an experiment. In Section 7.5 we point out, that due to the dependencies between meta-modeling, analysis, and design, results of experiments need to be carefully evaluated before conclusions are drawn.

Large parts of the explanations and discussions below are adopted from standard works such as Fang et al. [83], Kleijnen [167], and

Montgomery [211]. For the sake of readability we limit ourselves in referring continuously to the aforementioned authors. Instead a more detailed discussion on computer-based simulations and design and analysis of experiments can be found in the work of those authors.

7.1 Meta-Models

Generally, scientists use models to analyze and predict the behavior of the underlying system. This analysis provides the information basis for decision making, when the levels of input factors change. The relationship between input factors and a specific output variable of a computer experiment can be formalized as:

$$y = f(x_1, \ldots, x_k) = f(\boldsymbol{x}), \quad \boldsymbol{x} = (x_1, \ldots, x_k)' \in D \tag{7.1}$$

where $\boldsymbol{x}$ is a vector of different input factors k, y is an output variable – often referred to as the response, the function f may have an analytic formula, and D represents the experimental domain. This model can be regarded as a solution of a set of equations, including linear, nonlinear, ordinary, and/or partial differential equations. It is often not possible to determine an analytic solution for those equations. Therefore, scientists make use of computer simulations to explore the complex relationship between inputs and outputs, I/O-functions. In contrast to physical experiments, the outputs of a computer experiment are deterministic, i.e. there are no random errors. The model 7.1, therefore, does not provide a random error term on the right-hand side, see [83].

One of the goals of computer experiments is first to find an approximate model that is much simpler than the true (but complicated) model. The approximation of the functional relationship between input and output is conducted by the definition of a meta-model, which is assumed to best fit the underlying model, see Figure 7.2.

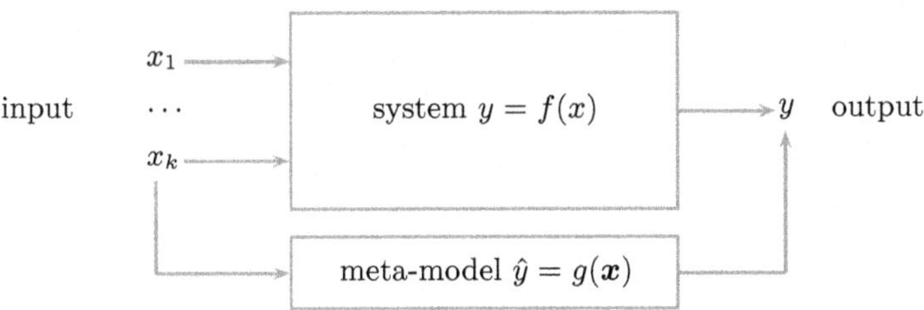

Figure 7.2: Relationship between input factors and output variable of the system and its simulated meta-model, Fang et al. [see 83, p.11].

However, for a given model $y = f(\boldsymbol{x})$ there are many different meta-models applicable. The determination of a simple meta-model $\hat{y} = g(\boldsymbol{x})$ that properly approximates the given model is a crucial task, the identification of the best meta-model g^* is even more difficult. A requirement of good modeling practice is to provide an evaluation of the confidence in the model. This allows the analyst to assess the uncertainties related to the modeling process and to the outcome of the model itself, see [83]. According to Fang et al. [83] and Kleijnen [167] the modeling of computer-based simulations can be viewed as linear regression on data without random errors. This assumption allows to apply fundamental ideas and concepts of statistical modeling. A linear combination of a set of specific bases is used to represent most meta-models, see [83]. Let $B_1(\boldsymbol{x}), B_2(\boldsymbol{x}), \ldots$ be a set of basis functions defined on the experimental domain D. A meta-model g thus can be written as:

$$g(\boldsymbol{x}) = \beta_1 B_1(\boldsymbol{x}) + \beta_2 B_2(\boldsymbol{x}) + \ldots \tag{7.2}$$

where β_j's are unknown coefficients to be estimated.

Widely used for the meta-modeling of computer-based simulations are polynomial models. These models apply a polynomial basis $x_1^{r_1} \dots x_k^{r_k}$, where $r_1, \dots, r_k$ are non-negative integers. The number of polynomial basis functions increases dramatically with the number of input factors and the degree of polynomial, [83]. Low-order polynomials such as the first-order polynomial model,

$$g(\boldsymbol{x}) = \beta_0 + \sum_{i=1}^{k} \beta_i x_i \tag{7.3}$$

or the second-order polynomial model

$$g(\boldsymbol{x}) = \beta_0 + \sum_{i=1}^{k} \beta_i x_i + \sum_{i=1}^{k} \sum_{j=1}^{k} \beta_{ij} x_i x_j \tag{7.4}$$

are the most popular meta-models for computer-based simulation [83, 167]. It is convenient to use *coded*, also *standardized* or *scaled*, factor values. If each factor has only two levels in the experiment, then these levels are denoted by -1 and $+1$. This linear transformation can be formalized as follows, see [167]:

$$x_{ij} = a_j + z_j \text{ with } a_j = \frac{l_j + u_j}{l_j - u_j};$$

$$b_j = \frac{2}{u_j - l_j}; \; j = 1, \dots, k; \; i = 1, \dots, n \tag{7.5}$$

which implies:

$$x_{ij} = \frac{z_{ij} - \bar{z_j}}{(u_j - l_j)/2} \tag{7.6}$$

and where z_j denotes the quantitative factor j measured on the original scale, l_j the lower value of z_j, u_j the upper value, and $\bar{z_j}$ the average value of input in a balanced experiment. A balanced experiment implies that each factor has the lower level in half of the n factor combinations. The difference $u_j - l_j$ is known as the *range* of input factor j.

Another approach to make numerical computation stable is the centralization of input factors around their average values in the experiment [83, 167]:

$$g(\boldsymbol{x}) = \beta_0 + \sum_{i=1}^{k} \beta_i(x_i - \bar{x_i}) + \sum_{i=1}^{k}\sum_{j=1}^{k} \beta_{ij}(x_i - \bar{x_i})(x_j - \bar{x_j}) \quad (7.7)$$

However, whenever multivariate inputs are assumed these basis functions need to be extended. Such an extension is difficult, because the number of terms in a input factor increases [83]. Therefore, techniques such as Kriging models, neural networks, and local polynomial models have been developed. They provide a more natural construct for the handling of multivariate basis functions. For further reading, consider Fang et al. [83].

7.2 Designs

A statistical design or *design matrix* denoted by *DM* represents a set of points of the experimental domain D which supports the construction of an approximate model based on the data set that is formed by *DM* and the output on *DM* [83]. A design of experiments can be perceived as the layout of a detailed plan for conducting experiments. It indicates the sequence of simulation runs that efficiently yields to meaningful results. The choice of an appropriate design depends on the meta-model, which is assumed to be valid, and on the intended target of the experiment. In Section 7.2.1 we discuss two major objectives, when running experiments. The efficiency of a computer-based experiment can be achieved by reducing the number of simulation runs, while still maintaining the significance of overall experimental results. In Section 7.2.2 we introduce different specifications of a prominent type of experimental designs often used for generating efficient layouts, namely *factorial designs.*

7.2.1 Purpose of Design

Screening

The choice of design strongly depends on the type of conclusion the analyst wants to draw. Whenever a bundle of factors is assumed to have an influence on the response, it is necessary to identify those factors that have a statistical relevance on the response. The motivation for this necessity derives from the curse of dimensionality [277]. Highly dimensional problems aggravate the identification of statistical relevant components. The *sparsity principle*, however, implies that the number of relatively important effects and interactions in a factorial design is very small [83]. The *parsimony* principle states that simpler theories should be preferred to more complex ones [167]. Additionally, Kleijnen [167] points out that it is valuable for the analyst to know which factors certainly do not affect the response. In order to enable the decision makers to discard irrelevant factors from their consideration and to concentrate any efforts on the management of relevant factors, appropriate statistical designs are needed.

Factor screening refers to a group of algorithms that seek to identify the most important factors influencing the outcome of experiments. Originally developed for real-world systems and physical experiments, screening algorithms are today commonly used to analyze factor effects of computational experiments with more than hundred varying factors, see Fang et al. [83]. The result of a screening algorithm is a so-called *screening design* that determines the factors and their corresponding levels to be investigated in the experimental setup.

The significance of factors depends on the experimental domain of the factors. It is the responsibility of the simulation analyst to provide adequate information like appropriate ranges of individual factors [167]. Therefore, the involvement of the decision maker is important for executing efficient experiments. Several types of screening designs are available and commonly used for the analysis of so-called black box approaches.

Trocine and Malone [314] derive criteria that mark good screening methods, namely: efficiency, effectiveness, robustness, and ease of use. Efficiency refers to the computational effort for an experiment. Screening designs should minimize the number of simulation runs while acquiring as much information as possible, which is defined by the effectiveness of a screening design. As in practical problems the effects of relevant and unimportant main or interaction factors are unknown, it is very difficult to measure the effectiveness of a screening design. The comparison of different designs for generated cases provides a first insight. However, analytical results cannot be generalized [314]. As we pointed out in the introduction of this chapter, the assumed meta-model, the design of an experiment, and the analysis of its results strongly depend on each other. Consequently, the application of specific designs demands for the existence of certain conditions within the underlying problem. These conditions, however, are what is sought while conducting the experiment [314]. Screening designs or procedures, therefore, need to work well in situations where deeper knowledge is missing. The ease of use is regarded as a desirable but not necessary criterion, especially as an easy to apply method should not offset efficiency, effectiveness, and robustness.

Prominent screening designs for factorial experiments are Placket-Burman [236], 2^{k-p} designs [211], and sequential bifurcation [33], some of which are introduced in Section 7.2.2. In addition there are some other approaches to be mentioned: one-factor-at-a-time designs [45], fold-over designs [220], methods based on frequency domain analysis [269, 214], edge designs [74], iterated fractional factorial designs [45] and the Trocine screening procedure [314]. For further details we refer to Fang et al. [83], Montgomery [211], Kleijnen [167], Trocine and Malone [313], and Trocine and Malone [314].

Response Surface Methodology

A factor is specified to have a few values in the experimental domain wherein the factor is tested. Screening designs consider two or three distinct factor levels in order to determine whether the response, y, significantly differs among these levels. A level combination is one of the possible combinations of factor levels. It is also called a treatment combination [83]. Besides determining the statistical significance of experimental factors, analysts are additionally interested in identifying functional relationships between many distinct factor level combinations and the response.

With the objective to identify treatment combinations that minimize or maximize the univariate output of the underlying system, the *response surface methodology* originated. It was introduced by Box and Wilson as an iterative heuristic for optimizing chemical systems [41]. Since then it developed into a collection of mathematical and statistical techniques that support the modeling and analysis of problems and the optimization of their response variable(s). Consider the example of Montgomery [211], in which a chemical engineer is interested in the level of temperature, x_1, and pressure, x_2, that maximize the yield of a process, y, see Montgomery [211] chapter 11. The process yield depends on the functional relationship between temperature and pressure:

$$y = f(x_1, x_2) + \epsilon \tag{7.8}$$

where ϵ represents the error in the response y. The expected response is denoted by $E(y) = f(x_1, x_2) = \eta$, then the surface is represented by:

$$\eta = f(x_1, x_2) \tag{7.9}$$

is called a *response surface.*

Usually, the response surface is represented graphically. Figure 7.3a visualizes η versus the levels of x_1 and x_2. Contour plots additionally help to visualize the response surface as can be seen from Figure 7.3b. Contour plots highlight the contour lines of constant response in the x_1, x_2 plane.

It can be assumed that in most problems the form of the relationship between the response and the design factors are unknown. Therefore, the first step is to find a suitable approximation for the real functional relationship. Often, a low-order polynomial is used to model the regions of the independent factors. If the response is modeled by a linear function the approximation would be a first-order model; if the response indicates a curvature a polynomial of higher-order is necessary, such as a second-order model. These two models are the most common approximations applied within response surface methodology. Montgomery [211] points out that it is unlikely that a polynomial model will be a reasonable approximation of the true functional response over the entire space of the independent factors, however, it might be a good fit for small regions.

The method of least squares, discussed in Section 7.3, is used to estimate the parameters in the approximating polynomials. In order to effectively determine the model parameters appropriate designs – so called response surface designs are needed. Proper designs for first-order models are *orthogonal first-order designs* and effective designs for second-order models are *central composite designs.* For each step of the response surface methodology procedure the factor levels need to change. To determine the direction of change, response surface methodology uses the gradient that is implied by the first-order polynomial fitted in the current step [167]. This gradient is used in the mathematical techniques of steepest descent (or steepest ascent, if output is to be maximized), see Montgomery [211]. The experiments terminate when no further decrease of response is observed on the path of steepest descent. A lack-of-fit of a first-order

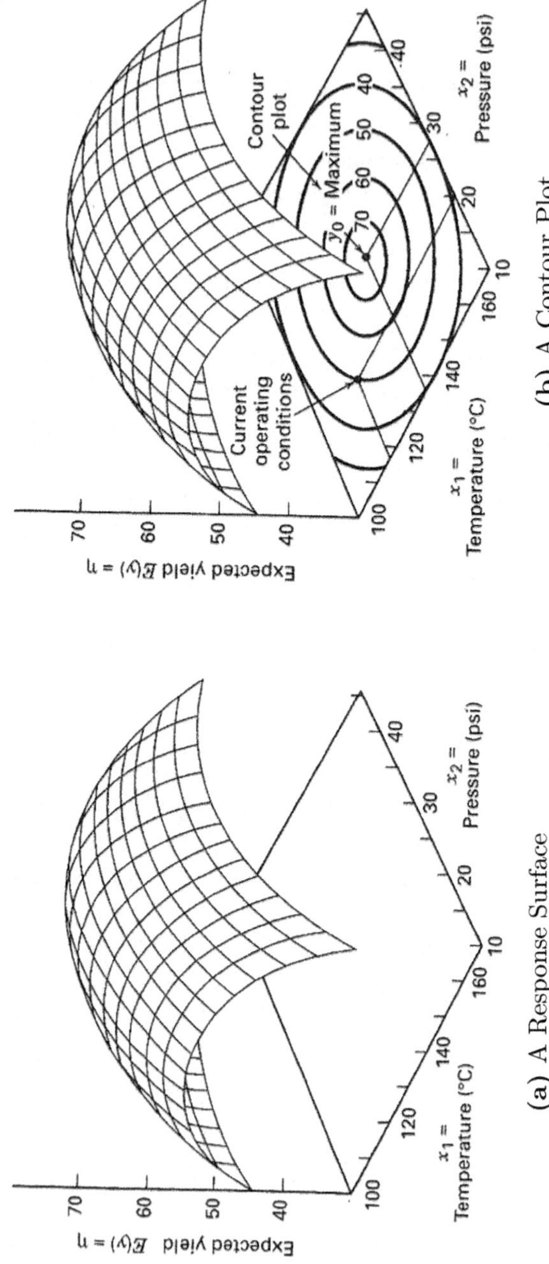

(a) A Response Surface

(b) A Contour Plot

Figure 7.3: A response surface visualizing the expected yield η as a function of temperature, x_1, and pressure, x_2, and the corresponding contour plot, see [211].

polynomial model indicates the possibility that the region of the optimum is reached. Then experiments with second-order polynomial models can be conducted to obtain a more precise estimate of the optimum.

There is a vast amount of literature discussing various topics of response surface methodology. For further reading we refer to general introductions such as Box and Draper [40], Khuri and Cornell [163], and Myers and Montgomery [220].

7.2.2 Classic Factorial Designs

Most prominent experimental designs are based on factors or design factors and called *factorial designs.* Therein a factor or design factor is a controllable variable that is of interest in the experiment. Factors that can be numerically measured are quantitative factors. Those factors whose values are categories are called qualitative factors. Variables that are not considered for the experimental analysis are set to fixed values. A factorial design is a set of level-combinations with main purpose of estimating main effects and some interactions between distinct factors [83].

2^k and 2^{k-p} Designs

Full factorial designs are experimental layouts that consider all potential factor level combinations. Clearly, the number of runs in a full factorial design should be $n = q^k$, where q is the number of factor levels – assuming that all factors have the same number of levels – and k is the number of factors. In physical experiments such designs are of mutual interest as the number of factors is small. As the number of factors increases the usage of *fractional factorial designs* (FFD) becomes of interest. In accordance with the *sparsity principle*, fractional factorial designs consider only a subset of all factor level combinations. Especially when high-order interactions are assumed to be negligible and information on effects of main and low-order interactions suffices, the execution of fractional factorial designs can be more efficient than running a full factorial design. The relatively smaller amount of observable responses compared to the set of factors, however, may result in *confounded effects.* In this case main as well as higher-order interactions cannot be clearly distinguished from each other, when fractional factorial designs are applied. In order to specify the degree of confounding the concept of *resolution* is used. A design is of resolution R, if no p-factor effect is aliased with another effect containing less than $R-p$ factors [211].

- Resolution III: No main effects are aliased with any other main effect, but main effects are aliased with two-factor interactions and some of them might be aliased with each other.
- Resolution IV: No main effects are aliased with any other main effect or with any other two-factor interaction, but two-factor interactions are aliased with each other.
- Resolution V: No main effects or two-factor interactions are aliased with any other main effect or two-factor interaction, but two-factor interactions are aliased with three-factor interactions.

The determination of a good subset out of the full factorial design is a difficult task. In literature the usage of orthogonal arrays is recommended [83]. When an analysis is intended for experiments with a great number of factors, FFD are not suitable [144].

Orthogonal Designs

An *orthogonal array* (OA) is a carefully selected combination of factor levels. An OA of strength r with n runs and k factors, denoted by $OA(n, k, q, r)$, is a FFD where any subdesign of n runs and m ($m \leq r$) factors is a full design. Strength two orthogonal arrays are extensively used for planning experiments in various fields [83]. An orthogonal design matrix, denoted by $L_n(q_1 \times \cdots \times q_k)$, is an $n \times k$

matrix with entries $1, 2, \cdots, q_j$ at the jth column such that each entry in each column appears equally often and each entry-combination in any two ($r = 2$) columns appears equally often [83].

Supersaturated Designs

Classic factor designs are referred to as *saturated.* Special cases of fractional factorials are supersaturated designs. Consider a design of n runs and k factors each having q levels. The design is called unsaturated if $n - 1 \geq k(q - 1)$; saturated if $n - 1 = k(q - 1)$; and supersaturated if $n - 1 \leq k(q - 1)$. Under the assumption of the sparsity principle supersaturated designs can be used to identify the most relevant factors out of a large set of factors [83, 211]. However, the application of supersaturated designs has not spread.

Plackett-Burman Designs

This group of designs is an alternative to fractional factorials with the purpose of factor screening. Plackett and Burmann [236] developed this type of designs for studying $k = n - 1$ factors in n runs, where n is a multiple of 4 rather than a power of 2 which defines the number of runs in fractional factorial designs. Especially for n equal to 12, 20, 24, 28, and 36, Plackett-Burman designs are of interest, because these designs cannot be represented as cubes and are therefore called *nongeometric designs.* However, these designs have disadvantageous confounding structures, which define the Plackett-Burman designs as *nonregular designs.* In contrast to *regular* resolution-three fractional factorial designs where two-factor interactions are indistinguishable from main effects, the two-factor interactions within Plackett-Burman designs are only partially confounded with main effects [211, 318].

Sequential Bifurcation

Originally developed by Bettonvil [33] this method was further extended by a few authors, [34, 333]. As the name implies sequential bifurcation is a sequential procedure that iteratively splits important from unimportant factors: The first step treats all factors as one factor and evaluates whether or not this factor has a relevant effect. If the aggregated factor (the group of all factors) has an important effect, then the algorithm bifurcates all factors in two subgroups and tests them for relevance. Then the algorithm continues iteratively, i.e. it splits important from unimportant factors and discards unimportant ones. In the last step, all individual factors identified as important are evaluated.

To keep computational effort low, Bettonvil [33] suggests to place and label individual factors in increasing order of assumed importance. With respect to supply chain analysis this sorting is very difficult, as the knowledge about the network and *all* of its factors might be small. Furthermore, the method assumes that the first-order polynomial model can be applied, which neglects the potential existence of interaction-effects.

7.2.3 Design construction

Construction of 2^{k-p}-Designs with Generators

The construction of 2^{k-p}-Designs requires the definition of p independent *generators*. Generators encompass those factors of a 2^{k-p}-Design that represent the $k-p+1$ to k factors. To illustrate the construction procedure consider the example of a 2^{4-1} fractional factorial design with factors A, B, C, and D. First, the full factorial design for the 2^3 factors is setup. The forth factor is then equated to the first three factors by the defining relation, $I = ABCD$, with I being the identity column:

$$D = ABC$$

In this example ABC is the generator for the forth factor D. Any other interaction such as AB, AC, or BC could also be used for generating the forth factor, D. Thus, generated factors are aliased with interaction effects. Without knowledge about the effects that are potentially important, it could happen that relevant factors are aliased with other relevant factors, which makes it difficult to properly identify these factors. In order to identify a *good* generator it is often suggested to use generators that maximize the resolution, because a high degree of resolution results in less confounded effects of low-ordered interactions. Besides resolution the criterion of *minimal aberration* has gained increased attention and developed into a popular criterion for comparing and assessing fractional factorial designs. Introduced by Fries and Hunter [95] the minimum aberration criterion minimizes the number of words in the defining relation that are of minimum length [211].

Foldover Designs

A *foldover* is a procedure that extends a fractional factorial design by adding columns with switched signs of one or more factors of a fractional factorial design. The intention of a foldover is to systematically isolate potentially important effects. A *single-factor foldover* adds a further fraction to the design with signs of one factor reversed. This extended experimental setup results in estimates of the main effect of that factor and its related two-factor interactions [211]. In order to break the alias chains between all main and their related interaction effects a *full foldover* design has to be executed.

Space-filling Designs

Space-filling designs spread the factor level combinations evenly throughout the entire experimental domain. This is especially valuable if the type of underlying model is extremely difficult to estimate or if different regions of the experimental domain are thought to be of interest. Space-filling designs are considered to be particularly appropriate for deterministic computer experiments and are widely used for response surface approximation.

One of the first space-filling designs was developed by McKay et al. [201] under the name *Latin hypercube design.* A Latin hypercube is a design containing n runs for k factors, where each column is a random permutation of the levels $1, 2, \cdots, n$ and are dependent. Latin hypercube sampling has been extensively used in deterministic computer experiments and many modifications have been proposed, for an overview we refer to Fang et al. [83]. Uniform designs spread the factor level combinations uniformly throughout the experimental domain. Originally these types of designs were proposed by Fang [82]. Ever since algorithms for the construction of uniform designs and corresponding measures of uniformity have been developed. [83] again provide a good overview of existing algorithms and measures.

7.3 Analysis

The analysis within an experimental setup provides a quantitative estimation of the effects of single factors as well as their interacting influence on targeted output variables. The quality of the effect estimates strongly depends on the validity of the chosen statistical model for representing the underlying model. Choosing a *good* representative model is, therefore, critical. The analysts have to carefully think of what they are expecting of the underlying model. Statistical models, especially polynomial models are evaluated by the means of standard regression analysis and by the analysis of variance (ANOVA).

Both types of analyses examine, whether a targeted output variable is affected by input factors. In contrast to the analysis of regression the ANOVA does not estimate a functional relationship. Instead the aim of ANOVA is to confirm initial conclusions by testing the significance of effect estimates.

While running a simulation experiment scenario-wise observations of the target value disperse around its mean. The dispersion can be referred back to the effects of considered factors. By examining different dispersion portions the effects of single factors as well as their interaction can be quantified.

7.3.1 Regression Analysis

Regression analysis is the basis for the design of experiments. The objective of regression analysis is to determine the functional relationship between the response, y, and k independent or regressor variables (factors). This relationship can be formulated by the means of a regression model. Low-order polynomial models are widely used to approximate the unknown relationship between the response and factors. Frequently regression methods are used to analyze data from unplanned experiments [211].

A linear regression model for the analysis of a response and k regressor variables can be described as

$$y = \beta_0 + \beta_1 x_1 + \beta_2 x_2 + \cdots + \beta_k x_k + \epsilon \tag{7.10}$$

where ϵ is the random error and $\beta_j, j = 0, 1, \ldots, k$ are called the *regression coefficients*. Each regression coefficient represents the expected change in response per unit change in the related factor, if the remaining independent factors are held constant. When interactions are assumed to be existent, still regression models can be used to analyze the functional relationship. Consider the existence of a two-factor interaction within a first-order polynomial model with two variables:

$$y = \beta_0 + \beta_1 x_1 + \beta_2 x_2 + \beta_{12} x_1 x_2 + \epsilon \tag{7.11}$$

We can rewrite this equation by substituting $x_1 x_2$ with x_3 and β_{12} with β_3:

$$y = \beta_0 + \beta_1 x_1 + \beta_2 x_2 + \beta_3 x_3 + \epsilon \tag{7.12}$$

which is a standard multiple linear regression model with three factors. Likewise, higher than first-order polynomial models can be reformulated. Generally, each regression model that is linear in the regression coefficients is a linear regression model irrespective of the shape of the response surface it models [211]. To estimate the regression coefficient the method of least squares is applied.

7.3.2 Method of Least Squares

Suppose the $(x_{i1}, \ldots, x_{ik}, y_i), i = 1, \ldots, n$ is a random sample from the linear model

$$y_i = \sum_{j=0}^{k} x_{ij} \beta_j + \epsilon_i \tag{7.13}$$

where ϵ_i is the random error. It can be assumed that random errors are uncorrelated random variables with mean 0 and common variance σ^2. Gauss advanced the method of least squares in the early 19th century. For the data set $(x_{i1}, \ldots, x_{ik}, y_i), i = 1, \ldots, n$, the method of least squares considers the deviation of each observation value y_i

from its expectation and finds the coefficient βs by minimizing the sum of squared deviations:

$$S(\beta_0, \ldots, \beta_s) = \sum_{i=1}^{n} (y_i - \sum_{j=0}^{k} x_{ij}\beta_j)^2 \tag{7.14}$$

With matrix notation

$$\boldsymbol{y} = \begin{pmatrix} y_1 \\ \vdots \\ y_n \end{pmatrix}, \boldsymbol{X} = \begin{pmatrix} x_{10} & \cdots & x_{1k} \\ \vdots & \cdots & \vdots \\ x_{n0} & \cdots & x_{nk} \end{pmatrix}, \boldsymbol{\beta} = \begin{pmatrix} \beta_0 \\ \vdots \\ \beta_k \end{pmatrix}, \boldsymbol{\epsilon} = \begin{pmatrix} \epsilon_1 \\ \vdots \\ \epsilon_n \end{pmatrix} \tag{7.15}$$

the model 7.13 can be rewritten as

$$\boldsymbol{y} = \boldsymbol{X}\boldsymbol{\beta} + \epsilon. \tag{7.16}$$

The matrix $\boldsymbol{X}$ is known as the design matrix and is of crucial importance in linear regression analysis. The $S(\boldsymbol{\beta})$ can be rewritten as

$$S(\boldsymbol{\beta}) = (\boldsymbol{y} - \boldsymbol{X}\boldsymbol{\beta})^{'}(\boldsymbol{y} - \boldsymbol{X}\boldsymbol{\beta}). \tag{7.17}$$

Differentiating $S(\boldsymbol{\beta})$ with respect to $\boldsymbol{\beta}$, we obtain the *normal equations*

$$\boldsymbol{X}^{'}\boldsymbol{y} = \boldsymbol{X}^{'}\boldsymbol{X}\boldsymbol{\beta} \tag{7.18}$$

If $\boldsymbol{X}^{'}\boldsymbol{X}$ is invertible, the normal equations yield the least squares estimator of $\boldsymbol{\beta}$ as a solution for 7.14

$$\hat{\boldsymbol{\beta}} = (\boldsymbol{X}\boldsymbol{X})^{-1}\boldsymbol{X}^{'}\boldsymbol{y}. \tag{7.19}$$

The least squares parameter estimates provide a simple method for estimating the regression coefficients [211].

7.3.3 Analysis of Variance (ANOVA)

Generally, the purpose of ANOVA is to test the statistical significant differences between means, which can be accomplished by comparing variances. The main fundamental concept of ANOVA is based on the characteristic that variances can be divided, i.e. partitioned. The significance test is based on the comparison of overall observations of the variance derived from the between treatment variability, called *Mean Square Effect*, with the within treatment variability, called *Mean Square Error*. Consider the null hypothesis stating that no mean differences between factor values in the experiment exist. Still, small random variations around the means for each factor value observations can be expected. Under the null hypothesis, the variance estimated based on the within treatment variability should equal the variance of the between treatment variability. Both estimates can be compared using the F-test (from the F-Distribution), which tests whether the ratio of the variance estimates is significantly greater than one. Thus, the purpose of ANOVA is to identify whether statistical significance of mean variations between factors exists. This analysis is conducted by partitioning the total variance into the part that can be referred to random error and the part that can be referred to differences between-factor means. The latter variance parts are tested for significance. If the variances is significant, the null hypothesis is rejected and the alternative hypothesis, which states that the means are different from each other, is accepted, see Hill and Lewicki [128].

7.3.4 Measures of Factor Effects

For the analysis of factor effects the measures *contrast* and *effect estimate* are used. For the analysis of their significance the ANOVA measures *sum of squares*, *degrees of freedom*, *mean squares*, *total sum of squares*, *error sum of squares* and *model sum of squares*. Note that, the measures of factor effects explained in the following are used for full factorial designs. Whenever fractional factorial designs are applied, the number of factors k needs to be substituted with the term $k - p$.

Contrast A contrast is a linear combination of factors, whose coefficients sum up to zero. Contrasts provide a means of comparing different treatments and are used for calculating estimated effects $AB \cdots K$ amongst other measures. Let $\hat{y}_1, \hat{y}_2, \ldots, \hat{y}_n$ be the responses of n different replicates and c_i be constants of the i's run representing the level of the factor considered. The sum

$$\sum_i c_i \hat{y}_i \tag{7.20}$$

is called a contrast if $\sum_i c_i = 0$. Two contrasts $\sum_i c_i \hat{y}_i$ and $\sum_i d_i \hat{y}_i$ are called *orthogonal* if $\sum_i c_i d_i = 0$. Tests performed on orthogonal contrasts are independent.

Effect Estimate The effect estimate of a factor $AB \cdots K$ is computed by the contrast of that factor. Let n be the number of replicates and k the number of factors [211].

$$EffectEstimate_{AB \cdots K} = \frac{2}{n2^k} Contrast_{AB \cdots K} \tag{7.21}$$

As computer-based simulation experiments are deterministic the number of replicates denoted by n equals 1. For the analysis of supply chain risk the supply chain planning engine functions as the black box. Whether the results of the supply chain planning engine are deterministic strongly depends on the optimization approach used for determining the supply chain planning solution.

Sum of Squares The computation formula for the sum of squares of an effect $AB \cdots K$ is as follows:

$$SS_{AB \cdots K} = \frac{1}{n2^k}(Contrast_{AB \cdots K})^2 \tag{7.22}$$

The Number of Degrees of Freedom The number of independent elements in the sum of squares is called the number of degrees of freedom. For each main effect the number of degrees of freedom equals the number of its levels minus one:

$$DF_k = q_k - 1. \tag{7.23}$$

For each interaction effect the number of degrees of freedom is calculated by the product of the number of degree of freedom of each main factor involved:

$$DF_{A \cdots K} = \prod_k (q_k - 1). \tag{7.24}$$

Mean Squares The mean squares of main and interaction effects are represented by the ratio of the sum of squares of the related effect and its number of degrees of freedom:

$$MS_{AB \cdots K} = \frac{SS_{AB \cdots K}}{DF_{AB \cdots K}}. \tag{7.25}$$

Total Sum of Squares Another result presentation of effect analysis is the total sum of squares. It is defined as the sum squared differences between each observation and the overall mean with regards to all observations. The total sum of squares for a 2^k and a

3^k design with factors A, B and A, B, C and number of factor levels a, b and a, b, c, respectively, are calculated as follows:

$$TSS_{AB} = \sum_{i=1}^{a}\sum_{j=1}^{b}\sum_{l=1}^{n} y_{i,j,l}^2 - \frac{y_{...}^2}{abn}, \tag{7.26}$$

$$TSS_{ABC} = \sum_{i=1}^{a}\sum_{j=1}^{b}\sum_{m=1}^{c}\sum_{l=1}^{n} y_{i,j,m,l}^2 - \frac{y_{....}^2}{abcn}. \tag{7.27}$$

Equally, the total sum of squares are:

$$TSS = SS_A + SS_B + \cdots + SS_K + SS_E. \tag{7.28}$$

Error Sum of Squares The error sum of squares equals to:

$$SS_E = TSS - SS_A + SS_B + \cdots + SS_K. \tag{7.29}$$

Model Sum of Squares The model sum of squares applies only the set of factors that is considered in the meta-model, for example:

$$SS_{Model} = SS_A + SS_B. \tag{7.30}$$

Residuals Residuals represent the variance in response values that can be explained by the model. The better the fit of the model, the smaller the values of the residuals. Residuals are calculated for factor level combination and each replicate. A residual, thus, is calculated by the deviation of an observed response value, y_i, from the predicted response value of the meta-model, $\hat{y}_i$:

$$e_i = y_i - \hat{y}_i. \tag{7.31}$$

F-Value The F-value is the ratio between two estimates of variance, the estimate for the variance derived from the between treatment variability, *Mean Square Effect*, and the estimate for the variance derived from the within treatment variability, called *Mean Square Error*. If both estimates are approximately equal, the F-value equals to one. This indicates that the means do not significantly differ from each other. If the F-value is, however, greater than one, this suggests that the means differ significantly.

$$F_0(AB \cdots K) = \frac{MS_{AB \cdots K}}{MS_E} \tag{7.32}$$

p-Value The statistical significance of a factor's effect is estimated by the p-value. The p-value represents a decreasing index of reliability of a result. The higher the value, the less significant the effect of the factor. A p-value of 5% is in many research areas treated as a "borderline acceptable" error level [128].

$$p_{AB \cdots K} = P(F) \tag{7.33}$$

7.4 Illustrative Examples

In order to consolidate the aforementioned steps of experimental analysis, we conduct a simple example adopted from Montgomery [211].

7.4.1 A 2^4 Full Factorial Experiment for the Analysis of Production Characteristics

The filtration rate of a chemical product is assumed to depend on four factors, namely temperature (A), pressure (B), concentration of formaldehyde (C), and a stirring rate (D). Each factor has two potential levels. Table 7.1 shows the design matrix and the response of a single full factorial 2^4 experiment.

Run number	Factor				Run Label	Filtration Rate
	A	B	C	D		
1	-	-	-	-	(1)	45
2	+	-	-	-	*a*	71
3	-	+	-	-	*b*	48
4	+	+	-	-	*ab*	65
5	-	-	+	-	*d*	68
6	+	-	+	-	*ac*	60
7	-	+	+	-	*bc*	80
8	+	+	+	-	*abc*	65
9	-	-	-	+	*d*	43
10	+	-	-	+	*ad*	100
11	-	+	-	+	*bd*	45
12	+	+	-	+	*abd*	104
13	-	-	+	+	*cd*	75
14	+	-	+	+	*acd*	86
15	-	+	+	+	*bcd*	70
16	+	+	+	+	*abcd*	96

Table 7.1: Design matrix of a 2^4 full factorial design [211].

Table 7.2 presents the matrix for the constant contrasts for the 2^4 design. Based on the contrasts different measures can be estimated. As can be seen from Table 7.3 the important effects are the main effects A, C, and D and the AC and AD two-factor interaction effects. However, the importance of main effects decreases when they are involved in significant interactions. Interaction plots provide further insights for determining the significance. Figure 7.4 shows that main factor A has limited influence on the response when the main factor C is at the high level or the main factor D is at the low level, respectively. The analysis emphasizes that the best filtration

Run Label	A	B	AB	C	AC	BC	ABC	D	AD	BD	ABD	CD	ACD	BCD	ABCD
(1)	-	-	+	-	+	+	-	-	+	+	-	+	-	-	+
a	+	-	-	-	-	+	+	-	-	+	+	+	+	-	-
b	-	+	-	-	+	-	+	-	+	-	+	+	-	+	-
ab	+	+	+	-	-	-	-	-	-	-	-	+	+	+	+
d	-	-	+	+	-	-	+	-	+	+	-	-	+	+	-
ac	+	-	-	+	+	-	-	-	-	+	+	-	-	+	+
bc	-	+	-	+	-	+	-	-	+	-	+	-	+	-	+
abc	+	+	+	+	+	+	+	-	-	-	-	-	-	-	-
d	-	-	+	-	+	+	-	+	-	-	+	-	+	+	-
ad	+	-	-	-	-	+	+	+	+	-	-	-	-	+	+
bd	-	+	-	-	+	-	+	+	-	+	-	-	+	-	+
abd	+	+	+	-	-	-	-	+	+	+	+	-	-	-	-
cd	-	-	+	+	-	-	+	+	-	-	+	+	-	-	+
acd	+	-	-	+	+	-	-	+	+	-	-	+	+	-	-
bcd	-	+	-	+	-	+	-	+	-	+	-	+	-	+	-
abcd	+	+	+	+	+	+	+	+	+	+	+	+	+	+	+

Table 7.2: Contrast constants for a 2^4 full factorial design [211].

Model Term	Effect Estimate	Sum of Squares	Percent Contribution
A	21.625	1,870.560	32.64%
B	3.125	39.063	0.68%
C	9.875	390.062	6.81%
D	14.625	855.563	14.93%
AB	0.125	0.063	0.00%
AC	-18.125	1,314.060	22.93%
AD	16.625	1,105.560	19.29%
BC	2.375	22.563	0.39%
BD	-0.375	0.563	0.01%
CD	-1.125	5.063	0.09%
ABC	1.875	14.063	0.25%
ABD	4.125	68.063	1.19%
ACD	-1.625	10.563	0.18%
BCD	-2.625	27.563	0.48%
$ABCD$	1.375	7.563	0.13%

Table 7.3: Effect estimates and sums of squares for the 2^4 factorial experiment [211].

rate can be achieved when main factor A and D are at the high level and C is at the low level.

The factor effect estimates suggest that main factor B has neither a main effect nor an interaction effect on the response. The resulting analysis of variance of factors except B is provided in Table 7.4.

The results based on the analysis indicate that the significant factors are: $A = 21.625$, $C = 9.875$, $D = 14.625$, $AC = -18.125$, and $AD = 16.625$. With an average response of 70.063, the expected filtration response can be represented by:

$$\hat{y} = 70.063 + \frac{21.625}{2}x_1 + \frac{9.875}{2}x_3 + \frac{14.625}{2}x_4 - \frac{18.125}{2}x_1x_3 + \frac{16.625}{2}x_1x_4 \tag{7.34}$$

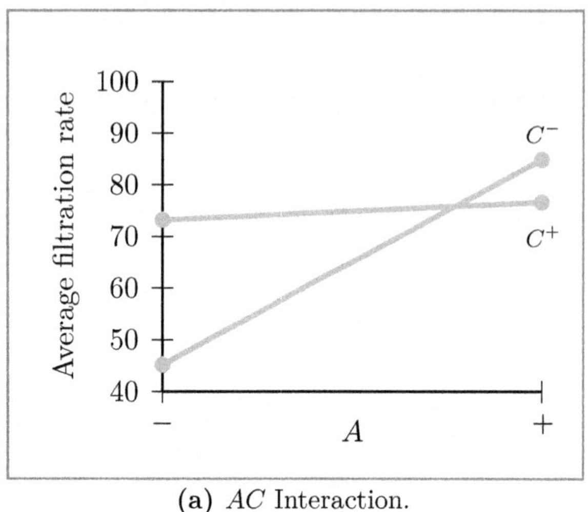

(a) *AC* Interaction.

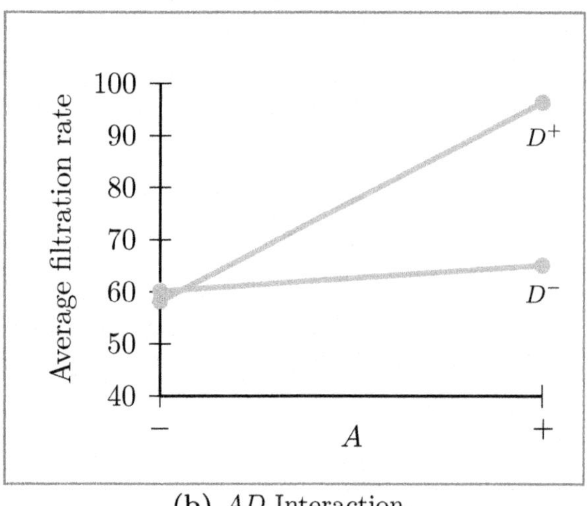

(b) *AD* Interaction.

Figure 7.4: Interaction plots [211].

The coded variables x_1, x_3, x_4 represent the factors A, B, and C and take values between -1 and 1. The values of the residuals and their corresponding normal probability plot is shown in Figure 7.5.

Source of Variation	Sum of Squares	Degress of Freedom	Mean Square	F_0	P-Value
A	1870.56	1	1870.56	83.36	<0.0001
C	390.06	1	390.06	17.38	<0.0001
D	855.56	1	855.56	38.13	<0.0001
AC	1314.06	1	1314.06	58.56	<0.0001
AD	1105.56	1	1105.56	49.27	<0.0001
CD	5.06	1	5.06	<1	
ACD	10.56	1	10.56	<1	
Error	179.52	8	22.44		
Total	5730.94	15			

Table 7.4: Analysis of variance table.

The residual values are reasonably close to the linear relation, which support the conclusion on the significant effects.

7.4.2 A 2_{IV}^{4-1} Fractional Factorial Experiment for the Analysis of Production Characteristics

This example is based on the identical circumstances described in the previous example. Instead of using a full factorial design for the analysis of effects on the filtration rate, we use a fractional factorial design. The defining relation is $I = ABCD$, because this results in the highest possible resolution, IV. First, we determine the basic design, i.e. 2^3. Next, we need to define the fourth factor D. The generator, $D = ABC$, defines the factor D to equal the factor combination ABC. The level of D in each run is determined by the product of of A, B, and C, respectively. The design matrix of this experiment and its related responses are visualized in Table 7.5.

Run number	Factor A	B	C	D=ABC	Run Label	Filtration Rate
1	-	-	-	-	(1)	45
2	+	-	-	+	ad	100
3	-	+	-	+	bd	45
4	+	+	-	-	ab	65
5	-	-	+	+	cd	75
6	+	-	+	-	ac	60
7	-	+	+	-	bc	80
8	+	+	+	+	abcd	96

Table 7.5: Experimental design matrices for a 2_{IV}^{4-1} fractional factorial design [211].

Based on the generator and the resulting resolution we know that each main factor is aliased with a three-factor interaction, namely $A = BCD$, $B = ACD$, and $C = ABD$, as well as every two-factor interaction is aliased with another two-factor interaction, namely $AB = CD$, $AC = BD$, and $AD = BC$.

Model Term	Effect Estimate	Alias Structure
A	19.00	A → A + BCD
B	1.50	B → B + ACD
C	14.00	C → C + ABD
D	16.50	D → D + ABC
AB	-1.00	AB → AB +CD
AC	-18.50	AC → AC + BD
AD	-19.00	AD → AD + BC

Table 7.6: Effect estimates and sums of squares for the 2_{IV}^{4-1} fractional factorial experiment [211].

The effect estimates shown in Table 7.6 indicate the large influence of the main factors A, C, and D on the model response. It can be concluded that the two-factor interactions AB and CD have minor effect on the model's response, because of the small estimates of the AB-CD alias chain. Additionally, the AC and AD estimates have significant influence. The results of the 2^k full factorial design confirm these conclusions. Although the effect estimates slightly differ from those of the 2^k analysis, the prediction equation looks similar to the 2^{k-1} model:

$$\hat{y} = 70.75 + \frac{19.00}{2}x_1 + \frac{14.00}{2}x_3 + \frac{16.50}{2}x_4 - \frac{18.50}{2}x_1x_3 + \frac{19.00}{2}x_1x_4 \tag{7.35}$$

7.5 Cautions with the Design of Experiments

We introduced several basic concepts related to the three main steps of experimental setup: meta-modeling, design, and analysis. Several assumptions need to hold such that conclusions based on the interaction of those steps are valid, because different designs are based on different mathematical assumptions concerning the *smoothness* of the I/O-function implied by the underlying simulation model, which is explained by Kleijnen [167].

We pointed out that the choice of the meta-model is especially important as a wrong meta-model can result in misleading conclusions with regard to the prediction of model outputs. In this thesis the focus is firstly set to the determination of factors' relevance rather than approximating the response for the entire experimentation domain. Therefore, the choice of an appropriate design that supports the identification of significantly relevant factors, is more critical for the overall goal of supply chain risk analysis.

Remember that efficient experimentation reduces the computational efforts necessary for the evaluation. As computer experiments are endowed with numerous factors of potential relevance, it is even more important to use designs that appropriately reduce the number of runs while acquiring as much information as possible. However, reducing the number of runs comes along with new assumptions. The Plackett-Burman design, for example, is based on the assumption that (higher-order) interactions can be neglected. The type of design results in long aliases chains that aggravate a dependable determination of main factor interactions. Montgomery et al. [212] show by the means of a specific example that the analysis of a 2^{k-p}_{III} design can outperform a Plackett-Burman design, when the true underlying model contains interaction effects. Whenever analysis results clearly indicate the relevance of certain effects, the experimenter should keep in mind that it can still be possible that results may be not consistent with reality. It can be the case that we screen out relevant factors.

Besides design construction and meta-model selection it is the analysis step, which can result in misleading interpretations. Especially, if the experimenter requires statistical significance for result interpretations, it should be considered that analysis methods are based on the assumption that model outputs are normally distributed. Kleijnen [167] discuss in depth how realistic the normality assumptions are with respect to the underlying problem and how the I/O-data can be transformed such that the normality assumptions hold. In this thesis the types, characteristics of factors and their influence on the experiments output are considerably different such that it is highly questionable, if the normality assumption holds. Nevertheless, in this thesis we implemented factorial designs with the purpose to screen irrelevant factors out. When it comes to quantification, which is a major objective of risk analysis, we apply approaches of response surface approximation and develop algorithms that are not based on the normality assumption.

Run label	y	$\hat{y}$	$e = y - \hat{y}$
(1)	45	46.25	-1.25
a	71	69.38	1.62
b	48	46.25	1.75
ab	65	69.38	-4.38
d	68	74.25	-6.25
ac	60	61.13	-1.13
bc	80	74.25	5.75
abc	65	61.13	3.87
d	43	44.25	-1.25
ad	100	100.63	-0.63
bd	45	44.25	0.75
abd	104	100.63	3.37
cd	75	72.25	2.75
acd	86	92.38	-6.38
bcd	70	72.25	-2.25
$abcd$	96	92.38	3.62

(a) Residuals of 2^4 factorial experiment.

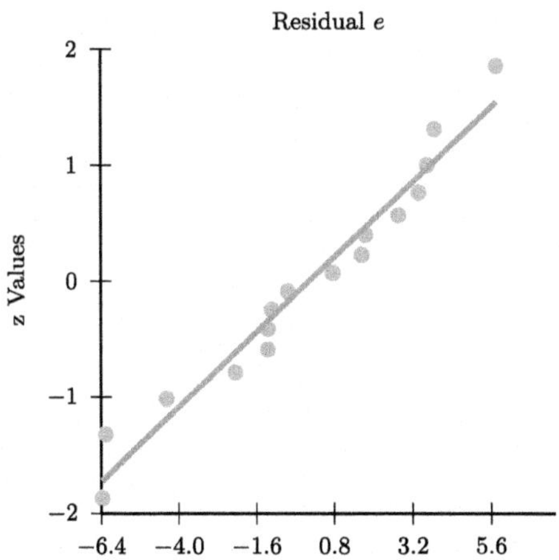

(b) Normal probability plot.

Figure 7.5: Residuals and normal probability plot of 2^4 factorial experiment [211].

8 A Simulation-based Approach for Supply Chain Risk Analysis (*SimSCRF*)

"Turn the question around and ask:
What chance of the uncertain event
would make you change your decision?"

Sam L. Savage

The literature on supply chain risk analysis is mostly of anecdotal or case-based nature [56, 225, 348] and only few authors present empirical research [328], see Chapter 3. While the results of the former type of analysis reveal the need for an improved management of supply chains newly facing disruptions, the latter provides rationalizations and best practices of historical events. However, conclusions of both analyses are not by implication transferable to other supply chains, other circumstances or other incidents. Insights based on empirical data have to be handled with care as they are often specific for the business, geographic and industrial environment as well as on internal dynamics of the supply chain affected. Similarly conclusions drawn by experts are subjective and often not re-producible in face of newly emerging supply chain risks. Quantitative, systematic and reliable analyses are scarce, see Chapter 5. Mathematical optimization approaches call for specific solution methods tailored for the underlying problem. Simulation is a suitable methodology to model numerous interacting characteristics. In Chapter 6 we discussed the appropriateness of simulation as a method to model and analyzed complex systems.

In this chapter we seize the idea of Sam L. Savage and ask: Which scenarios would result in predefined unappreciated outcomes and, thus, would demand for risk countermeasures? Following this idea we developed a new simulation-based conceptual approach for the analysis of supply chain risk. In Section 8.1 we briefly discuss the main requirements for the development of dependable simulation-based risk analysis. The following section presents the main procedures the simulation model is endowed with. Section 8.3 summarizes the main characteristics of the approach presented.

8.1 Requirements

Based on the extensive literature review we identified that supply chain risk depends on several distinct conceptual entities, see Chapter 3. The levels of all three entities, risk exposition, risk objectives and risk attitude, determine the level of current supply chain risks, whose evaluation is the purpose of risk analysis. When decision makers want to fully understand the genesis and the exacerbation of supply chain risks, then approaches are needed that support the identification and assessment of the underlying dynamics. More precisely, models are needed that support:

- the identification of influence of potential triggers on supply chain processes,
- the identification of dynamics between supply chain processes,
- the assessment of supply chain risk,

- the identification of influence of potential countermeasures on supply chain processes, and
- the assessment of the degree of supply chain risk reduction becoming effective due to the implementation of selective countermeasures.

In the following we refer to this bundle of characteristics as *risk-aware* characteristics.

Several studies identify further requirements for risk-aware decision tools. To ensure that supply chain risk management can be realized as a continuous process, supply chain managers seek solutions that integrate supply chain risk analysis in their routines and planning processes [140]. The Risk Response Network of the World Economic Forum highlights the need for scenario-based and business continuity planning as core risk management priorities [248]. Most-often scenarios are used to capture the shape of threating situations and evaluate their consequences on the supply chain. Those "what-if"-analyses are largely used in planning, but they are often conducted by defining individual scenarios, rather than by elaborated scenario generation.

As risk largely depends on what we value or which impacts are considered as harmful, supply chain risk depends on the specific supply chain strategy and goals. Therefore, the importance of performance indicators in the supply chain risk assessment may differ from supply chain to supply chain and from decision level to decision level. Consider an example from daily operational supply chain planning. The operator uses a system for short-to-mid-term planning to manage changes and deviations. For him, supply chain vulnerability relates to order fulfillment or capacity utilization. For a risk officer, who typically focuses on a mid-to-long-term horizon, supply chain vulnerability relates to performance indicators like costs of goods sold. The integration of both perspectives, roles and time scales would provide reliable risk results.

Based on this discussion we derive the following characteristics for the development of supply chain risk analysis:

- risk-aware,
- scenario-based, and
- comprehensive for decision makers on different decision levels.

8.2 A New Approach for Supply Chain Risk Analysis – Basic Models

So far no unanimous method has been developed to explicitly identify underlying dynamics and quantify supply chain risk. In this section we introduce a basic approach that allows the decision maker to define his expectations about the future and evaluate the resulting impact on the supply chain performance. In our work, we combine simulation and supply chain planning to support decision makers on different levels of decision making.

8.2.1 Scenario-based Procedure

The main challenge of the *SimSCRF* approach is to appropriately model the entities that define supply chain risk. We defined supply chain risk as a function that depends on the interaction between potential triggers, the constitution of the underlying supply chain, and the degree of target achievement, which is assumed to be influenced by the risk attitude of the decision maker, see Chapters 3 and 4.

Based on Figure 3.2 the relationship of supply chain risk defining entities is highlighted in Figure 8.1. Therein the occurrence of time-dependent risk exposition determines the level of supply chain objectives. Whether this target achievement is good enough for the underlying supply chain is evaluated by the decision makers' risk attitude. If they assess the level of target achievement as sufficient, there is no supply chain risk. If they assess the degree of performance as critical, supply chain risk exists for the underlying supply chain.

The risk exposition is further defined by potential triggers and the present supply chain constitution. Figure 8.2 visualizes the relationship between the conceptual approach and the methodological foundation.

The theoretical basis of *SimSCRF* is the assumption that potential triggers have an indirect and/or direct influence on supply chain processes. Supply chain processes are described by supply chain factors: a production process at production plants, for instance, can be defined through supply chain factors like production capacity, setup times, campaign duration, lot size, or production costs. Due to potential triggers these factors may change, which is depicted in different scenarios.

Definition 8.1: Scenario

A scenario is defined as a description of a prospective situation in terms of supply chain factors. Each scenario consists of a (predefined) set of supply chain factors and related factor values, which may or may not differ from their initial values.

While potential triggers are modeled by the means of modified factor values, the resulting constitution of a supply chain is depicted by the result of a supply chain planning run. The purpose of supply chain planning systems is to balance demand and/or forecasts with available resources of production, transportation, and inventory. With the objective to optimize user-defined terms, e.g. cost minimization, maximization of profit or customer satisfaction etc., planning runs determine the optimal resource allocation. As these planning results

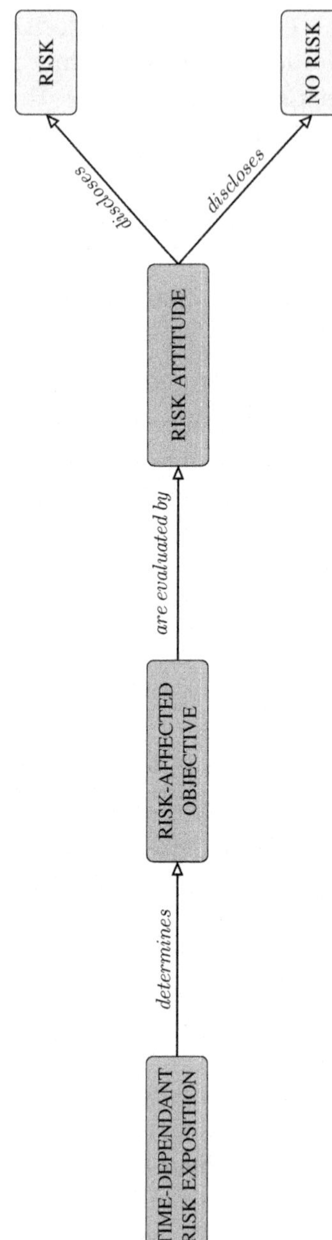

Figure 8.1: Relationship between supply chain risk defining entities.

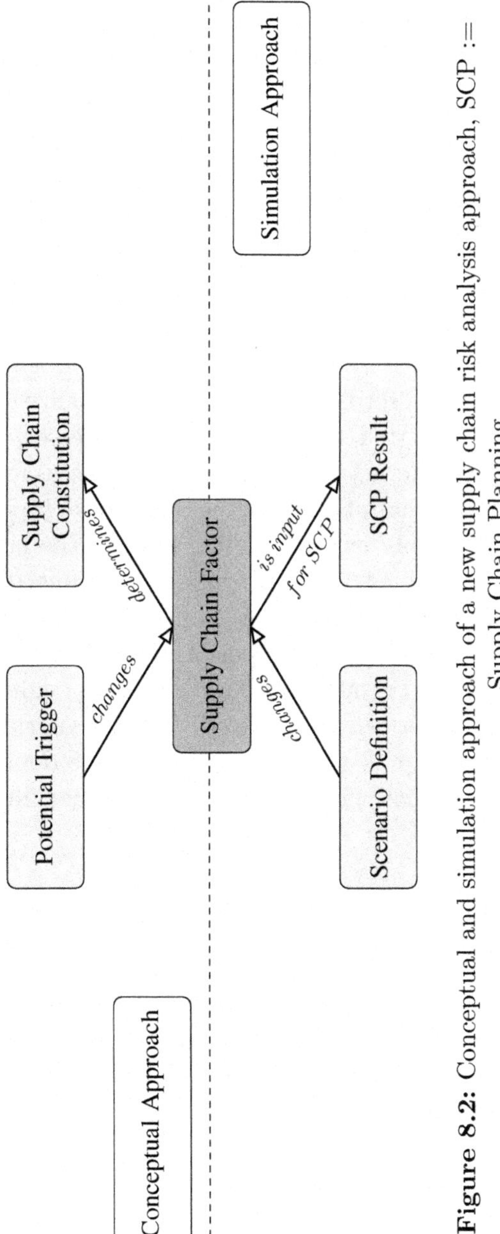

Figure 8.2: Conceptual and simulation approach of a new supply chain risk analysis approach, SCP := Supply Chain Planning.

are normally implemented and executed, they legitimately represent a good *snapshot* of the current workload of the underlying supply chain.

Definition 8.2: Supply Chain Snapshot

A supply chain snapshot displays the structure and the current resource availability of the underlying supply network. It subsumes the description and quantification of supply chain factors.

Supply chain factors describe the degree of availability and the amount of operating costs related to supply chain processes, but they can additionally define the actual state of resource's usage. While the former set of supply chain factors defines the set of input parameters forwarded to the supply chain planning engine, the latter describes the set of result variables to be determined (optimized) by the planning engine. Modified input factor values, hence, lead to different planning results. The impact on performance is quantified by simulating a scenario in the supply chain planning engine so that the potential deterioration can be assessed. If the scenario performance is better than or equal to the accepted level, the deviations of supply chain factors applied within the scenario do not impose a supply chain risk.

Process Flow

The process used to join the aforementioned thoughts is shown in Figure 8.3. Three main entities determine the work flow of the simulation: the decision maker, the simulation model and the planning engine. The simulation model is further divided into two sections. The front-end has an interface for communication with the decision maker and the back-end works as an interpreter between front-end,

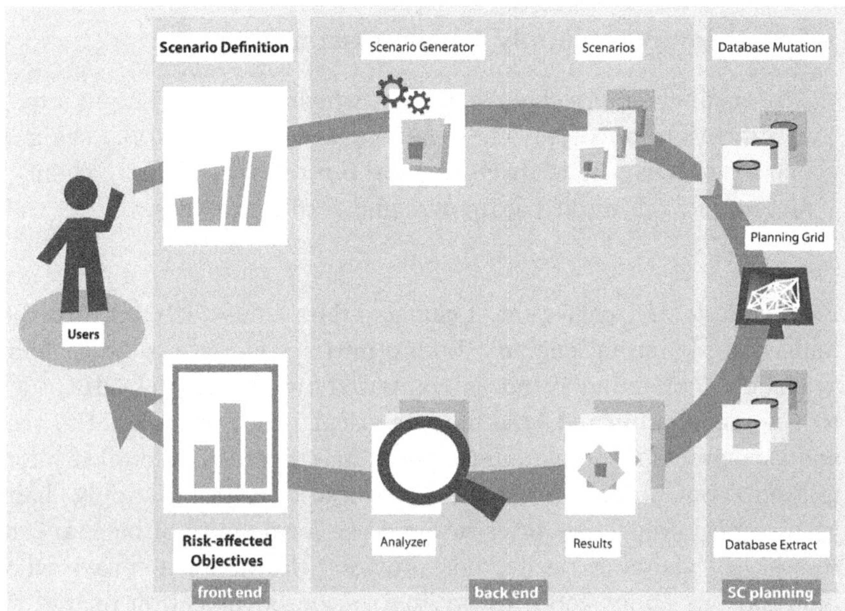

Figure 8.3: Basic process flow of a new supply chain risk analysis model.

the simulation kernel generating the set of scenarios and the planning engine. The process starts with the scenario definition. The decision maker defines the set of supply chain factors regarded as uncertain and specifies potential value modifications for each factor. The front-end passes the definitions to the back-end, which in turn translates decision maker's specifications to valid information streams for the scenario generation step. Based on this information the scenario-generator creates repository-valid scenario samples. As each scenario is represented by a set of data tables, these samples correspond to a series of manipulations of the *supply chain master pattern*.

Definition 8.3: Supply Chain Master Pattern

The original supply chain snapshot, which does not contain any modifications on supply chain factors, is called the supply chain master pattern. It is specified by the total set of supply chain factors of both input parameters and result variables.

Each sample, i.e. collection of changed data tables, is passed to the underlying planning engine. Taking into account the supply chain snapshot a planning result is computed by the engine. In order to get meaningful and credible analytical results through the risk analyses-process, the planning system has to provide detailed information about both material and order flow through the supply chain with respect to process priorities and the availability of backup processes. A planning result thus provides the decision maker with informations about good (or optimal) resource allocation related to production, transportation, and inventory. We differentiate between the reference plan and scenario-wise planning results.

Definition 8.4: Reference Plan & Scenario Plan

A reference plan is defined as a planning result that is based on initial, unmodified factor values. A scenario plan refers to a planning result related to modified supply chain factors.

Planning results are extracted from the repository of the planning engine, analyzed and prepared for comprehensive reports in the risk analyzing component. The user is provided with tables and figures highlighting how performance indicators changed due to factor modifications.

8.2.2 Screening Procedure

A major goal of supply chain risk analysis is to provide the decision maker with information about vulnerable supply chain processes. In the previous section we introduced a concept that supports decision makers with defining their expectations about future factor modifications and their potential impact on supply chain performance. However, this approach only supports the evaluation and identification among those processes that have been considered by the decision maker. In this section we introduce an extension of the former basic approach. The extended approach supports the identification of those processes that enhance the vulnerability of complex supply chain systems and that – if affected by disruptive triggers – most certainly result in the deterioration of supply chain performance.

A scenario-by-scenario evaluation provides decision makers with the possibility to better understand the results of single factor modifications. Additionally, they can evaluate the consequences of new supply chain strategies, policies and detailed risk-reducing arrangements. However, this type of analysis does not support a consistent evaluation of the underlying dynamics. It might be the case that the formulation of one scenario does not seriously affect supply chain performance, but a marginal increase of one supply chain factor included in the scenario results in a severe performance deterioration. It might also be the case that a lead time increase of one transportation link does not affect target achievement, but the increase of a consecutive transportation lead time does. As the number of all factors describing a supply chain system is huge and in order to evaluate which supply chain factor does seriously affect the functionality or profitability, the simulation model executes a screening process. The screening identifies which supply chain factors have a meaningful influence on the specified performance indicator.

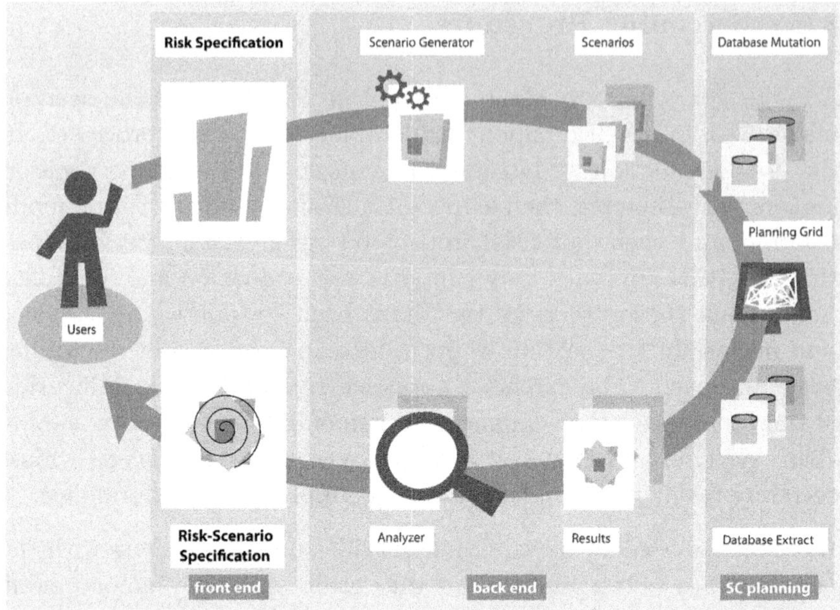

Figure 8.4: Process flow of the screening procedure within the supply chain risk analysis model.

Process Flow

The screening procedure uses the same main entities and data processing as the basic scenario-based approach. The scenario generation and analysis of planning results, however, are enhanced with a new methodology, which is explained in more detail in the following section. Additionally, at the beginning of the process the users have the possibility to specify they expectations about risk-enhancing supply chain factors. They express their expectations by selecting only those factors for the risk analysis that they assume to have a relevance for the target achievement. The result of this risk analysis procedure provides information about the potential effect of selected supply chain factors on the selected performance indicators.

8.2.3 Procedure for Risk Quantification

Following the prevalent event-based approaches described in Part I, often supply chain managers try to identify the most important potential disruptive events, such as labor strikes or earthquakes, and concentrate on defining adequate scenarios representing the characteristics of each potential trigger. This procedure consumes considerable amount of time and effort, and the results may not be helpful, as a large set of potential triggers – and an even larger set of factors – needs to be modeled and evaluated, although they do not have a considerable impact on performance. Typically, decision makers already know the acceptable deterioration level of relevant performance indicators. They accept increasing costs, decreasing capacity utilization, or reduced service level while the related tolerance range is still met. The target level of the risk objectives are specified by the user. Note that, by allowing the users to specify the amount of performance deterioration they are willing to accept, they are implicitly able to express their own risk attitude. Instead of defining scenarios and evaluating their impact individually, we thus propose to start with the definition of accepted performance deterioration and to continue with the subsequent identification of those scenarios that make the specified deterioration effective.

If supply chain decision makers knew which supply chain processes have an influence on performance indicators and if they knew how much supply chain factors, that describe these processes, need to change such that performance is deteriorated, they would be able to concentrate solely on those processes. One weakness of the contemporary risk analysis is the dependence on decision makers imagination or creativity. If they were not able to imagine causes for specific events, they would not have been able to define correspondent scenarios and most probably the supply chain would not have been prepared. The advantage of the advanced approach introduced is the possibility to overcome this dependence by a reversed simulation work flow. This process finds those input variable values that best fit a given objective without evaluating each assignment. This approach has just recently been coined by the misleading notion of simulation optimization, see Chapter 6.

Process Flow

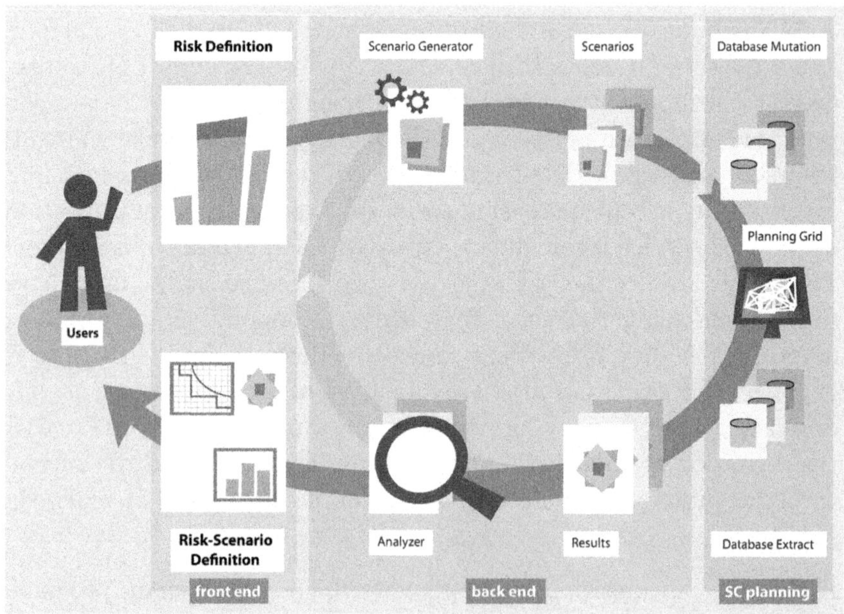

Figure 8.5: Process flow of the risk quantification procedure: a) sequential screening procedure (dark gray) and b) iterative risk quantification procedure (dark gray and light gray).

The analysis approach has now two objectives: First, it seeks to identify the set of supply chain factors that have a significant influence on relevant performance indicators, as described in the previous section. The process flow of this type of analysis follows a sequential procedure, see dark cycle of Figure 8.5. Second, for those supply chain factors that have been identified as influential, value levels need to be quantified that would result in an unacceptable supply chain performance deterioration. Therefore, a set of scenarios is generated at the beginning of the analysis run and all scenario-based results are evaluated by the means of statistical methods referred to the Design and Analysis of Experiments [211].

Quantification of the Risk Line

The screening procedure filters out irrelevant supply chain factors. Relevant factors have an influence on the performance indicator specified by the decision maker at the beginning of the analysis. The purpose of the risk quantification procedure is to assess the factor level combinations that result in the non-achievement of a user-defined target level. For further explanations consider Figure 8.6.

For the sake of simplicity this figure shows only two factors: the x-axis shows factor values for the lead time between node i and j at time period t, $L_{i,j,t}$ from right to left, and the y-axis shows factor values for the inventory level at node j at time period t, $I_{j,t}$ from the bottom up. The decision maker is willing to accept a deterioration of 3% of the performance indicator service level, SL. Assume that the relationship between the factor values could be represented by the decreasing gray line in Figure 8.6 a)-c). Every factor value combination above this isoline would result in a service level greater than 97% which is good. Every factor value combination below this isoline would result in a service level less than 97% which is critical. Within the figure unit steps are represented by dotted lines. The decision maker wants to identify the values defining the cube wherein the service level isoline is placed, see Figure 8.6 b). These value combinations that are just critical determine the risk line.

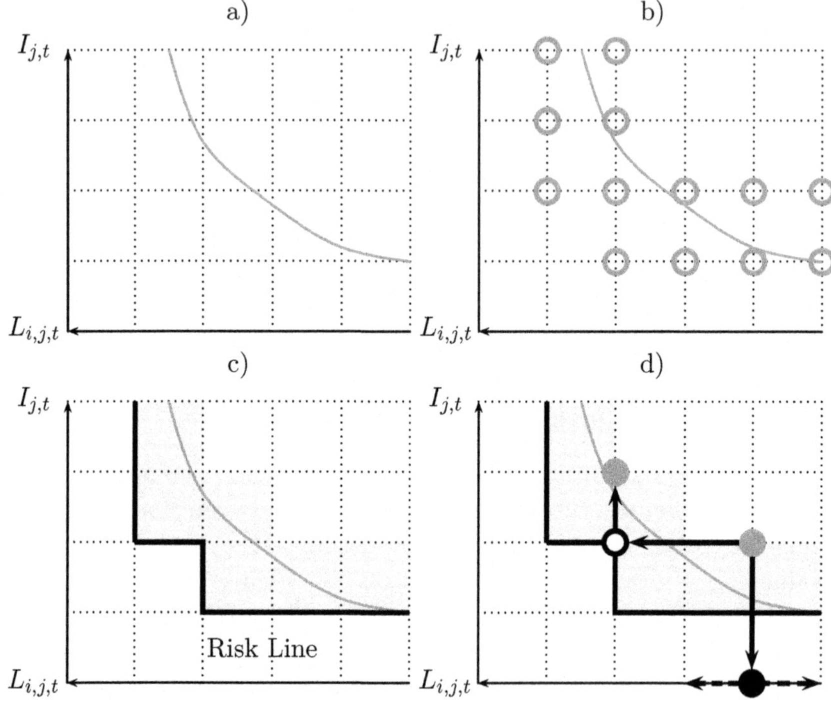

Figure 8.6: Risk line.

Definition 8.5: Risk Line

The risk line defines those factor level combinations, which result in a deterioration of the selected supply chain performance indicator.

The knowledge of the risk line provides the decision makers the opportunity to better understand which modifications of supply chain processes need their intervention. Assume, for instance, the lead time of the transportation process increases by two units compared to the actual lead time. In Figure 8.6 d) this modification of factor values is highlighted by the change from the light gray circle to the black ring. This point is below the accepted level of target deterioration. If the decision maker is able to increase the inventory level of one unit of measurement by specific risk-reducing arrangements the service level could be traced back to acceptable levels, highlighted by the second gray circle.

The risk line gives also insight about factor modifications that cannot be handled by adjusting other factors. Assume the inventory level to drop from its actual level to a lower one, visualized by the black circle in Figure 8.6 d). Any decrease of the lead time would not be able to absorb the inventory fall. The risk line, thus, indicates which factor changes can be compensated on a tactical basis and which must be considered at higher planning levels.

8.3 Summarized Main Features of the Approach

The main goal of the *SimSCRF* approach is to provide the user with valid and credible implications on the dynamics that drive the underlying supply chain and that potentially make supply chain risk effective when disturbances occur. Simulating disruptions by factor changes allow the decision makers to be better prepared, when critical situations come into existence. For the sake of conceptual and methodological consistency the risk analysis approach models and respects the defining entities of supply chain risk. As the simulation model is built around a tactical planning system, the decision maker is able to establish a continuous improvement process: Lessons learned from the risk analysis can be adopted for risk-reducing measures in the tactical system. Note that, this is only possible, because both systems access the same database. In addition to the property of data consistency, the scenario generation processes provide support for the identification and assessment of underlying dynamics. The screening procedure separates relevant from non-relevant supply chain factors. Based on the set of relevant or user-defined supply chain factors, the procedure for risk quantification identifies the combination of factor values that result in the non-achievement of performance targeted levels. The important performance indicators as well as their accepted level of deterioration are specified by the decision makers. They are thus able to express their risk attitude by specifying the level of deterioration, they are willing to accept.

Briefly, the main features of the simulation model are its capabilities of:

- respecting and modeling risk defining entities,
- providing data consistency between risk analysis and tactical planning,
- offering risk quantification procedures.

The proposed simulation model is a tool for the quantitative assessment of supply chain risks. It supports the users in their risk assessment through the definition of plausible scenarios, planning and scenario-evaluation according to their risk attitude. Formally, the framework can be classified as a combined approach of discrete-event simulation and supply chain optimization.

The main goal of this Chapter was to introduce the functionality of this new conceptual approach, whose objective is the analysis of supply chain risks. In order to demonstrate the functionality of the framework, we elaborate a case study in Chapter 11.

9 Representative Master Planning Module for Supply Chains

"Always, always have a plan."

Rick Riordan

The need for the evolution of supply chains and for the development of methods to *manage* them efficiently arises due to the fact that markets are increasingly delivered by internationally acting corporations and are visited by globally-spread customers. In this fierce business environment it is ambitious to become or to stay competitive. Corporations strive for cost reduction and service level increase. The effective integration of processes and operations provides the opportunity to reduce time and capacity buffers. Hence, single enterprises can achieve benefits when they are efficiently integrated in a supply chain system. Supply chains provide the opportunity for all partners to make benefits effective, but the interrelation of processes makes planning and surveillance of the supply chain systems difficult. Numerous proprietary software tools are available to be aimed at overcoming these difficulties by accomplishing the tasks of supply chain design, configuration and planning. Diverse software providers, for example, offer mid-term planning models as more or less standardized modules known under the name of *master planning*. Although offered by different providers master planning modules deliver akin information for mid-term supply chain plans. Due to the logistical focus and due to the high degree of standardization master planning modules are especially suitable for continuous supply chain risk analysis. The simulation framework presented in Chapter 8 is developed with the awareness of the structures that form contemporary master planning modules.

This chapter is intended to introduce a representative master planning model that replaces the (black box) proprietary planning tool within the *SimSCRF* approach. We start by classifying the main planning tasks along the supply chain and available software modules with respect to the planning horizon. Therein, we briefly refer to the fact why the master planning module presents a good snapshot of the logistical constitution of the underlying supply chain and is, therefore, suitable for supply chain risk analysis. Next, we introduce the mathematical formulation for an exemplary master planning problem. This model is used in Chapter 11 to evaluate the *SimSCRF* approach for supply chain risk analysis.

9.1 Planning Tasks of Supply Chains

The supply chain has to fulfill several functions to successfully accomplish its diverse objectives. These functions are split into four main supply chain processes with substantially different tasks, namely: procurement, production, distribution, and sales [254]. The *procurement* task is responsible for the acquisition of production relevant resources such as material and personnel. *Production* uses the limited resources for building products. *Distribution* bridges the distance between production sites and customers. The *sales* process serves as a trigger for the three aforementioned logistical processes by determining demand forecasts and customer orders [291].

	procurement	production	distribution	sales
long-term	materials programms supplier selection cooperations	plant location production system	physical distribution structure	product programme strategic sales planning
mid-term	personnel planning material requirements planning contracts	master production scheduling capacity planning	distribution planning	mid-term sales planning
short-term	personnel planning ordering materials	lot-sizing machine scheduling shop floor control	warehouse replenishment transport planning	short-term sales planning

Figure 9.1: Supply chain planning matrix [254].

Rohde et al. [254] combine the four main tasks of supply chain functions into the *supply chain planning matrix*. Classified by the planning horizon and the supply chain process under consideration, the supply chain planning matrix presents typical tasks occurring in most of current supply chain types, see Figure 9.1.

Today powerful decision support systems are needed and widely used for dealing with these tasks. These so called *Advanced Planning Systems (APS)* are composed of different, most-often hierarchically arranged planning modules. The supply chain planning matrix provides a means of systematically positioning different APS software vendors and their solutions, because distinct modules cover a certain range of planning tasks [254]. Figure 9.2 shows which planning steps are covered by respective software modules [208].

Thus, how major supply chain tasks are executed and coordinated, is determined by single modules of advanced planning systems. The master planning module can be regarded as the builder for the current image of the underlying supply chain from a logistical point of view, because it encompasses all three logistical processes procurement, production, and distribution. Therefore, its planning results provide a *good* view over the current supply chain constitution.

9.2 Mathematical formulation of a Master Planning Problem

The main mathematical formulations of the model below are based on prominent advanced planning models provided by the reviews of Alicke [9] and Stadtler [291] and by the references therein. The purpose of the planning model is to provide the decision maker with information about production allocation, business-to-business material flows, and the range of inventory levels across the supply network. The supply chain model is used for the planning of an integrated multi-echelon, multi-product, and multi-period transportation and

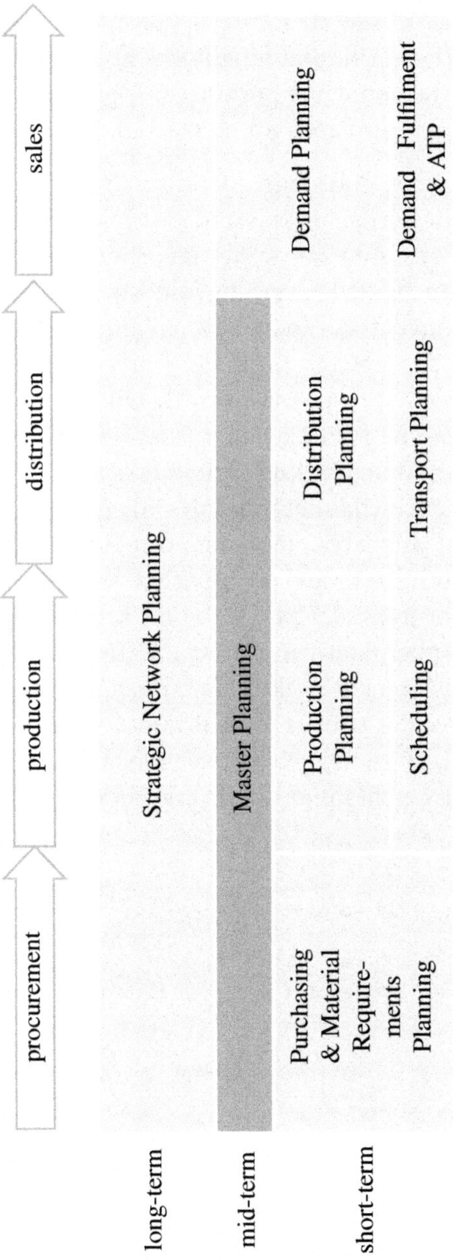

	procurement	production	distribution	sales
long-term	Strategic Network Planning			
mid-term	Master Planning			Demand Planning
short-term	Purchasing & Material Require-ments Planning	Production Planning	Distribution Planning	
		Scheduling	Transport Planning	Demand Fulfilment & ATP

Figure 9.2: Software modules covering the SCP-matrix [208].

production network, whose structure is considered to be given and deterministic over the entire planning horizon, T. The planning horizon is divided into discrete time periods, t, wherein sequence-related considerations and set-up-times are neglected.

The set of nodes, $\mathbb{N}$, is split into locations, $\mathbb{L}$, and transshipment nodes, $\mathbb{H}$. While the former is referred to nodes directly concerned with the material consumption or storage, the latter refers to nodes concerned with material flow handling. Subsets of locations are end-customers, $\mathbb{C}$, and inventory nodes, $\mathbb{IV}$. The latter are further classified into production sites, $\mathbb{S}$, producing pre- or end-products and distribution centers, $\mathbb{DC}$, responsible for distributing products to the markets. For this model formulation we assume that customer's demand are explicitly fulfilled by the regional distribution center. Decisions about distribution channels are forestalled by the consideration of a parameter that allocates customer to regional distribution centers, $cDC_{dc,c}$. Within this model formulation we differentiate original equipment manufacturers (OEM), $\mathbb{OS}$, and pre-product production sites or component manufacturing sites, $\mathbb{PS}$. Responsible for the material flow are transshipment nodes, more precisely by ports, $\mathbb{PH}$, and by airports, $\mathbb{AH}$. Besides transshipment nodes related transports via airplane or ship, direct transports between locations is possible. The composition of nodes is highlighted in Figure 9.3.

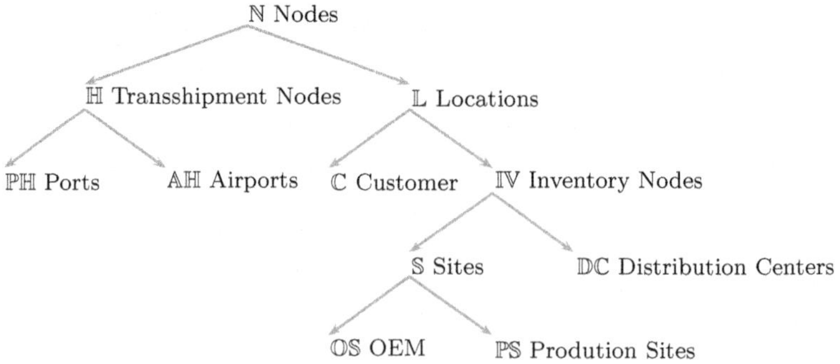

Figure 9.3: Set of nodes.

The replenishment time is divided into the lead time of transportation and of production, respectively. As origin-destination pairs in an internationally distributed supply network have to overcome long-distances, transports normally do not start in every period, e.g. container ships do not leave ports every day. Instead of modeling transportation or production lead times directly, the supply chain planning model considers input factors indicating start-time of transportation, $tST_{n,nn,tm,t,tt}$. This input factors depend on the origin, the destination, mode of transport and on the start as well as end-time of the transportation process. The introduction of different transportation modes increases the degree of freedom within the model as each type of transportation mode is subject to different restrictions and objectives. Similarly, the model considers the ratio of production time on the total replenishment time by introducing an input factor, $tSP^{mach}_{m,t,tt,p}$, indicating the start time of production with respect to the resource or machine, m, period in time of production start, t, and end, tt, and product to produce, p.

The sets and their related indices used by the model are summarized in Table 9.1.

9.2.1 Determinants

The determinants of the model are defined by the non-negative decision variables defined in Table 9.2 and by the input factors presented in Table 9.3.

Decision Variables

Model Identifier	Name	Description
$bl_{c,t,i,o}$	backlog	amount of unsatisfied demand of customer c for order o and end-product i at time period t

$fD_{c,t,i,o}$	fulfilled demand	amount of satisfied demand of customer c for order o and end-product i delivered to customer c at time period t
$out_{dc,t,i,o}$	outgoing goods	outgoing quantity at distribution center dc at time period t of end-product i for order o
$in_{dc,t,i,o}$	goods received	incoming quantity at distribution center dc at time period t of end-product i for order o
$f^{order}_{l,ll,tm,t,p,o}$	location transport	transportation quantity between locations l and ll with transportation mode tm of product p starting at time period t for order o
$f_{n,nn,tm,t}$	transport	transportation quantity between nodes n and nn with transportation mode tm starting at time period t
$I_{inv,t,p}$	inventory level	quantity of stock keeping units at inventory inv at time period t of product p
$I^{sw}_{inv,t,p,o}$	stock withdrawal	quantity of stock keeping units of product p used for production or demand fulfillment of order o from inventory inv at time period t
$I^{sp}_{inv,t,p,o}$	stock pilling	quantity of stock keeping units of product p placed into inventory inv evoked by order o at time period t
$X_{w,t,p,o}$	production output at site	amount of units produced of product p and finished at time period t at production site w for order o
$x_{m,t,p,o}$	production output at machine	amount of units produced of product p and finished at time period t at machine m for order o

$y_{w,t,pp,o}$	gross requirements	amount of gross requirements of pre-product pp for order o at time period t at site w
$proc_{w,t,pp,o}$	procurement	amount of net requirements needed to be procured of pre-product pp for order o at time period t at site w
$\sigma_{t,p,pp,o}$	product/pre-product usage	binary variable, equals 1 iff for order o product p is produced with pre-product pp at time period t
$\kappa_{p,pp,o}$	alternative product used	binary variable, equals 1 iff for order o product p is produced with the alternative pre-product pp
$\alpha_{l,ll,tm,t}$	auxiliary (direct) transport variables	binary variables, equals 1 iff direct transport takes place between location l and location ll at time period t
$\gamma_{h,hh,tm,t}$	auxiliary (transship-ment) transport variables	binary variables, equals 1 iff transshipments transport takes place between transshipment node h and transshipment node hh at time period t
$\phi_{m,t}$	capacity consumption	amount of capacity used on machine m at time period t

Table 9.2: Decision variables of the supply chain planning model.

Index Symbols	Set Symbol	Description
t, tt	$\mathbb{T}$	Periods
o	$\mathbb{O}$	Orders
m	$\mathbb{M}$	Machines/ Resources
n, nn	$\mathbb{N}$	Nodes
l, ll	$\mathbb{L}$	Locations $\subseteq$ Nodes
c	$\mathbb{C}$	Customers $\subseteq$ Locations
v, vv	$\mathbb{IV}$	Inventory-nodes $\subseteq$ Locations
dc	$\mathbb{DC}$	Distribution Centers $\subseteq$ Inventory-nodes
w, ww	$\mathbb{S}$	Sites $\subseteq$ Inventory-nodes
ow	$\mathbb{OS}$	OEMs $\subseteq$ Sites
pw	$\mathbb{PS}$	Production Sites $\subseteq$ Sites
h, hh	$\mathbb{H}$	Transshipment Node $\subseteq$ Nodes
hp, hpp	$\mathbb{PH}$	Ports $\subseteq$ Transshipment Node
ha, haa	$\mathbb{AH}$	Airports $\subseteq$ Transshipment Node
inv	$\mathbb{INV}$	Inventories
p	$\mathbb{P}$	Products
i	$\mathbb{EP}$	End-products $\subseteq$ Products
pp	$\mathbb{PP}$	Pre-products $\subseteq$ Products
q	$\mathbb{AG}$	Alternative Groups
tm	$\mathbb{TM}$	Transportation Modes

Table 9.1: Sets and indices of the supply chain planning model.

Input Factors

Model Identifier	Name	Description
Order parameters		
$D_{c,t,i,o}$	demand	requested quantity of end-product i for date required t for customer c and for order number o

RD_o	required date	required date for order delivery of order o
RC_o	customer order	customer c triggering order o
RP_o	product ordered	end-product i of order o
Resource or Machine parameters		
$mP_{m,p}$	production options on machine	binary parameter, equals 1 iff machine m produces product p
$sP_{w,t,p}$	production options at site	binary parameter, equals 1 iff site w produces product p at time period t
$Cap_{m,t}$	capacity	quantity of available capacity on machine m at time period t
$Con_{m,t,p}$	consumption	quantity of capacity consumed by machine m for producing of product p at time period t
$tSP^{mach}_{m,t,tt,p}$	start of production on machine	equals 1 iff time of production start at machine m in tt is possible such that production is finished in tt
$tSP^{site}_{w,t,tt,p}$	start of production at site	equals 1 iff production starts in time period t at site w such that production is finished in time period tt
Location parameters		
$\mathbb{AH}_l$	airport-location assignment	set of airports assigned to location l

$\mathbb{PH}_l$	port-location assignment	set of ports assigned to location l
$cDC_{dc,c}$	customer markets	binary parameter relating customers to distribution centers
Inventory parameters		
$\mathbb{INV}_l$	inventories at location	set of inventories inv allocated to location l
$iniI_{inv,p}$	initial inventory	quantity of stock keeping units of product p at inventory inv at the beginning of the planning horizon
$maxI_{inv,t}$	maximum inventory	maximum quantity of stock keeping units allowed at inventory inv at time period t
$vINV_{v,p}$	storage capability	equals 1 iff inventory node v is capable to store product p
Product parameters		
$\mathbb{AG}_q$	alternative products assignment	set of alternative preproducts pp enclosed by auxiliary product q
$pAG_{p,q}$	alternative products identifier	binary parameter, equals 1 iff product p is assigned to auxiliary product q
$a_{p,pp}$	demand coefficient	amount of preproduct pp needed to produce one unit of product p
Transportation parameters		

$TiMa_{n,nn,t}$	Time Matrix	transportation time between node n and node nn at transportation start t
$tST_{l,ll,tm,t,tt}$	start of transport	equals 1 iff transportation starts in time period t in transportation mode tm between locations l and ll such that transport is finished in time period tt
$minf_{n,nn,t}$	minimum transportation	minimum quantity on transports between nodes n and nn at time period t
$maxf_{n,nn}$	maximum transportation	maximum quantity on transports between nodes n and nn at time period t

Table 9.3: Input factors of the supply chain planning model.

9.2.2 Objective Function

Under the consideration of typical inventory balance and capacity restrictions, the objective function may vary between cost minimization, profit maximization, minimization of order backlogs or service level maximization. The formulation below minimizes the quantitative backlog over the entire planning horizon.

$$\text{minimize} \sum_c \sum_t \sum_i \sum_o bl_{c,t,i,o} \tag{9.1}$$

The backlog of each order o with respect to the end-product i is defined for each time period t that exceeds the required date of order fulfillment, RD_o.

9.2.3 Restrictions

Production and Resource Planning Constraints

The main set of constraints defines the production and resource planning necessary for producing the ordered end-product on time. For a comprehensive visualization of the main constraints, we refer to Figure 9.4.

$$fD_{c,t,i,o} = D_{c,t,i,o} - bl_{c,t,i,o} + bl_{c,t-1,i,o} \qquad \forall \quad c,t,i,o \quad | \quad RC_o{=}c \wedge RP_o{=}i \wedge RD_o{\geq}t \tag{9.2}$$

Constraint 9.2 defines the order fulfillment of each order and each customer. If the amount of delivered end-product does not satisfy the demand, $fD_{c,t,i,o} \neq D_{c,t,i,o}$, a backlog arises. A backlog can only emerge, if the required date of order fulfillment is reached $RD_o \geq t$. The constraint takes only those products and those customers into account that are allocated to the correspondent order, $RP_o = i$ and $RC_o = c$.

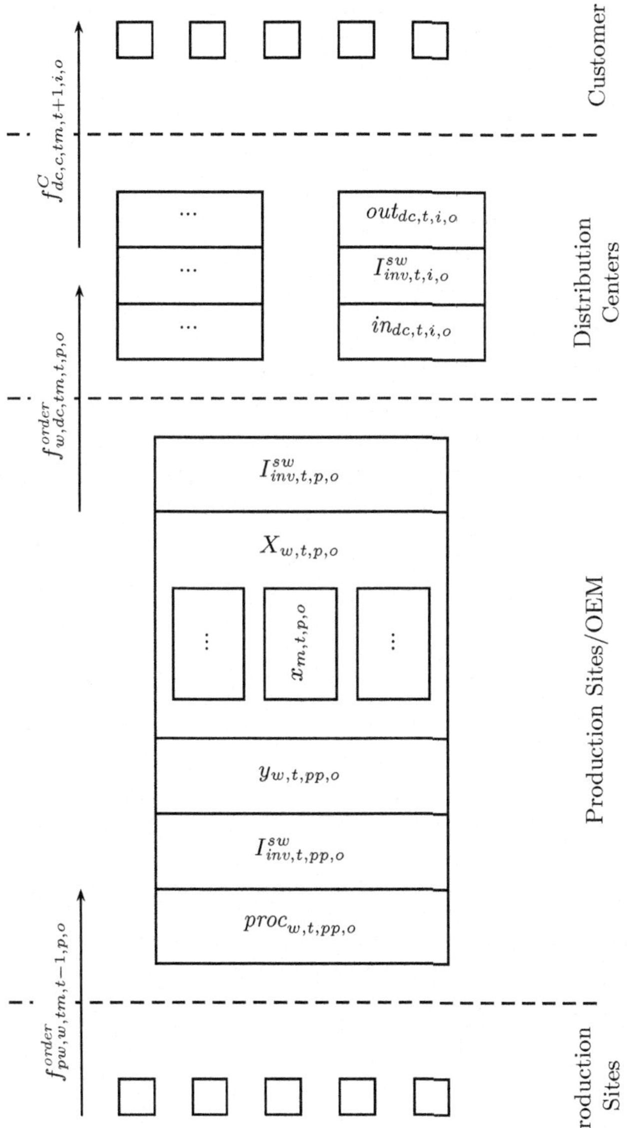

Figure 9.4: Visualization of the production and resource planning Variables.

$$\sum_{dc|cDC_{dc,c}=1} \sum_{tm} \sum_{tt|tST_{dc,c,tm,tt,t}=1} f^{order}_{dc,c,tm,tt,i,o} = fD_{c,t,i,o} \quad (9.3)$$

$$\forall \quad c,t \quad | \quad vINV_{dc,i}=1 \wedge RP_o=i \wedge RC_o=c$$

$$out_{dc,t,i,o} = \sum_{c|cDCdc,c=1} \sum_{tm} f^{order}_{dc,c,tm,t,i,o} \quad (9.4)$$

$$\forall \quad dc,t,i,o \quad | \quad vINV_{dc,i}=1 \wedge RP_o=i \wedge RC_o=c$$

Delivered demand to the customer originates from distribution centers that are allocated to the market region of the customer, $cDC_{dc,c} = 1$. The distribution to the customer is possible over different transportation links, see 9.3 and 9.4. Since transportation over links does not start at each period in time, the time of transportation is represented by a parameter that defines the start times, t, of different transportation modes, tm, and its corresponding time of arrival, tt, $tST_{dc,c,tm,t,tt}$.

$$in_{dc,t,i,o} = out_{dc,t,i,o} + \sum_{inv|inv \in \mathbb{INV}_{dc}} (I^{sp}_{inv,t,i,o} - I^{sw}_{inv,t,i,o}) \quad (9.5)$$

$$\forall \quad dc,t,i,o \quad | \quad vINV_{dc,i}=1 \wedge RP_o=i$$

Constraint 9.5 defines the amount of end-product needed at the distribution center, $in_{dc,t,i,o}$. By balancing the inventory at each distribution center with the distributed amount the needed amount of each end-product is determined.

$$\sum_{ow}\sum_{tm}\sum_{tt|tST_{ow,dc,tm,tt,t}=1} f^{order}_{ow,dc,tm,tt,i,o} = in_{dc,t,i,o} \tag{9.6}$$
$$\forall \quad dc,t,i,o \quad | \quad vINV_{dc,i}=1 \wedge RP_o=i$$

The needed end-product at each distribution center is transported via available transportation links from production plants 9.6.

$$\begin{aligned} X_{ow,t,i,o} &= \sum_{dc}\sum_{tm} f^{order}_{ow,dc,tm,t,i,o} \\ &+ \sum_{inv|inv\in\mathbb{INV}_{ow}} (I^{sp}_{inv,t,p,o} - I^{sw}_{inv,t,p,o}) \end{aligned} \tag{9.7}$$
$$\forall \quad ow,t,i,o \quad | \quad sP_{ow,t,i}=1 \wedge RP_o=i$$

$$\sum_{pp|pp\in\mathbb{AG}_q}\sum_{tt|tSP^{site}_{w,tt,t,p}=1} (y_{w,tt,pp,o}/a_{p,pp})\sigma_{t,p,pp,o} = X_{w,t,p,o} \tag{9.8}$$
$$\forall \quad w,t,p,q,o \quad | \quad sP_{w,t,p}=1 \wedge a_{p,pp}>0 \wedge pAG_{p,q}=1$$

$$\sum_{pp|pp\in\mathbb{AG}_q} \sigma_{t,p,pp,o} = 1 \tag{9.9}$$
$$\forall \quad t,p,q,o \quad | \quad pAG_{p,q}=1$$

A plant is able to deliver the required amount, if either sufficient inventory is available or production provides additional amounts (9.7). For the production of each product a certain amount of pre-products is needed, which can be determined by the bill of materials (9.8). The amount of pre-product, *pp*, which is necessary to produce one unit of the subsequent product, *p*, is quantified by the demand-coefficient, $a_{p,pp}$. With respect to the availability of production resources for product p, $sP_{w,t,p} = 1$, and the availability of pre-products, $a_{p,pp} > 0$, production is possible.

Often products are substitutable by other products of lower quality or less equipped. If the availability of the preferred (pre-)product is limited, the usage of a substitute (pre-)product can also become necessary. Nearly all types of industry, such as computer, automotive, mechanical engineering as well as chemical or pharmaceutic industry, profit from substitute products. In Chapter 11 we evaluate the *SimSCRF* approach for a supply chain derived from chemical industry. This supply chain model, however, does not consider alternative products. Nevertheless, we provide the opportunity to include the consideration of substitute products within the model formulation as follows. We extend the idea of Cardeneo and Held [46] by introducing sets that encompass all products, which are substitutable among each other. The set $\mathbb{AG}_q$ defines a group, q, of alternative pre-products, pp, that can be considered as convertible. Figure 9.5 highlights the structure of the bill of material and visualizes the resulting modeling approach for an exemplary bill of material containing two products. The decision variable $\sigma_{t,p,pp,o}$ retains which pre-product, pp, is used for the production of product, p (9.9).

$$\sum_{tt|tSP^{site}_{w,t,tt,p}=1} y_{w,tt,pp,o} = X_{w,t,p,o} a_{p,pp} \kappa_{p,pp,o} \tag{9.10}$$

$$\forall \quad w,t,p,pp,o \quad | \quad sP_{w,t,p}=1 \wedge a_{p,pp}>0$$

$$\sum_{pp|pp \in \mathbb{AG}_q} \kappa_{p,pp,o} = 1 \tag{9.11}$$

$$\forall \quad p,q,o \quad | \quad pAG_{p,q}=1$$

Substitute products provide the opportunity to use available products instead of waiting for the preferred product. With respect to the customer it can be necessary to deliver only one distinct version of end-product. The composition of all required products should be

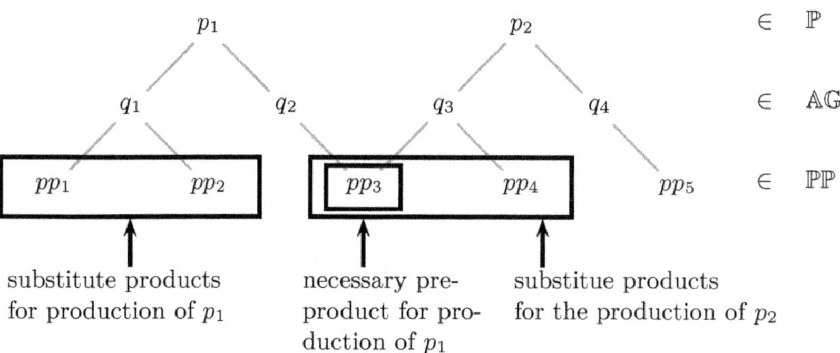

Figure 9.5: Visualization of modeling logic for substitute products.

identical. Constraints (9.10) and (9.11) limit the usage of alternative (pre-)products for a single order to one.

$$proc_{w,t,p,o} = y_{w,t,p,o} + \sum_{inv|inv \in \mathbb{INV}_w} (I^{sp}_{inv,t,p,o} - I^{sw}_{inv,t,p,o}) \tag{9.12}$$

$$\forall \quad w,t,p,o \quad | \quad vINV_{w,p}{=}1$$

$$\sum_{pw|pw<>w} \sum_{tm} \sum_{tt|sP_{pw,t,p}=1 \wedge tST_{pw,w,tm,tt,t}=1} f^{order}_{pw,w,tm,tt,p,o}$$

$$= \quad proc_{w,t,p,o} \tag{9.13}$$

$$\forall \quad w,t,p,o$$

$$X_{pw,t,p,o} = \sum_{w|w<>pw} \sum_{tm} f^{order}_{pw,w,tm,t,p,o} + \sum_{inv|inv \in \mathbb{INV}_{pw}} (I^{sp}_{inv,t,p,o} - I^{sw}_{inv,t,p,o}) \qquad (9.14)$$

$$\forall \quad pw,t,p,o \quad | \quad sP_{pw,t,p}=1$$

In the same way the amount of required finished products has to be balanced with available inventory, so has the amount of pre-product to be balanced with available amounts of pre-product inventory (9.12). The net demand for pre-products is shipped via different transportation links originating from production plants upstream the supply chain (9.13). Therein, the production of pre-products is determined by the difference between the sum of necessary products to ship and the amount transferable from outbound inventories.

Frozen Periods

In order to cope with uncertain developments planning is often conducted on a rolling horizon basis. A rolling horizon allows to control and revise planning results. In master planning modules the planning horizon is typically divided into months. At distinct planning points a plan is determined that covers the current planning horizon. However, only those periods are actually put into practice that have been *frozen* by the decision maker. At the next planning point actual developments evolved during the frozen periods can be considered for updates of relevant parameters such as demand forecasts. For further explanations on frozen periods we refer to Stadtler and Kilger [291]. In order to freeze planning results, $(decision\ variables)^f$, for certain time periods a frozen horizon, T^f, is introduced.

$$
\begin{aligned}
fD_{c,t,i,o} &= fD^{f}_{c,t,i,o} && \forall \quad c,i,o,t<T^f && (9.15)\\
out_{dc,t,i,o} &= out^{f}_{dc,t,i,o} && \forall \quad dc,i,o,t<T^f && (9.16)\\
in_{dc,t,i,o} &= in^{f}_{dc,t,i,o} && \forall \quad dc,i,o,t<T^f && (9.17)\\
f_{n,nn,tm,t,p,o} &= f^{f}_{n,nn,tm,t,p,o} && \forall \quad n,nn,tm,p,o,t<T^f && (9.18)\\
I^{sw}_{inv,t,p,o} &= I^{f,sw}_{inv,t,p,o} && \forall \quad inv,p,o,t<T^f && (9.19)\\
x_{m,t,p,o} &= x^{f}_{m,t,p,o} && \forall \quad inv,p,o,t<T^f && (9.20)\\
y_{w,t,pp,o} &= y^{f}_{w,t,pp,o} && \forall \quad w,pp,o,t<T^f && (9.21)\\
proc_{w,t,pp,o} &= proc^{f}_{w,t,pp,o} && \forall \quad w,pp,o,t<T^f && (9.22)
\end{aligned}
$$

Linearization

Due to the non-linearity of constraints (9.8) and (9.10) they are replaced by linearization constraints (9.23) – (9.25) and (9.26) – (9.28), respectively. These constraints follow the general linearization rule defined, for example, in Williams [337].

to be linearized: $y = X\theta$

$$
\begin{aligned}
y - M\theta &\leq 0\\
y - X &\leq 0\\
X - y + M\theta &\leq M
\end{aligned}
$$

$$X_{w,t,p,o} - M \sum_{pp|pp \in \mathbb{AG}_q} \sigma_{t,p,pp,o} \quad \leq \quad 0 \tag{9.23}$$

$$\forall \quad w,t,p,q,o \quad | \quad sP_{w,t,p}{=}1 \wedge a_{p,pp}{>}0 \wedge pAG_{p,q}{=}1$$

$$- \sum_{pp|pp \in \mathbb{AG}_q} \sum_{tt|tSP^{site}_{w,tt,t,p}=1} y_{w,tt,pp,o}/a_{p,pp} + X_{w,t,p,o} \quad \leq \quad 0 \tag{9.24}$$

$$\forall \quad w,t,p,q,o \quad | \quad sP_{w,t,p}{=}1 \wedge a_{p,pp}{>}0 \wedge pAG_{p,q}{=}1$$

$$\sum_{pp|pp \in \mathbb{AG}_q} \sum_{tt|tSP^{site}_{w,tt,t,p}=1} y_{w,tt,pp,o}/a_{p,pp} - X_{w,t,p,o} + M \sum_{pp|pp \in \mathbb{AG}_q} \sigma_{t,p,pp,o} \quad \leq \quad M \tag{9.25}$$

$$\forall \quad w,t,p,q,o \quad | \quad sP_{w,t,p}{=}1 \wedge a_{p,pp}{>}0 \wedge pAG_{p,q}{=}1$$

$$\sum_{tt|tSP^{site}_{w,tt,t,p}=1} y_{w,tt,pp,o} - M\kappa_{p,pp,o} \quad \leq \quad 0 \tag{9.26}$$

$$\forall \quad w,t,p,pp,o \quad | \quad a_{p,pp}{>}0 \wedge sP_{w,t,p}{=}1$$

$$- X_{w,t,p,o}a_{p,pp} + \sum_{tt|tSP^{site}_{w,tt,t,p}=1} y_{w,tt,pp,o} \quad \leq \quad 0 \tag{9.27}$$

$$\forall \quad w,t,p,pp,o \quad | \quad a_{p,pp}{>}0 \wedge sP_{w,t,p}{=}1$$

$$X_{w,t,p,o}a_{p,pp} - \sum_{tt|tSP^{site}_{w,tt,t,p}=1} y_{w,tt,pp,o} + M\kappa_{p,pp,o} \quad \leq \quad M \tag{9.28}$$

$$\forall \quad w,t,p,pp,o \quad | \quad a_{p,pp}{>}0 \wedge sP_{w,t,p}{=}1$$

Transportation Constraints

$$f^{order}_{ha,haa,tm,t,p,o} = \sum_{l|\mathbb{AH}_l=ha} \sum_{ll|\mathbb{AH}_{ll}=haa} f^{order}_{l,ll,tm,t,p,o} \tag{9.29}$$

$$\forall \quad ha,haa,tm,t,p,o \quad | \quad ha \neq haa \wedge tm=airfreight$$

$$f^{order}_{hp,hpp,tm,t,p,o} = \sum_{l|\mathbb{PH}_l=hp} \sum_{ll|\mathbb{PH}_{ll}=hpp} f^{order}_{l,ll,tm,p,o} \tag{9.30}$$

$$\forall \quad hp,hpp,tm,t,p,o \quad | \quad hp \neq hpp \wedge tm=shipfreight$$

$$f_{n,nn,tm,t} = \sum_{o} \sum_{p} f^{order}_{n,nn,tm,t,p,o} \tag{9.31}$$

$$\forall \quad n,nn,tm,t \quad | \quad n \neq nn$$

In order to integrate production and resource planning with transportation planning constraints (9.29) to (9.31) link demands for transportation, such as $f^{order}_{l,ll,tm,t,p,o}$, with the execution of transports, $f_{n,nn,tm,t}$.

$$f_{l,ll,tm,t} \geq minf_{l,ll,t} \alpha_{l,ll,tm,t} \tag{9.32}$$

$$\forall \quad l,ll,tm,t \quad | \quad l \neq ll \wedge TiMa_{l,ll,t}>=0 \wedge tm=direct$$

$$f_{l,ll,tm,t} \leq maxf_{l,ll,tm,t} \alpha_{l,ll,tm,t} \tag{9.33}$$

$$\forall \quad l,ll,tm,t \quad | \quad l \neq ll \wedge TiMa_{l,ll,t}>=0 \wedge tm=direct$$

Constraints (9.32) and (9.33) limit the lower and upper transportation amount, respectively, for each origin and destination pair with respect to the transportation mode and time period.

$$f_{h,hh,tm,t} \geq minf_{h,hh,t} \gamma_{h,hh,tm,t} \qquad (9.34)$$
$$\forall \quad h,hh,tm,t \quad | \quad h \neq hh \wedge TiMa_{h,hh,t} >= 0$$

$$f_{h,hh,tm,t} \leq maxf_{h,hh,tm,t} \gamma_{h,hh,tm,t} \qquad (9.35)$$
$$\forall \quad h,hh,tm,t \quad | \quad h \neq hh \wedge TiMa_{h,hh,t} >= 0$$

Similarly, constraints (9.34) and (9.35) define the limits for transports between transshipment nodes.

Inventory Constraints

$$I_{inv,t,p} = I_{inv,t-1,p} + \sum_{o} (I^{sp}_{inv,t,p,o} - I^{sw}_{inv,t,p,o}) \qquad (9.36)$$
$$\forall \quad inv,p,t$$

$$\sum_{p} I_{inv,t,p} \leq maxI_{inv,t} \qquad (9.37)$$
$$\forall \quad inv,t$$

The inventory constraints calculate the overall inventory level (9.36) and limit the maximal allowed inventory level (9.37).

Machine Constraints

$$X_{w,t,p,o} = \sum_{m | mP_{m,p}=1} x_{m,t,p,o} \qquad (9.38)$$
$$\forall \quad w,t,p,o \quad | \quad sP_{w,t,p}=1$$

$$\phi_{m,t} = \sum_{o} \sum_{p|mP_{m,p}=1} x_{m,t,p,o} Con_{m,t,p} \quad \forall \quad m,t \quad | \quad Cap_{m,t}>0 \tag{9.39}$$

$$\phi_{m,t} - Cap_{m,t} \leq 0 \quad \forall \quad m,t \quad | \quad Cap_{m,t}>0 \tag{9.40}$$

The overall production amount at each site is generated by distinct machines allocated at each site, $sP_{w,t,p} = 1$. Machines differ in their features or production specifications, $mP_{m,p} = 1$. Both characteristics limit the set of products that can be produced at the machine, see constraint (9.38). The capacity consumption of each production process depends on the product to be produced and the aforementioned specification of a machine, $Con_{m,t,p}$. Constraint (9.39) calculates the resource consumption, which needs to be limited by the maximal permitted capacity consumption formulated in constraint (9.40). The capacity restriction could also be formulated as a soft constraint, in this model, however, we regard the maximum capacity level as a hard limit that can not be exceeded.

Initialization and Termination Constraints

The model formulations require some initialization and termination constraints.

$$I_{inv,p,t} = iniI_{iv,p} \quad \forall \quad inv,t,p{=}0 \tag{9.41}$$

$$f_{v,vv,tm,t,p,o} = 0 \quad \forall \quad v,vv,tm,t{=}0,p,o \tag{9.42}$$

$$y_{w,t,pp,o} = 0 \quad \forall \quad w,t{=}T,pp,o \tag{9.43}$$

$$f_{v,vv,tm,t,p,o} = 0 \quad \forall \quad v,vv,tm,t{=}T{-}TiMa_{v,vv},p,o \tag{9.44}$$

We implemented this representative master planning model using the Java optimization modeling library of the IBM ILOG Concert Technology. In Chapter 11 we apply this model within the *SimSCRF* approach and evaluate a given exemplary supply chain derived from chemical industry. Planning runs were solved with ILOG CPLEX 12.6, on an Intel Core i7-2640M PC with 2.8 GHz processors and 7,88 GB RAM.

10 A Conceptual Information Meta-Model for Supply Chains

"We have more information than we have skills to turn it into useful knowledge."

Mark Rolston

Enterprises invest considerable amounts of money for supply chain information technologies, which vary in scale, usage, and level of technology. These systems include repositories, Enterprise Resource Planning (ERP), Advanced Planning Systems (APS), and other information systems. Supply chain management needs to access these systems for its original tasks of planning, monitoring, and control. Additionally, it can be necessary to retrieve specific data entries from distinct systems and process an updated data set to a business-specific planning tool that is dedicated for solving smaller problem instances or problems with different scope and objective. In situations, in which IT systems have to communicate with each other or with derived sub-systems, approaches are needed that support this domain-specific information and knowledge transfer.

Supply chain ontologies have lately been proposed as a mean for solving the interoperability problem of supply chain information systems

– simple as well as highly sophisticated systems [84]. In computer science the concept of ontologies is defined as "a formal, explicit specification of a shared conceptualization" [293]. It often refers to different terms such as data dictionary, taxonomy, information or data model, and conceptual schemas. Generally, it encompasses the knowledge about a specific domain. An ontology includes a vocabulary of terms and specifications of their meaning. This implies definitions of concepts and their relations, which both build a domain-specific data structure and restrict the meaning of terms [320].

In this chapter we approach the development of an ontology for supply chains by offering an information meta-model. It formalizes a set of supply-chain-specific terms and interactions, denoted by concepts, properties, and relations. The remainder of the chapter is organized as follows. Section 10.1 briefly summarizes the main motivation and major requirements for applying an information meta-model in the context of the *SimSCRF* approach. Section 10.2 presents related work. In the subsequent section the concepts, properties, and relations of the meta-model are introduced. The vocabulary defined within the meta-model is then used to create an instance of a supply chain, which we simply denote as *Supply Chain Model.* The chapter closes by visualizing this concrete instance of the meta-model.

10.1 Requirements for a Supply Chain Information Meta-Model

The main motivation for the application of a supply chain meta-model arises from the request to offer risk analysis for different planning engines. Distinct planning tools are composed by different rationales that underlie the mathematical model formulation and that result in different data structures encapsulating planning relevant data. Although the information needed for conducting supply chain planning is structured differently among distinct planning engines, the meaning included in the data refers to common concepts. Resources, for example, are endowed with capacity values that restrict their degree of usage. The resource-specific capacity consumption can depend on the item that uses the capacity, the point in time the capacity is accessed, the location of the resource, or others. The specific circumstances vary with respect to the planning engine and the industrial context. The semantic meaning of the resource capacity however remains the same and needs to be arranged properly within the *SimSCRF* data structure.

Thus, instead of modeling an interface that directly relates planning data to the internal representation of the *SimSCRF* model, an additional layer is used. It serves not only as a data processor, but also as an information interpreter and data validator. The implementation of a meta-model for supply-chain-specific planning offers the possibility to more easily switch between different planning engines, and as a result conduct risk analysis for different supply chain planning problems and engines. The internal supply chain model representation is then hardly influenced.

We summarize the resulting requirements for the information meta-model as follows:

- Abstraction: The meta-model should encapsulate the meaning of supply-chain-specific terms and their interactions, such that it formalizes supply chain knowledge and is applicable for different planning problems or engines.
- Efficiency: Planning repositories contain technical information, which are not specific for the supply chain domain. The meta-model and concrete model instances should not mirror the whole data base, but retrieve and formalize solely supply-chain-specific data.
- Effectiveness: The meta-model should embrace the information about logistical processes. Model instances need to reflect insights of *all* structured logistical activities.

Note that, the meaning of the concepts efficiency and effectiveness is different from those described in Chapter 3 with respect to core characteristics of supply chain risk.

10.2 Related Work

An international effort for standardizing the representation of supply chain operations has been conducted by the Supply Chain Council (SCC). In 1996 the SCC initially developed the Supply Chain Operations Reference (SCOR) model. It is a reference business process model widely used in practice [295]. Since then it was continuously updated with respect to new developments in the supply chain environment or due to new progress in research or technology. The SCOR is considered to provide the widest view on supply chains, because they capture (most of) the supply chain processes by categorizing them according to the perspectives: plan, source, make, deliver, and return. With respect to the modeling of information directly derived from supply chain planning and applied for supply chain risk analysis the SCOR model does not provide appropriate characteristics. It especially lacks to represent material or process flows which are indispensable for risk analysis. The reason for that can be referred to the primary focus of the model, which is to present a benchmark framework for the description and assessment of supply chain processes, rather than conceptualizing supply chain entities and their relations.

While the SCOR model is intended to be a benchmark framework for the description and assessment of supply chain processes, supply chain ontologies aim to describe *all* entities and relationships of supply chains. Generally, an ontology seeks to formally model the structure of a system, whose relevant entities and relations need to be identified. The construction of an ontology requires to organize relevant entities into *properties* and *relations* [289]. An ontology captures the attributes of an entity and inheritance relationships comparable to object-oriented programming [84]. Due to these characteristics, ontologies have been proposed as a mean to communicate between different computer systems [84] and to solve information systems interoperability issues [112]. The review by Grubic and Fan [112] analyzes the available literature on supply chain ontologies. Due to the limited work within this field, the authors identify numerous research gaps. Major gaps relate to the limited scope of application with respect to logistical perspectives as well as to time horizons. Nearly all of the identified supply chain ontologies are limited to a strategic horizon. Along with this detection comes the identification that most ontologies are only applicable for one- rather than multi-period considerations. A multi-period setting is, however, vital for supply chain risk analysis.

Additionally, further approaches have been developed, but yet not been widely applied. The *Supply Chain Modeling Language (SCML)* for example is a platform- and methodology-independent Extensible Markup Language (XML)-based markup language and encompasses supply chain structural as well as managerial information [52]. The SCML does not provide a compact meta-model and does not relate supply-chain-specific processes to structural components. Stumpp [294] deduced a *Concept and Property Model*, which contains structural, operational, and resource-specific concepts. Wiedenbruch [335] recently developed a process-oriented *Modeling Language for Supply Chain Event Management* intended to support supply chain event management. These approaches are promising with respect to their target field of application. To the best of our knowledge there have been no further efforts presented in the research literature of supply chain ontology or supply chain information modeling that focus on the interoperability of supply chain planning and supply chain analysis or even risk analysis tools. In the subsequent section we present a supply chain meta-model which combines ideas of the aforementioned existing supply chain models and ontologies.

10.3 Modeling Supply Chain Information

As discussed in Chapter 9 tactical supply chain planning provide the decision maker with information about how to accomplish supply chain's major tasks: procurement, production, distribution, and sales. The efficient planning of these tasks uses supply-chain-specific information about network structure, resource specifications, and operational activities as well as information about planning-related technical input. In the following we present the concepts, the properties, and the relations that describe these information for a supply-chain-specific meta-model.

10.3.1 Concepts

The supply chain meta-model consists of seven concepts classified into five concept types. *Structural concepts* are composed of the concepts *Node* and *Link*. The supply chain meta-model is endowed with an *operational concept* related to supply chain activities. *Resource-related concepts* address the capabilities of each resource. *Object-related* concepts are *Product* and *Gadget*. The *Resource Usage* is referred to as a *Technical concept.*

The concepts of the derived information meta-model for supply chains are visualized in Figure 10.1 and described in more detail in the following paragraphs.

A **Node** is a structural concept and refers to different types of facilities located within a supply chain network. A **Link** is a structural concept and connects two nodes. A link contains the information about its source and its end node. **Activities** are operational concepts and describe dynamic actions on different supply chain processes. Distinct activity types included in the meta-model are: *order*, *store*, *transport*, and *produce*. **Capabilities** are resource-related concepts and describe the capabilities of a resource with respect to the activity that is executed on the resource. Capability types include:

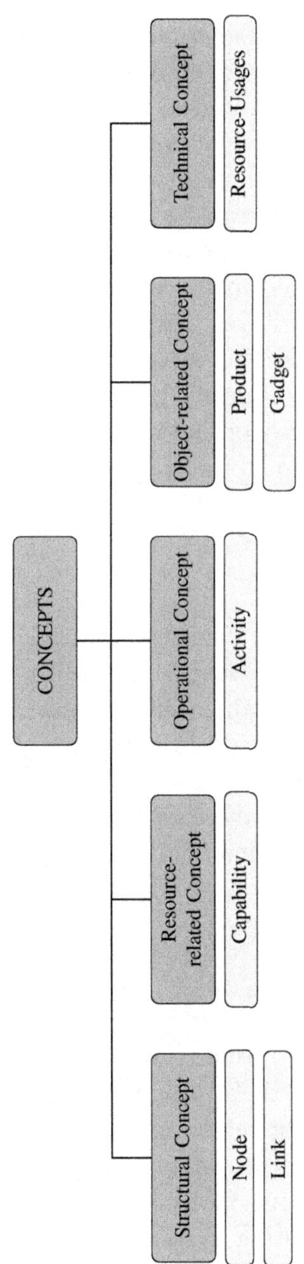

Figure 10.1: Concepts of the deduced information meta-model for supply chains.

Inventory, *Shipping*, and *Production*. **Products** are object-related concepts and are items that are stored as finished goods inventories or input material, that are produced as final product or intermediate product, that are transported as final product or pre-product, that are requested by production facilities or customers. **Gadgets** are object-related concepts and can be used as a containment of products like vehicles, palettes, or boxes. (Gadgets are not used for the supply chain model applied in the *SimSCRF* model and, therefore, they are not further described.) The **Resource-Usage** is a technical concept and is used for the initialization of the planning engine. This concept refers to the already given allocation of activities like for example initial inventory or given resource allocations of a supply chain plan that is fixed up to the frozen period.

10.3.2 Properties

Concepts are endowed with one or several properties that further describe the meaning of the concept. Each property is specified by a name, a unit, and a related value. Different classes of properties have been deduced for the supply chain meta-model: *Location* describes the geographical position of a node or facility. *Dates* refer to specific points in time. Contrary, a *duration* describes the length of a time period. *Quantity* defines numerical values. Finally, *costs* embrace monetary costs.

10.3.3 Relations

Concepts are connected to other types of concepts by relations. A common structure within the supply chain model is the relation between a structural concept, a resource-related concept, and an operational concept. A node is related to a production or inventory capability. These capability concepts are further related to activities such as producing and storing, respectively. Whenever activities are initialized or restricted within certain time periods, they are related to a resource-usage concept. For example, the storing activity is related to an inventory resource-usage concept. The relations used for the supply chain model are visualized in the next section.

10.3.4 Constraints

Apart from concepts and properties that define the vocabulary of the information meta-model as well as relations that connect different concept types, the meta-model assumes formal constraints. These constraints specify how the different terms in the vocabulary can be used together. With respect to the network structure the structural concepts node and link are assumed to be aligned in a specific context. Each link has a source node, which is declared by the relation "FROM_NODE", as well as a end node, specified by the "TO_NODE" relation. Similarly, each node is assumed to be connected to a link by an "INCOMING_LINK" relation and a "OUTGOING_LINK" relation, respectively. The interrelation is visualized in Figure 10.2

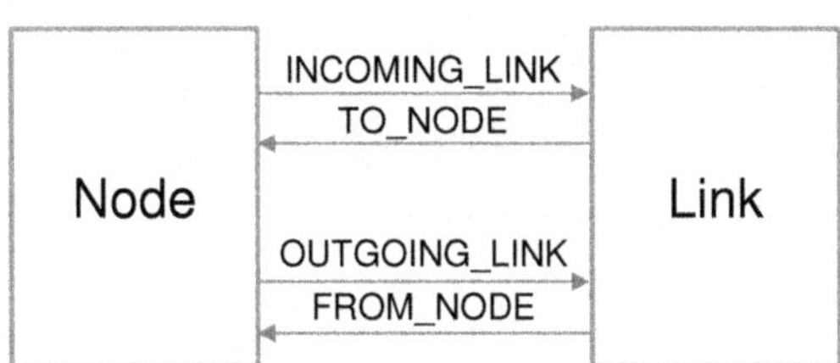

Figure 10.2: Link-node constraint.

The main tasks of a supply chain are explicitly concerned with the creation of a product and its enhancement of value. The product concept is a central component of the supply chain. Activity concepts like physical handling, storing, producing, and shipping, they all refer to products. Additionally, activities can only be executed, if they are related to a resource endowed with activity-specific capacities. Thus, a central constraint of the supply chain model is the combination of the capability-, activity-, and product concept. This is highlighted by Figure 10.3

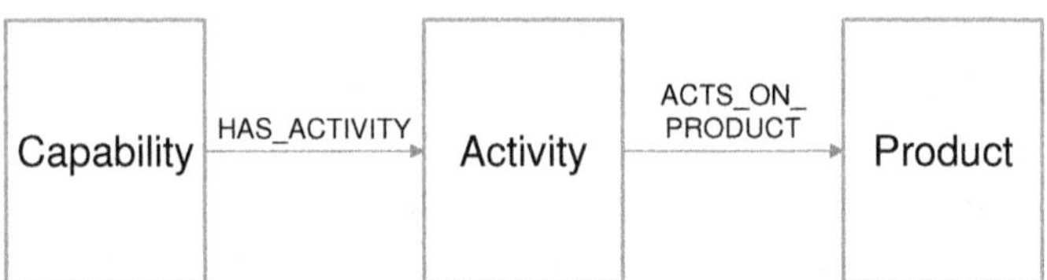

Figure 10.3: Capability-activity-product constraint.

Applied to real case supply chains this combination allows to distinguish different setups. Consider the example of the inventory capability, which is related to the storing activity. In process industries, like chemical industry or steel industry, products or input material are stored in silos. A supply chain (information) model representing this situation consists of a specific realization of the capability-activity-product combination. The inventory capability is not endowed with further properties, but with several storing activities, each of which is related to a different product. The activity concept of storing is endowed with properties like maximum capacity or inventory costs. Contrary, the inventory setup of discrete industries, like automotive or mechanical engineering, assumes the storage of products in common storehouses. Products, thus, compete for stockyard. Then, the inventory capability itself is endowed with properties like costs or capacities.

The data granularity mainly depends on the underlying supply chain planning engine and its data repository. With respect to model time-based characteristics, declared as a core characteristic of supply chain risk, we assume that the underlying supply chain consists of time-dependent activities or capabilities and we further assume that the planning tool is able to model multi-period supply chain processes.

To allow a multi-period consideration of supply chain properties, the date property *validity* is introduced. The validity property allows to model concepts whose properties are valid at distinct points in time. Water carriage for example starts in weekly intervals. Capacities can be restricted to be valid at a certain point in time. Additionally, we use this property for the resource-usage concepts to model resource allocations of a supply chain plan that is fixed up to the frozen period.

10.4 A Supply Chain Model

In this section we apply the information meta-model for supply chains to the representative master planning model introduced in Chapter 9. We introduce the supply chain model, which is instantiated by the information meta-model, by briefly explaining the main concepts, properties, and relations. The descriptions are enhanced by comprehensible visualization schemes.
Except for the concept gadget each of the afore introduced concepts were used for the supply chain model. Table 10.1 summarizes property types that have been applied for the supply chain model.

Class	Name	Unit
Costs	SELLING_PRICE	EURO
Costs	PURCHASE_PRICE	EURO
Costs	HANDLING_COSTS	EURO
Costs	FIXED_HANDLING_COSTS	EURO
Costs	TRANSPORTATION_COSTS	EURO
Costs	FIXED_TRANSPORTATION_COSTS	EURO
Costs	PRODUCTION_COSTS	EURO
Costs	FIXED_PRODUCTION_COSTS	EURO
Costs	INVENTORY_COSTS	EURO
Costs	FIXED_INVENTORY_COSTS	EURO
Costs	OBSOLESCENCE_COSTS	EURO
Date	REQUEST_DATE	TIME_PERIOD
Date	VALIDITY	TIME_PERIOD
Duration	TRANSPORT_DURATION	TIME_PERIODS

Duration	PRODUCTION_TIME	TIME_PERIODS
Location	LATITUDE	DEGREE
Location	LONGITUDE	DEGREE
Quantity	MINIMUM_HUB_CAPACITY	AMOUNT
Quantity	MAXIMUM_HUB_CAPACITY	AMOUNT
Quantity	MINIMUM_TRANSPORT_CAPACITY	AMOUNT
Quantity	MAXIMUM_TRANSPORT_CAPACITY	AMOUNT
Quantity	MINIMUM_PRODUCTION_CAPACITY	AMOUNT
Quantity	MAXIMUM_PRODUCTION_CAPACITY	AMOUNT
Quantity	PRODUCTION_CAPACITY_CONSUMPTION	AMOUNT
Quantity	MINIMUM_STORAGE_CAPACITY	AMOUNT
Quantity	MAXIMUM_STORAGE_CAPACITY	AMOUNT
Quantity	STORAGE_CAPACITY_CONSUMPTION	AMOUNT

Table 10.1: Property types deduced for the supply chain model.

Figure 10.4 shows the conceptual modeling of the transportation task. The whole transportation process is modeled by a combination of capabilities, activities, resource-usages, properties, and defining relations. Note that, the shadowed properties related to the capability of shipping represent a collapsed view. Each of this properties is implemented by defining two subsequent capabilities. The second capability is endowed with the amount and validity properties. The first represents the set or containment of all those capabilities. Similarly, the overall resource-usage concept is modeled by two subsequent concepts. The first represents the containment of all following order-specific as well as validity-specific resource-usage concepts.

Figure 10.5 represents the conceptual modeling of the production task. The representative master planning module models the production process through different machines. Machines are endowed with variable and fixed production costs as well as minimum and maximum production capacities. Contrary to a transportation process, the production time does not only depend on the resource, but also on the product that is produced by the activity. Therefore, the properties capacity consumption and production time are directly related to the activity of producing, which in turn refers to a specific product. The meta-product concept of type product is used to describe the overall amount that has to be produced at once at distinct machines. The amount property can be understood as the lot-size parameter, which equals in this case to one.

Figure 10.6 shows the conceptual modeling of the storing task. Similarly to transportation and production the inventories and their characteristics are modeled by a combination of capabilities, activities, resource-usages, properties, and relations. In contrast to those supply chain tasks, the inventory level is non-order-specific.

The supply chain information meta-model was implemented in Java as an object oriented model of the supply chain. The data repository is given as a relational database, therefore, the model builds upon an object-relational mapping. The presented realization of the meta-model is used in Chapter 11 to execute the *SimSCRF* model for a real case supply chain problem.

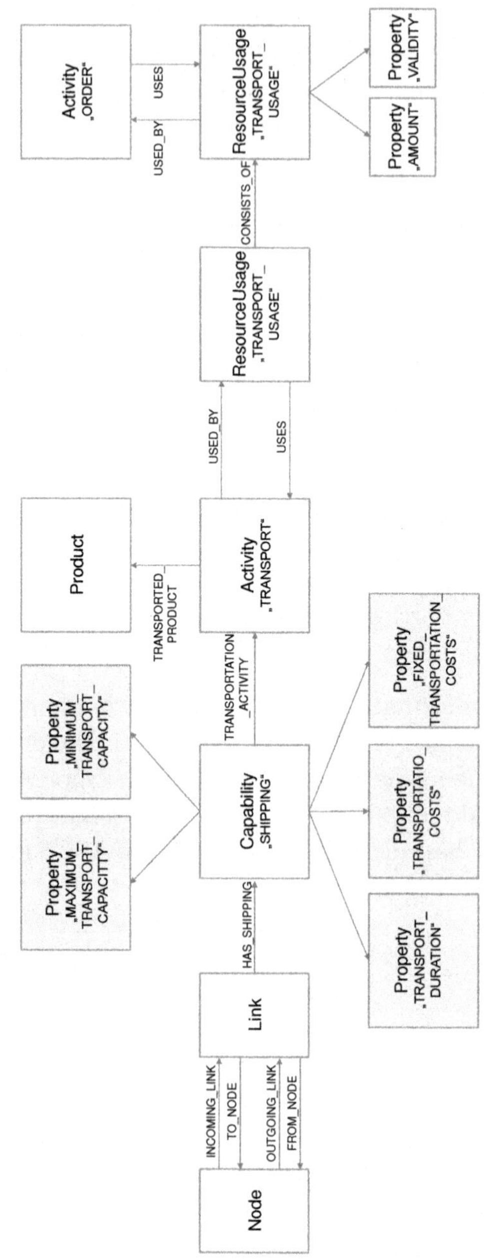

Figure 10.4: Conceptual modeling of the supply chain task transport.

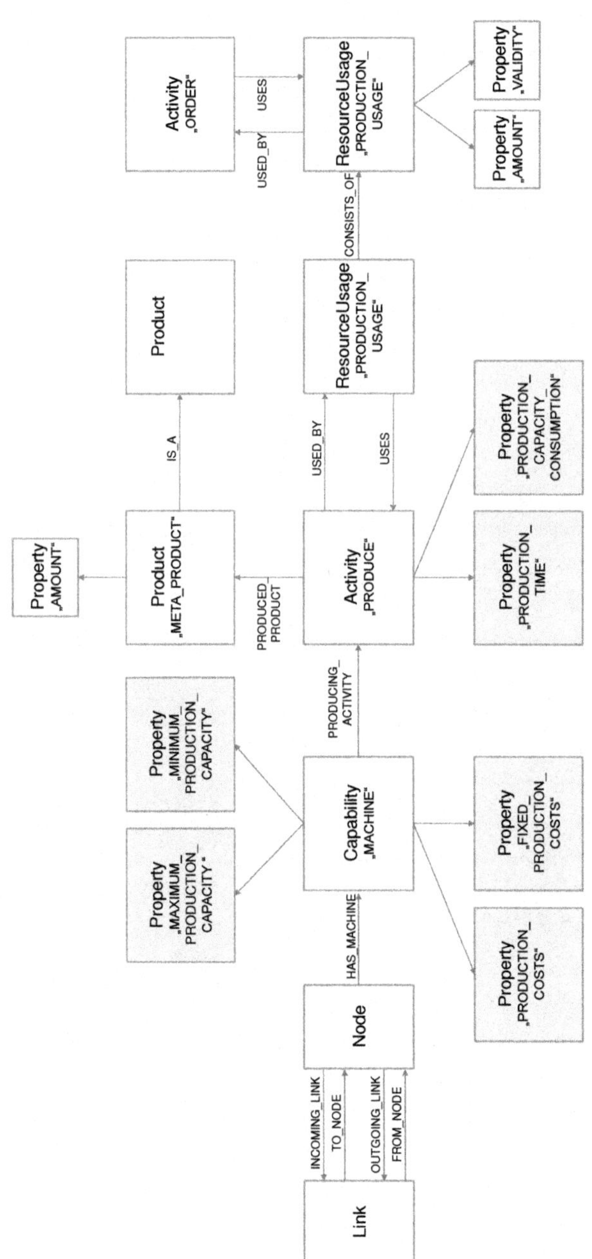

Figure 10.5: Conceptual modeling of the supply chain task production.

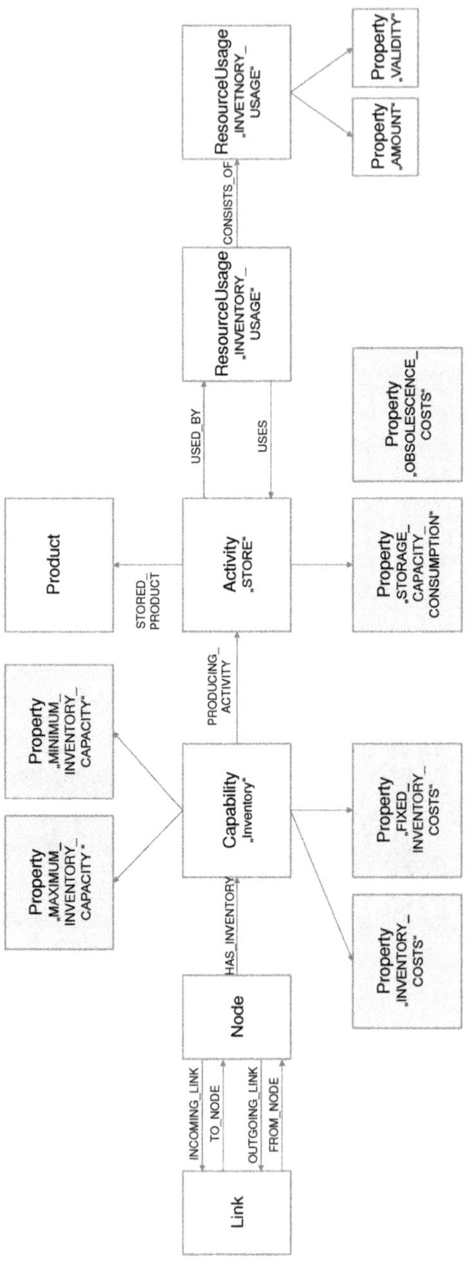

Figure 10.6: Conceptual modeling of the supply chain task storing.

11 A Real Case Evaluation of the *SimSCRF* Approach

"Es ist nicht genug, zu wissen, man muss auch anwenden. Es ist nicht genug, zu wollen, man muss auch tun."

"Knowing is not enough. We must apply. Willing is not enough. We must do."

Johann Wolfgang von Goethe

Given an economy, which is based on global division of labor, today's logistics systems – in particular production and supply networks – belong to the most complex technical systems. Tools for their planning and control are available and continuously developed further [254, 290, 291]. In view of the occurrence of minor and major disruptions that reveal the existence of supply chain risk, supply chain complexity is ever-expanding and asks for high-sophisticated planning tools. Interestingly, the aspect of risk management is scarcely considered and more or less addressed on a conceptual level [58, 149, 330]. The theoretical analysis of Chapter 4 concluded that the consideration and understanding of supply chain dynamics that result in supply chain risk is vital for the installation of selective mitigation measures.

Dependable tools that provide decision makers with the capability to quantitatively identify, assess, and control supply chain risks are still missing. Decision models for production, transportation, and supply network planning are available on the market, but these solutions do not consider risk and are predominantly deterministic. Additionally, the potential set of uncertain parameters is often explicitly limited to customer demands. Planning accuracy also in the light of supply chain risk is regarded to solely depend on demand forecasting methods, deviations of other supply chain characteristics from their nominal values is mostly neglected. Available risk analysis systems are build on strategic data models. Conclusions made in the supply chain risk analysis thus have to be re-interpreted for the supply chain planning tasks, systems, and corresponding data models.

In this chapter we present and apply the simulation-based framework (*SimSCRF*) derived in Chapter 8 for the quantitative analysis of supply chain risks. The *SimSCRF* framework offers the decision makers the opportunity to simulate future developments and to assess their influence on supply chain performance. Money, time and effort have been invested for the development, implementation, configuration, and customization of deterministic planning models, which limit the motivation of integrating new but risk-aware planning tools. Therefore, the framework provides the possibility to conduct supply chain risk analysis on the basis of a proprietary deterministic planning tool. This allows the decision maker to directly transfer conclusions derived from the analysis to the underlying planning task of the supply chain.

The chapter is organized as follows: Section 11.1 introduces the supply chain under investigation. Next, we discuss how supply chain risk has to be quantified with regard to the contemporary supply risk perception. Section 11.3 briefly recaps the motivation for the *SimSCRF* model and explains the underlying rationals. Based on the real case supply chain example, Section 11.4 presents the conduction of a set of risk analyses and evaluates their results. Finally, conclusions and a path for future research are given in the last section.

11.1 The Case

The supply chain under investigation originates from the chemical process industry and represents a typical supply chain of a major chemical company. We organize our explanation by starting to present the network structure, highlighted in Figure 11.1 and continuing with explaining the production process and product recipes.

We consider a supply chain that produces a set of products for satisfying distinct customer markets. Six production facilities are distributed among five customer regions. Each facility is able to produce the set of requested products for the assigned customer market. Internal transfers between production sites do not exist. Reactors or production lines can produce more than one product, but product changeovers result in setup times that limit the available production capacity. Since the supply chain planning is aligned for tactical horizons, setup times and changeover restrictions are not considered. To capture setup times, the overall production capacity of every reactor is instead reduced by a constant amount that represents the loss of capacity due to an average number of changeovers with average setup time. Raw materials are procured from an external main supplier and are only needed for the production of the main core pre-product. This product is shipped to other production facilities or further processed within its own place of production. Subsequent production steps following the production of this main pre-product constitute of refinement stages and do not need additional raw materials that have to be taken into account. The multi-stage production process for each requested or produced product is described by product-specific recipes. Each recipe specifies the amount of pre-product needed to complete the production step of the specified product. Prior to the customer delivery products are transfered into warehouses for intermediate storage or customer specific packaging.

The main pre-product is denoted by PP_B1 in the supply chain example. Figure 11.2 plots the recipes of the supply chain products

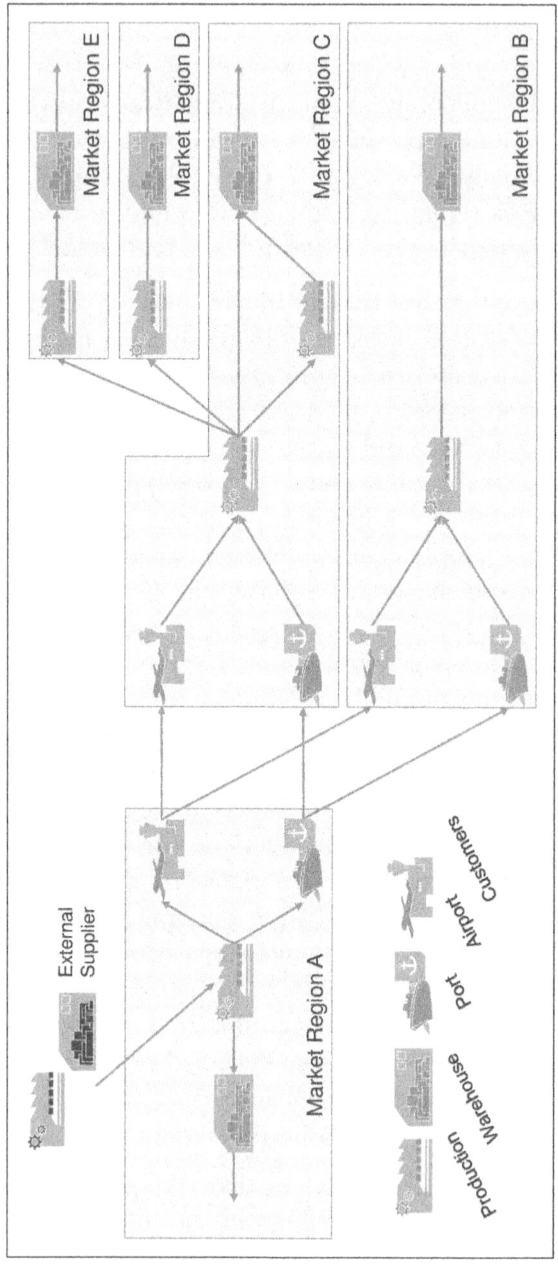

Figure 11.1: Supply chain under investigation: physical view.

on the network structure. The figure highlights whether products are produced, stored, or shipped at the related location.

Note that, pre-product PP_B1 is shipped from market region A to market region C. The subsequent production facility uses the main pre-product to produce further pre-products which in turn are used for the end-product refinement. In addition PP_B1 can be stored prior to shipment towards subsequent production facilities.

11.2 Contemporary Risk Quantification

The Risk Initiative of the World Economic Forum identifies the development of reliable supply chain risk metrics as the top priority concern, see [248], because quantification metrics especially tailored for supply chain risk are missing in literature. The majority of contemporary approaches uses deviation metrics, like variance or expected loss, and downside risk metrics, like value-at-risk or conditional-value-at-risk, to capture the extent of supply chain risk (see Chapter 5.3). Based on the supply chain example presented in the previous section, we present several aspects that reveal the boundedness of existing risk metrics intended to quantify and assess supply chain risk. Consider, for example, the change of production capacity at the facility that is located at market region A. Assuming a production shortfall of three days, we want to assess supply chain risk by the means of the most prominent quantification metrics value-at-risk and the product of probability of occurrence of a disruptive trigger and its related impact.

Starting with the latter, the probability of occurrence and the related impact of a three day production shortfall determine the level of risk. We assume that the probability of a production shortfall within the regarded time horizon equals to 0.1%. Furthermore, we consider the capacity to drop from initially 100.000 units per day to zero. In terms of effectiveness, supply chain risk would equal to $0.001 \times$

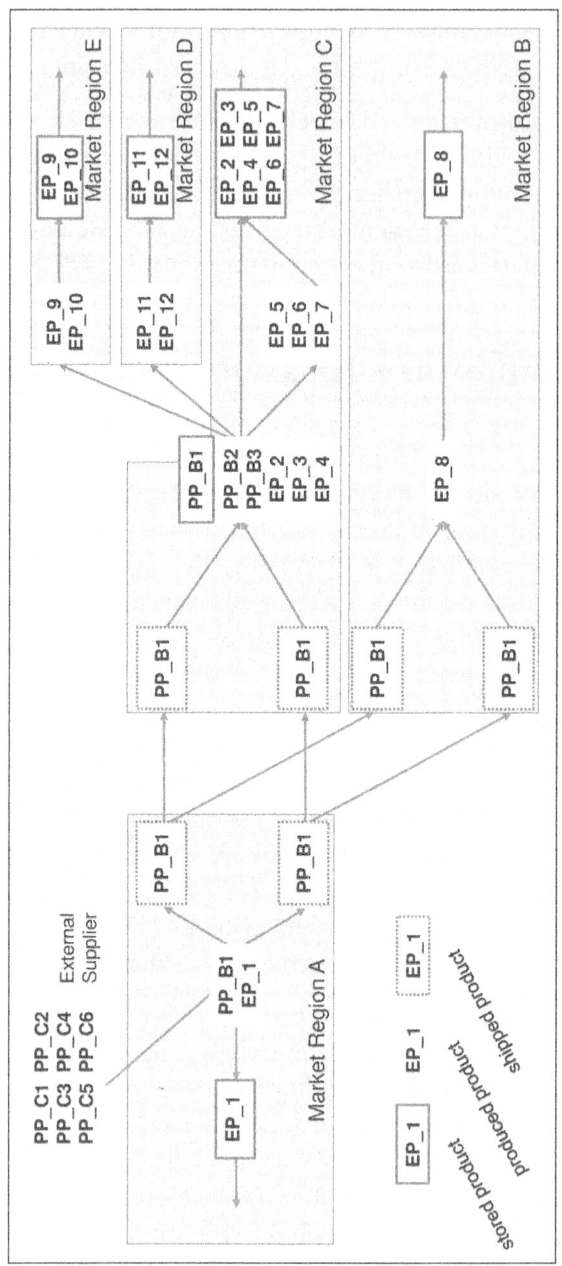

Figure 11.2: Supply chain under investigation: product view.

$100,000 = 100$ per day, thus, 300 units are potentially lost. In terms of efficiency, the unitary potential loss needs to be transfered into a monetary value. The costs of working capital are often used as an evaluation factor. Assume that the value added to the product EP_1 up to this supply chain level and location equals to $c_{i=X}^{cwc} = 120e$ per unit. Supply chain risk in terms of efficiency would equal to $300 \times 120e = 36,000e$.

Risk evaluation with the value-at-risk or conditional-value-at-risk measures is more complex. Generally, these measures can be computed in three different ways: using historical data, by analytical assessment, or with Monte-Carlo Simulation. Historical information about past production shortfalls are rare and if available this information does not predict future outcomes. Analytical assessment requires parameters that describe the shape of a probability distribution like the mean and the standard deviation. Value-at-risk determines the worst potential loss at a given confidence interval over a given time period. It is analytically calculated through: $VaR = -\mu + \alpha \times \sigma$. Assuming that the mean, μ, of additional percentaged costs equals to zero, which reflects a normal and undisrupted situation, and the standard deviation, σ, of increased percentaged costs equals to 1%. Both parameters are considered to be given and valid for monthly consideration over one year. A confidence interval of 95% of the standard normal distribution results in a z-score or number of standard deviations, α, equal to 1.645. Thus, the value-at-risk results in a value of $VaR = 0.01645$. This is the percentaged value-at-risk. Assuming monthly costs of one Million e the overall cost-related value-at-risk results in $16,448e$ per month. Similarly, the value-at-risk could be applied for evaluating supply chain risk in terms of effectiveness. It could, for example, evaluate the worst potential loss of service level.[1] In this example the value-at-risk describes the potential loss during a month, i.e. there is a 5% chance

[1] Note that, the value-at-risk level is not comparable with the measure evaluating probability of occurrence and its impact.

to lose 16,448e or more during a month. The vale-at-risk does not estimate the potential loss, when this bar is exceeded.

Generally, value-at-risk (as well as conditional-value-at-risk) is a financial, thus, monetary concept. Derived from financial management those metrics were developed to measure financial risks. With respect to supply chain risk, money is not (always) the right unit to measure potential losses. We intensively discussed the objectives of supply chains and potential losses with respect to different supply chain objectives in Chapters 3, 4, and 5. The criticism on the choice of an accurate unit of measurement coincidence with a further conclusion that can be drawn from this exemplary risk assessment. Standardized risk measures provide a local assessment, which misses to respect the overall condition of the supply chain. Assume that customers of market region A in total request 200 units of end-product EP_1 during the disrupted period. The distributing warehouse of this region stores 100 units of this product and the production facility holds again 100 units. The production shortfall can easily be compensated. The inventory levels at subsequent processes and nodes within the network are high enough to absorb a production halt and to preserve customer satisfaction. Even considered monetary, supply chain risk would not exist. The risk measures overestimated the potential loss. While the consideration of the afore described risk measures could be widened to cover the whole market region, risk assessment reaches its limits, if the whole supply chain needs to be considered.

Accordingly, supply chain risk can be underestimated by the afore described financial risk measures, whenever demand exceeds potentially existing buffers. Assume the production shortfall to last four instead of three days. The risk evaluated by the product of probability and impact equals to $4 \times 0.001 \times 100,000 \times 120e = 48,000e$. The value-at-risk does not change, but the actual loss would be quite different. The combined stock level of end-product EP_1 does not suffice to satisfy customer demand, which equals to 267 units for the four days period. Additionally, the production halt affects the supply of pre-product PP_B1 for subsequent production facilities at other markets. Assuming that their buffers could easily compensate a three days supply shortage of product PP_B1, but they fail to absorb an additional day of inventory stock-out. Consequently, they cannot produce market related end-products and customers cannot be satisfied. If market regions have to satisfy similar end-product requests like market region A and are endowed with equal inventory levels, the total backlog sums up to $67*5 = 335$ units of end-products. If end-products are sold at 150e, the overall potential loss equals to $335 * 150 = 50,250e$.

In summary, the afore described risk metrics provide mainly local assessment tailored for monetary quantification. Their calculation depends on the availability of parameters that describe the shape of a probability distribution or on the probability value of occurrence related to a specific event. Often this information is not available. Even when information is given, the risk assessment is exposed to the possibility of over- or underestimation. Following our supply chain risk definition derived in Chapter 3, the below presented approach supports decision makers in evaluating and assessing the supply chain risk in terms of its core characteristics. This approach not only seeks to operationalize supply chain risk, but also provides decision makers with reliable insights on the consequences of unexpected disruptions.

11.3 A new View on Supply Chain Risk Analysis

Some supply chains have the potential to absorb deviations within their processes from routine execution.

Example 11.1

The course of events after the eruption of the Icelandic volcano Eyjafjallajökull reveals that different supply chains although exposed to similar market conditions were affected quite differently from missing production materials. BMW for instance suffered from shortages of electronic packages and had halt production in three major German car assembly plants. Missing air-freight transportation capacities for gears from Germany to the United States caused the slowing down of production in one major US car assembly plant, too. On the other side Daimler and Ford suffered from shortages too, but the impact on their logistic processes was not serious for production.

Whenever we think of supply chain risk, we have in mind events, like labor strikes, extreme weather conditions, volcanic eruptions, earthquakes, piracy attacks, oil prices and exchange rate volatilities. The ash-cloud example reveals that supply chain risk does not solely depend on the occurrence of these so-called triggering events, but additionally on the supply network itself. Our extensive literature review identified additional core characteristics that all together determine the level of supply chain risk (see Chapter 3). Supply chain risk is defined as a functional relationship that depends on the interaction between potential triggers, the constitution of the underlying supply chain, and the degree of target achievement, which is assumed to be influenced by the risk attitude of the decision maker (see Chapters 3 and 8). In order to identify and assess risk these core characteristics need to be modeled. For a detailed description of the modeling of supply chain risk's core characteristic, we refer to Chapter 8.

The main assumptions that underlie the *SimSCRF* approach presented in Chapter 8 are summarized in the following: Typically, disruptive triggers have a direct or indirect influence on supply networks. The impact is visible in changes of supply chain factors that describe supply chain processes. A transportation process between two production plants, for instance, can be defined through supply chain factors like transportation time, transportation capacity, and transportation costs. Due to disruptive events factor values may change. Consider again the example of the eruption of the Icelandic volcano Eyjafjallajökull, whose ash emission led to an European no-fly zone. The immediate impact of this event led to a change of the transportation process for air-delivered products. In terms of transportation capacity the no-fly zone can be expressed by a capacity decrease down to zero. In terms of transportation lead time the impact can be depicted as an increase of three days. Whether these changes result in a deteriorated performance level depends on the dynamics that drive supply chain processes. The course of such events affect the constitution and consequently the target performance level of the underlying supply chain. Supply chain master planning uses supply chain factors as an input and determines the resulting optimal resource allocation. Both the constitution and the target performance is depicted by a supply chain planning run. Figure 8.2 visualizes the relation between risk core characteristics and the modeling approach used in our approach to operationalize supply chain risk.

The simulation-based approach presented in this chapter manipulates the input data for supply chain master planning to represent disruptive triggers and evaluates planning results as images of supply chain's constitutions. By evaluating the achieved performance level with the individual risk attitude of the decision maker, supply chain risk can be identified. Although this approach could be used for *what-if* analysis, i.e. specifying deviations for factor values in different scenarios and evaluating outcomes, we employ an approach denoted in literature as simulation optimization [97, 308], see Section 6.3. Simulation optimization seeks to reach inputs within a predefined optimality gap that result in a predefined output. For the developed approach this methodology allows to identify those scenarios that lead to a deterioration of supply chain performance whose target value is specified by the decision maker. Figure 8.5 shows the main step of out simulation-based approach.

Central to our approach is the usage of a supply chain master planning tool. Although we already made experiments with proprietary planning tools, the experiments conducted in this chapter are based on formulations and descriptions of Alicke [9], Stadtler and Kilger [291], and Stadtler [290], which we combined, adapted, and developed further to derive a formulation of a representative master planning model, see Chapter 9.

11.4 Supply Chain Risk Analysis

In this section we present how the *SimSCRF* conducts supply chain risk analysis. First, we explain in more detail the work flow of the simulation-based approach with special focus on the input needed from the user. Next, a screening analysis is performed on the basis of the real case supply chain presented in Section 11.1. Similarly, the last paragraph of this section explains the execution of a risk-line analysis and discusses its results with respect to the underlying supply chain.

11.4.1 Work Flow

Analyzing supply chain risk with the *SimSCRF* approach requires some preliminary work. First, the supply chain data stored within the master planning repository has to be modeled in terms of concepts, properties, and relations as defined in the supply chain information meta-model presented in Chapter 10. The resulting supply chain model provides the reference to the supply chain under investigation and describes different supply chain tasks and their related processes. The *SimSCRF* model seeks to systematically modify supply chain factors, which specify supply chain processes. Therefore, the decision makers have to define different supply chain factors with the vocabulary given by the supply chain information meta-model. Accordingly, they have to provide a definition of the (set of) performance indicator(s), whose deterioration is regarded as critical.

Having set up the *SimSCRF* model, the users have to prepare the analysis run. A supply chain consists of a great number of supply chain processes and consequently the number of related supply chain factors, which defines these processes, is large. Additionally, some supply chain factors can be assumed to be certain, i.e. their development of the planning horizon is deterministic. At the preparation step the decision makers, therefore, can specify, which supply chain factors should be regarded as uncertain within the analysis run. In order to evaluate the effect of each factor the response of the planning engine has to be evaluated in terms of a single target performance indicator. Thus, besides supply chain factor specification, the decision makers have to declare which performance indicator is used as response function. Along with the specification of supply chain factors comes the valuation of the frozen horizon. Master planning modules generally offer the possibility to fix the decisions of precedent planning runs by indicating a frozen horizon. Then planning decisions of the previous run (for the frozen horizon) cannot be changed in subsequent planning runs. We exploit this characteristic for the *SimSCRF* approach as explained next. When manipulating the values of supply chain factors the input data for the supply chain planning module is changed as well. The master planning tool, however, follows a deterministic approach. If the decision makers want to analyze a capacity shortfall at the middle of the planning horizon, which is certainly not known at the beginning, production decision prior to the shortfall occurrence have to remain constant. The frozen horizon refers to the point in time, when information about the disruption emerges. A re-planning, which adjusts to new supply chain factor values, is only possible after the emergence of disruption information.

The relationship between frozen horizon, the emergence of disruption information, and modifications of supply chain factors are visualized in Figure 11.3. It is possible that a disruption, expressed as an unexpected factor change, has already started before supply chain decision makers are informed. Disruptions occur unexpectedly like earthquakes or short circuits at production facilities, but sometimes there is some evidence prior to the beginning like announcements of labor strikes or weather reports. Nevertheless, the *SimSCRF* approach is used as a method to simulate disruptions before they occur and assess their influence on the overall supply chain performance. Therefore, we emphasize that it is justifiable that disruptions are known prior to their entrance within the *SimSCRF* environment.

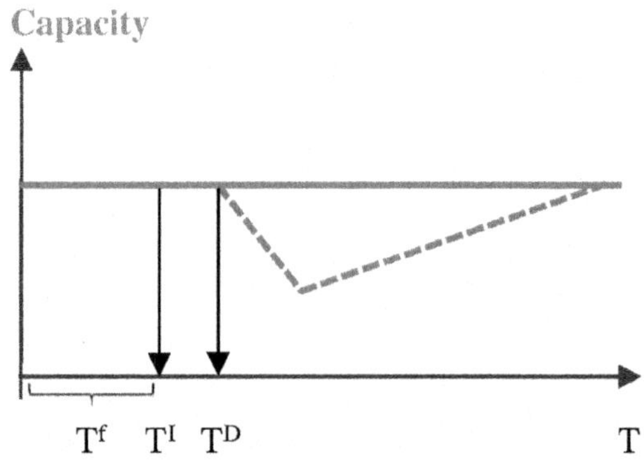

Figure 11.3: Relationship between frozen horizon, T^f, the emergence of disruption information, T^I, and the start of modifications, T^D, of supply chain factors (dashed line).

Before the risk analysis starts with planning and evaluating different scenarios, an initial planning is executed on the reference of the underlying supply chain, namely the supply chain model. Afterwards, planning results, which are covered by the frozen horizon, are added to the related resource usage concepts of the supply chain model and considered as initial values for the scenario-wise planning.

Moreover, the *SimSCRF* framework offers three modes of analysis.

The first mode is designated for the analysis of one single scenario. Although we emphasize that reliable risk assessment calls for a systematic analysis of a set of scenarios, the *SimSCRF* offers this mode, because it provides an in-depth analysis of the results of a single scenario. We denote this mode as *single-scenario mode (SSM)*. A visualization of the planning results is offered for the SSM analysis mode. It provides a view on the supply chain that is enhanced with the possibility to choose a base data or performance indicator report, see Figure 11.4 and Figure 11.5.

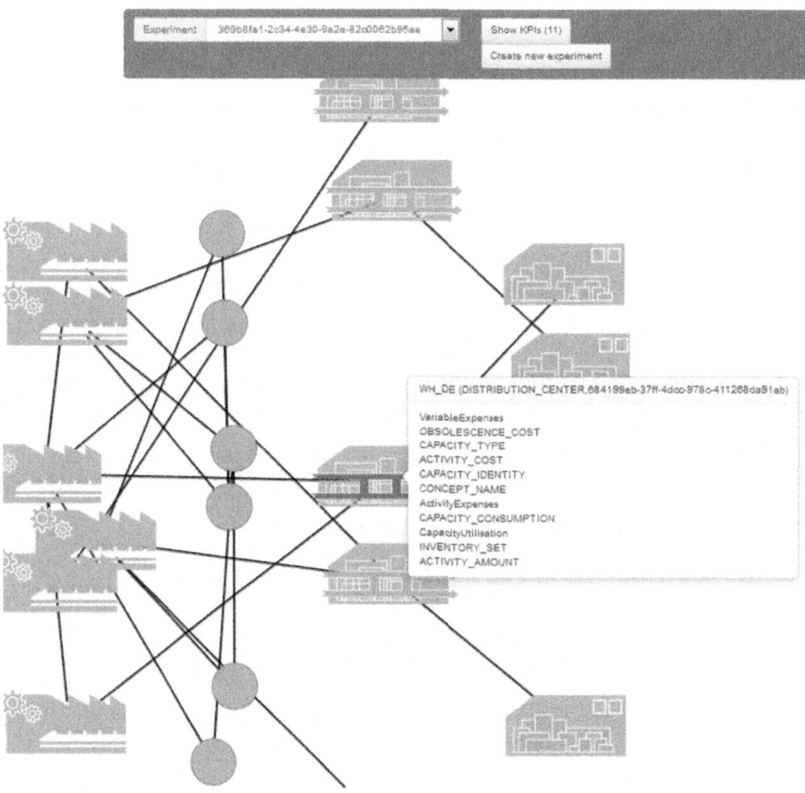

Figure 11.4: Planning reports for the reference supply chain and a single-scenario supply chain: network view.

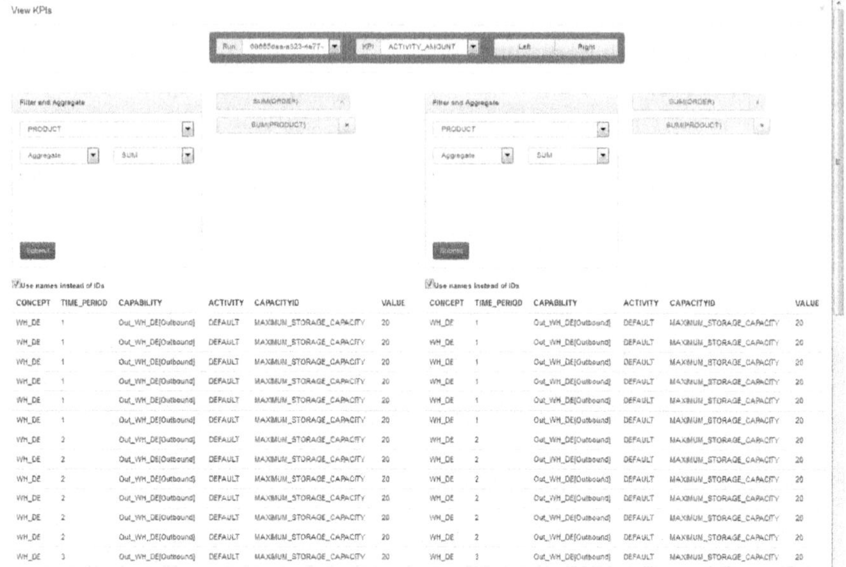

Figure 11.5: Planning reports for the reference supply chain and a single-scenario supply chain: KPI view.

The second mode refers to the effect analysis which is conducted by screening designs. This mode is denoted as *screening-analysis mode (SAM)*. Besides the mode of analysis, the user can specify the screening design used for the analysis. The third mode covers the identification and quantification of the risk line and is consequently denoted as *risk-line-analysis mode (RLAM)*. For the risk-line analysis the user has to additionally commit information about the acceptable level of supply chain performance as well as on the granularity of the risk-line approximation. The preparation step is concluded by starting the execution of the analysis. The analysis step is a fully automated procedure and does not need any interaction with the user.

The necessary user input aligned to the overall work flow described above is depicted in Figure 11.7. Over the next paragraphs we explain the definition of supply chain factors and performance indicators as well as the choice of analysis mode in more detail. In the following paragraphs we describe in more detail the definition of supply chain factors and performance indicators. The formulations of factors and indicators are governed by the vocabulary used to define the supply chain (information) model. Figure 11.6 supports in understanding the following explanations. For the sake of readability we replicate this figure here.

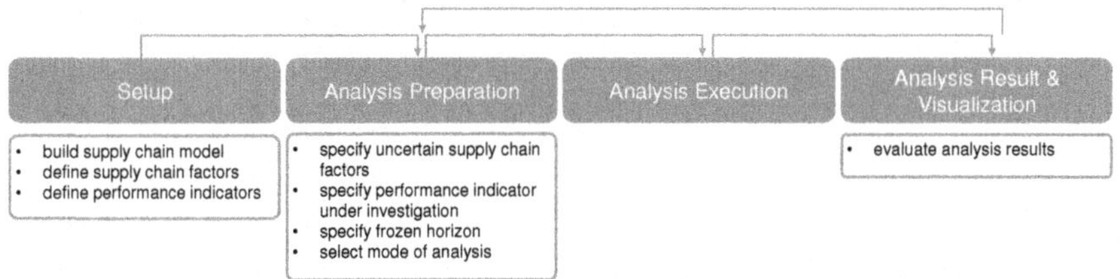

Figure 11.7: User input aligned to the work flow of the *SimSCRF* model.

Definition of Supply Chain Factors

Prior to user selection, supply chain factors have to be defined. By the means of the vocabulary of the supply chain meta-model properties are used to define commonly named supply chain factors, such as lead time, production and transportation capacity, as well as various cost factors. Within the definition process the level of granularity related to supply chain factors plays an important aspect. With respect to the representative master planning model a production process, for example, is specified by the combination of machine, product, and time period. Each combination is a potential representative for a single supply chain factor, which should be investigated. The level of granularity related to supply chain factors strongly depends on the underlying master planning tool and the derived supply chain model. However, sometimes users may not want to define highly granular supply chain factors, but rather aggregated overall supply

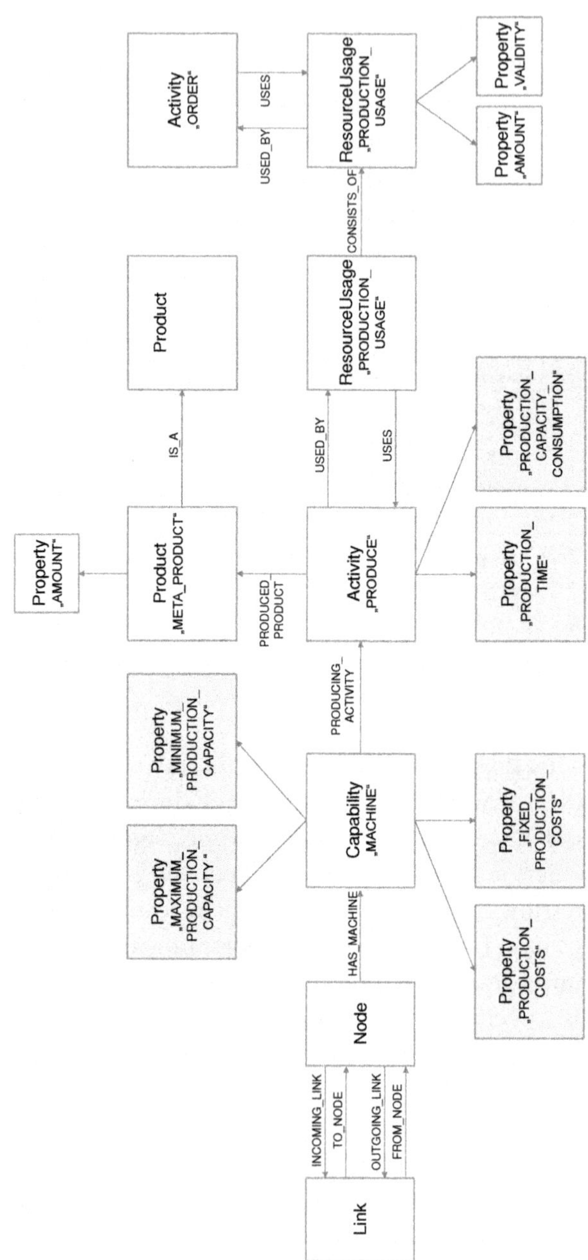

Figure 11.6: Conceptual modeling of the supply chain task production (replicate).

chain factors. The production capacity within a specific country, for example, might be of more interest than the production capacity at a specific machine. The *SimSCRF* approach, therefore, allows to filter for specific aspects of the accessed properties and it, additionally, allows to specify how values should be shared among aggregated factors.

Figure 11.8 shows a script template for the supply chain factor maximum production capacity. Line 4 of the factor definition template indicates, how the factor values are passed to each property. In this case the aggregation type "single" is set, which means that each property is set to the same value determined during scenario generation. Lines embraced by "{{ }}" indicate optional attributes, i.e. the users can filter for the country, but they do not have to. Parameters embraced by "%" have to be set by the user during the preparation step. The users do not only label the supply chain factor by a representative name, but more important they specify minimum and maximum values for the supply chain factor. The screening analysis uses these values as representatives of plus and minus signs of the experimental design. The risk-line analysis applies these values as natural limits related to the factors under investigation. Lines 6 to 10 define the set of capabilities that refer to a production capability. Lines 12 to 14 then depict the result set, i.e. the set of property values whose level is up for analysis. This set can be further restricted to properties of a user-specified time period or set of time periods.

```
name := {{%%NAME%%}}
min := {{%%MIN%%}}
max := {{%%MAX%%}}
aggregationType := SINGLE

prodMaxCapa := SELECT NODE
  ->CAPABILITY["HAS_MACHINE"]
  ->CAPABILITY["HAS_MAXIMUM_CAPACITY"]
  ->CAPABILITY["CONSISTS_OF"]
{{COUNTRY|WHERE NODE.LOCATION["COUNTRY"].VALUE = "%%
    COUNTRY%%"}}

result := SELECT CAPABILITY.QUANTITY["AMOUNT"] WHERE
    CAPABILITY IN prodMaxCapa
{{TIME_PERIOD|WHERE CAPABILITY.DATE["VALIDITY"].VALUE = "
    %%TIME_PERIOD%%"}}
{{TIME_PERIODS|WHERE CAPABILITY.DATE["VALIDITY"].VALUE IN
     %%TIME_PERIODS%%}}
```

Figure 11.8: Factor template for supply chain factor maximum production capacity.

These templates are accessed during the preparation step, when the user specifies which of the overall available supply chain factors should be regarded as uncertain.

Definition of Performance Indicators

As the master planning module is a black box, decision makers do not completely know the terms included in the objective function, nor do results of the master planning certainly provide the desired performance indicators. Therefore, the *SimSCRF* framework offers the possibility to define individual and user-specific performance indicators.

Defining a set of performance indicators, that have been determined to evaluate supply chain risk in terms of efficiency or effectiveness, is a two-step procedure. First, planning results are accessed and stored within *base data* objects. Given the vocabulary of the supply chain meta-model, the needed information is fetched from the resource-usage concepts and encapsulated in properly defined and named sets. Typically, performance indicators do not only depend on plain planning results, but also on planning input. The performance indicator logistics costs, for example, is determined by the product between produced, stored, and transported amount of products within the network and the costs related to each supply chain task. While the former is determined through the planning run, the latter is given as a property within the supply chain model. Figure 11.9 presents a script that defines the planned amount related to each activity. More precisely, the script shows an extract that refers to the amount produced at each machine within the supply network.

The first row defines the name of base data, which is needed for subsequent steps of the performance indicator definition. The second row defines the primary key that specifies the data points of highest granularity for each activity. In the third line a counter is created, which serves as an identifier for each entry. The subsequent lines basically represent the path from each node to the resource-usage concept of the supply chain activity of producing. The conceptual modeling of the production task is given in Figure 11.6 and can be used as a guideline for defining comparable base data related to the producing activity. Besides the amount of produced products, the base data script additionally contains activity amounts referring to transport, inventory, and handling of products.
The calculation of logistics costs requires information about the process related costs. Figure 11.10 shows the defining script of the base data related to the activity costs. Within the underlying supply chain model costs are defined as properties of the capability concepts as can be seen from Figure 11.6.

After having defined the access to the result and input data, the performance indicator can be defined. Figure 11.11 contains the definition of the performance indicator activity expenses. The definition is given in terms of highest granularity, i.e. expenses are calculated

```
PUT ''RESULT'' ''NAME'' ''ACTIVITY_AMOUNT''
PUT ''RESULT'' ''COLUMNS'' ''CONCEPT|ORDER|PRODUCT|
    TIME_PERIOD|CAPABILITY|ACTIVITY|CAPACITYID|VALUE''
CREATECOUNTER ''ROW''
FORCONCEPTS NODE
  PUT ''TMP'' ''NODE'' ''%CONCEPTUUID%''
  FORRELATIONS ''HAS_MACHINE'' CAPABILITY
    PUT ''TMP'' ''MACHINE'' ''%RELATEDCONCEPTUUID%''
    FORSUBTREE ''HAS_MAXIMUM_CAPACITY'' ''
        MAXIMUM_CAPACITY'' ''CAPACITY''
      GETCONCEPTATTRIBUTE ''CONCEPTUUID''
      PUT ''CAPA_TMP'' ''%PROPERTYVALUE[VALIDITY]%'' ''%
          POPSTACK%''
    FORRELATIONS ''HAS_PRODUCING_ACTIVITY'' ACTIVITY
      PUT ''TMP'' ''ACTIVITY'' ''%RELATEDCONCEPTUUID%''
      GETRELATEDCONCEPT ''PRODUCED_PRODUCT''
      GETRELATEDCONCEPT ''IS_A'' ''RELATEDCONCEPTUUID''
      PUT ''TMP'' ''PRODUCT'' ''%POPSTACK%''
      POP
      FORRELATIONS ''USED_BY'' RESOURCEUSAGE
        FORRELATIONS ''CONSISTS_OF'' RESOURCEUSAGE
          GET ''TMP'' ''NODE''
          PUT ''CONCEPT'' ''%CTR:ROW%'' ''%POPSTACK%''
          GETRELATEDCONCEPT ''USED_BY'' ''
              RELATEDCONCEPTUUID''
          PUT ''ORDER'' ''%CTR:ROW%'' ''%POPSTACK%''
          GET ''TMP'' ''PRODUCT''
          PUT ''PRODUCT'' ''%CTR:ROW%'' ''%POPSTACK%''
          GETPROPERTY ''VALIDITY'' ''PROPERTYVALUE''
          GET ''CAPA_TMP'' ''%TOPOFSTACK%''
          PUT ''CAPACITYID'' ''%CTR:ROW%'' ''%POPSTACK%''
          PUT ''TIME_PERIOD'' ''%CTR:ROW%'' ''%POPSTACK%'
              '
          GET ''TMP'' ''MACHINE''
          PUT ''CAPABILITY'' ''%CTR:ROW%'' ''%POPSTACK%''
          GET ''TMP'' ''ACTIVITY''
          PUT ''ACTIVITY'' ''%CTR:ROW%'' ''%POPSTACK%''
          GETPROPERTY ''AMOUNT'' ''PROPERTYVALUE''
          PUT ''VALUE'' ''%CTR:ROW%'' ''%POPSTACK%''
          INCREASECOUNTER ''ROW''
```

Figure 11.9: Extract of the definition script for base data activity amount.

for each concept (link or node), for each order, for each product, for

```
PUT ''RESULT'' ''NAME'' ''ACTIVITY_COST''
PUT ''RESULT'' ''COLUMNS'' ''CONCEPT|PRODUCT|TIME_PERIOD|
    CAPABILITY|ACTIVITY|VALUE''
CREATECOUNTER ''ROW''
FORCONCEPTS NODE
  PUT ''TMP'' ''NODE'' ''%CONCEPTUUID%''
  FORRELATIONS ''HAS_MACHINE'' CAPABILITY
    PUT ''TMP'' ''MACHINE'' ''%RELATEDCONCEPTUUID%''
    FORSUBTREE ''HAS_PRODUCTION_COSTS'' ''
        PRODUCTION_COSTS'' ''COSTS''
      PUT ''COST_TMP'' ''%PROPERTYVALUE[VALIDITY]%'' ''%
          PROPERTYVALUE[AMOUNT]%''
    FORRELATIONS ''HAS_PRODUCING_ACTIVITY'' ACTIVITY
      PUT ''TMP'' ''ACTIVITY'' ''%RELATEDCONCEPTUUID%''
      GETRELATEDCONCEPT ''PRODUCED_PRODUCT''
      GETRELATEDCONCEPT ''IS_A'' ''RELATEDCONCEPTUUID''
      PUT ''TMP'' ''PRODUCT'' ''%POPSTACK%''
      FORMAP ''COST_TMP''
        GET ''TMP'' ''NODE''
        PUT ''CONCEPT'' ''%CTR:ROW%'' ''%POPSTACK%''
        GET ''TMP'' ''PRODUCT''
        PUT ''PRODUCT'' ''%CTR:ROW%'' ''%POPSTACK%''
        PUT ''TIME_PERIOD'' ''%CTR:ROW%'' ''%KEY%''
        GET ''TMP'' ''MACHINE''
        PUT ''CAPABILITY'' ''%CTR:ROW%'' ''%POPSTACK%''
        GET ''TMP'' ''ACTIVITY''
        PUT ''ACTIVITY'' ''%CTR:ROW%'' ''%POPSTACK%''
        PUT ''VALUE'' ''%CTR:ROW%'' ''%VALUE%''
        INCREASECOUNTER ''ROW''
```

Figure 11.10: Extract of the definition script for base data activity costs.

each time period for each capability and activity. Nevertheless, the *SimSCRF* offers the users the possibility to aggregate performance indicators or restrict the consideration to a single supply chain task.

```
#define Columns (CONCEPT, ORDER, PRODUCT, TIME_PERIOD,
    CAPABILITY, ACTIVITY, VALUE);
#define Set X from BaseData(ACTIVITY_AMOUNT, CONCEPT,
    ORDER, PRODUCT, TIME_PERIOD, CAPABILITY, ACTIVITY);

ActivityExpenses((con, ord, pro, t, capab, act) in X) =
        ACTIVITY_AMOUNT(SUM:VALUE,
          CONCEPT=con,
          ORDER=ord,
          PRODUCT=pro,
          TIME_PERIOD=t,
          CAPABILITY=capab,
          ACTIVITY=act)
        * ACTIVITY_COST(VALUE,
          CONCEPT=con,
          PRODUCT=pro,
          TIME_PERIOD=t,
          CAPABILITY=capab,
          ACTIVITY=act);
```

Figure 11.11: Definition script for the performance indicator activity expenses.

11.4.2 Effect Analysis

Factorial and fractional factorial designs where all factors have two levels are widely used at the beginning of experimental analysis with the purpose to screen all factors for their significance. Many factors need to be investigated and it can be assumed that only a small number of factors is really important for the response of the underlying system. The significant factors are usually analyzed in more depth in subsequent experiments that operate on more comprehensive approaches such as those of response surface methodology, as it is explained in the next paragraph.

Designs of the 2^{k-p} family belong to the most frequently used screening designs. However, the number of runs of these designs is always a power of 2 and up to $n-1$ factors can be analyzed in n runs in a saturated design. Other screening designs such as those based on frequency domain, sequential bifurcation or supersaturated designs seem not appropriate for the analysis of supply chain networks. Within this thesis we implemented general 2^k, 2^{k-p}, and Plackett-Burman designs. For the subsequent analysis we apply a 2^4 design.

Inventory levels affect different risk objectives in terms of both efficiency as well as effectiveness. Endowing the underlying supply chain network with appropriate inventory levels is a crucial task, especially when production and procurement are time consuming and when costs of working capital are large. The underlying supply network is endowed with a central product PP_B1, which is used as an input in all recipes. Additionally, the central facility at market region C delivers pre-products, like PP_B1, to the production facilities in market region E, D, and C, respectively. Thus, the storage of this pre-product is crucial for subsequent production and transportation steps. Assume, that market region E is faced with large customer demands, which makes it particularly dependent on appropriate inventory levels. To decouple production from the central pre-product, the storage of highly-requested products seems reasonable. In the following we, therefore, conduct a risk analysis with four inventory related factors: PP_B1 at the inbound inventory at production facility of market region E (Factor A), EP_9 in the outbound inventory of the same facility (Factor B), EP_9 at the warehouse of market region E (Factor C), and PP_B1 at the central facility in market region C (Factor D). The factor levels of the product-inventory combinations are assumed to have zero minimum values and equal maximum values. The performance to be evaluated are overall logistics costs.

Note that, due to the large number of parameters the presentation of all input parameters and their related values is beyond the scope of this chapter. Similarly, the examination of numerous performance indicators exceeds the limit of the intended contribution of this thesis. A visualization of input parameters, performance indicators, along with the results of the analysis are presented at the following weblink: http://dol.ior.kit.edu/SimSCRF.php.

For the purpose of illustration we briefly explain the main setup and the results of the risk analysis. The scenario generation provides a design matrix comparable to the design matrix presented in Table 7.1 and is given in Table 11.1 along with the responses, i.e. logistics costs, of each scenario run. Table 11.2 shows the results of the risk analysis.

	Factor					
Run number	A	B	C	D	Run Label	Logistics Costs
1	-	-	-	-	(1)	34860
2	+	-	-	-	*a*	34788
3	-	+	-	-	*b*	34784
4	+	+	-	-	*ab*	34788
5	-	-	+	-	*d*	34860
6	+	-	+	-	*ac*	34788
7	-	+	+	-	*bc*	34860
8	+	+	+	-	*abc*	34788
9	-	-	-	+	*d*	34973
10	+	-	-	+	*ad*	35006
11	-	+	-	+	*bd*	34973
12	+	+	-	+	*abd*	35006
13	-	-	+	+	*cd*	34973
14	+	-	+	+	*acd*	35006
15	-	+	+	+	*bcd*	34973
16	+	+	+	+	*abcd*	35006

Table 11.1: Experimental design matrices for the 2^4 factorial screening analysis.

According to these results the main effect of factor D, i.e. the outbound inventory level of product PP_B1 at the central production facility of market region C, seems to have a large impact on overall logistics costs. The fact that all these inventories are in a line of subsequent facilities that aim to deliver a specific end-product, thus they are not distributed over the network to serve distinct markets,

Model Term	Effect Estimate	Sum of Squares	Percent Contribution
A	-10	400	0.3%
B	-9.5	361	0.3%
AB	9.5	361	0.3%
C	9.5	361	0.3%
AC	-9.5	361	0.3%
BC	9.5	361	0.3%
ABC	-9.5	361	0.3%
D	175	122500	91.0%
AD	43	7396	5.5%
BD	9.5	361	0.3%
ABD	-9.5	361	0.3%
CD	-9.5	361	0.3%
ACD	9.5	361	0.3%
BCD	-9.5	361	0.3%
$ABCD$	9.5	361	0.3%

Table 11.2: Results of the 2^4 factorial screening analysis.

reinforces the results of the screening risk analysis: As expected the supply with PP_B1 is of prime importance.

11.4.3 Risk Line Identification

In the following we describe a sequential procedure that seeks to approach the risk line, i.e. identify those factor value combinations that result in a deterioration of the acceptable level of supply chain performance, $aSCP_D$. The major assumption of this approach is the monotony of the response function. If a factor value increases then the response value has to increase, too. If a factor level, a, leads to a supply chain performance, which is smaller than the acceptable level of performance, $SCP < aSCP_D$, then every other value smaller then a results in a supply chain performance smaller than the acceptable level, too. Modification of factor value combinations evoke the same implication. Similarly, level combinations that result in a supply chain performance greater than the acceptable performance level dominate those combinations with higher values.

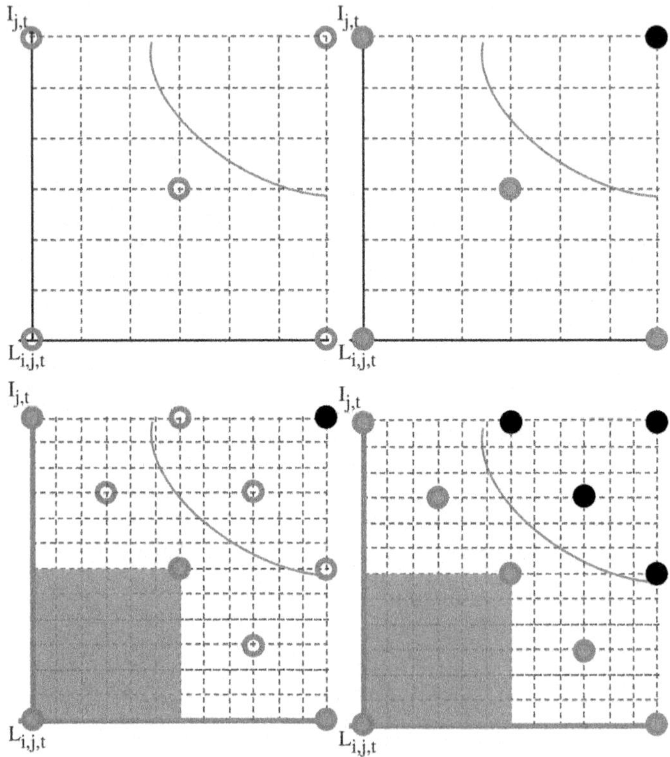

Figure 11.12: Visualization of risk line quantification (A).

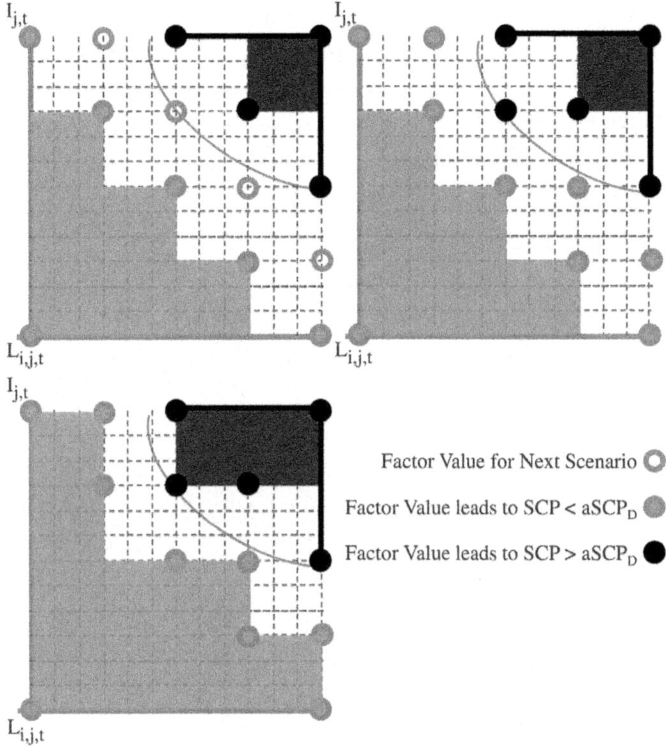

Figure 11.13: Visualization of risk line quantification (B).

The sequential approach splits the overall factor space in equal subspaces and evaluates the response of these factor value combinations with respect to the acceptable level of supply chain performance. Whenever the analyzed level combination results in a supply chain performance smaller than the acceptable performance, the dominated space of factor combinations smaller than the initial one, is not taken into account for the generation of subsequent scenarios. Figures 11.12 to 11.13 visualize the scenario generation and evaluation procedure for two factors in accordance to the description in Chapter 8. The target supply chain performance indicator is assumed to be the service level. While the left side of each figure represents the scenario generation step, the right side shows the evaluation step. Open circles present scenarios that are planned and evaluated during the next experiment. Closed green circles indicate planned and analyzed scenarios, whose level combination leads to a performance smaller than the acceptable performance, $SCP < aSCP_D$. Orange closed circles represent level combinations that lead to a performance level higher than the acceptable performance, $SCP > aSCP_D$, respectively.

The screening risk analysis indicates that Factor D, i.e. the outbound inventory level of product PP_B1, has a large effect on overall logistics costs. With a minor effect, but however still noticeable is the impact of factor A, i.e. inventory level of PP_B1 at the inbound inventory at production facility of market region E. We conducted the afore described risk-line analysis on both factors with a target overall logistics costs of 3500e. Figure 11.14 presents the resulting risk line for factor A and D.

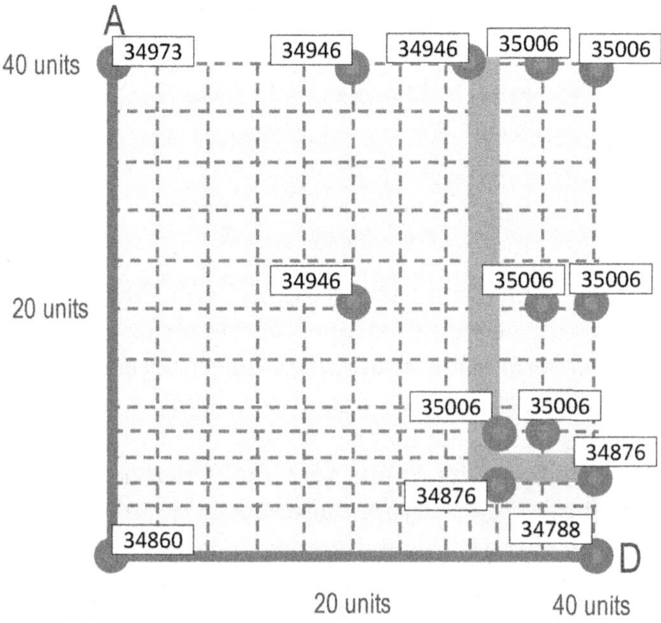

Figure 11.14: Risk line for factor A and D

The risk line shows areas, in which risk materializes and areas where it does not. Whenever the levels of the two inventories is at a point above the risk line, risk would materialize, because these points lead to logistic costs higher than 35000*e*. Whenever the inventory buffer of the outbound inventory of product PP_B1 exceeds 30 units, this can only be compensated by decreasing the inbound inventory of product PP_B1 down to 6 units. The identification of the risk line, thus, is relevant for logistical insights especially when tailored for mitigation options.

11.5 Conclusions and Outlook

The main contribution of this chapter is given by the presentation of a new simulation-based approach for supply chain risk analysis. It is based on the assumptions that disruptions have an immediate impact on supply chain processes and that the impact can be interpreted by modifications of supply chain factor values.

The *SimSCRF* framework has three objectives: First, the framework provides network visualization and report presentation of selected base data and performance indicators, which both improve decision makers comprehension of the underlying supply network. A single-scenario analysis mode enables the decision maker to define a specific scenario and compare its results with the underlying reference plan. Next, it supports in identifying those supply chain factors that have an influence on the user-defined supply chain performance. Third, it is endowed with an algorithmic sequential procedure that is based on principles of response surface approximation. The algorithm seeks to systematically identify those factor values that yield to a deterioration of the user-defined target level of supply chain performance.

Three levels of evaluation have to be considered for the *SimSCRF* approach:

- feasibility & re-usability,
- target achievement, and
- implementability.

First, from a technical point of view the framework offers the possibility to conduct scenario-wise planning on top of a master planning model. The implementation of an additional layer serving as a knowledge and information processor supports the definition of a supply chain (information) model as well as related supply chain processes and factors. Additionally, the *SimSCRF* model supports a systematic scenario generation and evaluation. As the execution of several analysis runs is possible, we declare the approach to be feasible. Still, a lot of work has to be put into the development of user-friendly visualization as well as simplified user input for factor, indicator, and scenario-generation definition. Besides improvement for user handling, the main concept has to be evaluated with different supply chain planning tools.

Second, the main motivation for the development of the *SimSCRF* framework was the need for enabling quantitative supply chain risk analysis. Although the afore described analysis does not imply a large number of supply chain factors, the real case evaluation nevertheless demonstrates that the approach leads to plausible and interesting results. Conclusions, which can be drawn form the *SimSCRF* analysis, have the potential to outperform commonly applied supply chain risk measures. Future work should concentrate on the investigation of larger instances, the development of risk-line identification algorithms tailored for supply chain risk, and systematic recommendations for the implementation of mitigation options.

Finally, a master planning is used as it encompasses the planning of all three logistical tasks: procurement, production and distribution. The results of the master planning provide a good view on the constitution of the underlying supply chain. Many module vendors boost their APS for a seamless integration of business functions [290]. However, information for input factor values of master planning are sometimes inconsistent, incorrect or missing (instead default values are used for planning), which make a direct transfer to physical supply chain processes difficult. Additionally, prior to a seamless integration, master planning results need to be validated by operational planning modules such as production, transportation, or distribution. Nevertheless, the *SimSCRF* approach is able to operationalize supply chain risk and offers precious insights on its extent.

Part III

Strategic Supply Chain Risk Mitigation – Optimization Approaches

12 Embedding Comprehensive Risk in Supply Chain Network Design Models

"A successful model tells you things you didn't tell it to tell you."

Jerry P. Brashear

The management of supply chains seeks to plan, monitor, and control a network of interdependent organizations that facilitates different types of flows between the original producer to the final customer. The major objectives of supply chain management are the maximization of profitability and the achievement of customers' satisfaction [292]. As the determination of the best supply chain configuration that supports supply chain's goal achievement is an important task of the strategic planning process, facility location problems are of particular interest for supply chain management [205]. One of the core problems of facility location is the capacitated plant location problem (CPLP-T) also known as the fixed-charge facility location problem (FLP) [87]. With regard to the strategic planning of supply chains, it is especially suitable, because it respects capacity restrictions that can be referred to production, inventory or handling capacities.

In the presence of the continuously increasing fierce competition for customers and their profitable satisfaction, supply chain management needs to respect numerous optimization criteria. Besides different aspects of network complexity, stochastic parameters need to be considered on different planning levels of supply chain management. Over the last decade supply chain risk became increasingly relevant, although the notion of risk or more precisely supply chain risk was not clearly defined. Our extensive literature review on supply chain risk concluded that supply chain risk can be defined by three elementary characteristics, namely: risk objective, risk exposition, and risk attitude, see Chapter 3. Figure 12.1 presents the *Core Characteristics of Supply Chain Risk (CCSCR) Hierarchy* deduced in this review. A joint consideration of those characteristics provides the possibility to accomplish formalization and operationalization of supply chain risk.

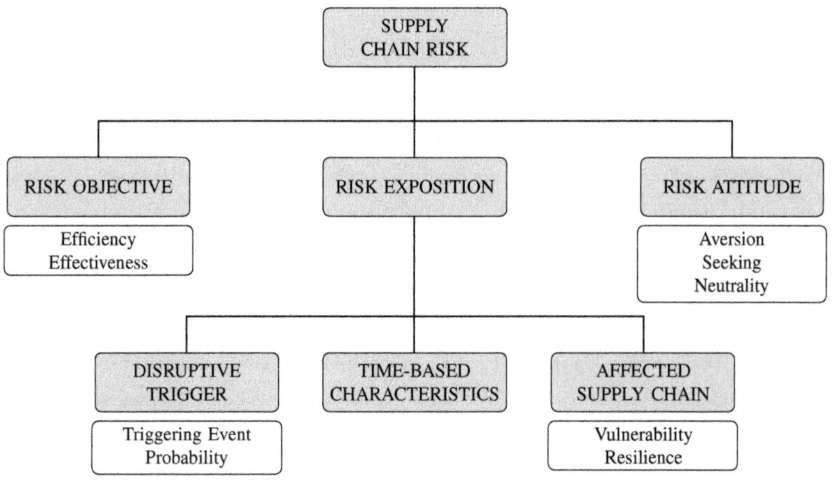

Figure 12.1: The core characteristics of supply chain risk (CCSCR) hierarchy [122].

Each of the supply chain risk core characteristics is exposed to uncertainty, whose consideration even aggravates decision making. For strategic problems under uncertainty, stochastic programming has been established as a mean to capture and model uncertainty. Wallace with different co-authors present numerous fields of application, such as product and financial management, logistics and health care [164, 332]. Stochastic programming has also been used for facility location problems, which is extensively discussed by Snyder [281]. Due to the complex structure of stochastic programs the scope of available models is still limited and especially lacks the consideration of risk, which has been pointed out by Melo et al. [205]. Approaches of stochastic programming explicitly referring to supply chain risk, though for a rather limited risk setting, were recently proposed by Azaron et al. [12], Babazadeh and Razmi [14], Huang and Goetschalckx [136], Goh et al. [106], Nickel et al. [224], and Soleimani and Govindan [287]. Nickel et al. [224] tackle risk within a multi-period supply network design problem and Azaron et al. [12] consider risk for a multi-objective supply chain design problem. The concept of risk used in their approaches entirely refers to financial risk as opposed to supply chain risk and therefore they do not address all the relevant core characteristics of supply chain risk. The other approaches tackle supply chain risk solely by defining plausible scenarios that capture future events.

The purpose of this chapter is to adopt the aforementioned core characteristics of risk to strategic supply chain decision problems, i.e. to a CPLP-T problem, by the use of stochastic programming principles.

The remainder of this chapter is organized as follows. In the next section we introduce the risk-aware capacitated plant location problem by following the CCSCR Hierarchy. In Section 12.2 an illustrative example is presented and sets the basis to determine the value of risk consideration and to quantify supply chain risk. Section 12.3 discusses preliminary computational results such as the expected value of perfect information and the value of the stochastic solution. As the focus is set to embedding a new risk concept in mathematical quantitative supply chain management Section 12.4 is dedicated to present possible extensions, which can be applied for different logistical settings. Conclusions are given in the last section.

12.1 Mathematical Model Formulations

In this section we propose a mixed-integer two-stage linear programming model for a risk-aware supply chain design problem. We therefore extend the capacitated plant location problem (CPLP-T) to the risk-aware capacitated plant location problem (CPLP-RISK). We start by introducing necessary notation and continue by presenting the initial location problem.

12.1.1 Notations

Sets

Index Symbols	Set Symbol	Description	Model
i	I	Facilities	c, c^T, c^{Risk}
j	J	Customers	c, c^T, c^{Risk}
t	T	Time periods	c^T, c^{Risk}
h	H	Expansion levels	c^{Risk}
s	S	Scenarios	c^{Risk}

Table 12.1: Sets and indices applied for the CPLP-T (c), CPLP-T (c^T) and CPLP-RISK (c^{Risk}) model.

Deterministic and Stochastic Parameters

Model Identifier	Name	Description	Model
f_i	Opening costs	Amount of costs related to the opening of each facility i	c, c^T, c^{Risk}
K_i	Capacity	Amount of capacity related to facility i	c, c^T, c^{Risk}

c_{ij}	Transportation costs	Amount of costs related to the transport between facility i and customer j	c, c^T, c^{Risk}
b_i	Costs of optional extra-capacity	Amount of costs related to installing optional extra-capacity at each facility i	c^{Risk}
r_j	Reward	Amount of reward related to demand fulfillment for customer j	c^{Risk}
u	Value of service level adherence	Amount of costs related to each unit of unreached target service level	c^{Risk}
ν_h	Expansion costs	Amount of costs related to each unit of extra-capacity of expansion level h	c^{Risk}
o_h	Expansion capacity	Amount of capacity related to each unit of extra-capacity of expansion level h	c^{Risk}
β^o	Target service level	Level of targeted service level	c^{Risk}
π_s	Scenario probability	Probability related to scenario s	c^{Risk}
d_{jts}	Customer demand	Amount of demand related to customer j in time period t and scenario s	c^{Risk}
γ_{its}	Capacity reduction	Amount of relative capacity reduction within facility i in time period t and scenario s	c^{Risk}

Table 12.2: Deterministic parameters applied for the CPLP-T (c), CPLP-T (c^T) and CPLP-RISK (c^{Risk}) model and stochastic parameters for the CPLP-RISK (c^{Risk}) model.

Decision Variables

Model Identifier	Name	Description	Model
y_i	Opening decision	Binary variable equal to 1 iff facility i is opened	c, c^T, c^{Risk}
x_{ij}	Transportation decision	Amount transported from facility i to customer j	c
x_{ijt}	Transportation decision	Amount transported from facility i to customer j in time period t	c^T
z_i	Installation decision	Binary variable equals 1 iff expansion options are installed at facility i	c^{Risk}
x_{ijts}	Transportation decision	Fraction of the demand of customer j in period t supplied from facility i in scenario s	c^{Risk}
φ_{jts}	Unsatisfied demand decision	Amount of unsatisfied demand related to customer j in time period t and scenario s	c^{Risk}
ω_{iths}	Expansion-level decision	Binary variable equals 1 iff in scenario s expansion level h is installed at facility i at time period t	c^{Risk}
β_s	Service level	Level of service level in scenario s	c^{Risk}
Δ_s	Service level deterioration	Amount of service level reduction in scenario s	c^{Risk}

Table 12.3: Decision variables for the CPLP-T (c), CPLP-T (c^T) and CPLP-RISK (c^{Risk}) model.

12.1.2 The Risk-aware Capacitated Plant Location Problem (CPLP-Risk)

In the following we extent the capacitated plant location problem (CPLP-T) to the risk-aware capacitated plant location problem (CPLP-RISK). A simple CPLP-T formulation is provided by the following model:

$$\text{minimize} \sum_{i \in I} f_i y_i + c_{ij} d_j x_{ij} \qquad (12.1)$$

(CPLP)

$$\text{subject to} \sum_{i \in I} x_{ij} = 1 \qquad \forall j \qquad (12.2)$$

$$\sum_{j \in J} d_j x_{ij} \leq K_i y_i \qquad \forall i \qquad (12.3)$$

$$x_{ij} \geq 0 \qquad \forall i, j \qquad (12.4)$$

$$y_i \in \{0, 1\} \qquad \forall i \qquad (12.5)$$

The basic CPLP-T model is formulated as a single-period problem. However, only a multi-period setting allows to further define time-based characteristics, which are of special importance for modeling disruptive triggers and supply chain resilience. In the light of risk it is indispensable to consider a multi-period horizon. The CPLP-T model is extended to a multi-period formulation that covers the decision of which facility to open as a strategic decision, which is made once at the beginning of the planning horizon. Tactical distribution decisions are made for each time period of the planning horizon. The time expanded CPLP-T model can be formulated as follows:

$$\text{minimize} \sum_{i \in I} f_i y_i + c_{ij} d_{jt} x_{ijt} \tag{12.6}$$

$$\text{(CPLP-T)} \quad \text{subject to} \sum_{i \in I} x_{ijt} = 1 \qquad \forall \quad j, t \tag{12.7}$$

$$\sum_{j \in J} d_{jt} x_{ijt} \leq K_i y_i \qquad \forall \quad i, t \tag{12.8}$$

$$x_{ijt} \geq 0 \qquad \forall \quad i, j, t \tag{12.9}$$

$$y_i \in \{0, 1\} \qquad \forall \quad i \tag{12.10}$$

Following the CCSCR-hierarchy we add constraints and variables to the CPLP-T formulation. For the sake of better comprehension we describe constraints of the CPLP-T model and compare them with the extended constraints of CPLP-RISK model, which are deduced from the CCSCR-hierarchy. The final CPLP-RISK model is presented at the end of this section.

Risk Objective

Traditionally, risk is perceived as financial risk and assessed with financial metrics like variance, mean-variance ratios, Value-at-Risk (VaR) or Conditional-Value-at-Risk (CVaR). In contrast to the overall corporate business objective the main task of a supply chain is to satisfy customers' demand. Therefore it seems at least imperfect that supply chain risk is solely evaluated in terms of financial risk, i.e. monetary loss. Nevertheless, for the sake of competitiveness supply chains need to accomplish the cost efficient execution of supply chain processes. While the availability of resources is captured by the concept of *effectiveness*, the possibility of competitive advantage is captured by the concept of *efficiency* (see Chapter 3). Therefore a supply chain has to fulfill two main objectives: efficiency

and effectiveness. The standard CPLP-T addresses the supply chain objective of efficiency through the consideration of costs related to the opening of facilities, f_i, and the transportation between facilities and customers, c_{ij}, in the objective function (see objective function (12.6)). For the CPLP-RISK model we add the consideration of effectiveness by introducing the evaluation of deviation of service level, β_s, from a targeted value, β^o, within the objective function, $u(\beta^o - \beta_s)$. In order to calculate the service level we allow the non-fulfillment of customers' demand, φ_{jts}, compare constraints CPLP-T 12.7 and CPLP-RISK 12.12. The service level is then calculated by $\beta_s = 1 - \frac{\sum_j \sum_t \varphi_{jts}}{\sum_j \sum_t d_{jts}}$ (12.16). The possibility of allowing unsatisfied demand has also been addressed for supply chain design problems in general and facility location problems in particular by a few authors like for example Cui et al. [67], Miranda and Garrido [209], and Sabri and Beamon [258].
Often it becomes necessary to decide which customer to serve when capacities become limited. For the CPLP-RISK model we therefore introduce a prioritization mean in terms of customer related reward for satisfied demand, r_j, see constraint CPLP-RISK (12.11). In that sense the model additionally allows that each customer can be served by several facilities, which is of particular interest, when disruptions impede supply from the major facility.

Risk Exposition

The risk exposition of the underlying supply chain is a core characteristic, which is further specified by time-based characteristics having tremendous impact on the severity, disruptive triggers occurring within or exterior to the supply chain and the constitution of the affected supply chain itself.

Disruptive Triggers A triggering event can impose the root cause of the non-achievement of targeted service level or increase of overall costs. A triggering event or a sequence of consecutive events is denoted as a disruptive event, when it results in the non-achievement of supply chain objectives. A disruptive trigger negatively affects one or several supply chain processes and its consequences propagate through the entire supply network. The initial impact of a disruptive trigger on the supply chain can be uncovered by its capability to influence supply chain processes. A disruptive trigger, for example, can result in a capacity reduction, γ_{its}, and/or simultaneously in increased customers' demand, d_{jts}. We consider the effects of a disruptive trigger on the capacities of facilities by introducing a capacity reduction parameter, γ_{its}. According to the future development depicted within different scenarios, this parameter reduces the capacity at each facility, $\gamma_{its}K_iy_i$, compare constraints 12.8 of CPLP-T and 12.13 of CPLP-RISK. Disruptive triggers that provoke a capacity reduction vary from natural disasters like earthquakes and flooding, technical failures to human errors. Similarly, the same disruptive trigger or another trigger occurring at the same time can lead to a demand shift, increase or decrease. The CPLP-RISK model allows to consider stochastic demand that is captured by a finite set of scenarios.

Affected Supply Chain Once an event has occurred it is irrelevant whether it has arisen within or external to the supply chain. It is the interplay of all supply chain processes and their actual states of supply chain characteristics that defines the resilience of a supply chain towards effectiveness and efficiency. This interaction determines whether the first impact of an initial event on the supply chain process provokes the dis-functionality or/and non-profitability of consecutive processes, propagates through the entire network and finally results in the non-achievement of supply chains goals in terms of efficiency or/and effectiveness. To endow supply chains with the ability to absorb or to flexibly adjust to consequences of disruptive triggers, two different types of decisions need to be done. First, it is necessary to assess the need to increase the supply chain resilience.

If the supply chain is considered to be robust against uncertainly occurring triggers, the installation of (further) risk countermeasures is not necessary. Otherwise supply chains need to be endowed with the possibility to occasionally and temporarily access additional capacities in terms of production capacity, inventory level, handling throughput, or time. Thus, the first decision determines whether the supply chain needs to be endowed with the possibility to access one or several other risk reducing options. Second, it is necessary to identify the right point in time, when and which of the available options should be used. As the execution of capacity increasing options like their installation is related with additional costs, both decisions need to be carefully balanced with the benefit they provide for supply chain resilience. We integrate these thoughts by introducing additional terms in the CPLP-RISK model. Therein each facility can be endowed with additional capacity extensions, z_i, that can be used whenever facilities are disrupted or demand volume is increasing, ω_{iths}, such that the overall capacity cannot fulfill overall customer demand. Capacity expansions have also been considered by Aghezzaf [5], Hugo and Pistikopoulos [137], Fleischmann et al. [90], Ko and Evans [172], Troncoso and Garrido [315] and been reviewed by Julka et al. [148]. Since we apply a stochastic program to encompass risk considerations, we define the decision of installing an option for capacity expansion as a first-stage decision and the decision when and which option level, h, to execute as a second-stage decision. Capacity expansions are intended to increase the available capacity level at the facilities, compare constraints CPLP-T 12.8 and CPLP-RISK 12.13. Expansions are, however, limited in their duration and number of times they can be executed. The CPLP-RISK model allows to execute only one type of capacity expansion, h, at each facility, i, in each period t, see CPLP-RISK 12.14. Capacity expansions come along with costs that depend on the expansion level selected, therefore the cost amount in the objective function is increased by $\sum_{i\in I}\sum_{h\in H}\nu_h o_h \sum_{t\in T}\omega_{iths}$.

Time-based Characteristics The literature on supply chain risk management has not yet considered in depth time-aspects, yet some authors point out their importance with respect to the modeling of supply chain risk [117, 188, 194, 270, 329]. Generic disruption profiles as introduced by Sheffi [270, 271] and discussed by several further authors [11, 28, 66, 192, 204, 282] present the relation between time and performance deterioration in more depth. With respect to the stochastic parameters introduced so far a triggering event can lead to a huge capacity reduction that slightly recovers over the planning horizon. It could result in a small reduction that can be compensated quickly within a small amount of time periods. Triggering events can occur more frequently in the considered planning horizon and they can of course consists of a mixture of the aforementioned characteristics. Besides the temporal development of distinct stochastic parameters, their common consideration is of great importance. Consider the case of the Thailand flooding in 2011, where an extreme capacity reduction for exporters of hard disk drives and solid-state drives was combined with an increased demand for the new solid-state drives. Within the CPLP-RISK model the capacity reduction and the demand modifications are multi-period parameters whose dependent developments are depicted in different scenarios. A common approach to pro-actively manage unpredictably occurring disruptive triggers is to install additional time or capacity buffers before a disruption has even occurred. However, so called robust approaches omit the dynamic nature of disruptive triggers and forestall the possibility to design the supply chain cost-efficiently for the times when no disruptive triggers occur. Therefore, the CPLP-RISK model is endowed with the first-stage decision of preparation for disruptive triggers, z_i, and the second-stage decision of executing a capacity extension of an appropriate level and duration, ω_{iths}.

Risk Attitude

The risk attitude of the decision maker is a core characteristic of supply chain risk as it reflects the level of risk the decision maker is willing to accept (see Chapter 3). When a decision maker is, for example, risk-seeking, he accepts higher degrees of value deterioration of a specific goal in exchange for the adherence or increase of an opposite one. The CPLP-RISK model has to consider two main objectives: customer satisfaction (an effectiveness-based objective) and cost minimization (an efficiency-based objective). The decision maker has to balance both objectives by evaluating how much he is willing to invest for capacity extensions with respect to the value of customer satisfaction. Whenever demand does not considerably increase over the planning horizon with regard to the overall available capacity, such that it would not have been necessary to install and execute capacity extensions, the invested money is somehow lost. Although we seek for a multi-objective formulation, we initially consider an objective-based balancing through scalarization. The input parameter u expresses the value of customer satisfaction with respect to the costs spent for capacity establishment and potential expansions.

CPLP-Risk Model Formulation

Finally, we can introduce the CPLP-RISK model, which is already the extensive form of the deterministic equivalent associated with the underlying stochastic program:

$$\text{minimize} \sum_{i \in I} (f_i y_i + b_i z_i)$$
$$+ \sum_{s \in S} \pi_s \left(u\Delta_s + \sum_{i \in I} \sum_{h \in H} \nu_h o_h \sum_{t \in T} \omega_{iths} \right. \tag{12.11}$$
$$\left. + \sum_{t \in T} \sum_{i \in I} \sum_{j \in J} (c_{ij} - r_j) d_{jts} x_{ijts} \right)$$

(CPLP-Risk)

subject to

$$\sum_{i \in I} d_{jts} x_{ijts} + \varphi_{jts} = d_{jts} \ \forall \ j, t, s \tag{12.12}$$
$$\sum_{j \in J} d_{jts} x_{ijts} \leq \gamma_{its} K_i y_i + \sum_{h} o_h \omega_{iths} \quad \forall \ i, t, s \tag{12.13}$$
$$\sum_{h \in H} \omega_{iths} \leq z_i \ \forall \ i, t, s \tag{12.14}$$
$$z_i \leq y_i \ \forall \ i \tag{12.15}$$
$$\beta_s = 1 - \frac{\sum_j \sum_t \varphi_{jts}}{\sum_j \sum_t d_{jts}} \ \forall \ i, s \tag{12.16}$$
$$\Delta_s = \beta^o - \beta_s \ \forall \ s \tag{12.17}$$
$$0 \leq \Delta_s \leq 1 \ \forall \ s \tag{12.18}$$
$$x_{ijts} \geq 0 \ \forall \ i, j, t, s \tag{12.19}$$
$$\varphi_{its} \geq 0 \ \forall \ i, t, s \tag{12.20}$$
$$z_i \in \{0, 1\} \ \forall \ i \tag{12.21}$$
$$y_i \in \{0, 1\} \ \forall \ i \tag{12.22}$$
$$\omega_{iths} \in \{0, 1\} \ \forall \ i, t, h, s \tag{12.23}$$

The decisions consist of first stage and recourse decisions. Initially, the opening and capacity expansion options are made for each facility, while minimizing the expected costs of the consequences of these

decisions. Opening and capacity expansion decisions are declared as first stage decisions. When uncertain parameters are disclosed, the recourse or second stage decisions lean on, improve or correct the decisions made at the first stage. The selection of the type of expansion level for every period depicts the second stage decision. It follows that the overall objective function minimizes the costs of the first and the expected costs of the second stage decision. Costs related to the opening of a facility and installing capacity options belong to the costs of the first stage decision. Costs related to the execution of available capacity options as well as the value of unsatisfied demand refer to costs of the second stage decision.
Demand constraint (12.12) equalizes demand fulfillment, $\sum_i d_{jts}x_{ijts}$, and unsatisfied demand, φ_{its}, with customer demand, d_{jts}. The capacity constraint (12.13) restricts the ratio of demand fulfillment of each facility to the available capacity at the facility considered. Facility-related capacity sums to the reduced capacity, $\gamma_{its}K_iy_i$, and the capacity extension units, $\sum_h o_h\omega_{iths}$. For each time period and facility only one extension level, h is allowed to be executed (12.14) if and only if a capacity extension option has been alloted to the facility (12.15). The amount of service level deterioration is calculated by (12.16)-(12.18). Additionally, variables are limited to appropriately accomplish the aforementioned requirements by (12.19)-(12.23).

12.2 Illustrative Example

The purpose of providing an illustrative example within this section is twofold. First, the example presents how the solution of the CPLP-RISK model differs from the basic multi-period CPLP-T model that does not encompass risk characteristics. Second, it highlights that the formulation of the CPLP-RISK as a stochastic program is most probably more appropriate than averaging the stochastic parameters and solve a deterministic problem.

12.2.1 Data Input

In the following paragraphs the model parameters and their values are introduced. For the illustrative purpose of this section, we limit the problem size to the consideration of two facilities and three customers. The deterministic parameter values are introduced first. Due to the specific characteristics of disruptions special attention is dedicated to the development of the stochastic parameters over time.

Deterministic Parameter Values

When we think of supply chain risk, we have disruptive triggers in mind such as earthquakes, tsunamis, European ash cloud, or the blowout of the Deep-Water-Horizon oil drilling rig. Often such incidents have an impact not only on different types of supply chain capacities, but also and especially on distinct cost drivers. Whenever infrastructure is destroyed, supply and distribution has to be organized by temporarily new and costly transportation means and occasionally new production sites or suppliers have to be acquired. Socio-geopolitical changes like the "Arabic Spring" can result in high oil price volatilities, which affect transportation and procurement costs as well, see Chapter 2. However, we emphasize that supply chain risk should not only be referred to catastrophic disruptions and big turmoils, but also to less well-known, initially smaller incidents like short circuits and machine failures at production facilities, reported for example by Norrman and Jansson [225]. These initially minor incidents typically do not affect cost parameters. We, therefore, consider all cost parameters in the CPLP-RISK model as deterministic and constant over time.

Moreover, we focus on the effects provoked by the demand shifts and capacity reductions, cost and capacity parameters are consequently set to reflect exemplary real world data structures and are not further

Facility i	1	2	
Opening costs f_i	100	200	
Costs for extra-capacity options b_i	100	200	
Capacity K_i	10	10	

Expansion Levels h	1 (small)	2 (medium)	3 (big)
Expansion capacity o_h	2	5	10
Expansion costs v_h	5	8	10

Customer j	1	2	3
Reward r_j	4	4	4

Transportation Costs c_{ij}	1	2	3
1	3	5	3
2	3	5	3

Table 12.4: Deterministic parameters and their values for the illustrative example.

examined. While the value of the service level adherence, u, is set to 30.000 and the length of the planning horizon to 12 periods, the other deterministic parameter values are summed up in Table 12.4.

Stochastic Parameter Values

The CPLP-RISK model allows time dependent stochastic parameters and provides the possibility to expand the capacity in each time period, when the available capacity cannot fulfill customers' demand. Note, that the CPLP-RISK model allows the execution of only one expansion for each facility at each time period. For a realistic evaluation of the model, it is necessary to describe the development of stochastic parameters accordingly. Instead of considering random erratic values for demand shifts and capacity reduction, we assume that the velocity to the full disruptive impact, the velocity to full recovery, the start of a disruption, and its end define different disruption profiles, see Figure 12.2. Different start times of a disruption and different durations are conceivable, see Figure 12.2 a). Additionally, a capacity reduction evoked by a disruptive trigger can, for example, evolve quickly into its minimum value and can recover more or less slightly back to its original level, see Figure 12.2 b). A disruptive trigger can also lead to a big or minor capacity reduction, see Figure 12.2 c). As discussed in Section 12.1 often the occurrence of a disruption has an influence on several supply chain processes. For the evaluation of the CPLP-RISK model we consider the case that a disruptive trigger has not only influence on capacity, but simultaneously causes a demand shift, see Figure 12.2 d). Capacity reduction affect both locations and demand shifts apply to all customers.

In order to consider different disruption profiles we base the scenario generation for capacity reductions on the start and end time of a disruption, the velocity of capacity decrease and recovery as well as on the absolute capacity minimum the disruption is intended to provoke. For the illustrative example we consider three different scenarios that differ in their absolute minimum. The velocity of capacity decrease equals to 2 per 10 time periods with respect to the duration of a disruption. This implies that the absolute capacity minimum is reached after two periods for a disruption lasting ten time periods. Similarly, the velocity of capacity recovery determines the period, where capacity is back to normal. A recovery velocity of 0.8 implies that capacity is back to normal 8 periods after absolute minimum. Within the illustrative example the disruption is assumed to start and end at period 2 and 10, respectively. Figure 12.3 shows the available overall capacity that results from the aforementioned

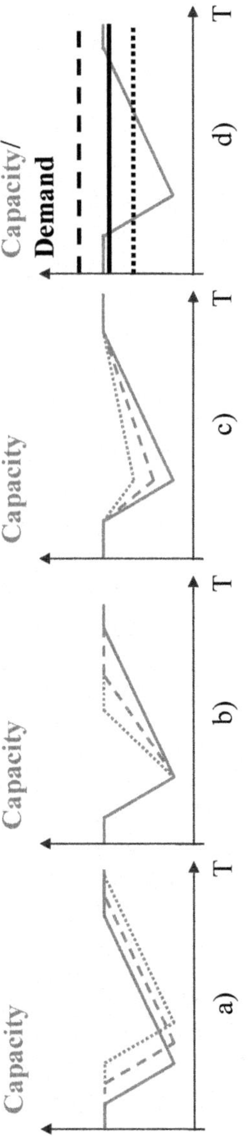

Figure 12.2: Development of stochastic parameters.

capacity reduction and additionally traces the overall demand for the three scenarios.

Scenario 1 reflects the situation of a major capacity reduction exposed to a minor fall in demand. This scenario is assumed to have a probability of 10%. Scenario 2 is defined by a less intense capacity reduction, but the reduction is combined with a demand expansion. This scenario is endowed with a probability of 40%. Scenario 3 more or less reflects a normal situation specified by a probability of 60%, where capacity remains constant over time and their overall availability exceeds customers demand.

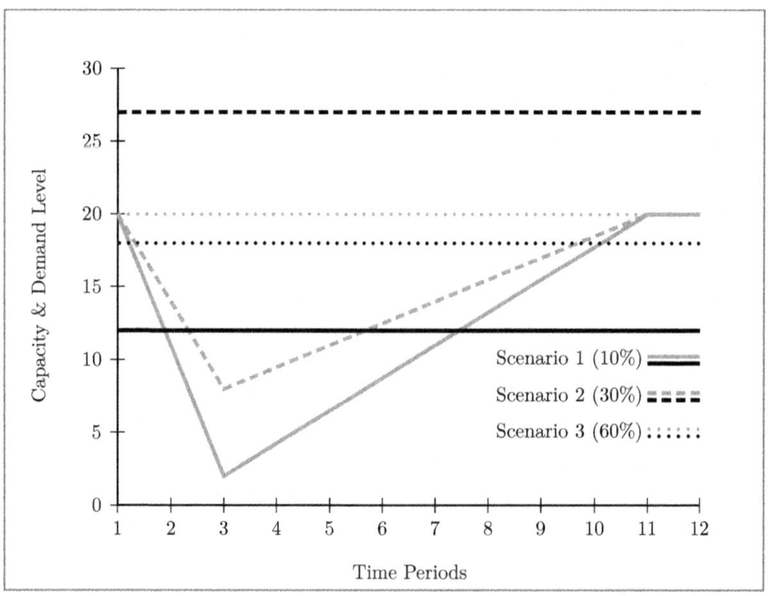

Figure 12.3: Development of overall capacity and demand for the illustrative example with two facilities and three customers: Start time of disruption is set to 1, velocity of capacity reduction equals 2, velocity of recovery equals 8, absolute minimum is reached in time period 3.

12.2.2 Solution Plausibility

To evaluate the solution of the stochastic model in terms of plausibility, we set the target service level to 100%. When considering the development of capacity and demand within the three different scenarios, see Figure 12.3, we expect that additional capacity is required in scenarios 1 and 2. In order to execute additional capacity options, facilities need to be endowed with this possibility at the beginning of the planning horizon. Table 12.5 summarizes the solution of the specified problem. For each scenario and each time period the overall available capacity, the consolidated demand, and the resulting capacity deficit is presented. For the sake of comprehension we do not only consider the solution of the stochastic program, CPLP-RISK, which is often difficult to interpret at the first sight, but also the solution of the scenario-wise problem, $CPLP^{Risk}(s)$, and the solution of the average problem, $CPLP^{Risk}(\hat{y}, \hat{z})$. The latter is determined by averaging the stochastic parameters, solving the model with averaged input, and apply the first stage decision, i.e. facility opening and installation of capacity options, in each scenario. The second stage decision, i.e. executing a specific type of capacity extension, is then determined based on the fixed first stage decision and in dependence of capacity needs. Whenever the first stage decision variables note to omit extra-capacity options, capacities cannot be applied at this facility (this case is marked by "na" in Table 12.5).

$\pi_{s=1} = 10\%$		t		1	2	3	4	5	6	7	8	9	10	11	12	β
	Capacity Decision provides Basis for Extension Decision	$\sum_i K_i$		20	11	2	4.25	6.5	8.75	11	13.25	15.5	17.75	20	20	
		$\sum_j \sum_t d_{jt}$		12	12	12	12	12	12	12	12	12	12	12	12	
		Capacity Surplus		**8**	**-1**	**-10**	**-7.75**	**-5.5**	**-3.25**	**-1**	**1.25**	**3.5**	**5.75**	**8**	**8**	
	Extension Decision	$CPLP^{Risk}(s)$	ω_{1th1}	na	na	na	na	na	na	na	na	na	na	na	na	
			ω_{2th1}		2	10	10	10	5	2						
		φ														**100%**
		$CPLP^{Risk}(\hat{y},\hat{s})$	ω_{1th1}	na	na	na	na	na	na	na	na	na	na	na	na	
			ω_{2th1}		2	10	10	10	5	2						
		φ														**100%**
		$CPLP^{Risk}$	ω_{1th1}		2	5	5	2	2	2						
			ω_{2th1}			5	5	5	2							
		φ														**100%**
$\pi_{s=2} = 30\%$		t		1	2	3	4	5	6	7	8	9	10	11	12	
	Capacity Decision provides Basis for Extension Decision	$\sum_i K_i$		20	14	8	9.5	11	12.5	14	15.5	17	18.5	20	20	
		$\sum_j \sum_t d_{jt}$		27	27	27	27	27	27	27	27	27	27	27	27	
		Capacity Surplus		**-7**	**-13**	**-19**	**-17.5**	**-16**	**-14.5**	**-13**	**-11.5**	**-10**	**-8.5**	**-7**	**-7**	
	Extension Decision	$CPLP^{Risk}(s)$	ω_{1th2}	2	10	10	10	10	5	5	10	5	5	2	2	
			ω_{2th2}	5	5	10	10	10	10	10	2	5	5	5	5	
		φ														**100%**
		$CPLP^{Risk}(\hat{y},\hat{s})$	ω_{1th2}	na	na	na	na	na	na	na	na	na	na	na	na	
			ω_{2th2}	10	10	10	10	10	10	10	10	10	10	10	10	
		φ			**-3**	**-9**	**-7.5**	**-6**	**-4.5**	**-3**	**-1.5**	**0**				**89%**

	$CPLP^{Risk}$	ω_{1th2}	2	10	10	10	10	10	5	2	5	5	2	5	
		ω_{2th2}	5	5	10	10	10	5	10	10	5	5	5	2	
	φ														**100%**
$\pi_{s=3} = 60\%$	t		1	2	3	4	5	6	7	8	9	10	11	12	
Capacity Decision provides Basis for Extension Decision	$\sum_i K_i$		20	20	20	20	20	20	20	20	20	20	20	20	
	$\sum_j \sum_t d_{jt}$		18	18	18	18	18	18	18	18	18	18	18	18	
	Capacity Surplus		**2**	**2**	**2**	**2**	**2**	**2**	**2**	**2**	**2**	**2**	**2**	**2**	
Extension Decision	$CPLP^{Risk}(s)$	ω_{1th3}	na	na	na	na	na	na	na	na	na	na	na	na	
		ω_{2th3}	na	na	na	na	na	na	na	na	na	na	na	na	
	φ														**100%**
	$CPLP^{Risk}(\hat{y}, \hat{z})$	ω_{1th3}	na	na	na	na	na	na	na	na	na	na	na	na	
		ω_{2th3}													
	φ														**100%**
	$CPLP^{Risk}$	ω_{1th3}													
		ω_{2th3}													
	φ														**100%**

Table 12.5: Solutions of capacity extensions decisions for the illustrative example with target service level of 100%: $CPLP^{Risk}(s)$ refers to the scenario-optimal solution, $CPLP^{Risk}(\hat{y}, \hat{z})$ presents the average solution, and$CPLP^{Risk}$ shows the solution of the stochastic program.

As can be seen from the results, the scenario-optimal solutions behave as assumed. Capacity extensions are provided in scenario 1 and 2. These capacity options are executed within the periods of capacity deficit and the type of extension is not over-dimensioned compared to the needed capacity. The average solution of the problem yields to unsatisfied demand, φ, in scenario 2. Generally, the average of stochastic parameters leads to an underestimation of uncertainty as intensively discussed for example in [263]. Here the averaging of the stochastic capacity reduction resulted in the non-installation of extra-capacity, which would have been necessary in scenario 2. The scenario-wise interpretation of the stochastic solution is more difficult, because the objective function of the stochastic program weights the costs related to each scenario-wise second stage decision with the scenario probability. The main goal of the plausibility check, however, is to determine whether the solution of the stochastic program provides capacity extension such that the target service level is reached. As this is the case we modify the target service level to 95%. Table 12.6 shows the results for this problem specification other parameter values being equal. Compared to the solution with 100% target service level, table 12.6 highlights that capacity expansions are realized such that the target service level can be met, while limiting the expenses for additional expansions.

Scenario				1	2	3	4	5	6	7	8	9	10	11	12	β'
$\pi_{s=1} = 10\%$	Capacity Decision provides Basis for Extension Decision	t		1	2	3	4	5	6	7	8	9	10	11	12	
		$\sum_i K_i$		20	11	2	4.25	6.5	8.75	11	13.25	15.5	17.75	20	20	
		$\sum_j \sum_t d_{jt}$		12	12	12	12	12	12	12	12	12	12	12	12	
		Capacity Surplus		**8**	**-1**	**-10**	**-7.75**	**-5.5**	**-3.25**	**-1**	**1.25**	**3.5**	**5.75**	**8**	**8**	
	Extension Decision	$CPLP^{Risk}(s)$	ω_{1th1}	na	na	na	na	na	na	na	na	na	na	na	na	
			ω_{2th1}			10	5	5	2							
		φ			**-1.00**	**0.00**	**-2.75**	**-0.50**	**-1.25**	**-1.00**						**95%**
		$CPLP^{Risk}(\hat{y}, \hat{s})$	ω_{1th1}	na	na	na	na	na	na	na	na	na	na	na	na	
			ω_{2th1}			10	5	5	2							
		φ			**-1.00**	**0.00**	**-2.75**	**-0.50**	**-1.25**	**-1.00**						**95%**
		$CPLP^{Risk}$	ω_{1th1}			2	2	2	2							
			ω_{2th1}			5	5	2	2	2						
		φ			**-1**	**-2.00**		**-0.5**								**98%**
$\pi_{s=2} = 30\%$	Capacity Decision provides Basis for Extension Decision	t		1	2	3	4	5	6	7	8	9	10	11	12	
		$\sum_i K_i$		20	14	8	9.5	11	12.5	14	15.5	17	18.5	20	20	
		$\sum_j \sum_t d_{jt}$		27	27	27	27	27	27	27	27	27	27	27	27	
		Capacity Surplus		**-7**	**-13**	**-19**	**-17.5**	**-16**	**-14.5**	**-13**	**-11.5**	**-10**	**-8.5**	**-7**	**-7**	
	Extension Decision	$CPLP^{Risk}(s)$	ω_{1th2}	2	5	10	10	10	5	5	5	5	2	2	2	
			ω_{2th2}	5	5	5	5	5	10	5	5	5	5	5	5	
		φ			**-3**	**-4**	**-2.5**	**-1**		**-3**	**-1.5**		**-1.5**			**94.9%**
		$CPLP^{Risk}(\hat{y}, \hat{s})$	ω_{1th2}	na	na	na	na	na	na	na	na	na	na	na	na	
			ω_{2th2}	10	10	10	10	10	10	10	10	10	10	10	10	
		φ			**-3**	**-9**	**-7.5**	**-6**	**-4.5**	**-3**	**-1.5**	**0**				**89%**

	$CPLP^{Risk}$	ω_{1th2}	5	5	5	10	5	5	5	5	5	2	5	2	
		ω_{2th2}	2	5	10	5	10	10	5	5	5	5	2	5	
	φ			**-3**	**-4**	**-2.5**	**-1**		**-3**	**-1.5**		**-1.5**			**95%**
$\pi_{s=3}$ = 60%	t		1	2	3	4	5	6	7	8	9	10	11	12	
Capacity Decision provides Basis for Extension Decision	$\sum_i K_i$		20	20	20	20	20	20	20	20	20	20	20	20	
	$\sum_j \sum_t d_{jt}$		18	18	18	18	18	18	18	18	18	18	18	18	
	Capacity Surplus		**2**	**2**	**2**	**2**	**2**	**2**	**2**	**2**	**2**	**2**	**2**	**2**	
Extension Decision	$CPLP^{Risk}(s)$	ω_{1th3}	na	na	na	na	na	na	na	na	na	na	na	na	
		ω_{2th3}	na	na	na	na	na	na	na	na	na	na	na	na	
	φ														**100%**
	$CPLP^{Risk}(\hat{y}, \hat{z})$	ω_{1th3}	na	na	na	na	na	na	na	na	na	na	na	na	
		ω_{2th3}													
	φ														**100%**
	$CPLP^{Risk}$	ω_{1th3}													
		ω_{2th3}													
	φ														**100%**

Table 12.6: Solutions of capacity extensions decisions for the illustrative example with target service level of 95%: $CPLP^{Risk}(s)$ refers to the scenario-optimal solution, $CPLP^{Risk}(\hat{y}, \hat{z})$ presents the average solution, and$CPLP^{Risk}$ shows the solution of the stochastic program.

Note that, in Table 12.6 we denote the unsatisfied demand by φ' and the service level by β', because the table presents the amount of unsatisfied demand that can be reached due to the available capacities. It does not reflect the unsatisfied demand of each solution. As the objective function strives for cost minimization and (only) punishes the non-achievement of the target service level, solutions certainly contain unsatisfied demand. Generally, decision makers strive for the fulfillment of *all* demands, even though the achievement of a specified target service level has priority. In order to motivate fulfillment of each customer demand, we could easily expand the objective function by an additional term punishing unsatisfied demand for the region between absolute demand fulfillment and the targeted demand fulfillment. As we consider and discuss the objective function in more detail in Section 12.4, we limit ourself by assuming that the achievement of the target service level is satisfactory for the decision maker.

12.2.3 The Value of Risk Consideration

After having determined the plausibility of the CPLP-RISK model, we want to assess the value of risk consideration. Consider the situation of a company that has not yet felt the need to consider supply chain risk. However, if uncertain and sudden developments of crucial supply chain parameters start to occur more frequently, it is reasonable to evaluate the necessity for risk reducing measures. The motivation and the need for a risk-aware supply chain design arises and manifests, when the consideration of supply chain risk has a positive value. In this paragraph we, therefore, compare the solution of the CPLP-RISK formulation with the deterministic time expanded formulation of the simple capacitated plant location problem CPLP-T. Both models are solved for the input data presented for the plausibility assessment. With the purpose to stronger differentiate between the opening of a facility and the installation of a capacity extension, the opening costs are increased to 1000 and 1500 for facility 1 and

2, respectively. The solution of the CPLP-RISK problem delivers the decisions for all of the three scenarios. The CPLP-T model provides the solution of one scenario and is solved for each of the three scenarios. Due to the scenario-wise disruption profile it is possible that a solution for the deterministic CPLP-T model – that does not capture supply chain risk – cannot be found, i.e. the problem is infeasible. The goal of this paragraph is, however, to evaluate how the consideration of supply chain risk core characteristics improve supply chain resilience and reduce supply chain risk. In order to provide this logistical insight we extend the CPLP-T model to allow unsatisfied demand, because it is then traceable to evaluate a solution (rather than assessing an infeasible problem). We weight the unsatisfied demand by parameter v, which equals 50 within the example. Note that, the deterioration of target service level is not included in the objective function, because this would result in a solution that allocates distribution decisions in a cost efficient or reward increasing way, which is initially not considered by the simple CPLP-T formulation. The resulting deterministic CPLP-T' model that is used for assessing the value of supply chain risk consideration is provided as follows:

$$\text{minimize} \sum_{i \in I} f_i y_i + c_{ij} d_{jts} x_{ijt} + v \varphi_{jt} \tag{12.24}$$

(CPLP-T')

subject to

$$\sum_{i \in I} d_{jts} x_{ijt} + \varphi_{jt} = d_{jts} \qquad \forall \quad j, t \tag{12.25}$$

$$\sum_{j \in J} d_{jts} x_{ijt} \leq \gamma_{its} K_i y_i \qquad \forall \quad i, t \tag{12.26}$$

$$x_{ijt} \geq 0 \qquad \forall \quad i, j, t \tag{12.27}$$

$$y_i \in \{0, 1\} \qquad \forall \quad i \tag{12.28}$$

The CPLP-T' model is solved for each scenario, s. The solution comparison is presented in Figure 12.4. The CPLP-RISK model suggest to open both facilities and installing capacity options at both sites – highlighted by additional circles around the facility locations. Contrary, in scenario 1 the CPLP-T' model suggests opening only one facility. The decisions determined by the CPLP-T' model reflect the situation of a company that has not felt the need to consider supply chain risk. Risk characteristics such as balancing efficiency- and effectiveness-related objectives are not applied for the model formulation. The deterministic solution for scenario 3, therefore, implies that all demands are fulfilled, because it is possible.

Definition 12.1: Value of Risk Consideration

The value of risk consideration (VRC) is defined as the difference between the objective function value of the optimal stochastic solution, $OV(CPLP^{Risk})$, and the weighted value of the scenario-wise optimal objective function values, $\sum_s \pi_s \quad OV(CPLP - T_s')$.

For the illustrative example presented above, the value of considering risk characteristics within the model formulation of the CPLP-RISK model compared to the risk-non-aware counterpart equals to:

$$VRC := \left(\sum_s \pi_s \quad OV(CPLP - T_s')\right) - OV(CPLP^{Risk}) \quad (12.29)$$

$$VRC = (0.1 \times 2725 + 0.3 \times 6100 + 0.6 \times 2500) - 3147$$

$$VRC = 3602,5 - 3147$$

$$VRC = 455,5$$

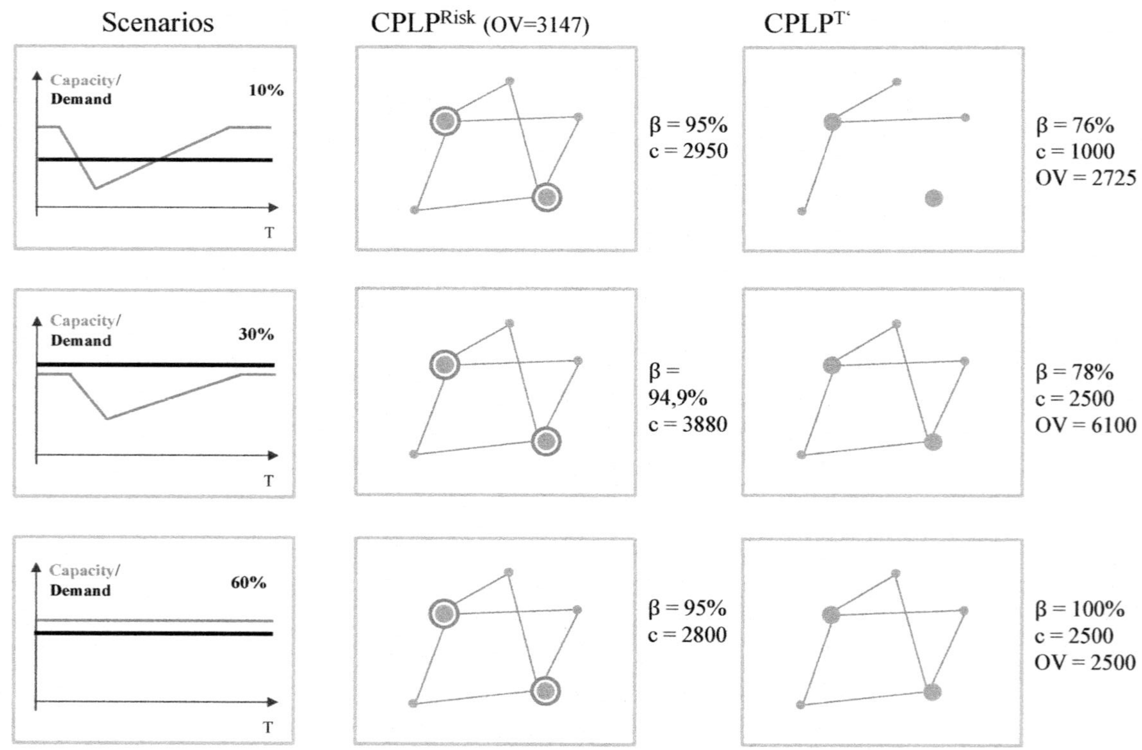

Figure 12.4: Solution comparison of deterministic CPLP-T' and stochastic CPLP-RISK model.

For the afore described business environment the value of risk consideration is positive and motivates the application of supply chain design formulations that model core characteristics of supply chain risk.

12.2.4 Quantification of Supply Chain Risk

Deduced from our extensive literature review, we determined the new supply chain risk definition: Supply chain risk is defined as the potential loss for a supply chain in terms of its target values of efficiency and effectiveness evoked by uncertain developments of supply chain characteristics whose changes were caused by the occurrence of triggering-events, see Chapter 3.

Based on the scenario-wise solutions of the deterministic problem and the stochastic problem provided in Figure 12.4 we can calculate the potential loss in terms of service level deterioration and logistic costs. We denote the capacity profile of each scenario, s, by $\mathbb{K}_s$, and the demand shift of each scenario, s, by $\mathbb{D}_s$, respectively. As we assume that the target service level equals to 95% for the deterministic problem as well, the supply chain risk in terms of effectiveness is calculated as the weighted difference between target and achieved service level. Supply chain risk in terms of effectiveness for the deterministic solution is calculated as follows:

$$\begin{aligned} SCR^{det}(\mathbb{K}_1, \mathbb{D}_1) &= u(\beta^o - \beta_1) \\ &= u(95\% - 90\%) = 30000 \times 0.05 = 1500 \\ SCR^{det}(\mathbb{K}_2, \mathbb{D}_2) &= u(\beta^o - \beta_2) \\ &= u(95\% - 78\%) = 30000 \times 0.17 = 5100 \end{aligned}$$

In scenario 3 there is no capacity deficit and therefore a potential loss, thus supply chain risk in terms of effectiveness, for this uncertainty development is equal to 0. The stochastic solution leads to supply chain risk in scenario 2 as follows:

$$\begin{aligned} SCR^{stoch}(\mathbb{K}_2, \mathbb{D}_2) &= u(\beta^o - \beta_2) \\ &= u(95\% - 94,9\%) = 30000 \times 0.01 = 300 \end{aligned}$$

The stochastic solution for scenario 1 and 3 results in the achievement of target service level and a minor deterioration in scenario 2, but this can only be achieved by additional costs. Supply chain risk in terms of efficiency is determined by the target logistic costs, which was not explicitly defined a priori. The degree of logistic costs deterioration was rather implicitly specified by the balancing parameter u. If we assume that the decision maker would have set the target logistic costs, c^o, to 2500 which equals to the opening costs of two sites, supply chain risk in terms of efficiency only exists for the stochastic solution and sums up to:

$$\begin{aligned} SCR^{stoch}(\mathbb{K}_1, \mathbb{D}_1) &= c_1 - c^o = 2950 - 2500 = 450 \\ SCR^{stoch}(\mathbb{K}_2, \mathbb{D}_2) &= c_2 - c^o = 3880 - 2500 = 1380 \\ SCR^{stoch}(\mathbb{K}_3, \mathbb{D}_3) &= c_3 - c^o = 2800 - 2500 = 300 \end{aligned}$$

However, the decision maker has expressed his risk attitude by parameter u, which denotes the decision maker's willingness to allow the deterioration of one target value in exchange for the improvement or achievement of another target value. In the illustrative example the stochastic solution suggests that the decision maker is willing to accept increased logistic costs up to 1380 in scenario 2 for the achievement of 94, 9% service level. Contrary, the deterministic solution of scenario 1 highlights that more money could have been invested in order to increase service level achievement. Thus, the risk-aware formulation allows to better model the degree of risk acceptance as the deterministic formulation and supports to define how much risk the decision maker is willing to accept in terms of effectiveness and efficiency, respectively.

12.3 Preliminary Computational Results

So far, we have seen that the CPLP-RISK model leads to both plausible and risk-aware solutions. In this section, we want to evaluate whether the formulation of the CPLP-RISK model as a stochastic program is reasonable and appropriate for the consideration of core characteristics of supply chain risk.

In the stochastic programming literature two evaluation indicators are used to describe the appropriateness of applying stochastic programs as method to capture uncertainty, namely, the expected value of perfect information (EVPI) and the value of the stochastic solution (VSS). The EVPI depicts the maximum amount the decision maker is willing to pay for the complete knowledge of the future. It is determined by the difference of the objective value of the stochastic problem, SP, and the expected value of the optimal solution, which is also denoted as the wait-and-see solution, WS. The wait-and-see solution is determined by solving the deterministic problem for each scenario and weighting the objective values by the scenario probabilities. For the CPLP-RISK formulation the EVPI is calculated as follows:

$$EVPI := SP - WS$$
$$EVPI := OV(CPLP^{Risk}) - \sum_{s} \pi_s \quad OV(CPLP^{Risk}(s))$$

The value of the stochastic solution is determined by the difference between the objective value of the stochastic problem evaluated in the optimal solution of the expected value problem, EEV, and the objective value of the stochastic problem, SP. For the CPLP-RISK this is formulated as follows:

$$VSS := EEV - SP$$
$$VSS := OV(CPLP^{Risk}(\hat{y}, \hat{z})) - OV(CPLP^{Risk})$$

The illustrative example presented above yields to an EVPI and a VSS greater than zero. This fact indicates the usefulness of applying a stochastic programming formulation for the risk-aware capacitated plant location problem. With the purpose to evaluate how the degree of uncertainty affects the development of EVPI and VSS in more detail, we set up an experiment that increases the degree of capacity and demand uncertainty in constant steps. The experimental input data leans on the illustrative example presented above with opening costs equal to 1000 and 1500 for facility 1 and 2, respectively. However, the stochastic parameters are initially set to the same values for each scenario. The demand is set to 6 and the capacity reduction to 0.5. Over the experimental runs the stochastic parameters are modified for two of the three scenarios. Their values are increased for the first and decreased for the third scenario. The values of second scenario are kept constant. With step-size 0.5 for the demand and 0.05 for the capacity reduction, the stochastic parameters are modified, i.e. increased and decreased, within each run. Additionally, the scenario-wise probabilities are modified such that each scenario has equal probability of occurrence. With this setup the second scenario always depicts the average scenario of the whole scenario set, which is especially suitable for the experimental execution and evaluation. Each stochastic parameter is modified in 10 steps; the resulting experiment, therefore, contains of 100 runs.

Table 12.5c and Figure 12.6 a) present the result of the EVPI and VSS evaluation. The number and the absolute values greater than zero of EVPI and VSS intensify in the bottom-left corner of the table. It can be assumed that a stochastic programming approach for modeling risk-characteristics is especially suitable, when decision makers expect high demand variability. With respect to today's planning procedures this result has an additional insight. As the value of the stochastic solution depicts the advantageousness of considering all potential developments of uncertain parameters rather than averaging out the stochasticity, demand uncertainty should not (only) be considered by demand forecasting, but should also be captured within planning models.

There are positive values for the expected value of perfect information in the up-right corner, which indicate that the stochastic programming approach might also be suitable, if capacity uncertainty increases or the input data changes. We, therefore, conducted two further experiments with modified facility opening costs; 500 and 600 for facility 1 and 2 within one experiment as well as 100 and 200 for facility 1 and 2 within another experiment. The results are presented in Table 12.5b and Table 12.5a as well as Figure 12.6 b) and 12.6 c), respectively. By decreasing the facility opening costs the capacity uncertainty becomes more important with respect to EVPI and VSS. This leads us to the conclusion that when capacity is cheap, but its degree of availability uncertain, it is more appropriate to consider models that include the stochasticity.
The conclusion seems to be quite reasonable, when we consider real case situations for facility location problems: The opening of a production plant is endowed with huge expenses in terms of monetary investments, but also in terms of legislative regulations. Once the capacity is installed, the range of cost minimizing actions in the presence of disruptions is limited, because the execution costs of extension options are comparably small. In this situation the application of stochastic programming compared to deterministic models seems to be less advantageous. Considering the installation of warehouses, which is much cheaper than the opening of production facilities, demand uncertainty, though it might be small, is intensified

Demand Steps	Capacity Steps 1		2		3		4		5		6		7		8		9		10	
	EVPI	*VSS*	*EVPI*	*VSS*	*EVPI*	*VSS*	*EVPI*	*VSS*	*EVPI*	*VSS*	*EVPI*	*VSS*	*EVPI*	*VSS*	*EVPI*	*VSS*	*EVPI*	*VSS*	*EVPI*	*VSS*
1	0	0	0	0	0	0	0	0	25	0	66	168	67	370	67	621	79	869	79	1119
2	0	0	0	0	0	0	0	0	0	0	67	18	67	244	67	472	66	726	66	1001
3	0	0	0	0	0	0	0	0	0	0	0	0	67	93	67	342	67	585	67	848
4	0	0	0	0	0	0	0	0	0	0	0	0	19	0	66	179	67	456	67	728
5	20	0	0	0	0	0	0	0	0	0	0	0	0	0	67	44	67	289	67	604
6	24	0	21	0	21	0	0	0	0	0	0	0	0	0	0	0	67	167	67	436
7	89	81	23	0	23	0	23	0	0	0	0	0	0	0	0	0	66	22	66	324
8	92	284	91	84	25	0	25	0	25	0	25	0	0	0	0	0	0	0	75	185
9	93	486	93	285	93	87	27	0	27	0	27	0	27	0	0	0	0	0	60	0
10	95	676	95	486	95	288	95	95	28	0	28	0	28	0	28	0	0	0	0	0

(a) Facility costs (100,200).

Demand Steps	Capacity Steps 1		2		3		4		5		6		7		8		9		10	
	EVPI	*VSS*	*EVPI*	*VSS*	*EVPI*	*VSS*	*EVPI*	*VSS*	*EVPI*	*VSS*	*EVPI*	*VSS*	*EVPI*	*VSS*	*EVPI*	*VSS*	*EVPI*	*VSS*	*EVPI*	*VSS*
1	0	0	0	0	14	0	27	0	11	0	21	0	34	0	39	0	150	0	232	37
2	38	0	19	0	0	0	0	0	2	0	0	0	0	0	0	0	8	0	33	0
3	100	0	80	0	71	0	51	0	31	0	10	0	0	0	0	0	0	0	0	0
4	131	41	124	28	114	18	101	11	91	1	78	5	54	0	42	0	22	0	9	0
5	173	155	136	98	133	81	126	68	116	58	103	51	93	41	134	0	114	0	80	0
6	177	401	174	305	174	171	138	138	131	109	121	95	118	91	114	82	196	0	188	0
7	242	646	176	608	176	487	176	353	139	223	136	161	133	145	123	133	216	22	212	5
8	245	997	244	891	178	874	178	744	178	614	178	484	141	357	134	234	128	171	228	51
9	246	1394	246	1301	246	1194	179	1184	179	1060	179	937	179	813	143	693	139	573	212	376
10	247	1740	247	1653	248	1558	247	1468	181	1463	181	1346	181	1228	181	1110	144	996	141	882

(b) Facility costs (500,600).

Demand Steps	Capacity Steps 1		2		3		4		5		6		7		8		9		10	
	EVPI	*VSS*	*EVPI*	*VSS*	*EVPI*	*VSS*	*EVPI*	*VSS*	*EVPI*	*VSS*	*EVPI*	*VSS*	*EVPI*	*VSS*	*EVPI*	*VSS*	*EVPI*	*VSS*	*EVPI*	*VSS*
1	0	0	0	0	0	0	0	0	0	0	0	0	0	0	0	0	34	0	103	0
2	0	0	0	0	0	0	0	0	0	0	0	0	0	0	0	0	0	0	0	0
3	0	0	0	0	0	0	0	0	0	0	0	0	0	0	0	0	0	0	0	0
4	5	0	0	0	0	0	0	0	0	0	0	0	0	0	0	0	0	0	0	0
5	160	0	67	0	47	0	27	0	7	0	0	0	0	0	0	0	0	0	0	0
6	411	0	313	0	179	0	109	0	73	0	48	0	42	0	29	0	28	0	21	0
7	576	146	510	108	496	0	362	0	196	0	130	0	110	0	89	0	70	0	51	0
8	577	498	578	391	511	374	511	244	511	114	495	0	332	0	202	0	132	0	113	0
9	580	894	580	800	579	694	513	683	513	560	513	437	513	313	476	193	473	73	422	0
10	581	1240	581	1153	581	1058	581	968	515	963	515	845	515	728	515	610	478	496	475	382

(c) Facility costs (1000,1500).

Figure 12.5: VSS and EVPI values for illustrative example with different facility costs

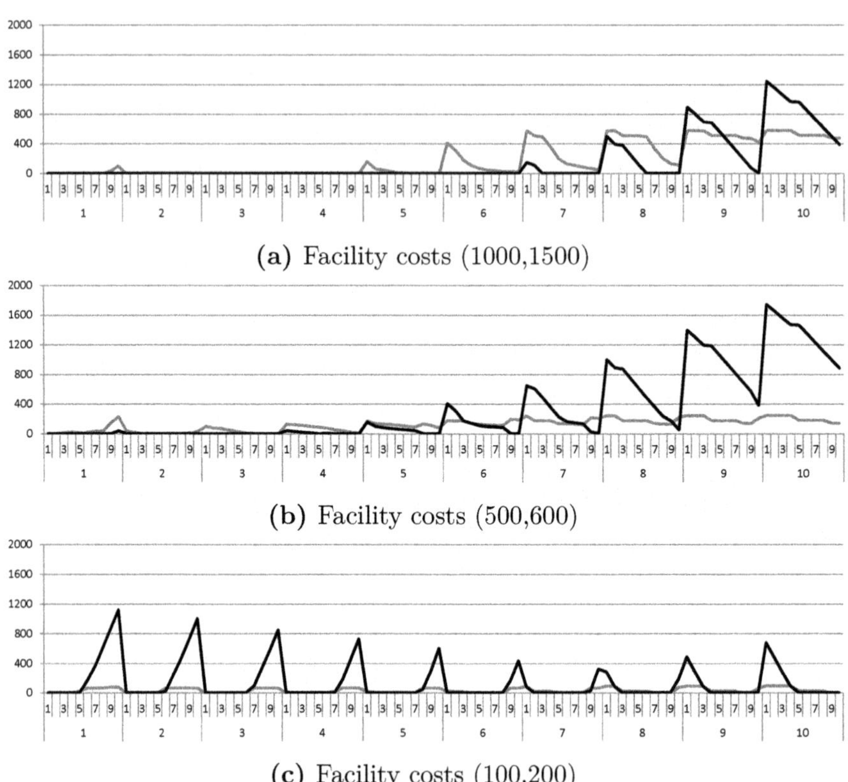

(a) Facility costs (1000,1500)

(b) Facility costs (500,600)

(c) Facility costs (100,200)

Figure 12.6: Development of VSS (♦) and EVPI (♦) values for illustrative example with different facility costs (x-Axis presents capacity (top) and demand steps (bottom)).

by capacity uncertainty. Hence, the existence of uncertainty of both parameters motivates the consideration of stochasticity within the planning process. Contrary, the installation of distribution centers or small regional warehouses is even cheaper, such that the allocation of capacity and capacity options has a wide range of possibilities. Then, increased capacity uncertainty more strongly motivates the application of stochastic programming. These presumptions are reasonable, but in order to provide dependable conclusions for the appropriateness of stochastic programming based on the logistical problem on hand more experiments are needed. Additionally as can be depicted from the solution tables, the VSS and EVPI matrix is sensitive towards modified opening costs. It can be assumed that the input data, especially the cost structure has enormous influence on the VSS and EVPI, respectively. Whether the formulation of the risk-aware CPLP as a stochastic program is useful, is assumed to depend on the cost structure as a whole. Again, more exhaustive computational experiments are necessary. We refer to a later publication on this topic.

Finally, Figure 12.7 plots the VSS and the computational run time needed to solve the stochastic problem and Figure 12.8 presents the computational run time for solving the stochastic compared to solving the deterministic problem. The model was implemented using the Java optimization modeling library of the IBM ILOG Concert Technology. The experiments were solved with ILOG CPLEX 12.6, on an Intel Core i7-2640M PC with 2.8 GHz processors and 7,88 GB RAM.

Figure 12.7 highlights that a problem setting yielding to a VSS greater than zero does not provoke considerable large computational efforts. The comparison of the computation time of the stochastic program and its deterministic counterpart shows, that – as could be expected – the solving time for the deterministic program is smaller, see Figure 12.8. The average value over all instances of the stochastic program equals to 134.7 compared to 47.5 for the deterministic program. The maximum values are given as 692 and 654, accordingly. With the goal to evaluate the development computation time in more detail, future work needs to conduct experiments with larger instances in terms of customers and facilities.

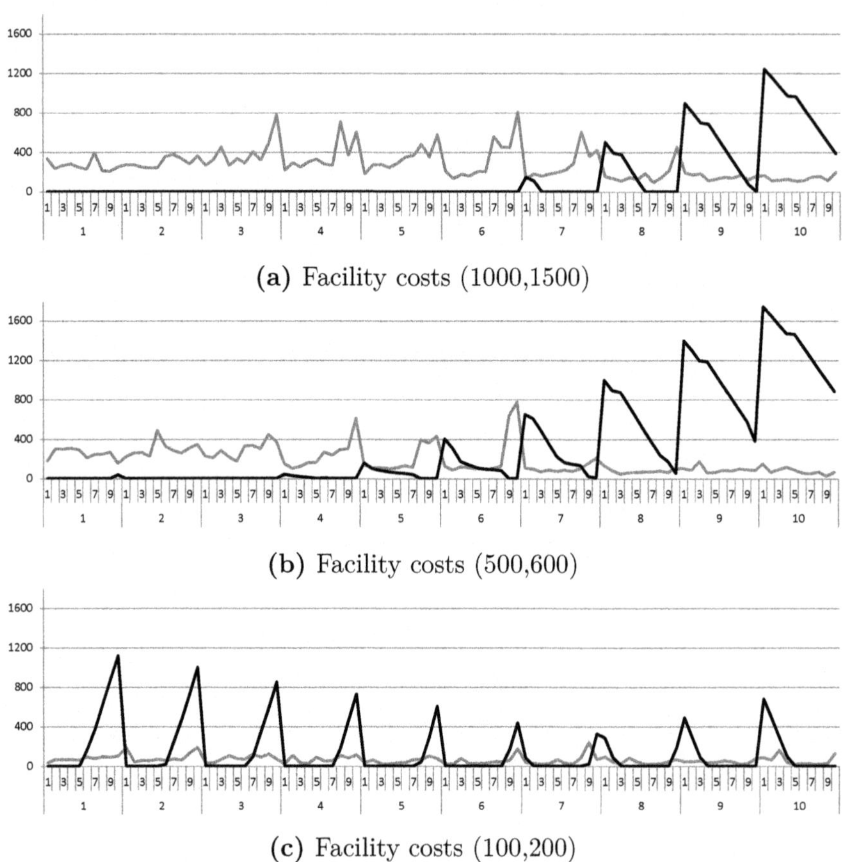

(a) Facility costs (1000,1500)

(b) Facility costs (500,600)

(c) Facility costs (100,200)

Figure 12.7: Development of computation time given in milliseconds (♦) and related VSS (♦) of the illustrative example with different facility costs (x-axis presents capacity (top) and demand steps (bottom)).

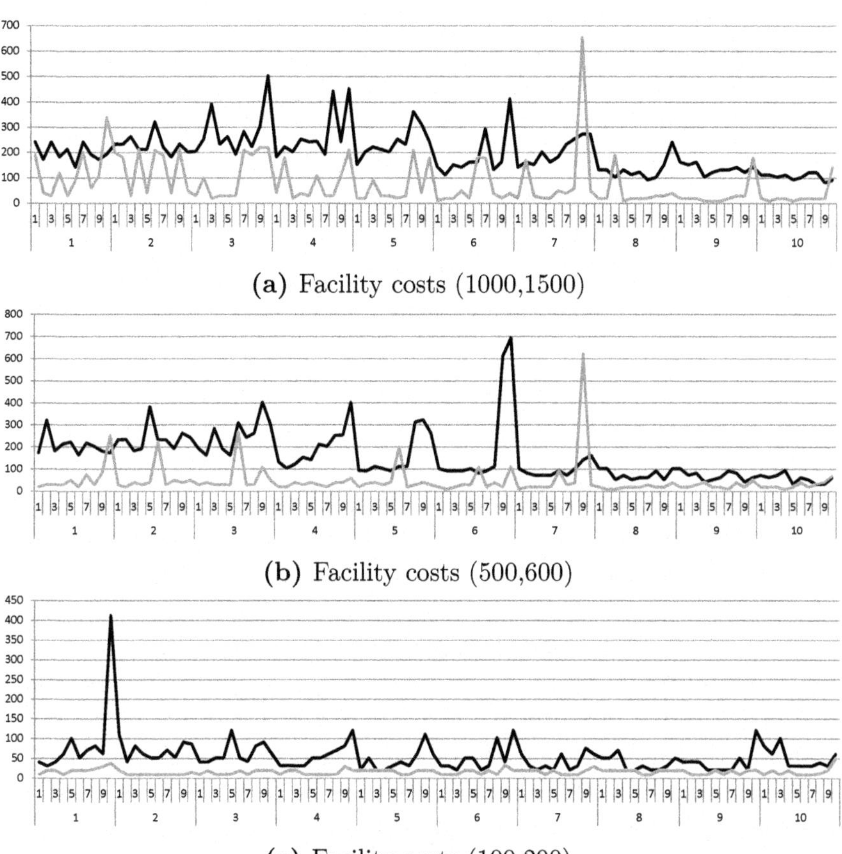

(a) Facility costs (1000,1500)

(b) Facility costs (500,600)

(c) Facility costs (100,200)

Figure 12.8: Development of computation time given in milliseconds of the stochastic program (♦) and its deterministic counterpart (♦) of the illustrative example with different facility costs (x-axis presents capacity (top) and demand steps (bottom)).

12.4 Model Extensions

The CPLP-RISK model provided so far is based on certain assumptions and specifications of the underlying supply chain. However, it offers extensions potentials with regard to the consideration of risk characteristics and the area of application. In this section we present potential extensions and discuss their value for strategic facility location problems.

12.4.1 Model Extensions for the Affected Supply Chain

The CPLP-RISK formulation as it is can be applied for a network of distribution centers, whose handling capacity is subject to uncertainty. Labor strikes or disease, like a flu epidemic, have the potential to decrease handling capacity and consequently reduce customer shipments. Companies can prepare such situations by closing contracts with external service providers. The possibility to occasionally access additional staff comes along with costs as well as the actual claim for extra-capacity. Different extension options reflect the specific range of available external employees. The type of capacity extension can refer to the number of additional handling teams or it can reflect the level of technical expertise. While the CPLP-RISK restricts the number of different capacity extension types to one for each time period, it is of course reasonable to allow a specific number of extensions, P, at each time period or a type specific number of extensions, P_h, for the whole planning horizon. In order to implement this simple model extension (12.14) should be re-formulated to match a limited number of extensions or a limited number of type specific extensions, respectively:

$$\sum_{h \in H} \omega_{iths} \leq z_i P \qquad \forall \quad i, t, s$$

or

$$\sum_{t \in T} \omega_{iths} \leq z_i P_h \qquad \forall \quad i, h, s$$

Capacity expansions can also be modeled for production facilities, whose manufacturing or production capacities are exposed to uncertainty. In case of a temporary or medium-term machine failures additional capacities can be acquired from contract manufactures or suppliers as observed at a Swiss chemical producer [189]. Direct and immediate access to production capacities asks for adequate preparations which again come along with costs prior to the capacity usage. In these situations it makes, however, sense to further limit the execution of previously installed capacity options. It might be reasonable to limit the type of extra-capacity, h, to one. Whenever the usage of capacity extension is worthwhile, the model has to determine which type of extra-capacity to choose. An additional binary variable κ_{ih} takes value of 1, if for location i the capacity expansion type h was chosen and 0 otherwise. Constraints (12.30) and (12.31) present the re-formulation of constraint (12.14) such that the aforementioned situation is captured:

$$\sum_{h} \omega_{iths} \kappa_{ih} \leq z_i \qquad \forall \quad i, h, s \tag{12.30}$$

$$\sum_{h} \kappa_{ih} \leq z_i \qquad \forall \quad i \tag{12.31}$$

Note that, this reformulation needs to be linearized as described in Chapter 9.

Furthermore, it can be necessary to restrict the duration of capacity usage. For example, an once executed option for extra-capacity has to last for a certain amount of periods or even the entire planning horizon. If we consider for example a network of regional warehouses, an additional capacity option can be provided by raising a new storage building. The preparation implies the purchase of additional property near the facility. When it becomes necessary to quickly raise an additional storage building, it is obvious that this building cannot be removed in the next period. To provide the possibility to limit the duration of an extra-capacity, we augment the indices for the decision variable ω_{iths} by an additional time index t'. The new expansion-level variable equals 1 if and only if in scenario s expansion level h is installed at facility i starting in time period t and lasting for t' time periods. The extension related to this situation affects the objective function, the demand and capacity restrictions, (12.12) and (12.13) respectively. The re-formulation for the objective function is as follows:

$$\sum_{i \in I} (f_i y_i + b_i z_i) \\ + \sum_{s \in S} \pi_s (u \Delta_s \quad + \sum_{i \in I} \sum_{h \in H} \nu_h o_h \sum_{t \in T} \sum_{t' \in T}^{T-t+1} \omega_{itt'hs} t' \\ + \sum_{t \in T} \sum_{i \in I} \sum_{j \in J} (c_{ij} - r_j) \, d_{jts} x_{ijts})$$

The extended demand and capacity restrictions equal to:

$$\sum_{j \in J} d_{jts} x_{ijts} \leq \gamma_{its} K_i y_i \\ + \sum_{h} o_h \sum_{t' \in T}^{t} \sum_{t''=t-t'+1}^{T-t'+1} \omega_{it't''hs} \quad \forall \quad i, t, s$$

$$\sum_{h \in H} \sum_{t \in T} \sum_{t' \in T}^{T-t+1} \omega_{itt'hs} \leq z_i \quad \forall \quad i, s$$

The duration of an expansion is then restricted to a certain amount of periods, T^d, or the rest of the planning horizon, $T - t$, through the following formulation:

$$\sum_{t \in T} \sum_{t' \in T}^{T-t+1} \omega_{itt'hs} t' \geq z_i (T - t)$$

or

$$\sum_{t \in T} \sum_{t' \in T}^{T-t+1} \omega_{itt'hs} t' \geq z_i T^d$$

In accordance with the specific logistical problem at hand, additional extensions to model the supply chain resilience in more detail can be formulated. We limit ourselves in having discussed some enhancement formulations applicable for the main supply chain capacity types: handling, production, and inventory.

12.4.2 Model Extensions for the Risk Objective

The CPLP-RISK model as it is captures only rudimentary the formulation of the risk objective, which is one of the core characteristic of supply chain risk. Considering risk appropriately implies to carefully balance several different objectives. We emphasize that supply chain risk needs to focus on two main types of supply chain goal achievement, namely, efficiency and effectiveness. While the CPLP-RISK model addresses one goal achievement for each of these two types, it can also be of interest to balance several different objectives of each type. The combined optimization of facility opening and option installation costs separated from distribution costs and capacity availability or customer satisfaction, can provide more insights in the *right* balance of supply chain resilience and supply chain vulnerability. The first step towards a more sophisticated consideration of the risk objective would be to introduce a bi-objective function and then proceed with the integration of additional defined terms of effectiveness, like capacity availability, and efficiency, like capacity utilization, that have the potential to draw opposite decisions.

12.4.3 Model Extensions for the Risk Attitude

Our extensive literature review revealed that the risk attitude of a supply chain decision maker has not yet been thoroughly discussed, see Chapter 3. We therein define the risk attitude with respect to the deterioration of target-values. A risk-averse decision maker only accepts a minor deterioration of target values of an efficiency- (or effectiveness-) based supply chain goal in exchange for the adherence or increase of an effectiveness- (or efficiency) based supply chain goal. Risk-seeking decision makers, however, accept higher degrees of value deterioration of a specific goal in exchange for the adherence or increase of an opposite one. Risk-neutral supply chain managers prefer neither of the two objective types, see Chapter 3. In order to introduce a more detailed consideration of the decision makers risk attitude, we emphasize that the risk attitude can change with both the value invested for the supply chain and on the past time since the last disruption has affected the supply chain:

- Risk attitude as a function of past time since the last disruption: Whenever disruptions or disasters occur, decision makers strive for better preparation or even full mitigation of such incidents. Decision makers' perceived risk attitude is risk-averse. However, it is quite common to observe that weeks or months after the disruption decision makers behave as if nothing had happened. They are more risk-seeking than right after the last disruption.
- Risk attitude as a function of investments: Similarly to the passing of time, the amount invested for the supply chain has an influence on the decision maker's risk attitude. With respect to the facility location problem such as the CPLP-T, a decision maker is risk-seeking, i.e. he is willing to spend money for the opening of facilities, because otherwise he could not enable the business.

From a certain amount of investments he becomes risk-neutral, i.e. he does not differ between investments for one or another target objective. After even more investments the decision maker becomes risk-averse, i.e. he is not willing to spent more money for increasing a specific target objective in exchange for another.

Both cases can be represented by a piecewise objective function. Different ranges (of investments or past time) represent distinct levels of risk attitude.

Besides various statistical metrics such as expected value, variance, or conditional-value-at-risk, which can assess different risk attitudes and hence the different parts of the objective function, a more simpler way is to define a utility function as objective. With the goal to assess different investment ranges, 0 to P_1, P_1 to P_2 or P_2 to P_3, differently weighting factors are introduced, δ_1, δ_2, and δ_3. The re-formulated objective function and accompanying constraints are formulated as follows:

$$\text{maximize} \quad \delta_1 q_1 + \delta_2 q_2 + \delta_3 q_3$$

$$\Phi = \begin{cases} \delta_1 \Phi & 0 \leq \Phi < P_1, \\ \delta_2 \Phi & P_1 \leq \Phi < P_2, \\ \delta_3 \Phi & P_2 \leq \Phi < P_3 \end{cases}$$

$$\begin{aligned} \Phi = \min \sum_{i \in I} (f_i y_i + b_i z_i) \\ + \sum_{s \in S} \pi_s \Big(u \Delta_s \quad & + \sum_{i \in I} \sum_{h \in H} \nu_h o_h \sum_{t \in T} \omega_{iths} \\ & + \sum_{t \in T} \sum_{i \in I} \sum_{j \in J} (c_{ij} - r_j)\, d_{jts} x_{ijts} \Big) \end{aligned}$$

$$q_1 + q_2 + q_3 = \Phi$$

$$\begin{aligned} \Phi &\leq P_1 + (1 - \alpha)M \\ q_2 &\leq (1 - \alpha)M \\ q_3 &\leq (1 - \alpha)M \\ P_1\beta &\leq \Phi \end{aligned}$$

$$\begin{aligned} \Phi &\leq P_2 + (1 - \beta)M \\ q_1 &\leq (1 - \beta)M \\ q_3 &\leq (1 - \beta)M \\ P_2\zeta &\leq \Phi \end{aligned}$$

$$\begin{aligned} \Phi &\leq P_3 + (1 - \zeta)M \\ q_1 &\leq (1 - \zeta)M \\ q_2 &\leq (1 - \zeta)M \end{aligned}$$

$$\alpha + \beta + \zeta = 1$$

12.5 Conclusions and Outlook

The CPLP-RISK model introduced in this chapter proves that it is possible to operationalize supply chain risk. The approach incorporates the core characteristics of supply chain risk derived for the *CCSCR Hierarchy* and thus provides risk-aware solutions for strategic facility location problems.

Results of the illustrative examples are reasonable with respect to the plausibility and the value of risk consideration of the CPLP-RISK formulation. Additionally, they provide the opportunity to quantify supply chain risk as defined in Chapter 3. Preliminary computational results are promising with respect to the value of the stochastic solution, the expected value of perfect information, and computational time, although more experiments with larger instances are needed for dependable conclusions for this category. First computational results show that a deterministic approach is not completely misleading, but that a stochastic formulation is still better even though the range of uncertainty is rather small.

Therefore, we emphasize that stochastic programming is especially suitable for the consideration of the supply chain risk core characteristics, because two-stage stochastic programs offer a preparedness stage for decisions that are valid prior to the occurrence of disruptive triggers and a recourse stage for decisions that adapt supply chain resilience to the realization of stochastic elements. Instead of implementing time and capacity buffers this approach allows to flexible adjust to the realization of stochasticity.

Finally, we provide possible model extensions with the purpose to enlarge the field of application as well as to draw a path for future work to improve the CPLP-RISK formulation with respect to supply chain risk incorporating characteristics.

13 Conclusions and Outlook

"Alles Wissen und alles Vermehren unseres Wissens endet nicht mit einem Schlußpunkt, sondern mit einem Fragezeichen."

"All our knowledge and all increase of our knowledge is not ending with a point, but with a question mark."

Hermann Hesse

Motivated by an ever increasing number of supply chain threatening incidents that constantly remind supply chain decision makers of the need to improve risk awareness and preparedness, the research field of supply chain risk management arose and ever since attracts the interest of both practitioners and researchers. This thesis raised the necessity and the topic of supply chain risk analytics defined herein as a subtheme of supply chain risk management and brought to application in two different settings. Based on the questions formulated in Chapter 1, which plotted the research path of this three-part thesis, the following paragraphs summarize major conclusions and disclose directions for future research.

13.1 Conlusions

Part I built a conceptual basis for supply chain risk, for supply chain risk analysis, for supply chain risk analytics, as well as for related terms.

Encouraged by a vast amount of publications that (unintentionally) miss to offer an explicit definition of supply chain risk, we conducted an extensive literature review of fundamental concepts and approaches that surround research in the field of supply chain risk management. With the goal to provide a complete foundation of nowadays understanding of supply chain risk, we studied not only mathematical approaches that originate from the operations research and management science community, but also conceptual and empirical publications. As supply chain risk is either ambiguously or incompletely defined the review did not only critically revise existing approaches, but also uncovered important core characteristics that drive the extent of supply chain risk. Arranged as the *Core Characteristics of Supply Chain Risk (CCSCR) Hierarchy* these elements underlie and strengthen our new definition of supply chain risk: *Supply chain risk is defined as the potential loss for a supply chain in terms of its target values of efficiency and effectiveness evoked by uncertain developments of supply chain characteristics whose changes were caused by the occurrence of triggering-events.*

Current supply chain risk analysis almost exclusively focuses on the identification of potential disruptive triggers within or external to the underlying supply chain. Supply chain risk is assessed and analyzed by simplified mechanisms that direct to misleading conclusions. Thus, as we concluded that supply chain risk is a multifaceted concept, whose degree of severity strongly depends on values of specific characteristics, we offered an analytical discussion of the dynamics that drive the extent of supply chain risk. The discussion was accompanied by additional definitions of related terms as well as logistical explanations. We emphasized that it is indispensable to know about and to understand these dynamics prior to the formulation of math-

ematical risk-aware supply chain models.
Modern supply chains are endowed with highly complex network structures, product portfolios, and production processes. Decision making in this environment is difficult and demands for the support of sophisticated planning models. The decision making process even aggravates, when supply chain risk needs to be incorporated. Mathematical approaches are needed that provide a basis for and trace a path towards the incorporation of risk into proprietary planning tools. Under the herein newly defined notion of supply chain risk analytics we subsumed mathematical approaches and measures tailored for the management of supply chain risk and associated sub themes. Risk preparedness comes along with additional costs; with the objective to assess the usefulness of supply chain risk analytics, we provided an analytical assessment of the costs related to different degrees of risk preparation. Consistently following preceding definitions and discussions, we offered an overview of existing literature of supply chain risk within the field of operations research and management science and disclosed relevant research gaps.

Having set the fundamental basis, we addressed the issue of incorporating supply chain risk first into a simulation and second into an optimization model.

The integration of new software tools into corporate routines and planning procedures is a time-consuming and expensive task. Therefore, in Part II of this thesis a new simulation-based procedure to identify and to assess supply chain risk is presented that offers the possibility to conduct supply chain risk analysis on top of a proprietary deterministic planning tool. We denoted this approach as *SimSCRF*. The main challenge of this approach was to appropriately model the entities that define supply chain risk. We solved this issue by underlying the framework with a theoretical basis, which assumes the following:

- Potential triggers have an indirect and/or direct influence on supply chain processes and provoke changes of the supply chain factors that specify these supply chain processes. The potential impact of triggers on supply chain factors is modeled by the means of distinct scenarios, each of which depicts a certain degree of factor value.

- The resilience of a supply chain towards factor changes is modeled by the result of a supply chain planning run. Due the fact that the purpose of supply chain planning systems is to balance demand with available resources, their results legitimately represent a good snapshot of the current workload, i.e. constitution, of the underlying supply chain.
- Supply chain decision makers know the acceptable deterioration level of relevant performance indicators. Since, modified input factor values, lead to different planning results, the impact on performance is quantified by simulating a scenario in the supply chain planning engine so that the potential deterioration can be assessed. A deviation from the used-defined target level of the objectives uncovers, whether the supply chain is exposed to supply chain risk.

By applying methods from design of experiments and response surface methodology the *SimSCRF* framework iteratively identifies those factors as well as their corresponding values that lead to the deterioration of the targeted supply chain performance. Formally, the framework can be classified as a combined approach of discrete-event simulation and supply chain optimization. We evaluated the *SimSCRF* approach on a real case supply chain originating from the chemical industry and determined the risk analysis to be plausible with respect to the identified supply chain factors. Additionally, the evaluation offered insights on potential conclusions for mitigation options.

Accompanying research was on the one hand intended to enable an efficient execution of the *SimSCRF* approach and on the other hand to provide a comprehensible evaluation. An efficient execution of the simulation framework was achieved by the application of an object-oriented information framework. The alignment of the data model for supply chain planning with the simulation-based representation of a supply chain problem provides the possibility to decouple risk analysis from the underlying supply chain planning tool. To evaluate the approach we set up a supply chain planning model, which serves as the proprietary planning tool in the *SimSCRF* approach. The developed planning model leaned on or applied formulations from well-known publications within the field of supply chain management.

The literature analysis of Part I led to the conclusion that most of the contemporary optimization approaches miss to quantitatively define and consistently model supply chain risk. It was the objective of Part III to overcome this research gap by providing a risk-aware supply chain design model. Following the developed *CCSCR Hierarchy* we deduced a mixed-integer two-stage stochastic programming model by extending the capacitated plant location problem. The deduced $CPLP^{Risk}$ model incorporates the newly defined concept of supply chain risk and therefore, provides a consistent operationalization of supply chain risk. For evaluation purposes – with respect to existing or future risk-aware models – we introduced the value of risk consideration, VCR, which is defined as the difference between the objective function value of the optimal stochastic solution, $OV(CPLP^{Risk})$, and the weighted value of the scenario-wise optimal objective function values, $\sum_s \pi_s \quad OV(CPLP_s^{T'})$. Preliminary computational results indicate the usefulness of the developed optimization model with respect to both the value of risk consideration and the application of stochastic programming principles.

In summary, this thesis provided:

- a careful literature analysis of existing supply chain risk definitions, related concepts, common risk measures, risk modeling approaches, as well as applied solution techniques,

- a new definition of supply chain risk and related terms, all arranged in the *Core Characteristics of Supply Chain Risk (CC-SCR) Hierarchy*,
- a discussion of contemporary risk rationales, resulting biases, and the influence of elementary risk characteristics on the overall extent of supply chain risk,
- a conceptual basis for supply chain risk analytics,
- a new approach combining discrete-event simulation with tactical supply chain planning that appropriately models supply chain risk,
- a two-stage stochastic programming model that shows the operationalization of supply chain risk and determines risk-aware supply chain designs, and
- a new measure to evaluate risk-aware solutions denoted as *value of risk consideration.*

13.2 Outlook

In the following we briefly summarize topics that have not been discussed in this thesis, that arise due to limitations of the afore presented concepts, approaches, and mathematical formulations, or that emerge at this point of research.

In this thesis we set the focus to supply chain risk analytics and particularly discussed the definition and assessment of risk. With respect to supply chains the definition deduced herein has been validated as being effective in two different settings. However, the identified core characteristics of supply chain risk do not seem to be specific for a supply chain environment. Although, the relevance of time-based characteristics has not been discussed extensively, it is quite common that every decision making process is exposed to an uncertain and unpredictable environment where unexpectedly occurring disruptive triggers affect the resilience of the underlying system. Irrespective of the present domain of decision making, the risk attitude almost always has an influence on the evaluation of overall objectives and consequently on the final decision. Thus, presumably this new risk concept can also be transferred to other domains covering risk. We formulate this as a future research question:

Can the risk definition as it was deduced in this thesis be transfered to other application domains?

For the nonce we assume that this risk definition can also be used for other sub-themes especially in the context of enterprise risk management. Consider for example the emergent interest for IT security. Contrary to supply chain specific issues, IT security primarily focuses on ensuring the effectiveness, i.e. functionality, of the underlying system. Efficiency is only of subordinate importance. Under the assumption that the relationship between efficiency and effectiveness can be displayed by Pareto-functions, a normalized Pareto split between efficiency and effectiveness would lie between 0 and 1, indicating the dis-functionality or functionality of the system, respectively. We assume that processes, sub-services, and their interrelation within IT systems can be modeled like supply chain networks. By transferring the theoretical concept of the *SimSCRF* model to the analysis of IT systems, it might be possible to identify and assess IT security risk. Assuming that the *SimSCRF* approach is enhanced with additional algorithms as concluded in Chapter 11, the research question can be given as:

Can the approach of the SimSCRF *model be applied for the identification and assessment of IT security risk?*

We additionally applied our supply chain risk definition to a stochastic programming formulation that offers quite promising results. The research path traced in Chapter 12 can lead to an even more sophisticated risk formulation. However, as extensively discussed in Part I of this thesis. Supply chain risk affects decisions for different logistical problems and on distinct planning levels. While the *SimSCRF* framework was developed to incorporate supply chain risk for tactical supply chain planning decisions, the $CPLP^{Risk}$ model was tailored for strategic supply chain design problems. It is an open question which logistical settings and types of decision problems would especially require or benefit from the consideration of supply chain risk. The suitability to tackle risk in other supply chain decision problems – with respect to the scope and planning horizon – needs to be carefully evaluated:

Which types of supply chain problems do especially benefit from the incorporation of supply chain risk?

The *SimSCRF* approach combines scenario-based simulation with strategic supply chain optimization. Most of contemporary combination approaches apply simulation and optimization in sequence from separated software programs. The integration of both methodologies within single mathematical formalism has already gained significant attention over the last decade [324]. Having developed a simulation-based supply chain risk analyzer as well as a risk-aware optimization model for supply chain design, it seems naturally to pose the question if their integration yields to even better supply chain planning tools.

Can an integration of the tactical SimSCRF *approach and the strategic risk-aware facility location model, yield to more risk-aware supply chains?*

Finally, this thesis does not intend to and never can be the end of the research line of risk in general or supply chain risk in particular, nor does it provide quantum leaps. As business and logistics concepts will further develop, provoking new requirements for supply chain management and hence demanding new approaches for supply chain risk, the conclusions of this thesis are in itself "at risk".

Is the Core Characteristics of Supply Chain Risk Hierarchy expandable by upcoming topics within the field of supply chain risk analytics?

Bibliography

[1] Aarrow, K. J. (1982). Risk perception in psychology and economics. *Economic Inquiry 20*, 1–9.

[2] Aberdeen Group (2005). Supply risk management benchmark: Assuring supply and mitigating risks in an uncertain economy. Technical report, Aberdeen Group.

[3] Acerbi, C. and D. Tasche (2002). On the coherence of expected shortfall. *Journal of Banking and Finance 26*, 1487–1503.

[4] Adams, J. (1995). *Risk.* London: Taylor & Francis.

[5] Aghezzaf, E. (2005). Capacity planning and warehouse location in supply chains with uncertain demands. *Journal of the Operational Research Society 56*, 453–462.

[6] Ahuja, R. K., T. L. Magnanti, and J. B. Orlin (1993). *Network flows: Theory, algorithms, and applications.* Englewood Cliffs, New Jersey: Prentice Hall.

[7] Airmic (2012). Airmic review of the supply chain insurance market –review of recent developments in the supply chain insurance market. Technical report, Airmic Ltd. Available at `http://www.airmic.com/sites/default/files/Supply%20Chain%20insurance_1.pdf` last accessed July 2015.

[8] Al Jazeera (2010). US "knew" of al-Qaeda parcel plot. *Al Jazeera November.* Available at `http://www.aljazeera.com/news/middleeast/2010/11/20101124153682723 8.html` last accessed July 2015.

[9] Alicke, K. (2005). *Planung und Betrieb von Logistiknetzwerken*. Berlin, Heidelberg, New York: Springer.

[10] Arzu Akyuz, G. and T. Erman Erkan (2010). Supply chain performance measurement: a literature review. *International Journal of Production Research 48*(17), 5137–5155.

[11] Asbjornslett, B. E. (2009). Assessing the vulnerability of supply chains. In G. A. Zsidisin and B. Ritchie (Eds.), *Supply Chain Risk*, Volume 124 of *International Series in Operations Research & Management Science*, pp. 15–33. New York: Springer.

[12] Azaron, A., K. N. Brown, S. A. Tarim, and M. Modarres (2008). A multi-objective stochastic programming approach for supply chain design considering risk. *International Journal of Production Economics 116*(1), 129–138.

[13] Bañuls, V. A. and M. Turoff (2011). Scenario construction via Delphi and cross-impact analysis. *Technological Forecasting and Social Change 78*(9), 1579–1602.

[14] Babazadeh, R. and J. Razmi (2012). A robust stochastic programming approach for agile and responsive logistics under operational and disruption risks. *International Journal of Logistics Systems and Management 13*(4), 458–482.

[15] Baffes, J. and T. Haniotis (2010). Placing the 2006/08 commodity price boom into perspective. *The World Bank – Development Prospects Group July*. Available at `http://economistsview.typepad.com/economistsview/2010/07/placing-the-200608-commodity-price-boom-into-perspective.html`, last accessed July 2015.

[16] Baghalian, A., S. Rezapour, and R. Z. Farahani (2013). Robust supply chain network design with service level against disruptions and demand uncertainties: A real-life case. *European Journal of Operational Research 227*(1), 199–215.

[17] Banks, J. (Ed.) (2007). *Handbook of Simulation: Principles, Methodology, Advances, Applications, and Practice.* John Wiley & Sons, Inc., Hoboken, NJ.

[18] Banks, J., J. S. I. Carson, and B. L. Nelson (2005). *Discrete-Event System Simulation.* Harlow, Essex: Prentice Hall.

[19] Barnes, P. and R. Oloruntoba (2005). Assurance of security in maritime supply chains: conceptual issues of vulnerability and crisis management. *Journal of International Management 11*, 519–540.

[20] Baron, D. (1977). On the utility-theoretic foundation of mean-variance analysis. *Journal of Finance 32(5)*, 1683–1697.

[21] Barroso, A., V. Machado, and V. Cruz Machado (2009). Identifying vulnerabilities in the supply chain. In *The IEEE International Conference on Industrial Engineering and Engineering Management*, pp. 1444–1448. IEEE.

[22] Basel Committee on Banking Supervision (2006). International convergence of capital measurement and capital standards. Technical report, Bank for international settlements, Basel. Available at `http://www.bis.org/publ/bcbs128.pdf` last accessed July 2015.

[23] Batty, D. (2010). Spanish airports reopen after strike causes holiday chaos. *The Guardian.* Available at `http://www.theguardian.com/world/2010/dec/04/spanish-airport-strike-state-emergency`, last accessed July 2015.

[24] BBC News (2010a). Recriminations grow over airline costs. *BBC News April.* Available at `http://news.bbc.co.uk/2/hi/europe/8633451.stm` last accessed July 2015.

[25] BBC News (2010b). Striking spain air traffic controllers return to work. *BBC News December.* Available at `http://www.bbc.com/news/world-europe-11918008` last accessed July 2015.

[26] Beamon, B. M. (1998). Supply chain design and analysis: Models and methods. *International Journal of Production Economics 55*(3), 281–294.

[27] Beamon, B. M. (1999). Measuring supply chain performance. *International Journal of Operations & Production Management 19*(3), 275–292.

[28] Behdani, B. (2013). *Handling Disruptions in Supply Chains: An Incidenttegrated Framework and an Agent-based Model.* Ph. D. thesis, Technische Universiteit Delft, The Netherlands.

[29] Bell, D. (1996). Measuring risk and return of portfolios. In R. Zeckhauser, R. Keeney, and J. Sebenius (Eds.), *Wise Choices: Decisions, Games, and Negotiations.* Boston, MA: HBS Press.

[30] Ben-Tal, A., B. D. Chung, S. R. Mandala, and T. Yao (2011). Robust optimization for emergency logistics planning: Risk mitigation in humanitarian relief supply chains. *Transportation research part B: methodological 45*(8), 1177–1189.

[31] Berdica, K. (2002). An introduction to road vulnerability: what has been done, is done and should be done. *Transport Policy 9(2)*, 117–127.

[32] Bernstein, P. L. (1998). *Against the Gods: The Remarkable Story of Risk.* New York: John Wiley.

[33] Bettonvil, B. (1990). *Detection of important factors by sequential bifurcation.* Ph. D. thesis, Tilburg University, The Netherlands.

[34] Bettonvil, B. and P. Kleijnen (1997). Searching for important factors in simulation models with many factors. *Journal of Operational Research 96(1)*, 180–194.

[35] Birkmann, J. (2006). *Measuring Vulnerability To Natural Hazards – Towards Disaster Resilient Societies*, Chapter Measuring vulnerability to promote disaster-resilient societies: Conceptual

frameworks and definitions, pp. 9–53. New Delhi: United Nations University Press.

[36] Boin, A. and A. McConnell (2007). Preparing for critical infrastructure breakdowns: the limits of crisis management and the need for resilience. *Journal of Contingencies and Crisis Management 15*(1), 50–59.

[37] Borgström, B. (2005). Exploring efficiency and effectiveness in the supply chain: a conceptual analysis. In *Proceedings from the 21st IMP Conference*, Rotterdam.

[38] Borshchev, A. and A. Filippov (2004). From system dynamics and discrete event to practical agent based modeling: Reasons, techniques, tools. In *The 22nd International Conference of the System Dynamics Society.*

[39] Bosman, R. (2006). Risk management in a global economy. Technical report, FM Global. Available at http://www.fmglobal.com/pdfs/ChainSupply.pdf last accessed July 2015.

[40] Box, G. E. and N. R. Draper (1987). *Empirical model-building and response surfaces.* New York, NJ: John Wiley & Sons, Inc.

[41] Box, G. E. and K. Wilson (1951). On the experimental attainment of optimum conditions. *Journal of the Royal Statistical Society. Series B (Methodological) 13*(1), 1–45.

[42] Breakwell, G. M. (2007). *The psychology of risk.* Cambridge: Cambridge University Press.

[43] Bundespolizeidirektion Stuttgart (2014). Zugunglück Mannheim Gemeinsame Presseerklärung Staatsanwaltschaft Mannheim und Bundespolizei. Technical report. Available at http://www.presseportal.de/polizeipresse/pm/74709/2801820/bpold-s-zugunglueck-mannheim-gemeinsame-presseerklaerung last accessed July 2015.

[44] Business Continuity Institute (2011). Supply chain resilience 2011. Technical report, Business Continuity Institute.

[45] Campolongo, F., P. Kleijnen, and T. Andres (2008). *Screening methods.* New York, NJ: John Wiley & Sons.

[46] Cardeneo, A. and T. Held (2009). Integrierte Planung von Produktion und Transport: Modellierung und Fallstudie zur zukünftigen Rolle von 4PL. In *Nachhaltigkeit in flexiblen Produktions- und Liefernetzwerken – 11. Paderborner Frühjahrstagung 2009*, pp. 119–134.

[47] Cardona, O. (2004). The need for rethinking the concepts of vulnerability and risk from a holistic perspective: A necessary review and criticism for effective risk management. In G. Bankoff, G. Frerk, and D. Hillhorst (Eds.), *Mapping Vulnerability: Disasters, Development and People*, pp. 37–51. London, UK: Earthscan Publications.

[48] Carvalho, H. and V. Cruz Machado (2011). Integrating lean, agile, resilience and green paradigms in supply chain management (larg-scm). In P. Li (Ed.), *Supply Chain Management*, pp. 66–76. InTech.

[49] Cavinato, J. L. (2004). Supply chain logistics risks. *International Journal of Physical Distribution & Logistics Management 34*(5), 383–387.

[50] Chanas, S. and P. Zieliński (2001). Critical path analysis in the network with fuzzy activity times. *Fuzzy sets and systems 122*(2), 195–204.

[51] Chapman, P., M. Christopher, U. Jüttner, H. Peck, and R. Wilding (2002). Identifying and managing supply-chain vulnerability. *Logistics & Transport Focus 4(4)*, 59–64.

[52] Chatfield, D. C., T. P. Harrison, and J. C. Hayya (2009). SCML: An information framework to support supply chain modeling. *European Journal of Operational Research 196*(2), 651–660.

[53] Chen, F. Y. and C. A. Yano (2010). Improving supply chain performance and managing risk under weather-related demand uncertainty. *Management Science 56*(8), 1380–1397.

[54] Chermack, T. J. (2004). Improving decision-making with scenario planning. *Futures 36*(3), 295–309.

[55] Chopra, S. and P. Meindl (2004). *Supply Chain Management.* New York: Pearson Education Inc.

[56] Chopra, S. and M. M. Sodhi (2004). Managing risk to avoid supply-chain breakdown. *MIT Sloan Management Review 46*(1), 53–61.

[57] Christopher, M. and H. Lee (2001). Supply chain confidence: The key to effective supply chains through improved visibility and reliability. Technical report, Cranfield University and Stanford University. Available at `https://www.gsb.stanford.edu/sites/gsb/files/publication-pdf/white-paper-supply-chain-confidence%20.pdf` last accessed July 2015.

[58] Christopher, M. and H. Peck (2004). Building the resilient supply chain. *International Journal of Logistics Management 15*(2), 1–13.

[59] Coleman, L. (2006). Frequency of man-made disasters in the 20th century. *Journal of Contingencies and Crisis Management 15*, 3–11.

[60] Comes, T., M. Hiete, N. Wijngaards, and F. Schultmann (2011). Decision Maps: A framework for multi-criteria decision support under severe uncertainty. *Decision Support Systems 52*(1), 108–118.

[61] Comfort, L. K. (2007). Crisis management in hindsight: Cognition, communication, coordination, and control. *Public Administration Review 67*, 189–197.

[62] Commission, I. E. (2006). Iec 60 050-351: International electrotechnical vocabulary part 351 – control technology. Technical report. Available at `http://www.electropedia.org/iev/iev.nsf/index?openform&part=351` last accessed July 2015.

[63] Computer Sciences Corporation (2004). Global survey of supply chain progress. Technical report, Supply Chain Mangement Review and Computer Sciences Corporation (CSC).

[64] Cox, D. (1967). *Risk-taking and information-handling in consumer behavior.* Boston: Harvard University Press.

[65] Cox, L. (2008). Why risk is not variance: An expository note. *Risk Analysis 28(4)*, 925–928.

[66] Craighead, C. W., J. Blackhurst, M. J. Rungtusanatham, and R. B. Handfield (2007). The severity of supply chain disruptions: Design characteristics and mitigation capabilities. *Decision Sciences 38*, 131–156.

[67] Cui, T., Y. Ouyang, and Z.-J. M. Shen (2010). Reliable facility location design under the risk of disruptions. *Operations Research 58*, 998–1011.

[68] de Finetti, B. (1940). Il problema dei pieni. *Giorn. Ist. Ital. Atturi 11*, 1–88.

[69] Dhaene, J., M. J. Goovaerts, and R. Kaas (2003). Economic capital allocation derived from risk measures. *North American Actuarial Journal 7*(2), 44–56.

[70] Eccles, R. G. (1991). The performance measurement manifesto. *Harvard Business Review 69(1)*, 131–137.

[71] Elkins, D., R. B. Handfield, J. Blackhurst, and C. W. Craighead (2005). 18 ways to guard against disruption. *Supply Chain Management Review 9*, 44–53.

[72] Ellis, S. C., R. M. Henry, and J. Shockley (2010). Buyer perceptions of supply disruption risk: a behavioral view and empirical assessment. *Journal of Operations Management 28*(1), 34–46.

[73] Elrod, C., S. Murray, and S. Bande (2013). A review of performance metrics for supply chain management. *Engineering Management Journal 25*, 39–50.

[74] Elster, C. and A. Neumaier (1995). Screening by conference designs. *Biometrika 82(3)*, 589–602.

[75] EM-DAT (2011). The international disaster database. Technical report. Available at `http://www.emdat.be/` last accessed July 2015.

[76] Ericson, C. A. (2005). *Hazard Analysis Techniques for System Safety.* Hoboken, NJ: John Wiley & Sons, Inc.

[77] Ermoliev, Y. M., T. Y. Ermolieva, G. J. MacDonald, V. I. Norkin, and A. Amendola (2000). A system approach to management of catastrophic risks. *European Journal of Operational Research 122*(2), 452–460.

[78] Eskew, M. (2004). Mitigating the supply chain risk. *CEO*, 25–26.

[79] Evans, J. R. (2012). *Business Analytics – Methods, Models, and Decisions.* Pearson.

[80] Falasca, M., C. W. Zobel, and D. Cook (2008). A decision support framework to assess supply chain resilience. In F. Friedrich and B. Van de Walle (Eds.), *5th ISCRAM Conference*, Washington, DC, USA, pp. 596–605.

[81] Fang, J., L. Zhao, J. C. Fransoo, and T. Van Woensel (2013). Sourcing strategies in supply risk management: An approximate dynamic programming approach. *Computers and Operations Research 40*(5), 1371–1382.

[82] Fang, K. (1980). The uniform design: application of number-theoretic methods in experimental design. *Acta Math. Appl. Sinicia 3*, 363–372.

[83] Fang, K., R. Li, and A. Sudjianto (2006). *Design and modeling for computer experiments.* London: Chapman & Hall/CRC.

[84] Fayez, M., L. Rabelo, and M. Mollaghasemi (2005). Ontologies for supply chain simulation modeling. In *Proceedings of the 2005 Winter Simulation Conference.*

[85] FAZ.NET (2011). "Keine Tabus" und "keinen Sicherheits-Rabatt". *Frankfurter Allgemeine Zeitung March.* Available at `http://www.faz.net/aktuell/politik/energiepolitik/merkels-atom-moratorium-keine-tabus-und-keinen-sicherheits-rabatt-1613323.html` last accessed July 2015.

[86] Federgruen, A. and N. Yang (2009). Optimal supply diversification under general supply risks. *Operations Research 57*(6), 1451–1468.

[87] Fernández, E. and M. Landete (2015). *Fixed-Charge Facility Location Problems*, pp. 47–77. Springer.

[88] Finkle, J. (2014). Hacker says to show passenger jets at risk of cyber attack. *Reuters.* Available at `http://www.reuters.com/article/2014/08/04/us-cybersecurity-hackers-airplanes-idUSKBN0G40WQ20140804` last accessed July 2015.

[89] Fishburn, P. C. (1984). Foundations of Risk Measurement. I. Risk As Probable Loss. *Management Science 30*(4), 396–406.

[90] Fleischmann, B., S. Ferber, and P. Henrich (2006). Strategic planning of bmws global production network. *Interfaces 36*, 194–208.

[91] Fleischmann, B., H. Meyr, and M. Wagner (2005). Advanced planning. In *Supply chain management and advanced planning*, pp. 81–106. Berlin, Heidelberg: Springer.

[92] Forrester, J. (1961). *Industrial Dynamics.* Cambridge: MIT Press.

[93] French, S. (2012). Cynefin, statistics and decision analysis. *Journal of the Operational Research Society 64*, 547–561.

[94] French, S., J. Maule, and N. Papamichail (2009). *Decision Behaviour, Analysis and Support.* Cambridge: Cambridge University Press.

[95] Fries, A. and W. G. Hunter (1980). Minimum aberration 2k-p designs. *Technometrics 22*, 601–608.

[96] Frosdick, M. (1997). The techniques of risk management are insufficient in themselves. *Disaster prevention and Management 6(3)*, 165–177.

[97] Fu, M. (2015). *Handbook of Simulation Optimization.* New York: Springer.

[98] Fujimoto, R. (1999). Parallel and distributed simulation. In *Proceedings of the 1999 Winter Simulation Conference*, pp. 122–131.

[99] Gan, B. P., L. Liu, S. Jain, S. J. Turner, W. Cai, and W.-J. Hsu (2000). Manufacturing supply chain management: distributed supply chain simulation across enterprise boundaries. In *Proceedings of the 2000 winter simulation conference*, San Diego, CA, USA, pp. 1245–1251. Society for Computer Simulation International.

[100] Ghadge, A., S. Dani, M. Chester, and R. Kalawsky (2013). A systems approach for modelling supply chain risks. *Supply Chain Management: An International Journal 18*(5), 523–538.

[101] Ghosh, S. and C. Rao (Eds.) (1996). *Handbook of Statistics 13: Design and Analysis of Experiments.* Amsterdam: Elsevier Science Pub Co.

[102] Gilovich, T., D. Griffin, and D. Kahneman (Eds.) (2002). *Heuristics and Biases: The Psychology of Intuitive Judgment.* Cambridge: Cambridge University Press.

[103] Glickmann, T. and S. White (2006). Security, visibility and resilience: The keys to mitigating supply chain vulnerabilities. *International Journal of Logistics Systems and Management 2(2)*, 10–119.

[104] Glover, F., J. P. Kelly, and M. Laguna (1996). New advances and applications of combining simulation and optimization. In *Proceedings of the 1996 winter simulation conference*, pp. 144–152.

[105] Goel, A., N. Moussavi, and V. N. Srivatsan (2008). Time to rethink offshoring. *The McKinsey Quarterly September.*

[106] Goh, M., J. Y. S. Lim, and F. Meng (2007). A stochastic model for risk management in global supply chain networks. *European Journal of Operational Research 182*(1), 164–173.

[107] Gollier, C. (2004). *The economics of risk and time.* Cambridge: MIT press.

[108] Goovaerts, M. J., F. d. Vylder, and J. Haezendonck (1984). *Insurance premiums : theory and applications.* Amsterdam: North-Holland.

[109] Götze, U. and B. Mikus (2007). Der Prozess des Risikomanagements in Supply Chains. In R. Vahrenkamp and C. Siepermann (Eds.), *Risikomanagement in Supply Chains*, pp. 29–58. Berlin: Erich Schmidt Verlag GmbH & Co.

[110] Griffin, J. (Ed.) (2010). *World Oil Outlook 2010.* Wien: Organization of the Petroleum Exporting Countries.

[111] Griffy-Brown, C. (2003). Just-in-time to just-in-case – managing a supply chain in uncertain times. *Graziadio Business Report 6(2).* Available at `http://gbr.pepperdine.edu/2010/08/just-in-time-to-just-in-case/` last accessed July 2015.

[112] Grubic, T. and I.-S. Fan (2010). Supply chain ontology: Review, analysis and synthesis. *Computers in Industry 61*, 776–786.

[113] Grundy, S., R. Pasternak, P. Greenland, S. Smith, and V. Fuster (1999). Assessment of cardiovascular risk by use of multiple-risk-factor assessment equations: A statement for healthcare professionals from the american heart association and the american college of cardiology. *Journal of the American College of Cardiology 34*(4), 1348–1359.

[114] Gurnani, H., A. Mehrotra, and S. Ray (2012). *Supply chain disruptions: Theory and practice of managing risk.* London: Springer.

[115] Habegger, B. (Ed.) (2008). *The International Handbook on Risk Analysis and Management.* Zurich: Center for Security Studies, ETH Zurich. Available at `http://www.css.ethz.ch/content/dam/ethz/special-interest/gess/cis/center-for-securities-studies/pdfs/RiA-HB-2008.pdf` last accessed July 2015.

[116] Hagmann, J. (2012). Fukushima: probing the analytical and epistemological limits of risk analysis. *Journal of Risk Research 15*(7), 801–815.

[117] Hahn, G. and H. Kuhn (2012). Value-based performance and risk management in supply chains: A robust optimization approach. *International Journal of Production Economics 139*(1), 135–144.

[118] Haimes, Y. Y., S. Kaplan, and J. H. Lambert (2002). Risk Filtering, Ranking, and Management Framework Using Hierarchical Holographic Modeling. *Risk Analysis 22*(2), 383–398.

[119] Hämäläinen, R. P., M. R. Lindstedt, and K. Sinkko (2000). Multiattribute risk analysis in nuclear emergency management. *Risk Analysis 20*(4), 455–468.

[120] Harland, C., R. Brenchley, and H. Walker (2003). Risk in supply networks. *Journal of Purchasing and Supply Management 9*(2), 51–62.

[121] Health & Consumer Protection Directorate-General (2000). First report on the harmonisation of risk assessment procedures. Technical report, European Commission. Available at `http://ec.europa.eu/food/fs/sc/ssc/out84_en.pdf` last accessed July 2015.

[122] Heckmann, I., T. Comes, and S. Nickel (2015). A critical review on supply chain risk – definition, measure and modeling. *Omega 52*(0), 119–132.

[123] Helbing, D., H. Ammoser, and C. Kühnert (2006). Disasters as Extreme Events and the Importance of Network Interactions for Disaster Response Management. In S. Albeverio, V. Jentsch, and H. Kantz (Eds.), *Extreme Events in Nature and Society*, The Frontiers Collection, pp. 319–348. Berlin, Heidelberg: Springer.

[124] Helbing, D. and S. Lämmer (2008). Managing Complexity: An Introduction. In D. Helbing (Ed.), *Managing Complexity: Insights, Concepts, Applications*, Volume 32 of *Understanding Complex Systems*, pp. 1–16. Berlin, Heidelberg: Springer.

[125] Hendricks, K. and V. Singhal (2003). The effect of supply chain glitches on shareholder wealth. *Journal of Operations Management 21(5)*, 501–523.

[126] Hendricks, K. and V. Singhal (2005a). Association between supply chain glitches and operating performance. *Management Science 51(5)*, 695–711.

[127] Hendricks, K. and V. Singhal (2005b). An empirical analysis of the effects of supply chain disruptions on long-run stock price performance and equity risk of the firm. *Production and Operations Management 14(1)*, 35–52.

[128] Hill, T. and P. Lewicki (2005). *Statistics: Methods and Applications.* Tulsa, OK: StatSoft Inc.

[129] Hillman, M. and H. Keltz (2007). Managing supply chain risk in the supply chain - a quantitative study. Technical report, AMR Research. Available at `http://www.scrlc.com/articles/AMR_Managing_Risk.pdf` last accessed July 2015.

[130] Hinsz, V. B., R. S. Tindale, and D. A. Vollrath (1997). The emerging conceptualization of groups as information processors. *Psychological Bulletin 121*(1), 43–64.

[131] Hodges, A. (2000). Emergency risk management. *Risk Management 2*(4), 7–18.

[132] Hopp, W. J. (2008). *Supply Chain Science.* Long Grove, IL: Wallace J. Hopp.

[133] Hotwagner, B. (2008). Supply Chain Risk Management und dessen systemische Umsetzung im Unternehmen. In *Supply Chain Risk Management*, pp. 23–41. Wien: Fachhochschule des bfi Wien GmbH.

[134] Hotz, I. (2007). *Simulationsbasierte Frühwarnsysteme zur Unterstützung der operativen Produktionssteuerung und-planung in der Automobilindustrie.* Ph. D. thesis, Otto-von-Guericke-Universität Magdeburg, Magdeburg.

[135] Håkansson, H. and F. Prenkert (2004). Exploring the exchange concept in marketing. In *Rethinking Marketing - developing a new understanding of markets*, pp. 75–97. Håkan Håkansson & Alexandra Walnuszewski.

[136] Huang, E. and M. Goetschalckx (2014). Strategic robust supply chain design based on the pareto-optimal tradeoff between efficiency and risk. *European Journal of Operational Research 237*(2), 508–518.

[137] Hugo, A. and E. Pistikopoulos (2005). Environmentally conscious long-range planning and design of supply chain networks. *Journal of Cleaner Production 13*, 1471–1491.

[138] Hull, J. (2006). *Options, futures, and other derivatives.* Upper Saddle River, NJ: Prentice Hall.

[139] Hull, J. (2012). *Risk Management and Financial Institutions.* Hoboken, NJ: John Wiley & Sons Inc.

[140] IBM Global Services (2009). Smarter Supply Chains: The Chief Supply Chain Officer Study. Technical report, IBM. Available at `https://www.ibm.com/smarterplanet/global/files/se__sv_se__none__smarter-sc_v2.pdf` last accessed July 2015.

[141] Ingalls, R. G. (1998). The value of simulation in modeling supply chains. In *Proceedings of the 1998 winter simulation conference*, pp. 1371–1376.

[142] International Organisation for Standardization (2007). Iso 14971:2007 – medical devices – application of risk management to medical devices. Technical report. Available at `http://www.iso.org/iso/catalogue_detail?csnumber=38193` last accessed July 2015.

[143] International Organisation for Standardization (2009). Iso/iec:31010 – risk management – risk assessment techniques. Technical report. Available at `http://www.iso.org/iso/catalogue_detail?csnumber=51073` last accessed July 2015.

[144] Ivanova, T., L. Malone, and M. Mansooreh (1999). Comparison of a two-stage group screening design to a standard 2^{k-p} design for a wholeline semiconductor manufacturing simulation model. In *Proceedings of the 1999 Winter Simulation Conference.*

[145] Jacobs, R., D. C. Whybark, and V. T. (2011). *Manufacturing planning and control for supply chain management.* New York: McGraw-Hill.

[146] Jaynes, E. (2003). *Probability Theory: the logic of science.* Camebridge: Camebridge University Press.

[147] Jenelius, E. and L.-G. Mattsson (2012). Road network vulnerability analysis of area-covering disruptions: A grid-based approach with case study. *Transportation Research Part A: Policy and Practice 46*(5), 746–760.

[148] Julka, N., T. Baines, B. Tjahjono, P. Lendermann, and V. Vitanov (2007). A review of multifactor capacity expansion models for manufacturing plants: Searching for a holistic decision aid. *International Journal of Production Economics 106*, 607–621.

[149] Jüttner, U. (2005). Supply chain risk management: Understanding the business requirements from a practitioner perspective. *The International Journal of Logistics Management 16*(1), 120–141.

[150] Jüttner, U. and S. Maklan (2011). Supply chain resilience in the global financial crisis: An empirical study. *Supply Chain Management 16*(4), 246–259.

[151] Jüttner, U., H. Peck, and M. Christopher (2003). Supply chain risk management: outlining an agenda for future research. *International Journal of Logistics Research and Applications 6*(4), 197–210.

[152] Kahneman, D. and S. Frederick (2002). Representativeness revisited: Attribute substitution in intuitive judgments. In *Heuristics and biases: The psychology of intuitive judgment.* Cambridge: Cambridge University Press.

[153] Kahneman, D. and A. Tversky (1979). Prospect theory: an analysis of decision under risk. *Econometrica 47(2)*, 263–292.

[154] Kajüter, P. (2003). Instrumente zum Risikomanagement in der Supply Chain. In W. Stölzle and A. Otto (Eds.), *Supply Chain Controlling in Theorie und Praxis*, pp. 107–135. Gabler Verlag.

[155] Kajüter, P. (2007). Risikomanagement in der Supply Chain: Ökonomische, regulatorische und konzeptionelle Grundlagen. In R. Vahrenkamp and C. Siepermann (Eds.), *Risikomanagement in Supply Chains*, pp. 13–27. Berlin: Erich Schmidt Verlag GmbH & Co.

[156] Kanitz, F. (2002). Logistik-FMEA für die Produktion. In W. F.-P. (Ed.), *Erfolgsfaaktor Logistikqualität*, pp. 112–118. Berlin: Springer.

[157] Kaplan, R. S. and D. Norton (1992). The balanced scorecard: Measures that drive performance. *Harvard Business Review 70(1)*, 71–79.

[158] Kelley, J. and M. Walker (1959). Critical-path planning and scheduling. In *Proceedings of the Eastern Joint Computer Conference*, pp. 160–173.

[159] Kelton, W. D. and A. M. Law (1991). *Simulation modeling and analysis*, Volume 2. Boston: McGraw-Hill.

[160] Kersten, W., M. Böger, P. Hohrath, and H. Späth (2006). Supply chain risk management: Development of a theoretical and empirical framework. In W. Kersten and T. Blecker (Eds.), *Managing Risks in Supply Chains - How to Build Reliable Collaboration in Logistics*, pp. 3–18. Berlin: Erich Schmidt Verlag GmbH & Co.

[161] Kersten, W., T. Blecker, and H. Flämig (Eds.) (2008). *Global Logistics Management – Sustainability, Quality, Risks.* Berlin: Erich Schmidt Verlag GmbH & Co.

[162] Kersten, W., T. Held, C. Meyer, and P. Hohrath (2007). Komplexitäts- und Risikomanagement als Methodenbausteine des

Supply Chain Managements. In I. H. . C. Mauch (Ed.), *Management am Puls der Zeit – Strategien, Konzepte und Methoden*, pp. 1569–1181. München: TCW – Transfer Centrum Verlag.

[163] Khuri, A. and J. Cornell (1996). *Response surface: design and analysis.* CRC press.

[164] King, A. J. and S. W. Wallace (2012). *Modeling with stochastic programming.* New York: Springer Science & Business Media.

[165] Klayman, J. and Y.-w. Ha (1987). Confirmation, disconfirmation, and information in hypothesis testing. *Psychological Review 94*(2), 211–228.

[166] Kleijnen, J. P. (2005). Supply chain simulation tools and techniques: a survey. *International Journal of Simulation and Process Modelling 1*(1), 82–89.

[167] Kleijnen, K. P. C. (2008). *Design and Analysis of Simulation Experiments.* Switzerland: Springer.

[168] Kleindorfer, P. R. and G. H. Saad (2005). Managing disruption risks in supply chains. *Production and Operations Management 14*(1), 53–68.

[169] Klibi, W. and A. Martel (2012). Scenario-based supply chain network risk modeling. *European Journal of Operational Research 223*, 644–658.

[170] Klinke, A. and O. Renn (2002). A New Approach to Risk Evaluation and Management: Risk-Based, Precaution-Based, and Discourse-Based Strategies. *Risk Analysis 22*(6), 1071–1094.

[171] Knight, F. (1921). *Risk, Uncertainty, and Profit.* Boston: Houghton Mifflin Co.

[172] Ko, H. and G. Evans (2007). A genetic algorithm-based heuristic for the dynamic integrated forward/reverse logistics network for 3pls. *Computers & Operations Research 34*, 346–366.

[173] Kohler, B. (2011). Verglüht. *Frankfurter Allgemeine Zeitung*. Available at `http://www.faz.net/aktuell/politik/atomdebatte-verglueht-1603852.html` last accessed July 2015.

[174] Kovacs, G. L. and P. Paganelli (2003). A planning and management infrastructure for large, complex, distributed projects–beyond ERP and SCM. *Computers in Industry 51*(2), 165–183.

[175] KPMG (2008). Risikomanagement – Von der Gesetzeserfüllung zum strategischen Steuerungsinstrument. Technical report, KPMG, Frankfurt.

[176] Kuhn, A. and B. Youngberg (2002). The need for risk management to evolve to assure a culture of safety. *Quality and Safety in Health Care 11*(2), 158–162.

[177] Kull, T. and D. Closs (2008). The risk of second-tier supplier failures in serial supply chains: Implications for order policies and distributor autonomy. *European Journal of Operational Research 186*(3), 1158–1174.

[178] Kumar, S. K., M. Tiwari, and R. F. Babiceanu (2010). Minimisation of supply chain cost with embedded risk using computational intelligence approaches. *International Journal of Production Research 48*(13), 3717–3739.

[179] Kupsch, P. (1995). Risikomanagement. In R. M. Corsten, H. (Ed.), *Handbuch Unternemehensführung. Konzepte - Instrumente - Schnittstellen.* Wiesbaden: Gabler.

[180] Lai, G., L. G. Debo, and K. Sycara (2009). Sharing inventory risk in supply chain: The implication of financial constraint. *Omega 37*(4), 811–825.

[181] Landsman, Z. and M. Sherris (2001). Risk measures and insurance premium principles. *Insurance: Mathematics and Economics 29(1)*, 103–115.

[182] Lapide, L. (2000). What about measuring supply chain performance? *Achieving Supply Chain Excellence Through Technology 2*, 287–297.

[183] Leadbetter, S. J. and M. C. Hort (2011). Volcanic ash hazard climatology for an eruption of hekla volcano, iceland. *Journal of Volcanology and Geothermal Research 199*(3–4), 230–241.

[184] Lempert, R. J. and D. G. Groves (2010). Identifying and evaluating robust adaptive policy responses to climate change for water management agencies in the american west. *Technological Forecasting and Social Change 77*(6), 960–974.

[185] Li, S., B. Ragu-Nathan, T. Ragu-Nathan, and S. Subba Rao (2006). The impact of supply chain management practices on competitive advantage and organizational performance. *Omega 34*(2), 107–124.

[186] Lin, F.-R. and M. J. Shaw (1998). Reengineering the order fulfillment process in supply chain networks. *International Journal of Flexible Manufacturing Systems 10*(3), 197–229.

[187] Liu, Z. and A. Nagurney (2011). Supply chain outsourcing under exchange rate risk and competition. *Omega 39*(5), 539–549.

[188] Lockamy III, A. and K. McCormack (2010). Analysing risks in supply networks to facilitate outsourcing decisions. *International Journal of Production Research 48*(2), 593–611.

[189] Logistik Heute (2010). Leihproduktion als Backup. *LOGISTIK HEUTE* (4), 54–55.

[190] Lohse, E. and M. Wehner (2011). Im Gespräch: Umweltminister Norbert Röttgen Können schneller aussteigen als bisher geplant. *Frankfurter Allgemeine Zeitung März.* Available at `http://www.faz.net/aktuell/politik/energiepolitik/im-gespraech-umweltminister-norbert-roettgen-koennen-`

schneller-aussteigen-als-bisher-geplant-1608605.html last accessed July 2015.

[191] Longo, F. (2011). Advances of modeling and simulation in supply chain and industry. *Simulation 87*(8), 651–656.

[192] Lynch, G. (2012). *Supply Chain Disruptions: Theory and Practice of Managing Risk*, Chapter Supply Chain Risk Management, pp. 319–337. London, UK: Springer.

[193] Mak, H.-Y. and Z.-J. Shen (2012). Risk diversification and risk pooling in supply chain design. *IIE Transactions 44*(8), 603–621.

[194] Manuj, I. and J. T. Mentzer (2008). Global supply chain risk management strategies. *International Journal of Physical Distribution & Logistics Management 38*(3), 192–223.

[195] Manyena, S. B. (2006). The concept of resilience revisited. *Disasters 30*(4), 434–450.

[196] March, J. G. and Z. Shapira (1987). Managerial perspectives on risk and risk taking. *Management science 33(11)*, 1404–1418.

[197] Markowitz, H. (1952). Portfolio selection. *The Journal of Finance 7*(1), 77–91.

[198] Martha, J. and S. Subbakrishna (2002). Targeting a just-in-case suppyl chain for the inevitable next disaster. Technical report, Supply Chain Management Review. Available at https://www.highbeam.com/doc/1G1-91562584.html last accessed July 2015.

[199] Maule, A. and G. Hodgkinson (2002). Heuristics, biases and strategic decision making. *The Psychologist 15*, 68–71.

[200] McGill, J. I. and G. J. Van Ryzin (1999). Revenue management: Research overview and prospects. *Transportation science 33*(2), 233–256.

[201] McKay, M., W. Conover, and R. Beckmann (1979). A comparison of three methods for selecting values of input variables in the analysis of output from a computer code. *Technometrics 21*, 239–245.

[202] McNeil, A. J., R. Frey, and P. Embrechts (2015). *Quantitative Risk Management: Concepts, Techniques and Tools.* Princeton University Press.

[203] Mearian, L. (2011). Hard drive prices slide as thai flood aftermath subsides. *COMPUTERWORLD.* Available at `http://www.computerworld.com/article/2500625/data-center/hard-drive-prices-slide-as-thai-flood-aftermath-subsides.html` last accessed July 2015.

[204] Melnyk, S., A. Rodrigues, and G. Ragatz (2008). Using simulation to investigate supply chain disruptions. In G. A. Zsidisin and B. Ritchie (Eds.), *Supply Chain Risk – A Handbook of Assessment, Management, and Performance*, Volume 124, pp. 103–122. Springer Science & Business Media.

[205] Melo, M., S. Nickel, and F. Saldanha-da-Gama (2009). Facility location and supply chain management - a review. *European Journal of Operational Research 196*, 401–412.

[206] Merriam-Webster (2013).

[207] Merz, M., M. Hiete, T. Comes, and F. Schultmann (2013). A composite indicator model to assess natural disaster risks in industry on a spatial level. *Journal of Risk Research 16*(9), 1077–1099.

[208] Meyr, H., M. Wagner, and J. Rhode (2005). Structure of advanced planning systems. In H. Stadtler and C. Kilger (Eds.), *Supply Chain Management and Advanced Planning – Concepts, Models, Software and Case Studies.* Berlin, Heidelberg: Springer.

[209] Miranda, P. and R. Garrido (2009). Inventory service-level optimization within distribution network design problem. *International Journal of Production Economics 122*(1), 276–285.

[210] Möller, K. E. K. and P. Törrönen (2003). Business suppliers' value creation potential: A capability-based analysis. *Industrial Marketing Management 32(2)*, 109–118.

[211] Montgomery, D. (2009). *Design and Analysis of Experiments.* John Wiley & Sons.

[212] Montgomery, D. C., C. M. Borror, and J. D. Stanley (1997). Some cautions in the use of plackett-burman designs. *Quality Engineering 10*(2), 371–381.

[213] Morgan, M. G. and M. Henrion (1990). *Uncertainty: A Guide to Dealing with Uncertainty in Quantitative Risk and Policy Analysis.* Cambridge: Cambridge University Press.

[214] Morrice, D. and I. Bardhan (1995). A weighted least-squares approach to computer simulation factor screening. *Operations Research 43(5)*, 792–806.

[215] Mula, J., D. Peidro, M. Díaz-Madroñero, and E. Vicens (2010). Mathematical programming models for supply chain production and transport planning. *European Journal of Operational Research 204(3)*, 377–390.

[216] Mullai, A. (2008). Risk management system - a conceptual model. In G. A. Zsidisin and B. Ritchie (Eds.), *Supply Chain Risk - A Handbook of Assessment, Management, and Performance*, pp. 83–102. Springer Science+Business Media.

[217] Munich Re (2007). Natural catastrophes 2006: Analyses, assessments, positions. Technical report, Munich Re. Available at `http://www.unisdr.org/files/1610_topics2006.pdf` last accessed July 2015.

[218] Munich Re Group (2004). Annual review: Natural catastrophes 2003. Technical report, Munich Re Group. Available at `http://www.sfu.ca/geog312/readings/Munich%20Re%282004%29.pdf` last accessed July 2015.

[219] Murray, A. T. and T. H. Grubesic (Eds.) (2007). *Critical Infrastructure – Reliability and Vulnerability.* Berlin, Heidelberg: Springer.

[220] Myers, R. H. and D. Montgomery (2002). *Response Surface Methodology: Process and Product Optimization Using Designed Experiments.* John Wiley and Sons.

[221] Nagurney, A., J. Cruz, J. Dong, and D. Zhang (2005). Supply chain networks, electronic commerce, and supply side and demand side risk. *European Journal of Operational Research 164*(1), 120–142.

[222] Neubürger, K. W. (1989). *Chancen- und Risikobeurteilung im strategischen Management: die informatorische Lücke.* Poeschel.

[223] Neyman, J. (1950). *First Course in probability and Statistics.* Henry Holt.

[224] Nickel, S., F. Saldanha-da Gama, and H.-P. Ziegler (2012). A multi-stage stochastic supply network design problem with financial decisions and risk management. *Omega 40*(5), 511–524.

[225] Norrman, A. and U. Jansson (2004). Ericsson's proactive supply chain risk management approach after a serious sub-supplier accident. *International Journal of Physical Distribution & Logistics Management 34*(5), 434–456.

[226] Oliveira, F., V. Gupta, S. Hamacher, and I. E. Grossmann (2013). A lagrangean decomposition approach for oil supply chain investment planning under uncertainty with risk considerations. *Computers and Chemical Engineering 50*, 184–195.

[227] Owen, S. H. and M. S. Daskin (1998). Strategic facility location: A review. *European Journal of Operational Research 111*, 423–447.

[228] Oxford Economics (2010). The economic impacts of air travel restrictions due to volcanic ash. Technical report, Oxford Economics, Oxford. Available at .

[229] Papadakis, I. S. (2006). Financial performance of supply chains after disruptions: an event study. *Supply Chain Management: An International Journal 11*(1), 25–33.

[230] Peck, H. (2005). Drivers of supply chain vulnerability: an integrated framework. *International Journal of Physical Distribution & Logistics Management 35*(4), 210–232.

[231] Peck, H. (2006). Reconciling supply chain vulnerability, risk and supply chain management. *International Journal of Logistics Research and Applications 9*(2), 127–142.

[232] Pedersen, C. S. and S. E. Satchell (1998). Choosing the right risk measure: A survey. Technical report. Available at `http://citeseerx.ist.psu.edu/viewdoc/download?doi=10.1.1.17.8559&rep=rep1&type=pdf` last accessed July 2015.

[233] Peng, M., Y. Peng, and H. Chen (2014). Post-seismic supply chain risk management: A system dynamics disruption analysis approach for inventory and logistics planning. *Computers and Operations Research 42*, 14–24.

[234] Petak, W. J. (1985). Emergency management: A challenge for public administration. *Public Administration Review 45*, 3–7.

[235] Pettit, T. J., J. Fiksel, and K. L. Croxton (2010). Ensuring supply chain resilience: Development of a conceptual framework. *Journal of Business Logistics 31*(1), 1 – 21.

[236] Plackett, R. L. and J. P. Burman (1946). The design of optimum multifactorial experiments. *Biometrika*, 305–325.

[237] Ponomarov, S. and M. C. Holcomb (2009). Understanding the concept of supply chain resilience. *International Journal of Logistics Management 20(1)*, 124–143.

[238] Poojari, C. A., C. Lucas, and G. Mitra (2008). Robust solutions and risk measures for a supply chain planning problem under uncertainty. *Journal of the Operational Research Society 59*(1), 2–12.

[239] Punter, A. (2013). Supply chain failures – a study of the nature, causes and complexity of supply chain disruptions. Technical report, Airmic – Sponsored by Allianz Global Corporate & Specialty & Lockton. Available at `http://www.airmic.com/sites/default/files/supply_chain_failures_2013_FINAL_web.pdf` last accessed July 2015.

[240] PwC (2011). Transportation & logistics 2030, volume 4: Securing the supply chain. Technical report, PwC. Available at `https://www.pwc.com/gx/en/transportation-logistics/pdf/tl2030_vol.4_web.pdf` last accessed July 2015.

[241] Quansah, J. E., B. Engel, and G. L. Rochon (2010). Early warning systems: A review. *Journal of Terrestrial Observation 2(2)*, 24–44.

[242] Ramos, M. (2004). *How to comply with Sarbanes-Oxley Section 404*. Wiley.

[243] Ray, B., C. Apte, K. McAuliffe, and L. Deleris (2008). Harnessing uncertainty: The future of risk analytics. Technical report, IBM Research Division. Available at `http://domino.research.ibm.com/library/cyberdig.nsf/papers/B910FD4421357445852574340053 49F4` last accessed July 2015.

[244] Renda, A. (2010). Protecting critical infrastructure in the EU. CEPS task force report, Centre for European Studies, Brussels. Available at https://www.ceps.eu/publications/protecting-critical-infrastructure-eu last accessed July 2015.

[245] Rice, J. and F. Caniato (2003). Building a secure and resilient supply network. *Supply Chain Management Review 7(5)*, 22–30.

[246] Richardson, G. (1991). *Feedback Thought in Social Science and Systems Theory.* University of Pennsylvania Press.

[247] Richey Jr, R. G. (2009). The supply chain crisis and disaster pyramid: a theoretical framework for understanding preparedness and recovery. *International Journal of Physical Distribution & Logistics Management 39*(7), 619–628.

[248] Risk Response Network (2011). New models for addressing supply chain and transport risk. Technical report, The World Economic Forum. Available at http://www3.weforum.org/docs/WEF_SCT_RRN_NewModelsAddressingSupplyChainTransportRisk_IndustryAgenda_2012.pdf last accessed July 2015.

[249] Risk Response Network (2013a). Building resilience in supply chains. Technical report, The World Economic Forum. Available at http://www3.weforum.org/docs/WEF_RRN_MO_BuildingResilienceSupplyChains_Report_2013.pdf last accessed July 2015.

[250] Risk Response Network (2013b). Global risks 2013. Technical report, The World Economic Forum. Available at http://www3.weforum.org/docs/WEF_GlobalRisks_Report_2013.pdf last accessed July 2015.

[251] Ritchie, B. and C. Brindley (2009). Effective management of supply chains: Risks and performance. In T. Wu and J. Blackhurst (Eds.), *Managing Supply Chain Risk and Vulnerability – Tools and Methods for Supply Chain Decision Makers.* Springer.

[252] Rockafellar, R. T. and S. Uryasev (2000). Optimization of conditional value-at-risk. *Journal of risk 2*, 21–42.

[253] Rogers, H., K. Pawar, and C. Braziotis (2012). Supply chain disturbances: Contextualising the cost of risk and uncertainty in outsourcing. In H. K. Chan, F. Lettice, and O. A. Durowoju (Eds.), *Decision-Making for Supply Chain Integration*, Volume 1 of *Decision Engineering*, pp. 145–164. London: Springer.

[254] Rohde, J., H. Meyr, and M. Wagner (2000). Die Supply Chain Planning Matrix. *PPS Management 5(1)*, 10–15.

[255] Rosenhead, J., M. Elton, and S. Gupta (1972). Robustness and optimality as criteria for strategic decisions. *Operational Research Quaterly 23*(4), 413–430.

[256] Ross, I. (1975). Perceived risk and consumer behavior: a critical review. *Advances in Consumer Research 2(1)*, 1–20.

[257] Ruta, A. (1999). *Fehlermöglichkeits- und Einflussanalyse FMEA füer die Produktionslogistik.* Ph. D. thesis, Universität Hannover.

[258] Sabri, E. and B. Beamon (2000). A multi-objective approach to simultaneous strategic and operational planning in supply chain design. *Omega 28*(5), 581–598.

[259] Sahay, B. and J. Ranjan (2008). Real time business intelligence in supply chain analytics. *Information Management & Computer Security 16(1)*, 28–48.

[260] Sahebi, H., S. Nickel, and J. Ashayeri (2014). Strategic and tactical mathematical programming models within the crude oil supply chain context. *Computers & Chemical Engineering 68*, 56–77.

[261] Sammonds, P., B. McGuire, and S. Edwards (2010). Volcanic hazard from Iceland: Analysis and implications of the

Eyjafjallajökull eruption. Technical report, University College London. Institute for Risk and Disaster Reduction, London. Available at https://www.ucl.ac.uk/rdr/documents/docs-publications-folder/icelandreport last accessed July 2015.

[262] Sarykalin, S., G. Serraino, and S. Uryasev (2008). Value-at-risk vs. conditional value-at-risk in risk management and optimization. In *Tutorials in Operations Research*, pp. 270–294. INFORMS.

[263] Savage, S. L. (2012). *The Flaw of Averages: Why We Underestimate Risk in the Face of Uncertainty.* John Wiley & Sons.

[264] Sawik, T. (2011). Selection of supply portfolio under disruption risks. *Omega 39*(2), 194 – 208.

[265] Sawik, T. (2013). Integrated selection of suppliers and scheduling of customer orders in the presence of supply chain disruption risks. *International Journal of Production Research 51*(23-24), 7006–7022.

[266] Sawik, T. (2014). Optimization of cost and service level in the presence of supply chain disruption risks: Single vs. multiple sourcing. *Computers and Operations Research 51*, 11–20.

[267] Schmitt, A. J. (2011). Strategies for customer service level protection under multi-echelon supply chain disruption risk. *Transportation Research Part B: Methodological 45*(8), 1266–1283.

[268] Schmitt, A. J. and M. Singh (2012). A quantitative analysis of disruption risk in a multi-echelon supply chain. *International Journal of Production Economics 139*(1), 22–32.

[269] Schruben, L. and V. Cogliano (1987). An experimental procedure for simulation response surface model identification. *Communications of the ACM 30(8)*, 716–730.

[270] Sheffi, Y. (2005). *The Resilient Enterprise: Overcoming Vulnerability for Competitive Advantage*, Volume 1 of *MIT Press Books*. Cambridge: MIT Press.

[271] Sheffi, Y. and B. Rice (2005). A supply chain view of the resilient enterprise. Technical report, MIT Sloan Management Review. Available at http://web.mit.edu/scresponse/repository/Sheffi_Rice_SC_View_of_the_Resilient_Enterprise_Fall_2005.pdf last accessed July 2015.

[272] Silver, E. A., D. F. Pyke, and R. Peterson (1998). *Inventory Management and Production Planning and Scheduling*. John Wiley & Sons.

[273] Simchi-Levi, D. (2010). *Operations rules*. Cambridge: MIT Press.

[274] Simchi-Levi, D., P. Kaminsky, and E. Simchi-Levi (2008). *Designing and Managing the Supply Chain*. McGraw-Hill/Irwin.

[275] Simchi-Levi, D., D. Nelson, N. Mulani, and J. Wright (2008a). Crude calculations – why high oil prices are upending the way companies should manage their supply chains. *The Wall Street Journal September*. Available at http://www.wsj.com/articles/SB122160061166044841 last accessed Juyl 2015.

[276] Simchi-Levi, D., D. Nelson, N. Mulani, and J. Wright (2008b). The impact of oil price on supply chain strategies: From static to dynamic. Technical report, Massachusetts Institute of Technology.

[277] Simpson, T., A. Booker, D.Ghosh, A. Giunta, P. Koch, and R. Yang (2004). Approximation methods in multidisciplinary analysis and optimization: a panel discrussion. *Structural and Multidisciplinary Optimization 27(5)*, 302–313.

[278] Singhal, P., G. Agarwal, and M. L. Mittal (2011). Supply chain risk management: review, classification and future research directions. *Int. Journal of Business Science and Applied Management 6*(3), 15–42.

[279] Skjong, R. (2005). Risk - a word from ancient greece. Technical report, DNV Managing Risk DNV.com. Available at http://www.dnv.com/focus/risk_management/more_information/risk_origin/ last accessed November 2012.

[280] Smith, J. C. (2010). *Basic Interdiction Models.* Wiley Encyclopedia of Operations Research and Management Science.

[281] Snyder, L. (2005). Facility location under uncertainty: a review. *IIE Transactions 38*, 537–554.

[282] Snyder, L. V., Z. Atan, P. Peng, Y. Rong, A. J. Schmitt, and B. Sinsoysal (2012). OR/MS models for supply chain disruptions: A review. *Available at SSRN 1689882*.

[283] Society of Risk Analysis (2014). *Glossary of Risk Analysis Terms.* Society of Risk Analysis. Available at http://www.sra.org/sites/default/files/docs/SRA_Glossary.pdf last accessed July 2015.

[284] Sodhi, M. S. (2005). Managing demand risk in tactical supply chain planning for a global consumer electronics company. *Production and Operations Management 14*(1), 69–79.

[285] Sodhi, M. S., B.-G. Son, and C. Tang (20012). Researchers perspective on supply chain risk management. *Production and Operations Management 21(1)*, 1–13.

[286] Sodhi, M. S. and C. Tang (2009). Managing supply chain disruptions via time-based risk management. In T. Wu and J. Blackhurst (Eds.), *Managing Supply Chain Risk and Vulnerability – Tools and Methods for Supply Chain Decision Makers.* Springer Science /& Business Media.

[287] Soleimani, H. and K. Govindan (2014). Reverse logistics network design and planning utilizing conditional value at risk. *European Journal of Operational Research 273*(2), 487–497. Article in Press.

[288] Souza, G. (2014). Supply chain analytics. *Business Horizons 57*(5), 595–605.

[289] Staab, S. and R. Studer (2010). *Handbook on ontologies.* Springer Science & Business Media.

[290] Stadtler, H. (2005). Supply chain management and advanced planning—-basics, overview and challenges. *European journal of operational research 163*(3), 575–588.

[291] Stadtler, H. and C. Kilger (Eds.) (2005). *Supply Chain Management and Advanced Planning – Concepts, Models, Software and Case Studies* (2nd ed.). Berlin, Heidelberg: Springer.

[292] Stock, J. and S. Boyer (2009). Developing a consensus definition of supply chain management: A qualitative study. *International Journal of Physical Distribution & Logistics Management 39(8)*, 690–711.

[293] Studer, R., V. R. Benjamins, and D. Fensel (1998). Knowledge engineering: principles and methods. *Data & knowledge engineering 25*(1), 161–197.

[294] Stumpp, M. (2010). A framework for statistical analysis of supply chain risks using factorial experiment designs - theory and application. Master's thesis, Karlsruhe Institute of Technology.

[295] Supply Chain Council (2008). Supply chain operations reference model 9.0 reference guide. Technical report.

[296] Supply Chain Digest (2009). The greatest supply chain disasters of all time. Technical report, Supply Chain Digest. Available at `http://www.scdigest.com/assets/news/09-05-07.htm\#FT` last accessed July 2015.

[297] Svensson, G. (2000). A conceptual framework for the analysis of vulnerability in supply chains. *International Journal of Physical Distribution & Logistics Management 30(9)*, 731–750.

[298] Svensson, G. (2002). Dyadic vulnerability in companies' inbound and outbound logistics flows. *Journal of Logistics: Research and Applications 5(1)*, 81–113.

[299] Svensson, G. (2004). Vulnerability in business relationships: the gap between dependence and trust. *Journal of Business & Industrial Marketing 19(7)*, 469–483.

[300] Takata, S. and M. Yamanaka (2013). BOM based supply chain risk management. *CIRP Annals - Manufacturing Technology 62*(1), 479–482.

[301] Taleb, N. N. (2007). *The Black Swan – The impact of the highly improbable.* Random House.

[302] Talluri, K. T. and G. J. Van Ryzin (2006). *The theory and practice of revenue management*, Volume 68. Springer Science & Business Media.

[303] Tang, C. and B. Tomlin (2008a). How much flexibility does it take to mitigate supply chain risk? In G. A. Zsidisin and B. Ritchie (Eds.), *Supply Chain Risk: A Handbook of Assessment, Management, and Performance*, Volume 124, pp. 155–174. Springer Science & Business Media.

[304] Tang, C. and B. Tomlin (2008b). The power of flexibility for mitigating supply chain risks. *International Journal of Production Economics 116*(1), 12–27.

[305] Tang, O. and S. Nurmaya Musa (2011). Identifying risk issues and research advancements in supply chain risk management. *International Journal of Production Economics 133*(1), 25–34.

[306] Tang, S. (2006a). Perspectives in supply chain risk management. *International Journal of Production Economics 103*, 451–488.

[307] Tang, S. (2006b). Robust strategies for mitigating supply chain disruptions. *International Journal of Logistics 9*, 33–45.

[308] Tekin, E. and I. Sabuncuoglu (2004). Simulation optimization: A comprehensive review on theory and applications. *IIE Transactions 36*(11), 1067–1081.

[309] Terzi, S. and S. Cavalieri (2004). Simulation in the supply chain context: a survey. *Computers in industry 53*(1), 3–16.

[310] The Open Group Trusted Technology Forum (OTTF™ (2011). Open trusted technology provider framework – industry best practices for manufacturing technology products that facilitate customer technology acquisition risk management practices and options for promoting industry adoption. Technical report, The Open Group.

[311] Tomlin, B. (2006). On the value of mitigation and contingency strategies for managing supply chain disruption risks. *Management Science 52*(5), 639–657.

[312] Trkman, P., K. McCormack, and M. P. V. de OliveiraAND Marcelo Bronzo Ladeira (2010). The impact of business analytics on supply chain performance. *Decision Support Systems 49*, 318–327.

[313] Trocine, L. and L. Malone (2000). Finding important independent variables through screening designs: A comparison of methods. In *Proceedings of the 2000 Winter Simulation Conference.*

[314] Trocine, L. and L. Malone (2001). An overview of newer, advanced screening methods for the initial phase in an experimental design. In *Proceedings of the 2001 Winter Simulation Conference.*

[315] Troncoso, J. and R. Garrido (2005). Forestry production and logistics planning: An analysis using mixed-integer programming. *Forest Policy and Economics 7*, 625–633.

[316] Tversky, A. and D. Kahneman (1974). Judgment under uncertainty: Heuristics and biases. *Science 185*(4157), 1124–1131.

[317] Tyler, R. (2004). BT fire brings chaos to Manchester. *The Telegraph.* Available at http://www.telegraph.co.uk/finance/yourbusiness/2882204/BT-fire-brings-chaos-to-Manchester.html last accessed July 2015.

[318] Tyssedal, J. (2008). Plackett-burman designs. In F. Ruggeri, R. Kenett, and F. Faltin (Eds.), *Encyclopedia of Statistics in Quality and Reliability.* Wiley.

[319] United Nations Inter-Agency Secretariat of the International Strategy for Disaster Reduction (UN/ISDR) (2004). *Living with risk: a global review of disaster reduction initiatives,* Volume II. New York, Geneva: United Nations publication. Available at http://www.unisdr.org/we/inform/publications/657 last accessed July 2015.

[320] Uschold, M. and R. Jasper (1999). A framework for understanding and classifying ontology applications. In *IJCAI99 Workshop on Ontologies and Problem-Solving Methods.*

[321] Van de Walle, B. and M. Turoff (2008). Decision support for emergency situations. *Information Systems and E-Business Management 6*(3), 295–316.

[322] Vanany, I., S. Zailani, and N. Pujawan (2009). Supply chain risk management: Literature review and future research. *International Journal of Information Systems and Supply Chain Management 2*(1), 16–33.

[323] VDI Guideline 3633 Part 1 (2010). Simulation of systems in materials handling, logistics and production fundamentals. Technical report, Verein Deutscher Ingenieure e.V. Available at https://www.vdi.de/uploads/tx_vdirili/pdf/1866575.pdf last accessed July 2015.

[324] VDI Guideline 3633 Part 12 (2010). Simulation und optimierung. Technical report, Verein Deutscher Ingenieure e.V.

[325] Venn, J. (1888). *The logic of chance.* New York: MacMi- MacMillan .

[326] Viceira, L. M. and J. Y. Campbell (2002). *Strategic asset allocation: portfolio choice for long-term investors.* Oxford University Press.

[327] Vollmann, T. E., W. L. Berry, D. C. Whybark, and F. R. Jacobs (2005). *Manufacturing planning and control for supply chain management.* New York: McGraw-Hill/Irwin.

[328] Wagner, S. and C. Bode (2006). An empirical investigation into supply chain vulnerability. *Journal of Purchasing and Supply Management 12(6)*, 301–312.

[329] Wagner, S. M. and C. Bode (2008). An empirical examination of supply chain performance along several dimensions of risk. *Journal of Business Logistics 29*, 307–325.

[330] Wagner, S. M. and C. Bode (2009). Dominant risks and risk management practices in supply chains. In G. A. Zsidisin and B. Ritchie (Eds.), *Supply Chain Risk*, Volume 124 of *International Series in Operations Research & Management Science*, pp. 271–290. Springer.

[331] Wakolbinger, T. and J. M. Cruz (2011). Supply chain disruption risk management through strategic information acquisition and sharing and risk-sharing contracts. *International Journal of Production Research 49*(13), 4063–4084.

[332] Wallace, S. W. and W. T. Ziemba (2005). *Applications of stochastic programming*, Volume 5. Siam.

[333] Wan, H., A. E., and B. Nelson (2006). Controlled sequential bifurcation: a new factor-screening method for discrete. *Operations Research 54(4)*, 743–755.

[334] Waters, D. (2007). *Supply Chain Risk Management.* Kogan Page Limited.

[335] Wiedenbruch, A. (2014). *A Modeling Language for Supply Chain Event Management.* Verlag Dr. Hut.

[336] Wille, J. (2011). Das Märchen vom Restrisiko. *Frankfurter Rundschau.* Available at `http://www.fr-online.de/energie/atomkraftwerke-das-maerchen-vom-restrisiko,1473634,8251762.html` last accessed July 2015.

[337] Williams, H. P. (1999). *Model Building in Mathematical Programming* (4th ed.). Wiley.

[338] Wilson, M. C. (2007). The impact of transportation disruptions on supply chain performance. *Transportation Research Part E: Logistics and Transportation Review 43*(4), 295–320.

[339] Wu, D. and D. Olson (2008a). Supply chain risk, simulation, and vendor selection. *International Journal of Production Economics 114(2)*, 645–655.

[340] Wu, D. and D. L. Olson (2008b). Supply chain risk, simulation, and vendor selection. *International Journal of Production Economics 114*(2), 646–655.

[341] Wu, Y. (2006). Robust optimization applied to uncertain production loading problems with import quota limits under the global supply chain management environment. *International Journal of Production Research 44*(5), 849–882.

[342] You, F., J. M. Wassick, and I. E. Grossmann (2009). Risk management for a global supply chain planning under uncertainty: models and algorithms. *AIChE Journal 55*(4), 931–946.

[343] Yu, H., A. Z. Zeng, and L. Zhao (2009). Single or dual sourcing: decision-making in the presence of supply chain disruption risks. *Omega 37*(4), 788–800.

[344] Yu, M. . and M. Goh (2014). A multi-objective approach to supply chain visibility and risk. *European Journal of Operational Research 233*(1), 125–130.

[345] Ziegenbein, A. (2007). *Supply Chain Risiken: Identifikation, Bewertung und Steuerung*, Volume 15. vdf Hochschulverlag AG.

[346] Zimmermann, H.-J. (2000). An application-oriented view of modeling uncertainty. *European Journal of Operational Research 122*, 190–198.

[347] Zipkin, P. (2000). *Foundations of Inventory management.* McGraw-Hill.

[348] Zsidisin, G., G. L. Ragatz, and S. A. Melnyk (2005). The dark side of supply chain management. *Supply Chain Management Review*, 46–52.

[349] Zsidisin, G. and B. Ritchie (2008). Supply chain risk management – development, issues and challenges. In G. A. Zsidisin and B. Ritchie (Eds.), *Supply Chain Risk – A Handbook of Assessment, Management, and Performance*, Volume 124. Springer Science & Business Media.

[350] Zsidisin, G. A. (2003). A grounded definition of supply risk. *Journal of Purchasing and Supply Management 9*(5), 217–224.

[351] Zuvela, M. (2010). Authorities review airport security after failed bomb plot. *Deutsche Welle.* Available at `http://www.dw.de/authorities-review-airport-security-after-failed-bomb-plot/a-6178554` last accessed July 2015.

Printed by Printforce, the Netherlands